African American
PSYCHOLOGY

To Our Watoto

Angela Ivy, Alexander Jaime, and Olivia Clare-Bernice

African American
PSYCHOLOGY
From Africa to America

FAYE Z. BELGRAVE ▪ KEVIN W. ALLISON

Virginia Commonwealth University

SAGE Publications

Thousand Oaks ▪ London ▪ New Delhi

For information:

Sage Publications, Inc.
2455 Teller Road
Thousand Oaks, California 91320
E-mail: order@sagepub.com

Sage Publications Ltd.
1 Oliver's Yard
55 City Road
London EC1Y 1SP
United Kingdom

Sage Publications India Pvt. Ltd.
B-42, Panchsheel Enclave
Post Box 4109
New Delhi 110 017 India

Printed in the United States of America

Library of Congress Cataloging-in-Publication Data

Belgrave, Faye Z.
African American psychology: From Africa to America/Faye Z. Belgrave, Kevin W. Allison.
    p. cm.
Includes bibliographical references and index.
ISBN 0-7619-2471-X (pbk.)
    1. African Americans—Psychology. 2. African Americans—Socialization. 3. African Americans—Social conditions. 4. United States—Civilization—African influences. 5. Afrocentrism. 6. Africa—Civilization. 7. Africa, West—Civilization. I. Allison, Kevin W. II. Title.
E185.625.B425 2006
155.8′496073—dc22   2005007118

This book is printed on acid-free paper.

05 06 07 08 09 10 9 8 7 6 5 4 3 2 1

Acquiring Editor:	Jim Brace-Thompson
Editorial Assistant:	Karen Ehrmann
Project Editor:	Beth Bernstein
Copy Editor:	Colleen Brennan
Typesetter:	C&M Digitals (P) Ltd.
Indexer:	Teri Greenberg
Cover Designer:	Janet Foulger
Cover Photography:	Janay Garrick

Contents

Preface

Why did we write this book? We have taught African American psychology for many years and wanted a text that would provide comprehensive and integrated coverage of the field of African American psychology. We also desired a book that would address and consider both African and American cultural perspectives.

Who should use this book? This book is for students interested in African American psychology. It is designed to be used as a semester-long textbook and covers 14 focal areas in African American psychology. The text can be used as a mid- to advanced-level undergraduate textbook and can also be used at the graduate level. In addition, those interested in understanding the psychology of African Americans may use the book in support of other courses and disciplines.

What are the unique aspects of this book? There are several unique features that the book contains. We begin each chapter with an African proverb that provides a framework and starting point for the chapter. Proverbs enrich us with lessons, rules, and wisdom for living our lives. We also begin each chapter with a news story that demonstrates the applicability of African American psychology to everyday life.

In each chapter, we provide a historical context that includes relevant information and literature from Africa, during the enslavement period, and at other critical historical time points. Because we believe in the idea of Sankofa, that it is important to look to the past to understand the present and consider the future, we relate the historical context of Africans and African Americans to the psychology of contemporary African Americans.

Each chapter begins with an introduction that defines terms and concepts. We have attempted to describe attributes of African and African American culture that impact the psychology of African Americans. Each chapter also has a methodological section that highlights methodological issues relevant to topics discussed in the chapter.

The book is organized in four sections. The first two chapters provide an introduction to, and a historical foundation for, the remainder of the book. Chapter 1 focuses on African American psychology as a discipline and provides a historical account of African Americans in the larger discipline of psychology. Chapter 2 is on Africentric psychology, which provides the framework for the study of people of African descent. The second section of the book focuses on social systems and structures and includes chapters on family, community, educational, and religious institutions and related processes. Chapter 3 describes the African American family and kinship, the primary agents of socialization. Educational systems and processes including schools and other institutions of learning are discussed in Chapter 4. African Americans live, work, and go to school in communities; this is the topic of Chapter 5. The third section of the book covers individual and developmental processes and includes chapters on interpersonal and close relationships; learning, cognition, and language; religion and spirituality; self-attributes and identity; and lifespan development. Our relationships with others are central to who we are and how we function. Interpersonal relationships including relationships with family, friends, romantic partners, and others are the focus of Chapter 6. Chapter 7 describes unique features of learning, cognition, and language among African Americans and discusses the relevance of these to creating positive learning environments for African American youth. Spirituality and religiosity are central beliefs of people of African descent; this topic is covered in Chapter 8. Self-attributes such as self-concept and ethnic identity define our thoughts and beliefs about who we are, which is the focus of Chapter 9. Chapter 10 covers developmental issues of African Americans throughout the life span. The fourth and final section of the book focuses on adjustment and adaptation and includes chapters on health, chronic illness, and disability; mental health; drugs and drug abuse; and aggression, crime, and violence. Chapter 11 discusses health, disability, and chronic illness from the perspective of African Americans attending to cultural and structural conditions that impact health conditions and how we adapt to chronic illness and disability. Mental health is the subject of Chapter 12 and provides an assessment of mental health conditions, mental health functioning, and culturally congruent models of mental health and adaptation. Drug use and abuse have serious adverse consequences for African Americans. These consequences are discussed along with strategies to prevent drug use and abuse in Chapter 13. Chapter 14 focuses on the adverse consequences of aggression, crime, and violence with attention directed toward ways violence can be prevented.

The Kenyan proverb "Having a good discussion is like having riches" exemplifies what we desire for the readers of this book. We hope that the readers of this book will have many riches as they read, review, challenge, and think about the materials in this book.

Acknowledgments

The journey toward the completion of this book has been a long one that has been filled with goodness. According to the Tanzanian proverb, "That which is good is never finished." So it is with our relationships and admiration for those who have joined us in this project.

Demetria Logan and Monica Jones contributed early on as research assistants when we first began this project. Tenea Johnson provided much editorial support in the revisions of the first draft. Crystal Awkward worked with us on the book until the end and gave countless hours doing library research and editing. We could not have done it without you. Karen Wilson and the staff at the Center for Cultural Experiences in Prevention at Virginia Commonwealth University forgave our absences and filled in for us on work tasks so that we could spend time on the book.

Jim Brace-Thompson from Sage encouraged us to go forward and provided never-ending support and encouragement. Thank you. Three reviewers who were anonymous to us provided critical and instructive feedback throughout this process. We appreciate your instructive wisdom and used it.

The writings and ideas of several psychologists have made a strong impact on each of us. Thank you, Reginald Jones, whom we will always admire for leading the way and writing the first book on African American psychology. We are eternally grateful to James Jones and Dalmas Taylor for supporting us and countless other African American psychologists through the American Psychological Association's Minority Fellowship Program. We would also like to thank scholars such as Linda Burton, Margaret Spencer, and William Cross for their conceptual and empirical contributions, scholarship, and support. And thank you, Na'im Akbar, for your influential writings and commentaries on African-centered psychology. We have learned so much.

Finally, thanks to all the friends, family, students, and colleagues who have cheered us along the way.

—Asante Sana

Section I

Introduction and Historical Foundation

Introduction to African American Psychology 1

If you know the beginning well, the end will not trouble you.

—Wolof proverb

In the Public Interest

Recognizing Kenneth B. Clark's Legacy

By Dr. Henry Tomes, APA Executive Director for Public Interest

Dec. 2002

Earlier this year, *The Review of General Psychology* issued its list of the top psychologists of the 20th century. As expected, Sigmund Freud, Ivan Pavlov and B. F. Skinner topped the list. I then scanned the list for Kenneth B. Clark. I was disappointed and surprised to find his name nowhere on that list of influentials.

The case for Clark

Why would I assume Kenneth Clark's name would be found in an article purporting to list eminent psychologists of the 20th century? There are several reasons. For one, Clark served as president of APA in 1970—the first African-American so honored. In 1994, he received APA's Lifetime Achievement Award, only the sixth time it had been bestowed.

But most importantly, Clark was central to one of the most significant U.S. Supreme Court decisions of the 20th century. When the court decided *Brown v. Board of Education* in 1954, one of the works cited was Clark's now-famous "Doll Study," which demonstrated the deleterious effects of racial segregation on the self-concept of black children. That research, conducted by Clark and his wife, Mamie Phipps Clark, not only influenced the Supreme Court justices to strike down the laws that mandated segregated schools, but arguably played a role in the demise of "separate but equal" in other areas of American life.

Never before had social sciences research been used by the highest court to make one of the most far-reaching decisions of the 20th century. Shouldn't that have helped Clark find a place, perhaps a reasonably high place, on a list of eminent and influential psychologists?

How did this happen?

The method used by the *Review of General Psychology* survey to generate the list of notables provides some clues as to how Clark was omitted. It relied heavily on the number of times an author was cited in journals and textbooks and on a survey of a sample of American Psychological Society members. Other factors were also taken into consideration, such as National Academy of Sciences membership, serving as APA president and being a recipient of the APA Distinguished Scientific Contribution Award. These criteria, particularly the number of journal and textbook citations, possibly worked against Clark. Certainly he was not short on honors and awards.

Still puzzled by his omission, I sought information about Clark from the Library of Congress, which, as it turned out, had quite a bit—168,500 items derived from publications, speeches, work papers and more that spanned 196 linear feet and occupied 500 boxes. Even a cursory review of these materials reveals a lot about how Clark spent his time. In addition to psychology, he worked with the National Association for the Advancement of Colored People, the Urban League and other groups involved with the civil rights movement of the 1950s and 1960s. He and his wife were involved in many organizations that benefited the New York community in which they lived.

It is likely that he was one of the most socially active psychologists of the era when minorities, primarily African-Americans, struggled for equal rights and justice in America.

So, after my investigations, the question remains: How could such a distinguished psychologist be omitted from such a list?

There are clearly honors for psychologists whose works are cited by others—that is how the discipline advances. But there are some acts and ideas that cannot be ascertained by numbers. Eminence may be one of them.

Kenneth Clark and his works, in my opinion, deserve better.

Introduction, Definition, and Conceptual Frameworks

The preceding article provides a brief narrative of one eminent African American psychologist and makes a convincing argument for why Dr. Kenneth Clark should be included as one of the top psychologists of the 20th century. Notably, Dr. Clark's work was a major contributing factor to one of the most significant U.S. Supreme Court decisions of the 20th century, and according to Tomes, he was one of the most socially active psychologists of the era. As we will see in this chapter, several African American psychologists along with Dr. Clark have made significant contributions in the field of psychology and in the wider society.

African American psychology encompasses many topics. In this chapter, we provide definitions and discuss conceptual frameworks for studying and understanding African American psychology. Then, we examine historical influences on the study of African American psychology. The contributions of African American psychologists in defining and conceptualizing African American psychology are discussed in a section on self-determination. Following that section, we review the current status of African American psychology. Methodological issues are addressed, and the chapter ends with a summary.

WHAT IS AFRICAN AMERICAN PSYCHOLOGY?

The fields of African American, Black, and African psychology have been defined by several scholars. Baldwin (1986)—a.k.a. Kambon—defines Black psychology this way:

> African (Black) Psychology is defined as a system of knowledge (philosophy, definitions, concepts, models, procedures, and practice) concerning the nature of the social universe from the perspectives of African cosmology. Black psychology is nothing more or less than the uncovering, articulation, operationalization, and application of the principles of the African reality structure relative to psychological phenomena. (p. 242)

African American psychology has been studied primarily from two perspectives. The first perspective is that psychological concepts and theories are universal and thus, African Americans can be studied using universal laws and principles. The second perspective, taken from Africentric scholars, is that African American psychology is the psychology of people of African descent and these beliefs and behaviors are central to the study of African Americans. In this book, we use a convergent approach that captures both perspectives.

Baldwin's definition encompasses an Africentric perspective. Africentric psychology is discussed in more detail in Chapter 2. Africentric psychology considers core values, beliefs, and behaviors found among people of African descent and central to understanding African Americans. Likewise, Azibo (1996) considers African American psychology to be African or Black psychology. He writes, "All human life processes including the spiritual, mental, biological, genetic, and behavioral constitutes African psychology" (pp. 6–7). In these definitions, Baldwin and Azibo do not make a distinction between African psychology and African American psychology, arguing that all people with origins in Africa are African.

One way of understanding the two perspectives in the psychology of African Americans is to consider differences between two schools of thought regarding Black/African psychology (Azibo, 1996). One school of thought is pro-Black and the other is pro-Africentric. In contrasting the two, Azibo notes that the pro-Black school of thought has focused on the

African in the U.S. experience and has not used the African structure to provide the patterns for interpreting the experience of African Americans. Although this school of thought has been useful in changing myths about Blacks based on a deficit model, it does not capture the core of the African experience. To capture the core African experience, Azibo advocates that an Africentric proactive school of thought be taken. This school takes the position that African philosophy is critical to understanding the psychology of Black/African people. To understand African American behavior, one must understand the behavior of Africans.

Baldwin similarly makes a distinction between Black psychology and African psychology (Baldwin, 1991). According to Baldwin, Black psychology was formed as a reaction to Western psychology. The Black psychological approach concerns itself with the psychological consequence of being Black in America. However, Baldwin argues that because African people preexisted European people as a distinct cultural group, it follows that a distinct African psychology existed, irrespective of when and how it was articulated by social scientists. Baldwin makes the point that indeed Black psychology is African psychology.

Aldelbert Jenkins (1995, 2004) takes a different approach in his study of the psychology of African Americans. Jenkins uses a humanistic perspective taken from Western psychology. A core assumption of the humanistic approach is that African Americans have always been and are currently active, planful, and proactive in shaping their destinies. Jenkins abandons the mechanistic conceptualization that posits that one's behavior is caused by external environmental forces. Instead he maintains that even under the most oppressive situations, individuals make choices and strive to exert some control over their outcomes. Jenkins notes that subtle efforts that have historically been and/or are currently being made by African Americans are often directed at resisting oppression. These efforts may not be conceived as logical from the perspective of Whites, but they have been useful in helping African Americans define themselves and have made possible an alternative conception of self. Jenkins provides the example of how money spent by a poor African American man on luxury items, such as an expensive car, may be seen as irrational behavior. However, according to Jenkins purchasing an expensive car could be an act of resistance for this individual. A luxury item may help him to define and express a sense of dignity that otherwise would not be obtained from an oppressive environment.

Convergent Perspectives

There are convergent viewpoints in conceptualizing the psychology of African Americans. Both perspectives acknowledge that African American psychology is a science and, consistent with a Western conceptualization of psychology, it is organized and structured. This means that there is a systematic approach to understanding the psychology of African Americans, although there may be disagreement on the methods used for conducting scientific work. Both perspectives consider the scope and content of African or African American psychology to be fairly broad and diverse. African/African American psychology includes the study of behaviors as well as thoughts, feelings, beliefs, attitudes, and ways of interacting and being. All perspectives underscore the importance of self-definition and self-determination. For example, from the perspective of Africentric scholars, self-knowledge is a requisite for achieving well-being. Jenkins's humanistic theory also acknowledges the striving for self-determination and mastery.

African and Western Psychology

African American psychology can be distinguished from Western psychology, not only by the population studied (i.e., African Americans), but also by the nature of the discipline. Azibo (1996) distinguishes African psychology from Western psychology by its nature and essence. According to Azibo, the essence of African psychology was seen in the practice of the people from Kemit (ancient Egypt, the place of original civilization). The Kemit approach to understanding humans was through self-realization, whereas Western psychology's approach was through domination (Kambon, 1998).

One feature of Western psychology is the importance that is placed on observable behavior. Although Freud's influence made the unconscious a part of the scope of Western psychology, psychology has primarily focused on that which can be observed. The focus on observable behavior is attributed to the great weight that Western psychology has placed on prediction and control of the behavior of people. African psychology considers self-knowledge and intuition to be as important as that which is observable (Grills, 2004; Myers, 1988).

In summary, there is no one definition of African American psychology. The definition depends on the perspective that is taken regarding the influence of African and American/Western cultures on the psychology of African Americans. We acknowledge both African and American influences on behavior.

Historical Perspective on the Psychological Study of African Americans

ORIGINS OF AFRICAN PSYCHOLOGY

African American psychology began in ancient Kemit (Egypt), a civilization that began in 3200 B.C. According to Azibo (1996), African psychology can be traced to the period in time in which Africans produced an "organized system of knowledge (philosophy, definitions, concepts, models, procedures, and practice concerning the nature of the social universe" (p. 4). From this perspective, African American psychology pre-existed Western psychology. African psychology is discussed in more detail in the next chapter.

EUROPEAN SCIENTISTS' CONTRIBUTION TO RACISM

In 1976, Robert Guthrie published the book *Even the Rat Was White*. The second edition was published in 1998. This book reviews the contributions of the European scientific community in influencing American psychology and beliefs about Blacks and how Blacks have been studied over the past two centuries. The book illustrates how scientific racism contributed to the perception of the inferiority of Blacks and justification for racism and oppression. Contributions from Guthrie's book are highlighted next.

Comparative Studies in Physical Anthropology

Studies done by physical anthropologists in the late 18th and 19th centuries compared differences in the physical attributes of Blacks and Whites (Guthrie, 1976/1998). These included skin color, hair texture, skull shape and size, facial structure, and posture. Observed differences were always found in favor of the superiority of Whites and the inferiority of Blacks. In studies that looked at skull size as an indicator of intelligence, it was concluded that the Black man's skull and brain were smaller and therefore less complex than the White brain.

In 1898, the Cambridge Anthropological Society began a cooperative venture between psychology and anthropology. When scientists were sent to New Guinea to study the mental attributes of its residents, they concluded that the natives of the South Pacific were inferior to Westerners on all traits, including intelligence. This study was the beginning of studies of racial differences.

Darwin's Survival of the Fittest

In 1859, Darwin published his theory on the survival of the fittest. The key assumption of this theory was that only the strongest and most intelligent could survive. According to Guthrie (1976/1998), this doctrine greatly influenced American psychology by emphasizing individual differences, an assumption that currently underlies much of the work in psychology. The vast majority of research on African Americans within the field of psychology during the first half of the 20th century looked at individual differences in the psychological attributes of African Americans and Whites. The findings generally showed African Americans to be inferior on individual difference variables.

Galton's Eugenics

Galton's work in the 19th century also contributed to promoting a belief in the racial inferiority of Blacks. Galton's theory was that intelligence and other personality attributes were inherited. If intelligence was inherited, then one would not expect those of lower intelligence to improve in ability (Guthrie, 1976/1998). Galton's theory of eugenics was promoted to improve the race through selective mating and sterilization. The improvement of the human race could be done by genetic control of those who were of inferior intelligence and those who were social deviants. The application of eugenics resulted in Blacks and other ethnic minorities being disproportionately included among those who were inferior and unfit.

AMERICAN SCIENTISTS' CONTRIBUTION TO SCIENTIFIC RACISM

Like their European counterparts, American scientists also conducted research to support the intellectual inferiority of African Americans (Guthrie, 1976/1998). The implication of this research on social policy has adversely affected African Americans.

Jensen's (1969) work on intelligence encouraged the belief that some people were genetically inferior to others. According to Jensen, intelligence was essentially determined at birth, and genetics or inheritance accounted for about 80% of intelligence. Note the similarity between this theory and that of eugenics.

In regard to public policy, a theory that intelligence is predetermined adversely affects people who may need environmental and social supports to improve their conditions. For example, compensatory programs such as Head Start were designed to provide economically disadvantaged children an academic boost prior to beginning school. However, if the reasoning is that intelligence is fixed at birth, there is little that can be done to change one's ability, and compensatory programs are not likely to do much good.

Research on the intellectual inferiority of African Americans is seen in more contemporary times in Herrnstein and Murray's (1994) book, *The Bell Curve*. These authors provided data that suggest that intelligence differs among racial groups and that African Americans are at the lowest end of the bell curve. A major point of the book is that most social problems, especially those found among economically and socially marginalized people, cannot be solved because they are linked to intelligence, which is mainly inherited. Therefore, environmental supports put in place to solve these problems will not be useful if the social problem is due to intelligence.

A broad implication of *The Bell Curve* is that the poor, the uneducated, and the unemployed—among whom African Americans constitute a sizable percentage—will live an unproductive life. Social programs cannot help these individuals, due to their lower intelligence (Haynes, 1995). Another implication of *The Bell Curve* is that people who are socially and intellectually inferior cause many of the social problems in this country.

The Bell Curve has been subject to intense scrutiny and criticism because of its erroneous assumptions and methodological flaws (Fairchild, 1994; Haynes, 1995). The inference of causality based on correlational data is a major methodological flaw as is the importance given to what an intelligence test means. That is, to assume that lower intelligence scores cause social problems is erroneous when cross-sectional correlational data are used to make these assumptions. Also, to assume that an intelligence test score is the best indicator of intelligence, adaptability, and general life success is flawed.

Intelligence Testing

Intelligence testing, according to Guthrie (1976/1998), was an important factor in perpetuating scientific racism during the first part of the 20th century. Binet and Spearman's work contributed to scientific racism in that intelligence testing was used to show intellectual differences between Blacks and Whites.

In 1904, Alfred Binet, a French physician, developed the Simon-Binet Scale, the forerunner of the Stanford-Binet test of intelligence that is still in use today. Charles Spearman developed the two-factor theory of intelligence that says that mental tests measure two factors: a general factor and a specific factor. The assumption is that the general factor measures general intellectual capability. The problem with this conception of a general factor of intelligence is that it emphasizes the general intellectual capacity while de-emphasizing other mental attributes that may be more contextual or culturally specific (Williams, Williams, & Mitchell, 2004).

The earliest test of racial differences in intelligence was done using the Binet scales in 1912. In this study, Alice Strong measured the intelligence of 225 White children and 1,125 Black children. Black children were also categorized according to skin color (dark, medium, and light). Strong (as quoted in Guthrie, 1976/1998) noted that the "colored children excelled in rote memory . . . however, they are inferior in aesthetics judgment, observation, reasoning, motor control, logical memory, use of words, resistance to suggestion, and in orientation or adjustment to the institutions and complexities of civilized society" (p. 64). In other words, the Black children were inferior to Whites on conceptual and intellectual attributes.

In 1916, Ferguson published a study titled *The Psychology of the Negro: An Experimental Study.* This study was considered a classic. It reported that the Negro had deficits in abstract thinking, but was very capable in sensory and motor abilities. Given capacity in these types of skills, Negroes should be useful for doing manual work. Overall, much of the early work of American scientists perpetuated the myth of Black inferiority.

STUDY OF AFRICAN AMERICANS IN AMERICAN PSYCHOLOGY

In American psychology, studies of Negroes, Coloreds, Blacks, Afro-Americans, and African Americans have been conducted throughout the last century in the United States. Often, theories and conceptual frameworks that may be useful for Western psychology have been erroneously applied to the psychology of African Americans. For example, consider the concept *self-esteem*, a frequently studied topic in Western and American psychology. In understanding what self-esteem is from an African and Western perspective, one must understand the difference between Western and African conceptions of the self. Using a Western perspective, self-esteem can be defined as a feeling of liking and regard for one's *self*. From an Africentric perspective, the personal self is indistinguishable from the self that is derived from membership in the African community (Nobles, 1991). Therefore, one's affiliation to one's group defines one's view of self. The African proverb "I am because we are and we are because I am" characterizes this notion of the self. Thus, the conceptualization of people of African descent may be different from that of Whites, and it also may function differently for African Americans than for Whites (see Chapter 9 for a more detailed discussion).

Another approach taken by American psychology has been to use information gathered from White populations as the norm and then to compare African Americans with Whites. This approach is seen with the use of measures that have been developed to assess individual difference traits. For example, continuing with the example of self-esteem, a measure of self-esteem that does not include the collective nature of self-esteem may not be relevant for African Americans. Given the problem of non-normative data, we have seen, over the past two decades, more effort directed at the inclusion of African Americans and other ethnic and cultural groups within normative samples when measures are developed.

A related problem is when methods that are based on Western psychology are used to study African Americans. As will be discussed in Chapter 2, the method for acquiring knowledge may differ for different cultural groups. According to Africentric scholars, self-knowledge is the most important type of knowledge and is the basis for all knowledge. Self-knowledge then is more important than knowledge that is acquired from the external environment. In this regard, understanding how a person who participates in a research project perceives him- or herself may be just as important as seeing how he or she responds to external stimuli.

Within American psychology, the preferred methodology for conducting research has been the experiment. Experiments are believed to be superior in producing valid and factually correct information. Experiments also provide a context in which predictions—and subsequently control—can be more exact. Yet, experimentation may not be the best way to obtain information about African Americans. Other, more naturalistic methods such as interviewing and systematic observations may be more useful singularly or in conjunction with experimental approaches.

A large percentage of studies done in American psychology have focused on differences between African Americans and Whites. During the first part of the 20th century, most of the research conducted on African Americans involved comparative studies that contrasted African Americans and Whites on individual difference traits (Guthrie, 1976/1998). This focus on differences led to African Americans being viewed as having deficits on many psychological characteristics. Studies that examine within-group differences among African Americans are just as important to aid in understanding why some African Americans do well and others do not. In the next section, we provide an overview of earlier comparative studies done on African Americans.

COMPARATIVE STUDIES

The vast majority of the studies conducted by psychologists on African Americans during the first half of the 20th century were studies that compared Colored, Negroes, and Blacks with Whites. For the most part, these studies examined differences between African Americans and Whites on intelligence, mental ability, and personality. Studies were conducted with children, adolescents, and adults. Studies on intellectual differences employed standard individual intelligence tests such as the Stanford-Binet, as well as group tests to assess mental functioning. One test used was the Army Classification Battery (ACB). The ACB was developed by the army to assess soldiers' aptitude on different assignments. The ACB test was used in several studies that examined differences in mental ability and intelligence between African Americans and Whites. One study that examined differences between Negroes and Whites on the ACB found that Negroes scored lower than Whites on intelligence (Roen, 1961).

Other studies conducted during the first half of the 20th century investigated differences between African Americans and Whites on personality attributes, traits, and temperaments. Findings from representative studies are reviewed next. The method used to carry out these studies was influenced by the social and political climate of the time, with most findings reflecting negatively on African Americans. These studies, which almost always found inferior traits among African Americans, contributed to the climate of racism and discrimination against African Americans.

A study published in the 1920s is illustrative of the studies of this era. Peterson (1923) tested White and Negro children using several group intelligence tests and individual learning tests. He found significant race differences, with White children scoring higher on both group and individual tests. He noted in his findings that the White 8-year-old children scored higher than the Negro 10-year-old children. Peterson pointed out that these differences were especially salient because of the fact that 60% of the White 8-year-old children came from poor sections of the city, whereas 97% of the 10-year-old Negro children came from one of the best Negroes schools in the city. He reported that about 83% of the Whites were smarter than the Negroes, and that only 15% to 18% of the Negroes were as smart as the Whites. According to Peterson, differences between the two groups were most striking on tasks that required abstract and logical thinking. In making recommendations stemming from his findings, he suggested that there be less abstract and conventional types of education for Negro children. Peterson did not mention that even though the Negro children may have attended one of the best Negro schools in town, these schools had substantially fewer resources than the poor White schools.

Findings of inferior functioning among African Americans were also seen in early studies on personality traits. Roen (1961) found that Negroes in his study lacked self-confidence more than did Whites. Furthermore, low self-confidence among Negroes was associated with lower intelligence test scores. Roen speculated that the lack of pride in historical achievement, coupled with a negative socioenvironmental context, had led to internalized intellectually defeating personality traits that contributed to lower intelligence scores.

Many studies found that African Americans had elevated scores for problem behaviors. For example, Hokanson and Calden (1960) found even when Negroes and Whites both came from predominately northern working-class settings, Negroes had personality deficits higher in several areas of the Minnesota Multiphasic Personality Inventory (MMPI). The authors suggested that special norms be developed for Negro and White subjects. Regarding general adaptation to society, studies found that White and Negro adolescents of similar mental ability differed in personal and social adjustment (Pierce-Jones, Reid, & King, 1964).

In a review of psychological studies published between 1943 and 1958, Dreger and Miller (1960) found that Whites were superior to Negroes on several attributes including psychophysical, psychomotor, intelligence, and temperament traits (i.e., neuroticism). They noted that differences between Negroes and Whites were smaller among young children. In none of these studies did the authors find superior performance among African Americans.

Given the findings from psychological studies, it is no wonder there was an assumption of African American racial inferiority during most of the 20th century. These studies were conducted by researchers at prestigious universities who had the authority of their position and "scientific" credibility for their work (Guthrie, 1976/1998).

In spite of the reports of inferior psychological attributes found in most psychology publications, some scholars as early as the 1940s were questioning the racial bias of psychological tests, especially intelligence tests. In commenting on why test items that differentiate between Blacks and Whites should be replaced, Pastore (1946) pointed out that test items that differentiate between boys and girls are eliminated because they are unfair. However, items that differentiate between Whites and Blacks have not been eliminated in intelligence testing. He concluded that this leads to no differences being seen for boys and girls, but differences being seen between Negroes and Whites.

A large amount of research on African Americans published during the first half of the 20th century was concerned with whether or not the results of differences between Blacks and Whites were due to genetic inferiority or the environment. Studies were cited to provide evidence for both positions. Those who made the argument that the environment was the cause of inferior performance among African Americans presented evidence that African Americans could learn when provided an opportunity. Witty (1945) argued that the scores for the Army General Classification test, a test of intelligence, were associated with educational opportunities for soldiers within their local communities. To support this statement, Witty provided evidence that Negroes improved in performance when given the opportunity. In a special training unit, illiterates were given an 8-week course to develop fourth-grade skills. The essential skills were attained by 87% of the Negroes and 84% of the Whites. He concluded that these findings showed evidence that Negroes are equal to Whites in the ability to learn.

In accounting for environmental influences on low Negro self-concept, Grambs (1965) wrote,

> It does not take much imagination to understand what generations of being told one is unworthy will do to a group's own validation of its worth. . . . The self-esteem of the Negro is damaged by the overwhelming fact that the world he lives in says, "White is right; black is bad." The impact on the Negro community is to overvalue all those traits of appearance that are most Caucasian. Evidence is clear that in almost every Negro family, the lighter children are favored by the parents. (p. 14)

The first part of the 20th century saw much work devoted to justifying the inferiority of Blacks within American psychology. However, during the second half of the century, this assumption began to be questioned.

Self-Determination

Several critical events provided the impetus for the development of a contemporary psychology of African Americans. A pivotal assumption was that African Americans had to define for themselves what constitutes the psychology of African Americans. The emergence of a voice among African American psychologists (albeit few in number) occurred during the sociopolitical struggles of the 1960s for civil rights and equality in all aspects of life. The demand for civil rights was seen in all institutions including educational institutions. Black Nationalism and the Black Power movement were also driving forces for self-determination during the 60s. These sociopolitical movements set the stage for self-determination.

AFRICAN AMERICAN PSYCHOLOGISTS IN THE EARLY 20TH CENTURY

During the first part of the 20th century, a few African Americans were beginning to enter the field of psychology. Despite many obstacles, African Americans managed to become psychologists (Guthrie, 1976/1998). Two of the major obstacles for African Americans were geographical location of graduate programs in psychology and the cost of graduate school. Most graduate-level universities in the South, where the majority of African Americans lived, did not admit African Americans. This meant that African Americans had to go north in order to attend graduate school. However, out-of-state tuition was expensive, as were travel costs to get there. This situation, along with the low incomes of most African Americans during this period, made it very difficult for African Americans to go to graduate school even if they were accepted.

At this time, most African Americans attended predominately Black colleges. White universities required African Americans who had received their bachelor degree from a predominately African American university to complete an additional year of undergraduate school to demonstrate that they had the ability for graduate school. This resulted in a longer period of matriculation for African Americans than for Whites (Guthrie, 1976/1998).

Despite these obstacles, a few African Americans managed to obtain a Ph.D. in psychology during the first quarter of the 20th century. Francis

Sumner was the first Black to receive a Ph.D. in psychology, in 1920, from Clark University in Massachusetts. Because of this distinction, Sumner is referred to as the Father of Black psychology. Sumner conducted his dissertation research on the psychoanalysis of Freud and Adler. He became chair of the Department of Psychology at Howard University in Washington, D.C. Howard became a leading university for providing training in psychology to African Americans at both undergraduate and graduate levels. Charles Henry Thompson was another early recipient of the Ph.D. in psychology. He received his Ph.D. in educational psychology from the University of Chicago in 1925. Dr. Thompson conducted his dissertation research on teacher curriculums.

In 1938, Herman Canaday at West Virginia State College convened Black professionals interested in Black psychology and established a Black psychologists committee within the American Teachers Association (ATA). The ATA was the professional organization for Black educators.

THE ASSOCIATION OF BLACK PSYCHOLOGISTS

The Association of Black Psychologists (ABPsi) was organized in 1968 when African American psychologists attending the predominately White American Psychological Association (APA) Conference reacted to what they felt were nonsupportive, if not racist, positions regarding ethnic minority concerns. A group of African American psychologists met during the 1968 APA meeting in San Francisco and generated a list of demands (Guthrie, 1976/1998). The reactionary position of African American psychologists at this meeting was consistent with the self-determination and protest ideology of the 1960s. African American psychologists were tired of being ignored and were fed up with research, policies, and programs that were discriminatory to African Americans.

The demands that African American psychologists made included the following:

1. The APA must integrate its own workforce with more African Americans.

2. The APA should work to gain the admittance of more African Americans in psychology graduate schools.

3. Racist content found in APA journals should be eliminated.

4. The APA should establish programs so that concerns specific to each minority group can be addressed.

Following the 1968 meeting, African American psychologists in attendance decided to form their own organization rather than to try to effect change within the APA.

The thrust of ABPsi today remains similar to that articulated over 35 years ago. Some of the agendas of the ABPsi today are as follows: First, to provide training and support to African American psychology students. The ABPsi encourages and promotes the professional development of African American undergraduate and graduate students through scholarships, support of students in their research activities, and publications directed at assisting students in their graduate education. The student committee of ABPsi provides support to and a forum in which students can address important topics facing them, the universities they attend, and communities in which they live. The student ABPsi has been especially beneficial to students who attend predominately White universities as it introduces them to African American psychologists.

Second, ABPsi has been engaged in strong advocacy against racist and discriminatory practices within the discipline of psychology as well as in other arenas. The ABPsi has emphasized the need for culturally competent practices, treatment, and services. As early as 1969, the year after the formation of ABPsi, African American psychologists were arguing against the use of culturally biased tests. Robert Williams, then chair of ABPsi, asked for an end to using tests that were not standardized on African Americans, arguing that they were not valid. To illustrate what he perceived as cultural bias in testing, Williams developed a test labeled the "Bitch" test, the Black Intelligence Test of Cultural Homogeneity. Williams showed that when the Bitch test was administered to White samples, they fared poorly in comparison to African Americans. The discriminatory nature of testing as it affects African Americans continues to be one of the major issues addressed by ABPsi.

ABPsi and/or its members have articulated positions on several other practices that are discriminatory against Black people and have promoted agendas that aid in improving the mental, physical, social, economic, and political status of all people of African descent. In this regard, ABPsi has developed position papers and press releases and has provided information to the general public on racist research, practices, and policies. For example, a special issue of the official journal of ABPsi, *The Journal of Black Psychology*, was dedicated to exposing the fallacies found in the book *The Bell Curve*, which promoted racial inferiority. A 2004 issue of *The Journal of Black Psychology* was devoted to HIV/AIDS epidemiology, prevention, and treatment for people of African descent.

Third, ABPsi has been active in addressing social, psychological, and health problems found among people of African descent through training, education, and programs at the local, state, and national levels. Training in topics related to mental health, substance abuse, HIV, and children and families are offered by local chapters, at the national convention, and by members throughout the country. ABPsi and its members provide health screenings, mental health assessment, expert testimony, consultation to agencies, and other activities in communities throughout the United States.

Fourth, ABPsi has promoted an awareness of the problems and concerns facing Blacks throughout the diaspora. A related mission is to increase connections and collaborations among Blacks throughout the world. For example, racial apartheid in South Africa, tribal conflict, and famine in African countries have been publicized through ABPsi. Annual national conferences of the ABPsi have included Blacks from other countries, and there have been collaborative activities with Blacks from other countries including the Caribbean, Africa, and South America. Two ABPsi annual conferences have been international conferences, held in Jamaica and Ghana.

TOWARD A BLACK PSYCHOLOGY

A seminal message that contributed to the recognition of the field of Black psychology was articulated by Joseph White (1970) in an Ebony magazine article titled "Toward a Black Psychology." A recent update to this article appeared as a chapter in the fourth edition of Reginald Jones's book *Black Psychology* (2004). In this article, Dr. White, a professor at the University of California, Irvine, explained how it was difficult, if not impossible, to understand the psychology of Black people using theories that were developed by White psychologists to examine White people (Guthrie, 1976/1998). In this article, White strongly advocated a Black psychology defined by Blacks.

This article received a lot of attention from the public. Some felt that the position of Joseph White was polarizing for African Americans. Others felt that this position dichotomized psychology into Black and White disciplines. Still others felt that a psychology formulated from the experiences of Blacks would marginalize Black psychology. The perspective that Black psychology was in some way different from White psychology was perceived by some as creating a lower-class psychology for Blacks. Others felt just as strongly as Professor White that it was time for Black psychology to be formulated for the authentic experiences of Blacks.

THE JOURNAL OF BLACK PSYCHOLOGY

The Journal of Black Psychology is the official journal of the ABPsi. The journal began in 1974, 6 years after the formation of the ABPsi, and has grown from publishing issues twice a year to publishing issues four times per year. In addition, special issues that focus on specific topics are published on a periodic basic. Some of the more recent special issue topics have included sickle cell disease, racial identity, African American children, HIV prevention, and substance abuse prevention. *The Journal of Black Psychology* publishes contributions within the field of psychology that are directed toward the understanding of the experience and behavior of Black populations. The major disciplines of psychology are represented in the journal, including clinical, counseling, social, educational, organizational, and cognitive psychology. Journal articles tend to be empirical but also include theoretical reviews, commentaries, case studies, and book reviews. *The Journal of Black Psychology* was relied on extensively in gathering research and literature for this book.

STUDIES OF AFRICAN AMERICANS IN OTHER JOURNALS

There have been an increasing number of studies on African Americans published in journals other than *The Journal of Black Psychology*. This increase has been partially due to the increase in African American psychologists and to an increasing awareness of cultural diversity. Publications have expanded the knowledge of African Americans and informed the psychological community on culturally congruent approaches to studying African Americans. The more recent writings have also focused more on understanding African American behaviors from a positive, culturally appropriate framework rather than a negative, culturally deviant framework.

INFLUENTIAL AFRICAN AMERICAN PSYCHOLOGISTS

Several African American psychologists have influenced the field of African American psychology. Next, we highlight individuals who have made important contributions. We selected these individuals based on several considerations: (a) These individuals were the first to obtain a doctorate in psychology or the first in other accomplishments; (b) they have developed new theories and conceptual frameworks; and (c) they have conducted research that has impacted social policy and improved conditions for African Americans. Some have been influential because they have advanced theories that have been a catalyst for others who have followed them; still others have had a large impact because of how prolific they were. Some are listed because they have directly and indirectly influenced our teachings and writings.

Francis C. Sumner

Sumner, the first African American to receive a Ph.D. in psychology in the United States (in 1920), is regarded as the Father of Black Psychology (Guthrie, 1976/1998). This accomplishment is noteworthy because at the time he received his degree, only 11 Blacks out of a total of 10,000 recipients had earned a Ph.D. between 1876 and 1920 in the United States. Working against many barriers, Francis Sumner earned his degree at Clark University in Massachusetts. At the age of 15, he enrolled as a freshman at Lincoln University in Pennsylvania after having passed an examination in lieu of a high school diploma. He enrolled in Clark College in 1915 and also received a degree in English.

Sumner joined the faculty at Howard University, Washington, D.C., in 1928 and was chair of the Department of Psychology from 1928 to 1954. During this period, he established strong graduate and undergraduate programs in psychology. Under his leadership, the department produced many influential Black psychologists and provided training, especially at the bachelor's and master's levels. Both Mamie Clark and Kenneth Clark, two other influential African American psychologists, received training at Howard University.

Mamie Clark and Kenneth Clark

This husband and wife team is best known for their work on racial preferences among Black children. Their classic doll studies were published in the 1940s and early 1950s. In these studies, Black children were shown Black and White dolls and told to choose the one that looked like them, the one they preferred, the one that was a good doll, and the one that was a bad doll. The Clarks concluded from their findings that Black children preferred White dolls. This classic study led the Clarks to argue that Black children who attended segregated schools had low self-esteem. The findings were used in arguments against racial segregation, the most famous of which was the 1954 landmark case *Brown v. Board of Education*. Prior to this, Blacks had received inferior education in segregated schools. The *Brown v. Board of Education* landmark decision ruled that separate but equal education was unconstitutional. That is, schools could not be separate and equal at the same time. Although there were several subsequent methodological criticisms of the Clark and Clark doll studies, they continue to be classic studies of racial identity and preferences. Kenneth Clark was the first and only Black to be president of the APA.

William Cross

William Cross's model of the development of racial and ethnic identity has generated a considerable amount of work over the past three decades and continues to do so today. Cross's model was labeled a "nigrescence" model. Nigrescence models accounted for the progression of African Americans through sequential stages to arrive at a healthy racial identity (Cross, 1978). These stages were subsequently labeled as pre-encounter, encounter, immersion-emersion, internalization, and internalization commitment.

Each stage is characterized by certain affective, cognitive, and behavioral reactions. Racial identity theory is discussed more extensively in Chapter 9. Cross's model has been revised and augmented by several other scholars including Janet Helms and Thomas Parham. The theory of racial identity has prompted much research (Cross, Parham, & Helms, 1998).

Reginald Jones

Reginald Jones is included as an influential psychologist because of the large amount of work he has published on Black psychology. Jones has published over 20 books on African American psychology and related topics, and his books have provided comprehensive coverage of Black psychology. Many of his works are edited volumes that include a variety of authors, perspectives, and topics. His book on Black psychology was the first to be published on the topic. The first edition of *Black Psychology* was published in 1972, and the fourth edition was published in 2004. *Black Psychology* includes chapters on several topics, including African philosophy, personality, assessment, intelligence assessment, counseling, racism, racial identity, cognition, and language. We frequently consulted Jones's *Black Psychology* when writing this book.

Some of the other books on African American psychology that Jones has edited include *African American Identity Development* (1998b); *Advances in African American Psychology* (1999); *African American Children, Youth, and Parenting* (1998a); *African American Mental Health* (1998c); *Black Adolescents* (1989); and *Handbook of Tests and Measurement for Black Populations* (1996). The books authored by Dr. Jones have been used in African American psychology classes and similar courses throughout the country. Dr. Jones is currently a professor emeritus at Hampton University in Hampton, Virginia.

James Jones

James Jones is included as an influential African American psychologist for two reasons. First, his book on *Prejudice and Racism*, originally published in 1972 and revised in 1997, is a classic examination of prejudice and racism. In this book, Jones provides an analysis of the different types of racism, that is, individual, institutional, and cultural.

Second, Dr. Jones has substantially impacted African American psychology in his role as the director of the APA's Minority Fellowship Program. In this position, Dr. Jones has been responsible for managing a program to increase the number of African American and other ethnic minority scholars who obtain doctorates in psychology. The mission of the minority fellowship program is to improve the quality of mental health treatment and research on issues of concern among ethnic minority populations in psychology by offering financial support and by providing guidance and training in becoming a psychologist. The minority fellowship program began in 1974 with Dalmas Taylor as the first director. James Jones became director in 1977 and continues to direct the program.

Africentric Psychologists

Beginning in the 1970s, several African American psychologists began writing and educating people about the importance of understanding African philosophy as a basis for understanding African American psychology. These include Na'im Akbar, Asa Hilliard, Wade Nobles, Joseph Baldwin (a.k.a. Kobi Kambon), Daudi Azibo, and Linda James Myers. The work of these psychologists is often published in *The Journal of Black Psychology*. Chapters were also published in Reginald Jones's edited book *Black Psychology*. Several of these psychologists are highlighted in Chapter 2.

AFRICAN AMERICANS' PRESENCE WITHIN THE AMERICAN PSYCHOLOGICAL ASSOCIATION

The APA is a membership organization of approximately 150,000 members. The mission of APA is to advance psychology as a science and profession as a means of promoting human welfare. Divisions within APA operate that are geared to disciplines and interests of APA members (APA, 2005).

Several components of APA represent the professional interests of African American psychologists. APA's Division 45, The Society for the Psychological Study of Ethnic Minority Issues, encourages research on ethnic minority issues and the application of psychological knowledge to addressing issues of ethnic minority populations. One distinction between APA's Division 45 and the ABPsi is that APA's Division 45 supports issues of all ethnic minority groups and ABPsi is more specifically focused on Black issues. The official journal of Division 45 is *Cultural Diversity and Ethnic Minority Psychology*. This journal is published quarterly.

The Office of Ethnic Minority Affairs at APA seeks to increase the scientific understanding of how culture pertains to psychology and how ethnicity influences behavior. It also focuses on promotion, recruitment, retention and training opportunities for ethnic minority psychologists, increasing the delivery of appropriate psychological services to ethnic minority communities, and promoting better inclusion of ethnic minorities in organized psychology (APA, 2004).

Status of African American Psychology Today

TEACHING AFRICAN AMERICAN PSYCHOLOGY

Today, African American psychology is taught at many colleges and universities. The course is often cross-listed with African American studies. Increased interest in African American psychology is attributed to several factors, including the growing appreciation for cultural diversity, increased enrollment of African American students, recognition of the contributions of African American psychology to general psychology, and increases in the number of African American faculty who can teach this course.

NUMBER OF AFRICAN AMERICAN PSYCHOLOGISTS

To date, data on the exact number of African American psychologists could not be obtained. However, statistics reported by APA show that there has been a shift in the number of Ph.D.-level psychologists of color. In 1977, 7.5% of the new doctorates in psychology were people of color. This number had increased to 17.7% by 2000 (APA Research Office, 2000b). Among Ph.D.s in the workforce, only 2% were people of color in 1973 compared with 9% in 1999. Although the increase has been fairly substantial, the percentage of people of color within psychology is still significantly less than one would expect given their representation in this country. Also, it is important to note that this number represents all people of color, including Hispanics, Asian/Pacific Islanders, Native American/Alaska Natives, and Blacks.

AFRICAN AMERICAN FACULTY AND GRADUATE STUDENTS IN GRADUATE DEPARTMENTS OF PSYCHOLOGY

The presence of African American faculty in psychology departments, specifically graduate departments, is important. Graduate departments provide training at the doctoral level. African American faculty are important insofar as they generally tend to encourage research on issues of concern to African Americans, assist in recruitment and retention of African American students, and teach classes and integrate material on African Americans in the curriculum of courses taught. An APA survey of departments of psychology gathered demographic data on faculty and graduate students (APA Research Office, 2000b). In 2000, racial/ethnic minority faculty represented approximately 10.5% of all full-time faculty in doctoral-level programs. Because all ethnic minority faculty are included in this figure, the number of African American faculty is much lower.

Statistics compiled by APA on the percentage of ethnic minority students in doctoral programs show that in 2000, 7.2% of first-year students in doctoral programs were African American, 6.3% of students were Asian, and 5.6% were Hispanic (APA Research Office, 2000b). Consistent with faculty, the number of students enrolled in graduate programs is not representative of the ethnic group representation in this country. One of the barriers to the enrollment of African Americans is the lack of mentoring at the undergraduate level for preparation for graduate schools. The lack of mentoring may occur at both predominately White and predominately African American colleges and universities. African Americans who attend predominately White institutions may not develop a relationship with faculty or be provided the type of guidance needed to prepare for graduate school. Students attending predominately African American schools may have more interactions with faculty, but because most African American universities are traditionally teaching universities, they may not be exposed to the research experiences that are often required for graduate school.

Methodological Issues

Some of the methodological issues that were historically problematic in studying African Americans remain today. The best methods for studying African American populations may differ from the methods for studying other ethnic groups. For example, the experimental method is the favored method in psychology and has been considered the gold standard for conducting research. However, it may not always be the best way to arrive at an understanding of the psychology of African Americans. Other methods such as interviewing and observation may be more appropriate, depending on what is being studied. African psychology (discussed in Chapter 2) considers self-knowledge and intuition to be as important a source of knowing as observable data. Self-knowledge is derived from asking people about themselves, not from observing them under experimental conditions.

Another methodological consideration is the relevance of the constructs that are being examined. A construct may not hold the same meaning for African Americans as other ethnic groups. An earlier example we used was how the concept of self-esteem is used. For people of African descent, the concept of self includes the collective as well as the individual self. From a Western psychological perspective, the self is individualized. Another construct that may differ is that of the family. Who constitutes the African American family? What is effective family functioning? The answers to these questions may be different for African Americans than for other groups. More research is needed to better understand when they are universal and when they are culturally specific to African Americans.

The relatively low percentage of African American psychologists contributes to some of these methodological issues. The problems and questions of interest are often identified and studied by those most affected. We return to methodological and conceptual issues throughout this book, pointing out how these issues affect the validity and practicality of studies conducted on African Americans.

Summary

The proverb at the beginning of this chapter suggests that when the beginning is understood, the end will be successful. This chapter was written to inform the reader about African American psychology, its origins, and historical events and people. By so informing the reader of the history, we hope that the reader will be successful in learning about this field of psychology.

The origin of the study of African American psychology can be traced to ancient Kemet in that it is during this period of time that Black people produced a systematic body of knowledge. European theories, including Darwin's survival of the fittest doctrine and Galton's eugenics, contributed to the belief in the inferiority of Blacks. This belief perpetuated discrimination and racism. Contemporary scientific work on racial inferiority is seen in Herrnstein and Murray's (1994) *The Bell Curve*.

During the first half of the 20th century, the study of African Americans in American psychology was largely comparative, and findings showed African Americans to be inferior to Whites on intelligence, personality, and general adaptation. Obtaining a Ph.D. in psychology was very difficult for Blacks. Frances Sumner obtained his degree in 1920 and is known as the Father of Black Psychology because of this achievement. In 1968, a period of self-determination began. The ABPsi was formed by African American psychologists who felt that the predominately White APA did not address the concerns of Black people. Since then, there has been an increase in culturally appropriate publications. There has also been an increase in the number of African American psychologists, and an increase in awareness of cultural diversity in psychology. The APA has offices (e.g., the Office of Ethnic Minority Affairs) and programs targeted at African American professionals and students. More college students are becoming familiar with African American psychology as many colleges and universities teach courses in it.

2 Africentric Psychology

Wood may remain ten years in the water, but it will never become a crocodile.

—Zairian proverb

Celebration of Kwanzaa Stresses Unity, Community, Focus on Family

By Maria Sonnenberg for *Florida Today*

Dec. 25, 2004

As the world around her swirls in the rush of holiday preparations, Laquasia Clinkscales remains calm, focused on the meaning of her favorite celebration.

Clinkscales and her family celebrate Kwanzaa, the African-inspired holiday of the self, the family, the community and the Earth. Created in 1966 by Dr. Maulana Karanga, chair of the Department of Black Studies at California State University, Kwanzaa grew from a decade of change. It is a cultural holiday deeply rooted in the African philosophy of respect for self and those around you. The name is derived from the "matunda ya kwanza," Swahili for "first fruits." "It is not religious at all," Clinkscales said. "Some friends of ours celebrate both Christmas and Kwanzaa."

According to founder Karenga, the holiday reflects the best of African thought in its reaffirmation of the dignity of the individual, the well-being of family and community, and the integrity of the environment. The focus of Kwanzaa is the seven principles known as Nguzo Saba, and the seven-day-long holiday provides a time for family gathering and introspection.

When Clinkscales first met her husband-to-be, Jalik, he was already celebrating Kwanzaa every year. Twenty-three Kwanzaas later, Clinkscales is still committed to the principles of the holiday. "My sons celebrated since they were children," Clinkscales said. "We wanted them to remember the principles." Her two sons, now in college and living on their own, look forward to coming home on Dec. 26 and joining in the festivities. They gather together around the holiday's seven basic symbols, which represent values and concepts reflective of African culture.

Introduction to the Africentric Worldview and Historical Framework

The news story that opens this chapter conveys how African Americans maintain a link with African beliefs, values, and behavior through practicing Kwanzaa. This is the focus of this chapter.[1]

The behavior of African Americans is rooted in both African and American culture. In this chapter, we discuss the influence of African culture and the Africentric worldview on the psychology of African Americans. The terms *Africentric*, *African*, and *Black* psychology are used interchangeably in this chapter according to the usage by scholars cited. Likewise, the terms *Africentric* and *Afrocentric* are used interchangeably, following the spelling used by the scholar cited. In this chapter, we begin with a definition of *worldview*, including the Africentric worldview, and we discuss the origins of Africentric psychology. We then describe the contributions of several Africentric psychologists. Africentric worldview dimensions are discussed next and the question as to whether or not an Africentric worldview can exist among contemporary African Americans is addressed. In the section on Africentric research, we discuss three areas of research: research on differences between African and European Americans on Africentric dimensions; studies on the relationship between Africentric values and other variables; and studies on Africentric-based approaches to prevention, interventions, and treatment. Methodological issues are addressed, including a review of some Africentric measures. The chapter concludes with a summary.

WHAT IS A WORLDVIEW?

A worldview is a way of thinking that organizes all aspects of one's life, including intra- and interpersonal thoughts and behaviors and one's functioning in social systems and institutions in the community (e.g., family, school, job, and church) and in larger society. Intrapersonal thoughts refer to one's attitudes, beliefs, values, and expectations. Interpersonal behaviors refer to one's interactions with others. Worldviews provide us with guidelines for living: They affect our perceptions, thoughts, feelings, inferences, and behaviors and how we experience the external world.

The Africentric worldview is the worldview of people of African descent. It consists of the values, beliefs, and behavior of people of African heritage. Butler (1992) characterizes the African worldview as follows:

> It represents a general design for living and patterns for interpreting reality. It is how someone makes sense of their world and their experiences—it determines which events are meaningful and which are not and provides the process by which those events are made harmonious with their lives. (p. 29)

Asante (2003) also defines Afrocentricity as an attitude and actions that promote the well-being of people of African descent. "Afrocentricity is a mode of thought and action in which the centrality of African interests, values, and perspectives dominate. . . . It is the placing of African people in the center of any analysis of African phenomena" (p. 2).

Likewise, Grills's (2004) conceptualization of African psychology focuses on defining African psychological experiences from an African perspective. According to Grills, the African paradigm consists of African values, ways of accessing knowledge, ways of defining reality, ways of governing and interpreting behavior, social relations, and designing environments to sustain healthy, adaptive functioning among people of African descent.

The Africentric worldview has been contrasted with a Eurocentric worldview that is derived from European culture. The Africentric worldview differs from a Eurocentric worldview along several dimensions such as spirituality, interdependence and collectiveness, time orientation, death and immortality, and kinship (Akbar, 1991a; Nobles, 1991). These dimensions will be discussed later. In general, the Eurocentric worldview provides a cultural template for people of European descent, whereas the Africentric worldview provides a cultural template for people of African descent.

It is important to note that there are variations in the Africentric and other worldviews, and individuals may function along a continuum, with some people of African descent having some Eurocentric worldview beliefs and some people of European descent having some Africentric worldview beliefs. However, in general it is expected that Africentric worldview dimensions will be found in some degree among most people of African descent.

BEGINNINGS OF AFRICENTRIC PSYCHOLOGY

Africentric psychology, as a topic and perspective, is fairly recent. Most literature on Africentric psychology has been published within the past 30 years. However, the study of African psychology as an organized and systematic study of African people has existed since ancient Kemet (3000 B.C.; Azibo, 1996). Although much of the scholarship on the Africentric worldview has come out of African Studies, several African American psychologists have also contributed to an understanding of the Africentric worldview.

During the 1960s and early 1970s, African American psychologists began to write about the Africentric worldview and how it could be used to understand the psychology of African Americans (Azibo, 1983; Nobles, 1976, 1986; White, 1972, 1984). These early writings coincided with other historical events such as the civil rights movement and the Black Power movement. Much of this earlier work focused on articulating what the Africentric worldview was and how it differed from the Eurocentric worldview.

Over the past 20 years, there has been much theoretical and empirical work directed at better understanding the Africentric worldview. African American scholars from various academic disciplines have contributed. Much of the work produced by African American psychologists has been published in *The Journal of Black Psychology,* the official journal of the Association of Black psychologists.

Other sources of information on Africentric psychology include journals such as *The Western Journal of Black Studies* and the *Journal of Black Studies.* Several books have also been written. A notable work is Molefi Asante's classic book, *Afrocentricity: The Theory of Social Change,* first published in 1980 and updated in 2003. Azibo's (1996) *African Psychology in Historical Perspective and Related Commentary* is a more recent addition to the understanding of Africentric psychology. Representative Africentric research will be discussed later in the chapter.

African American Psychologists and Africentric Psychology

Several African American psychologists have contributed to an understanding of the Africentric worldview. Six psychologists and their contributions are discussed next.

JOSEPH WHITE

White's chapter on the psychology of Black people (1972) is an important early work that challenged the use of traditional theories and frameworks to study African Americans. This work helped to reshape thinking of how African Americans should be studied. White wrote:

> It is very difficult, if not impossible, to understand the lifestyles of Black people using traditional theories developed by White psychologists to explain White people. Moreover, when these traditional theories are applied to the lives of black folks many incorrect, weakness-dominated, and inferiority-oriented conclusions come about. (p. 5)

White's book on Black psychology (coauthored with Thomas Parham, 1990), *The Psychology of Blacks,* was widely read by the academic community as well as the general public interested in African American psychology. This book advanced the understanding of the psychology of African Americans long before it was recognized as a discipline in psychology. A theme throughout the book is that Western models of human behavior are not appropriate for studying African Americans and that African Americans must define their paradigms. The book is now in its third edition (Parham, White, & Ajamu, 1999).

WADE NOBLES

Nobles advanced the understanding of the study of Black psychology in several ways, and his writings on African philosophy serve as the foundation for Black psychology (Nobles, 1980, 1991, 2004). Prominent in Nobles's contribution is his work on African philosophy and how this operates among Black cultures. Nobles's writings contribute to our knowledge of several aspects of African philosophy, including religion and philosophy, notion of unity, concept of time, death and immortality, and kinship.

Nobles (1991) addressed the question of how African perspectives of religion, unity, time, death/immortality, and kinship were maintained by Blacks in this country.

> An orientation stemming from a particular indigenous African philosophy could only be maintained when its cultural carriers were isolated from alien cultural interaction and if their behavioral expression of the orientation did not openly conflict with the cultural-behavioral elements of the host society. (pp. 47–63)

Isolation of Blacks through slavery and oppressive conditions in this country helped to preserve African values.

Nobles's contribution to Africentric psychology can be found in his conceptualization of the self from an Africentric perspective. According to Nobles, the individual self-concept is intricately linked to the collective self. Hence, the individual self cannot exist independently from the collective self. One's personal identity, esteem, and worth are tied to one's identity as a person of African descent. Nobles's work has encouraged several scholars to study the relationship between individual and collective selves among African Americans.

NA'IM AKBAR

Akbar has written and spoken extensively on the effects of oppression on African Americans and other Blacks. According to Akbar, many mental illnesses among African Americans are due to attempts to function within an oppressive and alien environment. Akbar has classified and described some of the mental conditions that result from functioning within an alien environment. One such disorder is called an alien-self disorder. This disorder is found among people who behave in ways counter to their natural disposition. A symptom of this would be materialism. On materialism, Akbar (1991b) writes, "African Americans have been socialized with materialistic goals and evaluate their worth by the prevalence of material accomplishments" (p. 343). Another disorder is the anti-self disorder. This disorder is found among persons who identify with the oppressor and who are hostile to and reject members of their own groups.

Akbar (1991a, 2004) is also known for his work on the developmental stages of the study of African Americans by African American psychologists. He notes that African American psychology has been studied from three perspectives—Eurocentric, Black, and African. The Eurocentric perspective holds as normative a model of the middle-class Caucasian male. When this model is used, African Americans are seen as deficient and inferior.

The approach of the Black perspective is to prove that Blacks are not inferior. However, this perspective is reactive rather than proactive. Psychologists taking this perspective assume that differences between African and European Americans are due to environmental and sociological differences. The socioenvironmental context for African Americans is primarily labeled as "low class" and "ghetto." This perspective does not recognize the vast diversity among African Americans. It also does not recognize that not all Blacks are from urban, low-income, inner-city environments.

According to Akbar, the African perspective is "nature-centric" and can be described as natural psychology. This perspective assumes that there are absolute standards and principles governing human behavior. One such principle is collective survival. From the perspective of this principle, a wide range of human behavior can be understood. It should be pointed out that there has been some disagreement among scholars regarding Akbar's assertion that there are absolute standards and principles governing human behavior.

DAUDI AJANI YA AZIBO

Azibo has advanced knowledge on African psychology in several ways. Azibo makes the assertion that Black psychology is African psychology. According to Azibo (1996), an understanding of African psychology requires one to examine the past, present, and future. Azibo asserts that the study of the psychology of Africans began with ancient Kemet (3000 B.C.). This was the time Blacks produced an organized system of knowledge. This organized system of knowledge enabled one to understand behavior.

Also notable among Azibo's contributions to Africentric psychology is his development of the Azibo nosology, a system for diagnosing diseases and disorders among Blacks with psychological problems (Atwell & Azibo, 1991). Unlike the *Diagnostic and Statistical Manual of Mental Disorders* (*DSM*), the standard psychological classification system, the Azibo nosology is culturally sensitive and addresses disorders that may exist among African Americans due to the unique historical, societal, and cultural factors that have helped shape their personality and behavior.

One question that has been raised is the application of the Azibo nosology and whether it reflects the real experiences and conditions of African Americans. A related question is whether therapists can utilize this system within clinical settings. Atwell and Azibo (1991) answered these questions using a case study approach. They examined two clients who had been previously diagnosed as having panic and conduct disorders based on the *DSM, third edition, revised* (*DSM-III-R*; 1987). Both were rediagnosed using the Azibo nosology. Findings indicated that the Azibo nosology accurately reflected the experiences of this client and that it could be used effectively by a therapist.

KOBI K. K. KAMBON (A.K.A. JOSEPH BALDWIN)

Kambon's contributions to Africentric psychology have been numerous. One major contribution has been in work on the African personality. Kambon distinguishes Africentric and non-Africentric theories of the African personality. Africentric theories assume that the African personality is core to people of African descent.

Kambon's research has examined components and correlates of the African personality. To measure the African personality, Kambon developed the African Self-Consciousness Scale (Baldwin & Bell, 1985). This scale has been used extensively in studies on Africentric psychology (Baldwin & Bell, 1985; Baldwin, Brown, & Rackley, 1990; Baldwin, Duncan, & Bell, 1992).

The African Self-Consciousness Scale assesses how African Americans feel about African/African American culture and societal issues that are related to racism. Using this scale, Kambon and others have examined the prevalence of African self-consciousness among African American college students in both predominately White and Black universities and within African American male-female relationships (Baldwin et al., 1992; Hamlet, 1998).

Among college students, Kambon concluded that African self-consciousness appears to be important in explaining differences between Blacks from various sociocultural environments; settings that reinforced cultural pride promoted healthy personality functioning (Baldwin et al., 1992). Regarding African American male-female relationships, findings suggest that individuals who have a high Africentric cultural consciousness prioritize qualities such as emotional and intellectual stimulation, commitment to the Black community, and family orientation; these are qualities identified by study participants when asked to describe an ideal mate (Hamlet, 1998).

Kambon's (2003) book, *Cultural Misorientation*, discusses forms of cultural misorientation found among contemporary African Americans. According to Kambon, cultural misorientation is a condition that drives African people to engage in anti-Black, racially disempowering, and self-destructive behaviors. It represents the basis for Black personality disorder. Examples of cultural misorientation can be seen in education, religious practices, and the media. For example, regarding the media, Kambon (2003) posits that media in America are controlled by and based on Eurocentric imagery. Africans subsequently accept Eurocentric media and perpetuate its imagery in Black-owned media as well.

LINDA JAMES MYERS

Myers's contribution is found in her writings on an optimal worldview (Myers, 1988). Although she examines the oppression of African Americans, her theory is not exclusive to this group. Rather, she promotes social change for all oppressed groups. Myers's optimal worldview theory helps to promote an appreciation of human diversity by encouraging an investigation of both human behavior and social roles such as gender and ethnicity.

In introducing an optimal worldview, Myers notes that our orientation is influenced by how we perceive the world. The world we see, hear, and feel through our senses is not an external world, but our own projection of reality. According to Myers, understanding the perceptual system of the dominant European culture is critical for understanding how knowledge about the external world is acquired.

The Eurocentric worldview places importance on the acquisition of material objects. Furthermore, external knowledge is assumed to be the basis for all knowledge. One acquires knowledge by attending to the external world. These values result in an identity or self-worth that is based on external criteria (e.g., what one owns, status symbols, job title, etc.). Myers maintains that these assumptions are the basis for racism and other -*isms*, all of which are suboptimal. According to Myers, everyone of European descent is not racist, but rather anyone buying into these assumptions is at risk for these consequences that naturally follow.

On the other hand, African knowledge is based on the ideas that reality is both spiritual and material, interpersonal relationships are valued, and self-knowledge is the foundation for all knowledge. Myers maintains that these assumptions result in an optimal worldview with resulting peace and happiness. Everyone of African descent does not have this worldview, but this optimal worldview may be generalized across many people of African descent.

These six psychologists have all made unique contributions to understanding Africentric psychology. They share several common features. They all assume that the study of African American psychology has to be based on an understanding of the African worldview and that this worldview is adaptive and functional for people of African descent. They assume that people of African descent are the best prepared to define and study African and African American people. Furthermore, they believe that the methodology for conducting research and acquiring knowledge cannot be based on Western paradigms. All are past national presidents of the Association of Black Psychologists, with the exception of Azibo.

African Worldview Dimensions

Africentric worldview dimensions have been described by several scholars (Akbar, 1991a; Azibo, 1996; Kambon, 2003; Myers, 1988; Nobles, 1991). These dimensions are assumed to exist among Blacks throughout the African diaspora to some degree.

Although the dimensions of the Africentric worldview are discussed separately here for the sake of clarity, these dimensions should not be considered independent. In fact, they are interdependent and highly correlated with one another. Central to Africentric thinking is the concept of holism. Holism provides an overarching framework for Africentric beliefs. All aspects of one's being are integrated, in harmony, and in balance.

The Africentric dimensions discussed next are not unique to people of African descent. Many of these dimensions are characteristic of other cultural groups. In sociological and psychological literature, the distinction has been made between individualistic cultures such as that of the United States and collectivist cultures such as those found in Asia (Triandis, 1995). African dimensions are likely to be found among people in collective cultures. Several non-Western cultural groups, including Latinos, Native Americans, and Asians, may hold worldview dimensions similar to African culture. For example, Zea, Quezada, and Belgrave (1996) noted several similarities within the belief systems of Latino and African cultures (i.e., extended family, spirituality, communalism).

SPIRITUALITY

Spirituality is a fundamental Africentric dimension and is interwoven in the lives of African people. Spirituality is a belief in a being or force greater than oneself. In the United States, spirituality is seen in religious worship and rituals such as attending church, prayers, and celebration of religious holidays. Within Western culture, spirituality is reflected in religiosity and is kept separately from other aspects of one's life. This separation is in part due to the separation of church and state. (See Chapter 8 for a fuller discussion of religion and spirituality in Africa.)

Spirituality is not separated from other aspects of one's life in African culture. One's spirituality is woven into one's daily activities. According to Nobles (1991), in traditional African culture, spirituality was such an integral part of one's existence that it could not be separated from the person. Spirituality was central in one's life from conception to post–physical death. One's being was in fact a religious experience. According to Akbar (1996), at the highest life form, man is essentially spirit.

Spiritual beliefs have been compared with materialistic beliefs. The highest fulfillment for those with a spiritual worldview is the development of the self into a spiritual being that exists in harmony with other aspects of the universe. In contrast, the fulfillment of a material worldview is the acquisition of material goods and services. Societies that have reached the highest levels of human refinement, sensitivity, and cultural dignity are those with a widely accepted and powerful image of God (Akbar, 1996).

Although spirituality and religiosity differ, they are correlated. Spiritual people are likely to engage in religious practices such as praying and attending church. Among present-day African Americans, a large percentage believe in God or a higher being and consider themselves religious. Taylor, Chatters, Jayakody, and Levin (1996) found that 80% of Blacks, compared with 51% of Whites, felt that religious beliefs were important.

African Americans are more likely than European Americans to report having religious beliefs. They also spend more time in church and other places of worship (Taylor et al., 1996). African Americans are also more likely to use spirituality as a framework for coping with stressful circumstances such as chronic illnesses and disabling conditions (Belgrave, 1998; Potts, 1996; Taylor et al., 1996). For example, parents of children with disabilities reported that they found meaning and a positive interpretation of their children's disability based on their spiritual beliefs (Belgrave, 1998). Among African Americans, spirituality is an important part of one's life regardless of circumstances. Spirituality exists across all socioeconomic levels, age-groups, and geographical locations.

COLLECTIVISM

A collective orientation is an Africentric dimension that reinforces interdependence, cooperation, and the motivation to work for the survival of the group rather than that of the individual. Significant others are considered in one's thoughts and actions.

The collectivistic orientation differs from the individualistic and competitive orientation found in Western culture. The collectivistic orientation is reflected by the saying, "I am because we are; and because we are, therefore, I am" (Mbiti, 1970). In a collective culture, the experiences of the individual influence the experiences of the group and vice versa. The individual does not exist apart from the group (Nobles, 1991). Competition is minimized in collective cultures, and harmony with the group is maximized. The collectivistic orientation values interpersonal relationships rather than the acquisition of material things. Relationships with other persons are important because one's own well-being is interwoven with that of significant others.

In African cultures, the collectivistic orientation helped to ensure the survival of the tribe. African tribes' strong commitment to kinship included the sharing of common beliefs, which helped sustain all members of the tribe (Nobles, 1991). When one member suffered, all suffered and when one member did well, all did well. Loneliness and alienation are not found in African cultural groups because the members of each tribe are interconnected and there is concern and responsibility for one another (White & Parham, 1990). Aggression and violence is minimized within tribes. From a collectivistic perspective, an act of aggression against another member of the tribe is viewed as an act of aggression toward oneself (Nobles, 1976).

Among present-day African Americans, collective orientation is reflected through strong commitment to the family, the extended family, and fictive kin (McAdoo, 1998; Nobles, 1991). Fictive kin are those individuals who are not biologically related or related through marriage but are treated as though they are. This collective orientation is reflected in African Americans' frequent contact with the immediate and extended family, the tendency of family members to live near one another, and the care provided for elderly and disabled family members (McAdoo, 1993).

The collectivistic orientation has important implications for studying and understanding the behavior of African Americans. The family and significant other members of the "family tribe" should be considered when one attempts to understand, diagnose, or treat individual-level problems. Within Western psychology, the unit of analysis has been based on the Eurocentric dimension of individualism. Consequently, much of Western psychology has focused on understanding and addressing problems at an individual level. This focus on individuation is not always appropriate for African Americans, as significant others should be included. For example, within African American communities, persuasive health care messages should promote good health practices by appealing to the family or community rather than the individual.

TIME ORIENTATION

Time is viewed differently in Western and African cultures. Time within Western culture is future oriented, whereas time within African culture considers the past and present to be of equal importance as the future. Time orientation determines the rhythm of one's life, one's rate and intensity of activity, as well as one's priorities (Akbar, 1991a).

Time for West Africans was experienced through the life of the tribe that went back many generations (Nobles, 1991). Time in African cultures is cyclical rather than linear. The past is important in African culture because it shapes the direction for present-day life experiences. African cultures make future decisions based on what has happened in the past.

In European culture, time is a concrete commodity to be bought and sold (Akbar, 1991a). It is seen as mathematical and bound by the clock. In contrast, time among Africans is flexible, elastic, and exists to meet the needs of the people. Time is experienced subjectively and reduces the need to impose one's own time on others. According to Akbar (1991a), Eurocentric future orientation creates urgency and pressure, as it is essentially impossible to ever catch up with the future.

Future time orientation is reflected in Western psychology's emphasis on prediction and control. This emphasis has resulted in the misunderstanding of cultures that do not emphasize control and prediction and have therefore been labeled deficient. For example, African Americans have been labeled as deficient because they lack a futuristic time orientation and are perceived as not having the ability to delay future gratification (Banks, McQuater, Anthony, & Ward, 1992). The emphasis on the past and present, relative to the future, is viewed as a negative personality trait. In a critical analysis of the delay of gratification literature, however, Banks et al. found that Blacks were no less future oriented than Whites. Rather, African Americans are more likely to focus on the past and present along with the future.

Among African Americans, time orientation can be captured by the cliché "colored people's time" (CPT). CPT means that arriving late is acceptable or that time must be experienced to be valid. A CPT orientation is found among Blacks throughout the diaspora. J. M. Jones (1994) commented on experiences with time in Trinidad. He noticed that people from Trinidad have personal control over time; they are not driven or made a slave by it. Things start when people arrive and end when they leave.

There is evidence of elastic and flexible use of time by African Americans when compared with European Americans. Rubin and Belgrave (1999) investigated differences in European and African American college students' responses to when they were likely to arrive at certain events (e.g., meet a professor, go on a job interview, arrive at a social dinner). They found that African American students used time in a more flexible way, and European American college students used time in a more mathematical or exact way. African Americans were more likely to respond that they would arrive at an event at an approximate time in contrast to European Americans, who indicated that they would arrive at an event at the exact time.

ORALITY

Orality is a preference for receiving stimuli and information from the external world orally. This orientation may be contrasted with one that prefers written stimuli. African cultures, compared with Western cultures, are more oral in orientation.

Orality is used in Africa when information is handed down from elders to members of the tribe. The culture of a tribe was orally transmitted from generation to generation. On coming to the New World, the oral orientation helped slaves to retain their African culture and to function in the New World since they were not allowed to read or write. The oral orientation is reflected in present-day African Americans' storytelling and rap music.

With technologically advanced ways of transmitting information (e.g., Internet, fax, etc.), it is possible to receive virtually all types of information without oral communication. These technologically advanced means of communication allow for quicker and faster dissemination of information, but they may be counter to the oral preference of people of African descent.

SENSITIVITY TO AFFECT AND EMOTIONAL CUES

The sensitivity to affect and emotional cues is an orientation that acknowledges the emotional and affective states of self and others. This dimension is related to the collective orientation, as it includes a consideration of other people. Among people of African descent, there is an extended sensitivity to the emotional and affective states of others (Boykin, 1983; Boykin & Ellison, 1995). This orientation places emphasis on receiving emotional receptivity and expressions. It is seen when one empathizes with and relates to others. From this perspective, one has the ability to feel the pain and the joy of others, and one expects others to feel his or her pain. Similarly, one's own affective states are linked to the affective states of significant others.

Sensitivity to others' orientation can be contrasted to an emotionally isolated orientation whereby one's affective state is determined by one's individual and personal level of functioning. Here, one's emotional and affective state is determined in isolation from the emotional state of others. The sensitivity to affect and emotional cue orientation leads to synchronicity between one's emotions and affective states and others' thoughts and behaviors. For example, if a person feels happy, he or she is more likely to engage in positive behavior. If unhappy, he or she is less likely to engage in positive behavior.

VERVE AND RHYTHM

The verve and rhythm dimension is reflected in behavior that is rhythmic and creative. This may be seen in movement, posture, speech patterns, and behavior. Verve can be considered an improvisational style among African Americans (Boykin, 1983). Verve and rhythm orientations are related to time orientations insofar as natural rhythm dictates how one functions and presents oneself (Nobles, 1991). A person with verve walks, talks, and presents him- or herself in a creative and expressive way.

Verve suggests a preference for several stimuli rather than a singular and routine stimulus. It is characterized by an increased appeal for stimuli that change by increases in energy level and pace. According to Boykin, verve is important in terms of how children learn. The didactic "teacher talks and students listen" mode of learning may not work as well with African American children as it does with European American children because of differences in verve and rhythm. African American children might learn better by multiple teaching and learning methods (interactions with each other, movement, touching, etc.).

BALANCE AND HARMONY WITH NATURE

In African philosophy, it is important to have balance and harmony with nature (Nobles, 1991). Balance and harmony are necessary for one's well-being, and it is necessary to have balance between one's mental, physical, and spiritual states. Within the African tradition, this assumes that the various aspects of one's self are intricately connected. Spiritual imbalance is reflected by a physical and mental imbalance and vice versa. The importance of living in harmony with nature is also seen in African cultures. Nature includes the animals, plants, and natural phenomena that constitute the environment in which humans live. The desired goal of life is not to conquer nature and the physical elements, but to live in harmony with them. According to Nobles (1991), everything in nature, including humans, animals, and plants, is functionally connected. Therefore, control and mastery over nature, which is a prominent theme in Western philosophy, does not exist in Africentric philosophy. Although these dimensions are not the only characteristics found among people of African descent, they are core to rendering this group distinct (Randolph & Banks, 1993).

OTHER ASPECTS OF AFRICENTRIC PSYCHOLOGY

In a thoughtful review of African psychology, Grills (2004) discusses seven related concepts that anchor and frame the study of African psychology.

- *Ma'at* is a cardinal principal that governs the dynamic functioning of the universe and refers to balance and cosmic order. There are seven cardinal virtues of Ma'at, including truth, justice, compassion, harmony, balance, reciprocity, and order. The more these virtues are practiced, the more developed the self becomes.

- *Maafa* is the term used to describe the enslavement of Africans by Europeans. The Maafa was designed to oppress, humiliate, and destroy African people. Critical to Maafa is the denial of the humanity of Africans. It is seen in present-day times by oppressive and discriminatory actions against African Americans.

- Veneration of the person assumes the value of all living beings. A person's life is interwoven with the lives of everyone else. This includes both the living and the departed. In short, life is venerated, cherished, and celebrated.

- Spiritness is a concept whose meaning is to be full of life—to have a mind, soul, energy, and passion. From the Africentric perspective, spirit is both real and symbolic and is the divine spark that makes humans who they are.

- Human authenticity is the condition of being sincere and being who you are meant to be. It is the quality of being genuine and free of imitation. When authenticity is absent, the threat of survival emerges, as one is not sure who to trust or rely on.

- Inclusive metaphysical epistemology refers to the use of both affective and cognitive syntheses of information as a way of knowing. Reality is not limited to what is understood by the five senses, and rational logic is not the only way of obtaining knowledge.

- *Sankofa* is an Akan Adrinkra symbol that means in order to go forward, one must look back. In contemporary African American culture, this means that one must look back at historical events to learn from them and to plan for the future. Sankofa also symbolizes one's return to African culture and identity for guidance.

According to Grills, the concepts of Ma'at, Maafa, veneration of the person, spiritness, human authenticity, and inclusive metaphysical epistemology, along with Africentric worldview dimensions, are central to understanding African psychology.

CAN AN AFRICAN WORLDVIEW EXIST AMONG CONTEMPORARY AFRICAN AMERICANS?

The belief that an African worldview exists among African Americans has been questioned for two reasons. One, people on the African continent are diverse and thus not likely to hold universal beliefs and values. Two, Africans in America have been socialized for several centuries in this country and may have lost African traditions in the socialization process. In addressing these issues, Nobles (1991) wrote that although many West African tribes have different languages, religions, and many unique customs, there are many similarities that suggest a common ethos among persons of African descent.

In the New World, enslaved Africans held on to the African worldview because it provided a familiar pattern of beliefs, habits, and ways of behaving that were adaptive in an oppressive environment (Nobles, 1991). Physical and environmental isolation helped Africans in the New World retain their culture. Blacks were cut off from the civilization of Europeans, and their culture was retained as a means of survival. Enslaved Africans were not allowed to read, and there were no televisions, radio, Internet, or other modes of transmission by which they could assimilate European culture. We see the continued physical and geographical isolation of African Americans in many urban areas today. African Americans almost exclusively populate some inner cities.

A second way of transmitting African values has been through the oral tradition. Enslaved Africans brought their oral tradition with them to the New World. Laws that did not permit slaves to read and write reinforced the retention of this tradition. Oral communication became essential for survival. This tradition has been passed down through the generations.

Spirituality also helped Africans in the New World to maintain the African worldview. Under harsh and oppressive conditions, spirituality provided a reason for living. This ideology continues in present-day beliefs. The fulfillment of the spiritual self is not linked to external criteria but to a relationship with God or a higher power. One's life is meaningful if one is spiritual and if one lives for a higher calling, regardless of social status.

The extended family and fictive kin helped Africans in the New World to maintain African values and beliefs. In Africa, members of a tribe worked and lived interdependently. On the plantation, biological families were separated and sold. Once sold, families often did not see each other again. Therefore, biologically unrelated slaves on the plantation related to one another as family. The inclusion of nonbiologically related persons as family is known today as fictive kinship (McAdoo, 1998; Nobles, 1991). Fictive kin are people who are not biologically related or related through marriage but who feel and function like family. African American families and kin have had to rely on each other due to economic hardships. This reliance has fostered collectivism.

Acculturation affects the extent to which African Americans have assimilated to the Eurocentric worldview. Acculturation is the degree to which a minority culture adopts the values and customs of the majority culture. There is a fair amount of acculturation among African Americans, with some individuals being more acculturated than others.

The degree to which enslaved Africans were acculturated was determined by their geographical location. For example, the Geeches, a geographically isolated group of African Americans who live on the Sea Islands of the coast of Georgia, have behaviors and language patterns in which African culture is highly evident. Their geographic isolation has resulted in a low level of acculturation (White & Parham, 1990). In more integrated and acculturated settings, the Africentric worldview may be present but more limited.

Some scholars note that acculturation and deviation from an African-centered perspective is at the root of many of the social problems African Americans face today, for example, drugs, violence, and child abuse and neglect (Akbar, 1991b; Azibo, 1996; Kambon, 2003). The loss of core Africentric values is attributed to many factors, including expansive indoctrination of European culture through the mass media.

Africentric Research With African Americans

Although research in Africentric psychology is limited, there has been a growing body of work on this topic over the past 20 years. Studies have (a) examined differences between African Americans and European Americans on Africentric worldview dimensions (Allen & Butler, 1996; Grills & Longshore, 1996; Rubin & Belgrave, 1999); and (b) examined the relationship between the Africentric worldview and other psychological and sociological variables, such as racial identity (Brookins, 1994; Jagers, Smith, Mock, & Dill, 1997), mental health (Dixon & Azibo, 1998), and drug use (Belgrave, Brome, & Hampton, 2000). A few recent studies have evaluated the effectiveness of Africentric-based programs for African Americans (Belgrave et al., 2000; Cherry et al., 1998; Harvey & Hill, 2004).

STUDIES ON DIFFERENCES BETWEEN AFRICAN AMERICANS AND EUROPEAN AMERICANS ON AFRICENTRIC DIMENSIONS

Several studies have looked at differences between African Americans and European Americans on Africentric dimensions. Others have examined whether or not Africentric worldview dimensions relate to adaptive functioning among African Americans and European Americans. One would expect favorable outcomes to be correlated with Africentric values for African Americans more so than for European Americans.

Research by Allen and Boykin (1991) showed that low-income African American children performed better on learning tasks when the learning context provided music and the opportunity for movement than when it did not. In a subsequent study addressing this same issue, Allen and Butler (1996) looked at the effects of music and movement opportunity on reasoning and learning tasks. Participants were 28 third graders attending a public school in a northeastern city. Fifteen of the children were African American and 13 were European American. African American children were from low-income families and European American children were from middle-income families.

The children were told two stories via an audiocassette. The two stories were told under two different learning contexts. In one learning context, children were told to sit or stand while they listened to a story. The story was read aloud by an adult who stood in front of the children. In this condition, the students could not move, and music was not provided. This condition was referred to as the low-movement expressive learning condition. In the other learning context, an adult read the story while a rhythmic tune played. The children were asked to stand or sit around the experimenter, and movement and clapping to the beat of the rhythmic tune were encouraged. This condition allowed the children to be movement expressive and allowed for a high level of stimulation.

The children listened to the stories under the movement expressive or no movement expressive conditions and completed a reasoning and learning test immediately following the story. Children were tested in race and gender homogeneous groups. The findings showed significant differences between African American and European American children in how well they performed under the two conditions. African American children's performance was significantly better under the high movement expressive learning condition than the low movement expressive learning condition. In contrast, the learning of the European American children was better under the low movement expressive context.

Allen and Butler (1996) concluded that African American children can perform at the level of European American children under learning conditions that are congruent with their culture. Although European American students in this study were from higher socioeconomic backgrounds and African American children were from lower socioeconomic backgrounds, they performed at similar levels.

A study on differences in how African Americans and European Americans use time provides a second example of research on ethnic differences in Africentric dimensions. Rubin and Belgrave (1999) examined differences between African American and European American college students in relative and mathematical time orientations. They hypothesized that African Americans would be more likely than European Americans to use relative time and that European Americans would be more likely to use mathematical time. Relative time was defined as elastic and flexible (i.e., not exact but approximate; e.g., very early, somewhat early, etc.), whereas mathematical time was defined as quantifying a specific time period (i.e., 15 minutes early, 10 minutes late, etc.). Participants were 55 students attending a midsize university on the East Coast.

Participants were asked to choose one time response that best corresponded to the time they would arrive at several events: (a) a family/cultural event, such as a worship service; (b) an academic-related event, such as a lecture; (c) a social event, such as going to a movie with friends; and (d) a work-related event, such as a job interview. These scenarios were grouped into formal or informal categories. An example of an informal family scenario was the following: "A holiday weekend is approaching and you are going home. Your family is going to have dinner together when you arrive. You arrive . . ." Each scenario was followed by 14 time choices with responses ranging from "very early" to "15 minutes late." Seven of the choices depicted relative or flexible time (e.g., "early" or "late"), while the other seven choices were clock time descriptors (e.g., "5 minutes late" or "10 minutes early"). Rubin and Belgrave (1999) found that African Americans were more likely than European Americans to use relative time for most occasions. European Americans, on the other hand, were more likely to use mathematical time. European Americans used relative time less than African Americans and when it was used, it was used for informal and unstructured events. African Americans were more likely than European Americans to use relative time for events that included attending a lecture, meeting a professor, going on a job interview, and going to work. Incongruent time orientations for African Americans and European Americans who work together may create conflicts when each assumes that the other is using time inappropriately. Cross-cultural training in time orientations may help each cultural group to better understand the cultural orientation for certain behaviors.

In yet another study of the differences between African Americans and European Americans, Logan and Belgrave (1999) administered a communalism scale (Boykin, Jagers, Ellison, & Allbury, 1997) and Belgrave's Africentric Worldview Scale (Belgrave, 2005) to 198 working and college-attending African American and European American adults. The findings revealed significant differences between the two ethnic groups on several dimensions. African Americans were more communal and spiritual and had a more flexible time orientation than did their European American counterparts.

THE RELATIONSHIP BETWEEN AFRICENTRIC BELIEFS AND OTHER VARIABLES

Studies have examined the correlation between Africentric beliefs and other psychological and sociological variables. Africentric worldview constructs have been correlated with racial identity (Brookins, 1994), academic attitudes (Jagers et al., 1997), imposter feelings (Ewing, Richardson,

James-Myers, & Russell, 1996), and drug attitudes and use (Belgrave et al., 2000).

Africentric Worldview and the Imposter Phenomenon

A study by Ewing et al. is illustrative of this research. Ewing and colleagues were interested in whether or not the Africentric worldview was correlated with the imposter phenomenon among African American graduate students. The researchers were also interested in how racial identity correlated with the imposter phenomenon.

The imposter phenomenon, defined as an inner experience of intellectual phoniness (Clance & Imes, 1978), has been linked to people with a higher level of education relative to others in their family, negative self-esteem, and uniqueness within their environment. The imposter phenomenon is a negative psychological state and interferes with one's ability to function competently.

Participants were 103 African American students enrolled in graduate or professional programs. Participants attended a large midwestern university and a midsize East Coast university that were predominately European American. The Belief Systems Analysis Scale by Montgomery, Fine, and James-Myers (1990) was used to measure an Africentric worldview; the Harvey Imposter Phenomenon Scale was used to measure imposter feelings (Harvey & Katz, 1985); and the Racial Identity Attitude Survey (Parham & Helms, 1981) was used to measure racial identity.

Findings indicated that the Africentric-based Belief Systems Analysis Scale was a significant and unique predictor of the imposter phenomenon. Those participants who scored higher on an Africentric belief measure scored lower on the imposter measure. Moreover, the results showed that the Africentric belief system, and not racial identity, was correlated with imposter feelings. Ewing et al. concluded that African Americans with Africentric worldview beliefs are less likely to experience imposter feelings in graduate school.

Africentric Worldview and Drug Use

A study by Belgrave et al. (2000) examined the extent to which the Africentric worldview was correlated with drug attitudes and behaviors among African American youth. The researchers assumed that Africentric beliefs would be protective and that strong Africentric beliefs would be negatively correlated with negative behaviors such as drug use.

Participants were 195 fourth and fifth graders attending public schools in two cities on the East Coast. Students were recruited to participate in a drug prevention program. Data reported for this study was pretest data collected prior to their participation in the drug prevention program. Participants were administered measures of Africentric values, drug attitudes, and drug use.

The findings indicated that Africentric beliefs were significant predictors of drug attitudes and use. Stronger Africentric beliefs and stronger religious beliefs were associated with attitudes that were intolerant of drugs and less drug use.

Africentric Worldview and Health and Stress

Logan (2000) examined the relationship between Africentric beliefs, health status, perceived stress, and drug use among African Americans. Logan hypothesized that high Africentric values would be associated with less stress, a more positive self-health rating, and less drug use.

Participants were 113 African American working and college-attending adults. The questionnaire consisted of self-report measures of Africentric values, perceived stress over the past 30 days, self-rating of physical health status, and 30-day drug use. The findings revealed significant relationships between Africentric values and stress, health, and drug use. Stronger Africentric values were related to less stress, better rating of health status, and less reported drug use.

RESEARCH ON AFRICENTRIC-BASED APPROACHES IN PREVENTION, INTERVENTION, AND TREATMENT

Research on the effectiveness of programs based on Africentric theory is fairly limited and only a few studies could be identified. Increased interest in Africentric beliefs should encourage work in this area.

A study by Cherry et al. (1998) titled "NTU: An Africentric Approach to Substance Abuse Prevention Among African American Youth" is an illustration of this developing body of work. Cherry and colleagues implemented a program to prevent drug use among African American youth by increasing resiliency factors and reducing risk factors. Africentric beliefs were considered a resiliency factor. The objectives of the prevention program were to improve knowledge of and increase intolerance of drugs; to increase Africentric values; to increase awareness of racial identity; to improve self-esteem; to increase knowledge of African culture; and to improve school behaviors.

Participants were 169 fifth- and sixth-grade African American youth considered at high risk for alcohol, tobacco, and other drug use because of their socioenvironmental context. Participants resided in areas with elevated levels of criminal and drug activity.

Africentric philosophy and worldview provided the conceptual framework for the development and implementation of intervention activities. The main intervention component was a rites of passage program. This program provided an opportunity for children to gain the skills, behaviors, and attitudes necessary to transition to a higher developmental stage. In this case, children were being prepared for transition from childhood to adolescence. Other intervention components were a substance abuse education program and an African education program.

The rites program used the principles of Nguzo Nane (seven principles of Kwanzaa) and Heshema (respect) to foster positive values and behavior. Students participated in several activities. Weekly rites sessions consisted of skill building and self-enhancing activities. Symbolic and ceremonial activities were designed to be congruent with Africentric methods. The rites of incorporation ceremony inducted youth into the program. The rites of separation ceremony allowed parents to symbolically give their children to the program staff to work with. A 2-day retreat was held to foster bonding and relationship building among youth and between staff and youth. A naming ceremony provided youth the opportunity to obtain an African name that reflected who they were and who they wanted to become. The final event was a graduation ceremony that completed the transformation into adolescence.

In addition to the rites program, there were weekly classes on African history and culture. These classes were designed to increase students' awareness and knowledge of the culture of Africa. There was a substance abuse course designed to teach students about drugs and how drugs affect the African American community.

Students participated in the program during their fifth-grade school year, attending sessions twice a week. During their sixth-grade year, they attended sessions once a week. There were two groups of participants. The intervention group consisted of fifth and sixth graders attending one school, and the comparison group consisted of the same-grade students attending a school that was in a demographically similar community. Data were collected at the beginning and the end of the program from both intervention and comparison groups.

Measures used to assess the effectiveness of the intervention included an attitude toward drugs test, the Africentric Value Scale for Children (described later in this chapter), a children's racial identity scale, a knowledge test about African culture, a self-concept scale, and a teacher rating scale.

Analyses were computed to determine if there were differences between the intervention and the comparison groups at posttest when controlling for pretest scores. The findings revealed significant improvement for intervention but not comparison youth in several areas including racial identity, knowledge of African culture, self-esteem, and school behaviors. Interestingly, there were no significant improvements in drug attitudes. Cherry et al. (1998) speculated this might be due to the fact that students in both groups had very negative attitudes toward drugs and little drug use at the beginning of the program because of their young age. The researchers concluded that an Africentric-based program seems promising for increasing resiliency factors for African American youth.

Similarly, Harvey and Hill (2004) found benefits of an Africentric-based youth and family rites of passage program. This program also targeted at-risk African American adolescent boys and their parents. It was a 3-year evaluation of a youth rites of passage demonstration project that used therapeutic interventions based on Africentric principles. The findings revealed that youth who participated in the program increased in self-esteem and accurate knowledge of the dangers of drug abuse.

Programs that use Africentric approaches tend to be better received by African American participants than those that do not (Chipungu et al., 2000). Chipungu reviewed 12 drug prevention programs that targeted African Americans. Chipungu and colleagues found that African American youth liked their Africentric prevention programs more than African American youth who were in other programs and non–African American program participants. Participants were also more likely to view the program as important to them if it used Africentric methods than if it did not.

In summary, studies that use Africentric methods in programs are increasing. This early work suggests a positive benefit to using these methods.

Methodological Issues

There are two central methodological issues to consider in Africentric psychology. One revolves around how we study people of African descent. The second issue is how we measure Africentric values, beliefs, and constructs. These are discussed next.

METHODS FOR STUDYING PEOPLE OF AFRICAN DESCENT

The psychology of African Americans cannot be studied with the same methodology used to study European Americans. Carruthers (1996) argues specifically against the use of the experimental method to study African Americans, noting that this method, with its emphasis on control and prediction, has been used to control oppressed people.

Kambon's (1998) analysis of Africentric and non-Africentric theories of African personality suggests another concern with the scientific method. The scientific method, in its attempt to isolate discrete cause and effect relationships between variables, may be inherently biased toward Eurocentric or non-Africentric explanations or perspectives of African behavior. Kambon asserts that non-Africentric (Eurocentric) theories of personality exclusively focus on the individual. Within Eurocentric psychology, each individual is seen as unique, with a personalized biopsychological condition that makes the person a distinguishable significant entity. Persons outside of this unique individual are not considered as they are in African psychology.

Semaj (1996) also rejects the use of the experimental method as the scientific method to study Black people. Semaj rejects as a myth that science is objective, culturally universal, and unemotional. He disputes the notion that science leads systematically to truth. According to Semaj, the knowledge gained from studying society can never be passive but is always active in maintaining or in destroying a social system. Semaj further points out that despite the many academic degrees awarded, the problems of society remain relatively unchanged. Semaj (1996, pp. 198–199) offers alternative guidelines for conducting research with people of African descent:

1. Self-knowledge should be of primary importance. "Know thyself."

2. There should be no artificial divisions via discipline; such divisions do not allow for the collective efforts that come about through diversity.

3. There should be no limitations on issues studied and methodologies used to study them. Scholars should be free to study that which is important and not just that which is dictated by one's discipline.

4. There should be no scientific colonization. Research should be conducted that will serve the interests of people rather than to advance a career or satisfy individual interests.

5. There should be concern with interpretation and application of data. The scientist should make sure that his or her findings are appropriately interpreted and applied.

6. The publication and dissemination of work should be done by those who share the vision of liberation.

7. Researchers should practice what they preach. The lifestyle of the researcher should be consistent with his or her work.

HOW IS THE AFRICENTRIC WORLDVIEW MEASURED?

Increased interest in the Africentric worldview has raised attention to methods of measuring it. There have been several scales developed to assess Africentric constructs over the past decade. Before describing the measures and the theoretical frameworks used to develop these scales, we must make a distinction between the Africentric worldview and racial identity attitudes, as these terms are sometimes used interchangeably. Both are relevant to understanding the beliefs, attitudes, and behavior of African Americans. As noted previously, Africentric values are those derived from people of African descent and are those values and beliefs that are reflected by the dimensions discussed previously (i.e., spirituality, collectivism, flexible time orientation, etc.). Ethnic identity consists of thoughts, behaviors, and feelings about being a member of a racial and ethnic group, and feelings of belonging and affiliation with one's ethnic group.

Substantially more work has been done on the conceptualization and measurement of ethnic and racial identity than Africentric values (Burlew & Smith, 1991; Helms, 1990; Roberts et al., 1999). We discuss some of the work on measurement of Africentric worldview next.

African Self-Consciousness Scale

Baldwin (a.k.a. Kambon) developed the African Self-Consciousness Scale (ASC) to assess dimensions of Black personality (Baldwin & Bell, 1985). This scale has been widely used with African American populations. According to Baldwin, the core of the Black personality is oneness of being that is reflected in an extension of self and a communal orientation. The ASC scale assesses self-extension and communal orientation.

Several dimensions core to African self-consciousness are captured in this measure, including awareness that one is of African heritage, priorities placed on Black survival and liberation, priorities placed on activities directed at self-knowledge and self-affirmations, and resistance toward anti-Black forces and threats to Black survival. These dimensions cover education; family, religious, and cultural activities; interpersonal relations; and political orientation areas.

The scale consists of 42 items. One such item is, "I don't necessarily feel like I am also being mistreated in a situation where I see another Black person being mistreated." A Likert-type format that ranges from 1 = "strongly disagree" to 8 = "strongly agree" is used. Higher scores represent stronger African self-consciousness.

Belief Systems Analysis Scale

The Belief Systems Analysis Scale (BSAS) was developed by Montgomery et al. (1990) to measure one's optimal worldview. The scale is based on the assumption that the optimal worldview beliefs are holistic and integrated into one's being. The suboptimal worldview is associated with fragmentation of one's self. High scores on the BSAS are associated with a high belief in an optimal worldview and low scores are associated with a low optimal worldview. The optimal worldview scale consists of five factors: (a) values for interpersonal relationships, (b) a de-emphasis on appearance, (c) integration of opposites, (d) satisfaction based on that which is nonmaterial, and (e) optimism.

The scale consists of 31 items. Respondents indicate the extent to which they agree or disagree with statements using a 5-point Likert scale format.

An example of an item is, "Working on a job with meaning is more important than the money received from a job."

The Communalism Scale

The Communalism Scale, developed by Boykin et al. (1997), assesses the Africentric dimension of communalism. Communalism is akin to collectivism. It reflects interdependence among people and is associated with cooperation, shared interests and activities, and concern for others. Communalism places greater emphasis on the survival of the group than of the individual. Communalism is a central dimension because it reinforces the other Africentric worldview dimensions.

The Communalism Scale measures how connected the respondent feels to others in his or her family, community, and other environments. The scale consists of 31 items that are rated based on Likert-type responses that range from 1 = "completely false" to 6 = "completely true." Nine filler items are included to reduce response set and social desirability. An example of a scale item is, "I place great value on social relations among people."

Africentrism Based on the Principles of Nguzo Saba

This scale was developed by Grills and Longshore (1996) to assess the principles of the Nguzo Saba, which correspond to Africentric beliefs. The seven principles of Nguzo Saba represent a set of guidelines and a value system for healthy living that African Americans should strive for and live by (Karenga, 1988; see news story at chapter opening). The principles of Nguzo Saba were originally intended to be celebrated during Kwanzaa, an African American celebration; however, they are believed to be universal guidelines and their usage is not restricted to African Americans or Kwanzaa celebrations. The principles of Nguzo Saba are as follows:

Umoja (unity): To strive for and maintain unity in the family, community, nation, and race.

Kujichagulia (self-determination): To define ourselves, name ourselves, create for ourselves, and speak for ourselves.

Ujima (collective work and responsibility): To build and maintain our community together by sharing our sisters' and brothers' problems and making an effort to solve them together.

Ujamaa (cooperative economics): To build and maintain our own stores, shops, and other businesses and to profit from them together.

Nia (purpose): To make our collective vocation the building and developing of our community and to restore our people to their traditional greatness.

Kuumba (creativity): To always do as much as we can, in the way we can, to leave our community more beautiful and beneficial than we inherited it.

Imani (faith): To believe with all our heart in our people, our parents, and our teachers, along with the righteousness and victory of our struggle.

The Africentrism scale consists of 17 items. A 4-point Likert scale format is used and items range from 1 = "strongly disagree" to 4 = "strongly agree." An example of a scale item is, "My family's needs are more important to me than my own needs."

Africentric Value Scale for Children

The measures discussed thus far are used with adolescents and adults. Much less has been done to assess Africentric constructs among children. This is partially due to the fact that an understanding of Africentric dimensions may be different for children than for adults. At the preadolescent stage, children are ego-centered. It may be difficult for them to respond to concepts of spirituality, unity, and collectivism if they have not yet formed a personal identity. On the other hand, there may be some internalization of Africentric beliefs, especially in a cultural context where children are socialized and surrounded by significant others who hold these beliefs.

The Africentric Value Scale for Children (AVS-C) was developed to meet the need for a measure to assess Africentric values following an Africentric-based program designed to infuse Africentric values among youth (Belgrave, Townsend, Cherry, & Cunningham, 1997). Like the Africentrism scale developed by Grills and Longshore (1996), items composing the scale were written to correspond to the seven principles of Nguzo Saba (Karenga, 1988). Factor analysis of 18 items resulted in three distinct factors: collective work and responsibility, cooperative economics, and self-determination. The collective work and responsibility subscale assesses the belief that African Americans are responsible for one another and should work together to improve their family and community. The cooperative economics subscale assesses the belief that resources should be shared and maintained within the African American community. The third subscale, self-determination, assesses the belief that African Americans should make decisions about what is best for them, their families, and their communities.

A Likert scale format is used with three response categories: "yes," "sometimes," and "no." An example of a scale item is, "African Americans should shop in African American owned stores whenever possible." The scale has been used with children between the ages of 9 and 14.

In summary, some measures for assessing the Africentric worldview exist. These measures are based on the Africentric dimensions and the principles of Nguzo Saba. In general, these measures are valid and reliable. Research on measuring Africentric constructs is likely to continue.

Summary

The proverb at the beginning of this chapter, "Wood may remain ten years in the water, but it will never become a crocodile," conveys the idea that although time and conditions change, core features of the person will remain the same. This is true of persons of African descent living in America.

The Africentric worldview is found among most people of African descent. A worldview consists of the values, beliefs, and behaviors of a group of people. African American psychologists began to write about the Africentric worldview in the late 1960s and early 1970s. Several psychologists have advanced our understanding of the Africentric worldview. Among them are Joseph White, Na'im Akbar, Wade Nobles, Daudi Ajani ya Azibo, Kobi Kambon, and Linda James Myers. Much of the work on Africentric psychology has been published in *The Journal of Black Psychology*.

The Africentric worldview is characterized by several dimensions that differ from the Eurocentric worldview. While there is a great deal of diversity among African Americans, the following dimensions are assumed to exist among most people of African descent to some degree: spirituality, collectiveness, flexible and past time orientation, orality, sensitivity to the emotional and affective state of others, verve and rhythm, and an orientation toward balance and harmony. Grills (2004) identified other concepts relevant to understanding African psychology, including Ma'at, Maafa, veneration of the person, spiritness, human authenticity, and Sankofa. Several conditions helped Africans in the New World to maintain African values and traditions.

Africentric research has examined differences between African Americans and European Americans on Africentric dimensions, the relationship between Africentric dimensions and other psychological and social variables, and the effectiveness of Africentric-based interventions. Several measures have been developed to assess Africentric worldview dimensions.

Note

1. An earlier version of this chapter was published as a supplement by authors F. Z. Belgrave, D. Logan, and R. Tademy (Thomson Publishing).

Section II

Social Systems and Structures

Kinship and Family 3

"It's a Family Affair," *The Washington Post*, September 7, 2001

Natalie Hopkinson

The seeds for this weekend's National Black Family Reunion Celebration were planted 16 years ago, in the mind of civil rights leader Dorothy Height. The now 89-year-old founder and president of the National Council of Negro Women read an article about the "dying Black family" and got mad about it.

"Her answer to that was that the African American family is not dying," explains Shiba Freeman Haley, the regional coordinator for the celebration. "Ours aren't always the typical mother, father, 2.3 children, but there is still much to celebrate." Height responded by organizing the first annual National Black Family Reunion Celebration on the Washington Monument grounds, not far from the council's Pennsylvania Avenue headquarters. In the tradition of summertime family reunions, the council invited families to spend the day outside, enjoy music and entertainment, and eat way too much food.

In addition to entertainment, ethnic foods, and an arts and crafts marketplace, the council organized activities aimed at strengthening the family unit, such as panels, seminars, and health screenings.

"We wanted to take all different aspects of the family—spiritual, health, economics, and so forth—and to have panel discussions and activities," Haley continues. "To look at what is different and good about black families."

Definitions and Historical
Background on African American Families

As indicated in the news story, African American families are not the typical husband, wife, and two children. African American families are varied and diverse as will be seen in this chapter. Many disciplines including sociology, anthropology, history, and psychology are interested in the African American family and kinships. The family is the most proximal influence for youth and the primary institution for socializing them. In this chapter, we cover structural (i.e., who the family consists of and what the family looks like) as well as functional (i.e., what purposes the family serves) aspects of the African American family. First, we provide definitions of terms-relevant to family. Then, we give a historical overview of how African American families have been studied, and we describe the functional and structural characteristics of Africans living in the New World during the period of slavery. We provide a snapshot of what African American families look like. We explore strengths and coping patterns among Black families and the impact of discriminatory institutional policies on them. Finally, we review methodological issues in studying African American families and summarize the main ideas of the chapter.

DEFINITIONS

More than half a century ago, the sociologist Murdock (1949) defined the family as a social group characterized by common residence, economic cooperation, and reproduction. A family, according to Murdock, includes adults of both sexes, at least two of whom have a sexual relationship, and one or more children, biological or adopted, of the sexually cohabiting adults. Murdock described the nuclear family as the most basic family structure, which consisted of a married man and woman with their offspring. Murdock's definition captures what has been thought of as a traditional family. As we will see, African American families differ substantially from the family described by Murdock.

Reiss's (1965) definition of the family focuses on its functional aspects. According to Reiss, the one universal function of the family is the socialization of the young. Reiss defines the family as a small kinship-structured group with the key function of providing nurturance and socialization of the newborn. He acknowledges that this group is commonly the parents in a conjugal relationship, but occasionally it is the mother and/or other relatives of the mother.

Hill's (1998) definition of the Black family emphasizes both functional and structural aspects. According to Hill, the Black family is a household related by blood or marriage or function that provides basic instrumental and expressive functions to its members. Families serve instrumental functions by providing for the physical and material needs of the family members, such as providing clothing, shelter, and food. The expressive functions of a family take into account the emotional support and nurturance needs met by the family.

The family network can include biological relations as well as non-biologically related members. The African American family is characterized as an extended family (Hill, 1998). The *extended family* is a network of functionally related individuals who reside in different households. The *immediate family* consists of individuals who reside in the same household, regardless of the number of generations within that household.

Fictive kin are often included as members of African American families. *Fictive kin* are those members of the family who are not biologically related nor related through marriage but who feel and function like family. Friends who are fictive kin are seen socially and emotionally as kin. A person who is considered fictive kin may be seen as a father, mother, grandmother, grandfather, uncle, aunt, sister, brother, or cousin, depending on the role he or she plays (Scott & Black, 1989). Fictive kin may be referred to as "play mother, play father, play sister," and so forth.

HISTORICAL APPROACHES TO STUDYING BLACK FAMILIES

Much of the early writings on the Black family are found in the domains of history and sociology. Du Bois authored the first books on the Black family, *The Philadelphia Negro* (1899) and *The Negro American Family* (1908). In these books, Du Bois draws on African and slave experiences in discussing differences between Black and White families. Du Bois disputes the then-existing myth that Africa was not a source of culture and civilization. He describes the cultural survival of Africans in the New World and discusses how their language, religion, and practices survived the Middle Passage to the United States (Gadsden, 1999).

Frazier's (1939) book, *The Negro Family in the United States*, is one of the first scholarly attempts to examine Black family life in the United States. In this book, Frazier describes the negative consequences of slavery on the disorganization of the Black family. According to Frazier, slavery created an unstable family unit that resulted in lasting damage to the African American family. During slavery, the biological family unit was not sacred. Children were sold from their biological parents, and male and female partners were kept from legal unions. The economical structure of slavery forced separations of male and female partners, from each other and from their children.

The lack of family stability with its resulting problems among African Americans continued after slavery, as Blacks began the migration from the South to the North. According to Frazier (1939), the social welfare measures to combat poverty in the 1930s had many negative consequences for families. Families became dependent on welfare and handouts and did not achieve self-sufficiency. Furthermore, many of the practices that were grounded in African traditions, useful in southern life, were not functional in the urban North. Frazier recommended that these practices be eliminated. He believed that a different approach was needed to survive in the urban North and that African American families could not progress until they changed their way of living.

The study of the African American family during the 1960s and 1970s was done in the context of the many social and economic barriers African Americans faced during this period. Two types of literature on the family were written during this period (Gadsden, 1999). One group of studies focused on the conditions and circumstances that prevented Blacks from social and economic mobility. Moynihan's (1965) commissioned paper, *The Negro Family: Case for National Action,* is illustrative of this approach. This paper portrayed Black families as pathological, with a structure that differs from the normative family structure within the United States. Normative family structure was based on middle-class European American family structure. According to Moynihan (1999),

> In essence, the Negro community has been forced into a matriarchal structure which, because it is so out of line with the rest of the American society seriously retards the progress of the group as a whole, and imposes a crushing burden on the Negro male, and in consequence, on a great many Negro women as well. (p. 7)

The theme in Moynihan's paper is congruent with Frazier's disorganization theme in accounting for the conditions of Black families. Moynihan's main point is that the deterioration of the Black family is responsible for the deterioration of Black society.

The second type of literature that emerged during the 1960s and 1970s used a strength model to describe Black families. These writings used new ways of understanding the experiences of African American families (Billingsley, 1968). The patterns and styles that had come to be associated with African American families were seen as adaptive and functional for the survival and well-being of members of the family. This new work viewed flexible family structure, such as the extended family, as functional. Authors of this type of literature discussed the dynamic and positive interactional patterns and support systems within African American families (McAdoo, 1998). This research tradition continues today.

Research on Black families in the 1990s and 2000s tends to focus on structural factors such as the marriage rate of African Americans (Gadsden, 1999). These studies include studies of structural patterns and socioeconomic indicators, such as female-headed households and poverty and adolescent mothers. Other current topics include African American extended families, child-rearing and socialization practices, poverty and vulnerability among Black children, and African American fathers.

African American Family Structure and Function

HISTORICAL PERSPECTIVE

Families During Enslavement

Although it has been assumed that there were no two-parent families during slavery, Burgess (1995) writes that the majority of families of African descent living in the United States in the 1700s and 1800s were two-parent households. By examining plantation records, Gutman (1976) observed the presence of nuclear families among enslaved Africans that resembled that of the slave masters. Using 1880–1885 census data collected from Blacks in several cities, Gutman found that the majority of Blacks of all social classes were in nuclear families. Gutman believed that slavery did not destroy the Black family and that in fact enslaved families were stronger than thought. Although there were nuclear families, other family forms also existed because enslaved families were often separated through sales.

During slavery, the mother-child relationship rather than the husband-wife relationship was primary to family life. Within slave communities, members helped to raise children of single mothers. When parents were sold to other slave owners, other adults in the slave community took care of the children left behind. The biggest fear of families was the threat of a child being sold.

Although enslaved families were able to function as adaptively as feasible given their circumstances, the consequences of slavery were nevertheless devastating on the African American family (Burgess, 1995). Enslavement had several pervasive, institutional, and long-term effects on the family. These included earlier ages of intercourse, childbearing, and establishing a household. In African communities, natural spacing techniques such as breastfeeding and polygamous unions allowed women to space childbearing. Within the New World, there was an emphasis on increased economic production and thus human reproduction. Therefore, enslaved African women began parenting at earlier ages and had greater numbers of children than did their foremothers in Africa.

Permanent unions and marriages were not possible because slaves could be sold at any time. Marriages between Africans in the United States received no legitimacy from slave owners. Slaves were required to get permission from their owners before they could marry, even though their marriages were not legally recognized.

Black Families During Emancipation and Reconstruction

During the period from 1865 to 1898, African Americans began to own small businesses and farms, and to develop churches and some banking systems. Colleges were created and some literacy was achieved. Fathers who had been sold and separated prior to the emancipation reestablished relationships with their families. After slavery, there was an increase in two-parent households, as fathers rejoined their families and couples were legally able to marry (Burgess, 1995).

Migration North

From 1910 to 1930, families began to leave the South for what they thought would be a better life in northern cities. Although there were harsh conditions and Blacks could only obtain menial jobs for the most part, they were able to find some form of employment. Some African Americans developed businesses and were able to take care of their families (Burgess, 1995).

The Black family migration north and urbanization changed the makeup of the Black family (Staples, 1999b). By 1925, Blacks in the urban North no longer had the cultural practices that had enabled them to survive in the South. Around this time, new phenomena surfaced: children reared by mothers only, welfare dependency, and juvenile delinquency. According to Staples, about 10% to 15% of all Black families experienced these problems in the 1950s. Social policies that included welfare and poverty programs were developed during this period. However, many of these programs did not consider other factors that affected the African American community. For example, social policies were based on a "bread-winner" model that assumed that husbands would provide the basic needs for their families. This model did not consider the low wages and the high level of unemployment among African American men that made it impossible for them to take care of their families (Burgess, 1995). Thus, some of the early programs that were supposed to benefit families may have encouraged fathers to be absent from the home. For example, public assistance requirements prohibited male presence in homes in which public assistance was received.

What Does the African American Family Look Like?

Structural aspects of the African American family are described by several scholars (e.g. Taylor, Tucker, Chatters, & Jayakody, 1997). These papers focus on with whom African American children live, the composition of households, family structure and poverty, and differences between African American and White family structure.

SINGLE PARENT–HEADED HOUSEHOLDS

There has been an increase in single-mother families over the past few decades for both White and African American households. In 2002 among Whites, 16% of families were headed by females compared with 48% for Blacks and 27% for Hispanics (see Table 3.1; Fields, 2003). Reasons for the increase in single female households differ for African Americans and Whites. Among White women, there has been an increase in divorce and a decrease in remarriage. Among African American women, the increase in single parent–headed households is due to the fact that there has been an increase in the number of never-married mothers. Never-married women tend to have less economic stability than married women, as they are more likely to be younger and to have less education.

A small proportion of African American children, 5%, live in single father–headed families (Fields, 2003). Single father–headed families tend to be more economically advantaged than single-mother families (McLanahan & Casper, 1995). Single father–headed families tend to have more support from others in the household than do single mother–headed families. About 80% of African American single fathers report they reside in either a subfamily, a cohabiting relationship, or with a related adult. This means that the majority of single African American males do not have the sole responsibility for child rearing, as is often the case with females who head households.

FAMILY STRUCTURE OF HOUSEHOLDS WITH CHILDREN

The household structure of the family that the child lives in is important to consider and has implications for the well-being of the child. For example, households with only one adult are more likely to be poorer and have fewer resources than households where there is more than one adult. Over the past decade, there has been a decline in two-parent African American households. Table 3.1 provides statistics on household structure by race.

As seen in Table 3.1, almost half (48%) of African American children live in households with a single mother, whereas 16% of White children live with a single mother. African American children are also more likely to reside in a home where a grandparent(s) is present than are White children (U.S. Census Bureau, 2002b; see Table 3.2). In about 11% of these households, grandparents are responsible for the care of at least one grandchild.

Table 3.1   Percentages of Children With Single Parents and Cohabiting Single Parents by Race

Characteristic	White	Black	Hispanic
Single Mother	16	48	25
Single Father	4	5	5
Single cohabiting mother	14	6	12
Single cohabiting father	29	30	46

Source: U.S. Census Bureau, Annual Demographic Supplement to the March 2002 Current Population Survey.

Table 3.2   Presence of Grandparents in the Household by Race

Characteristic	White	Black	Hispanic
Presence of grandparent	7.6	20.2	16.7
Presence of grandparent for at least one grandchild	3.0	11.0	6.1

Source: U.S. Census Bureau, Census 2002, special tabulation. Internet Release Date: March 16, 2004.

Family Structure and Childhood Poverty

Childhood poverty is linked to family structure. Poverty among children is highest among those who live in mother-only families. African American children who live with their mothers only are four times more likely to be poor than African American children who live with both parents (Hogan & Lichter, 1995).

Table 3.3 gives information on child poverty among children by household structure (Fields, 2003). As seen in Table 3.3, both African American and White children who live in married-couple families have less poverty than those who live in single-parent households. For example, in 2001, 7.8% of African American children in married-couple families lived in poverty compared with 35.2% of children in mother-only households. These large differences in poverty rates are also seen for White and Hispanic children who live in married-couple families versus female-headed families.

Consequences of Family Structure on Children's Outcomes

Although many children reared in mother-only households do well, there may be adverse consequences for others (Taylor et al., 1997). Research suggests that children who live in female-headed households do not do as well on several social indicators; for example, there is a higher

Table 3.3 Families in Poverty by Family Structure and Race

Type of Family	White	Black	Hispanic
All families	5.7	20.7	19.4
Married couple	3.3	7.8	13.8
Female householder	19.0	35.2	37.0

Source: U.S. Census Bureau, Current Population Survey, 2001 and 2002 Annual Demographic Supplements.

school dropout rate among these children, and daughters are at higher risk of becoming teen parents themselves. Juvenile delinquency may also be higher because there may be less parental supervision. Fewer resources in mother-only households account in part for these differences. Many of these adverse social indicators can be moderated by support from extended family and friends.

BIRTHS TO TEEN MOTHERS

Teen mothers have special challenges in that they are more likely to have economic challenges compared with older mothers. The teen years also present some developmental transitions in terms of social, emotional, and physical development. Teen births across all groups have declined over the past 10 years (Martin et al., 2003). The birth rate for African American teens in 2002 was 68.3 per 1,000 compared with a birth rate of 118.2 per 1,000 in 1991. In 2002, the teen birth rate for African Americans was more than double that for Whites but less than that for Hispanic females.

FOSTER CARE

Children are placed in foster care temporarily, and sometimes permanently, when their families cannot care for them. African American children are three times more likely than White children to be in foster care. A report from the Administration on Children, Youth, and Families indicates that 38% of the children in foster care in 2001 were Black (see Table 3.4).

Table 3.4 Teen Birth Rates for Teenagers by Race for 1991 and 2002

Year	White	Black	Hispanic
1991	43.4	118.2	104.6
2002	28.5	68.3	83.4

Source: Martin et al., 2003.
Note: Rate per 1,000 women aged 15–19 years in the specified group.

Table 3.5   Children in Foster Care by Race

Race	Percentage
White	37
Black	38
Hispanic	17

Source: Adoption and Foster Care Analysis and Reporting System (AFCARS) data submitted for the FY 2001, 10/1/00 through 9/30/01.

Table 3.5b   Children Who Exited Foster Care by Race

Race	Percentage
White	45
Black	30
Hispanic	15

Source: Adoption and Foster Care Analysis and Reporting System (AFCARS) data submitted for the FY 2001, 10/1/00 through 9/30/01.

Black children are also less likely than White and Hispanic children to leave foster care (see Table 3.5).

MARRIAGE, DIVORCE, REMARRIAGE, AND COHABITATION

Overall, marriage has declined for both African Americans and Whites. However, there are substantial differences in the marriage rates of African Americans and Whites. Among women aged 15 and older, White women are twice as likely as African American women to be married (Kreider & Simmons, 2003). In 2000, 27.5% of African American women and 34.2% of African American men were married with spouses present, compared with 53.2% of White women and 56.8% of White men (Kreider & Simmons, 2003; see also Table 3.6).

In studying the declining marriage rates among African Americans, James (1998) examined three economy-based explanations for declining marriage rates among African American men and women over the past few decades. One explanation focuses on declines in male economic viability. This explanation argues that the economic status of men contributes to marital outcomes. When economic opportunities are good, both men and women marry earlier. Subsequently, declines in marriage among African Americans may be due to a poor labor market for African American men. Over the past few decades, the increasing economic marginality of African

Table 3.6   Marital Status by Race

Characteristic	Married With Spouse Present	Never Married
Male		
White	56.8	27.3
Black	34.2	41.6
Hispanic	42.7	38.3
Female		
White	53.2	20.8
Black	27.5	39.7
Hispanic	46.2	30.0

Source: U.S. Census Bureau, Census 2000 special tabulation.

American men has made them less attractive as potential marriage mates. A second explanation for declining marriage rates is that African American women have become more economically independent and do not have economic needs that would typically be fulfilled within a marriage. This explanation focuses on the function of marriage in providing financial support for women. A third explanation for the declining marriage rate is that changes in African American sex ratios have contributed to more available women than available men as marriage partners.

James (1998) explored these explanations in a series of analyses that looked at individual and market level variables on marital outcomes. Data collected from the 1970 through 1990 censuses were used. James looked at the age at which individuals entered marriage between 1970 and 1980, mate availability (i.e., number of men and women within a geographical area), and economic opportunity (i.e., number of African American men who were not in school or working) as market variables. James found support for the explanation that economic viability or employment is a factor in whether or not men married during the period from 1970 to 1990. The author also found some support that suggested as women obtain more economic opportunities, marriage levels decline. She found that for each decade, the proportion of females who were working full-time was negatively correlated with the likelihood of marriage among men. Contrary to what has been written regarding male-female sex ratios, James did not find that the ratio affected marriage rates.

Divorce, Separation, and Remarriage

African Americans are more likely than Whites to be separated or divorced. When African Americans do separate, they tend to wait longer than Whites before they become divorced (Bramlett & Mosher, 2002). Only 30% of African Americans divorce within a year of separating, whereas 60% of Whites divorce within a year of separating (Bramlett & Mosher, 2002). The longer period of separation among African Americans may be because remarriage is not as likely to occur, so there may be less motivation to divorce.

African American women are not as likely as White women to remarry (Bramlett & Mosher, 2002). After 5 years of divorce, the probability of remarriage is 58% for White women and 32% for Black women.

THE AFRICAN AMERICAN EXTENDED FAMILY

The African American family is often extended and multigenerational, with a cooperative and collective family structure (Wilson et al., 1995). Included within the family network are immediate family members, extended members, friends, neighbors, fictive kin, and church members. There is diversity in living arrangements that goes beyond marriage, parentage, and children to include other adults and children in shared-residence situations. African American children may live in households with grandparents and other adults who are not members of the immediate family. Elderly African Americans are likely to be living with grandchildren. Young, low-income, and single mothers also are likely to be sharing a residence with other family members.

Wilson et al. (1995) note that extended family arrangements can provide resources and be a positive factor for African American families. The extended family members, particularly grandparents and adult siblings of single mothers, provide needed support and assistance in caring for, nurturing, and rearing children. The extended family promotes the welfare of dependent family members in dealing with both normal and unusual life events. The presence of an adult who is not the children's parent can provide additional financial and other types of help. The presence of a caring grandparent may be especially beneficial and serve to buffer children against stressors that may be in homes where a single parent may be rearing a child without adequate financial and emotional resources.

Studies show that emotional support from extended family members is helpful in child-rearing practices. In one study, mothers with higher levels of emotional support were less likely to scold or ridicule their children than those without emotional support (McLoyd, 1990a). Support from other adults may provide adults with the opportunity to discuss child-rearing practices such as discipline; it also may provide parents with an alternative interpretation of their child's behavior and give parents some help in supervising the child.

THE ROLE OF THE GRANDMOTHER

As noted previously, grandparents are present in the homes of many African American families. Grandmothers may provide an especially important form of assistance in child rearing (Wilson et al., 1995). Grandmothers may be the primary caregiver of the children as well as the secondary caregiver. Flaherty, Facteau, and Carver (1999) identify seven functions of grandmothers who care for their adolescent daughters' child. These are managing, caretaking, coaching, assessing, nurturing, assigning, and patrolling. Also, grandparents serve instructional (i.e., giving advice) and modeling functions for their teen or adult children. They tell their children what to do and show them how to do it.

However, grandparents may feel some strain and resistance when rearing grandchildren. Burton and Dilworth-Anderson (1991) found that while parenting grandchildren is emotionally rewarding, there are also psychological, physical, and social costs incurred with these roles. In some families, grandparents not only have primary roles in caring for their grandchildren but care for other family members as well. Under these conditions, caring for grandchildren may create additional stress for grandparents. Young grandparents may also resent the timing of the grandparental role and the association of grandparenthood with being elderly.

AFRICAN AMERICAN HUSBANDS AND FATHERS

Research on African American Fathers

There has been a recent increase in research on the role of fathers in families. Traditional portrayals of African American men as husbands and fathers have in general been negative, focusing on stereotypical images that include uninvolved and financially irresponsible fathers. Research has been consistent with this portrayal. Many studies have been conducted on social problems of adolescent fatherhood, out-of-wedlock paternity, and child support enforcement with a focus on young men or young fathers (Taylor & Johnson, 1997). This focus does not account for the broad diversity of family, spousal, and parental roles found among African American men.

Research by J. McAdoo (1988) is an exception. His work focuses on middle-income fathers who are involved in socializing their children. McAdoo's work indicates that African American fathers are actively involved in the socialization of their children.

African American Male Roles in the Family. Being an economic provider is a role that African American men identify as important. Taylor, Leashore, and Toliver (1988) found that older respondents and those with higher personal incomes are more likely to have positive provider role perceptions than those who are younger and with lower incomes.

Concerns about being able to fulfill the provider role are associated with marital problems (Veroff, Douvan, & Hatchett, 1995). These concerns, which center on income and employment problems, may contribute to the tendency for African American men to marry later than Whites and to more likely be single, separated, or divorced. African American fathers have had difficulties as primary providers due to historical changes in patterns of racial discrimination. As the employment difficulties have changed from low-skilled work to chronic joblessness, there have been increases in marital and family problems related to the provider role (Bowman & Forman, 1997).

Bowman and Forman conducted a study that looked at the instrumental and expressive family roles of fathers by analyzing data from the National Survey of Black Americans. They examined several issues related to father roles among African American men. They were interested in fathers' perception of their instrumental (i.e., financial provider) and expressive (i.e., nurturing and caring) roles. Bowman and Forman (1997) found that fathers had more personal income and less financial stress than did mothers. However, despite the higher income, they perceived greater difficulty than mothers as providers for their children. Fathers who were unemployed were the most worried about being able to provide financially for their families. However, unemployed fathers did not express difficulty in expressive roles. Perhaps, these fathers have more time to be with their children and to help them in their daily activities.

Quality of Life Satisfaction Among African American Fathers. Using data from the National Survey of Black Americans, Taylor and Johnson (1997) examined African American men's perception of parental and spousal roles and overall satisfaction with family life. They found that in general, African American husbands and fathers were satisfied with their spousal and parental roles and very satisfied with their family life. African American men reported that performing well in these roles was important to them.

One of the realities for African American men is that many do not live with their biological children. Therefore, traditional definitions of residential status and involvement may not adequately capture the extent to which African American fathers play critical roles in their children's development. One must consider the role of the father outside of the traditional residential living arrangement with his children.

In terms of satisfaction with family life, African American men show diversity according to their life experience. Being older, married, and parenting a minor child are associated with higher ratings of family satisfaction (Broman, 1988). Persons who are divorced have lower levels of family satisfaction.

AFRICENTRIC PERSPECTIVE ON
THE AFRICAN AMERICAN FAMILY

Structural and functional aspects of the contemporary African American family can be seen in the African family. Parham, White, and Ajamu (1999) offer an African-centered perspective for understanding the functioning and beliefs of African American families. According to these authors, African family values have been present among African Americans since the Middle Passage. These values illustrate African cultural presence in this country. One core value that captures the African American family is "spiritness." Spiritness has enabled families to be supportive and to work together for collective survival. According to Parham and colleagues, this spiritness captures members of individual family units but also helps to connect families across space and time. In other words, spiritness is an underlying process that is operative and connects all African American families irrespective of geographical location or time.

Another core value among African American families is the importance attached to children. Through socialization of children, families direct individual and collective purposes and goals. According to Parham and colleagues (1999), children represent the manifestation of the spirit because they "belong" and can "become." Children are believed to be the opportunity for the future and to represent what has occurred in the past.

Parham and colleagues discuss how cultural values and practices from traditional African families are seen among contemporary African Americans in their family practices. Values of interconnectedness, responsibility, and cooperation can be seen operating within African American families much as they operate in African families. The elders of the family, usually the oldest male, have the authority to make decisions. However, in the absence of males, the oldest female usually holds this authority. Child rearing in African families is done by the extended family, and extended family members are also responsible for disciplining and punishing the child. The functioning of the extended family in Africa is not dependent on the survival of the conjugal unions, and the family relationships are the most influential for socializing the child. These cultural child-rearing practices are also found among present day African American families. Family members besides the biological parents socialize and discipline children.

Strengths, Coping, and Parenting Patterns

STRENGTH AND RESILIENCY
AMONG AFRICAN AMERICAN FAMILIES

Over the past few decades, family scholars have moved from a deficit view of African American families to a strengths-based model. Strengths are viewed as culturally based beliefs and values unique to African Americans. Hill (1998) defines family strengths as those attributes that enable the family to meet both the needs of its members and the demands made on the family by outside forces.

Hill (1971) describes five strengths of African American families: (a) strong achievement orientation, (b) strong work orientation, (c) flexible family roles, (d) strong kinship bonds, and (e) strong religious orientation. According to Hill, these attributes are functional for the survival, stability, and advancement of African American families. While these attributes are found among other ethnic groups, they are likely to be expressed differently among African Americans because of their unique experiences in this country.

H. P. McAdoo (1998) also describes cultural patterns that contribute to strengths and resiliency among African American families. They include a supportive social network, flexible relationships within the family unit, a strong sense of religiosity, use of extended family, and the adoption of fictive kin. McAdoo cautions that although some commonalties exist, there is a great deal of diversity among African American families. She also believes that some of the cultural patterns that have promoted resiliency have been eroded because of poor economic conditions.

Resiliency Model of At-Risk Youth

McCubbin and colleagues' (1998) family resiliency model has been used to understand and work with African American at-risk youth, their families, and youth offenders. An assumption of the resiliency model is that even the most chaotic and dysfunctional family system has competencies and abilities. These strengths, even if limited, provide a mechanism for the family to improve itself.

McCubbin's resiliency model has been used in interventions with African American families and offending male youth in residential treatment. The model assumes that families with a youth member in residential care have to cope with the transitional problems that prompt changes in the way the family unit functions. The model also assumes that families have unique styles of functioning and patterns of behavior that can be identified. These patterns will affect the success of the treatment of youth. Also, youth along with their families have specific and predictable styles of functioning that will affect successful completion of treatment and long-term adaptation.

McCubbin (1998) examined more than 800 African American youth that were treated in the Michigan Boysville program, an agency that serves troubled youth. The Boysville treatment program emphasizes family therapy and the realignment of the family system for youth and adult participants. In this study, positive improvements among boys were associated with improvements among family members who successfully completed the program.

BUILDING STRONG AFRICAN AMERICAN FAMILIES

Parham et al. (1999) offer several recommendations for building healthy families. They note that current family structures differ from the family structure of the past in that modern families do not necessarily begin with marriage or living together. Therefore, building healthy families must start with appropriate socialization of African American youth. They recommend that families

1. Socialize youth to love themselves and to understand their relationship with the creator

2. Help youth to develop an identity and perspective of what it means to be a man or a woman that is culturally congruent and that affirms both males and females

3. Teach youth to recognize and model healthy family functioning; youth are often exposed to dysfunctional family functioning that provides a distorted view of how a healthy family should function

4. Teach youth how to be successful in male-female relationships; youth must be taught to relate to members of the opposite sex in a sincere, respectful, caring, and loving way and not to first focus on own needs

5. Teach children that relationships should be sustained through difficult periods; when relationships are challenged during stressful and difficult times, tolerance and perseverance are needed

6. Teach youth to develop personal insights into themselves and help them to understand how past experiences affect their current ways of behaving

COPING AND ADJUSTMENT AMONG AFRICAN AMERICAN FAMILIES

Strong support from the family can help family members who are experiencing stress. Support can be emotional such as affirmation and acceptance, instrumental such as lending money or helping with child care, or cognitive such as giving advice. Examples of these types of support are seen among African American families who assist family members to cope with chronic illnesses and disabilities (Belgrave, 1998) or to care for an elderly family member (Thornton, 1998). Many African American families have developed successful mechanisms for coping with stress caused by environmental challenges.

Care for Elderly Family Members

The family is the most important system within which health is maintained, and health decisions are made for the African American elderly by their families (Bowles & Kington, 1998). The family is the primary source of social support and care of the African American elderly. Who are the African American elderly, and why is the family so important to their well-being? African American elderly represented 8% of the total U.S. population aged 65 and older (McKinnon, 2003).

There may be few economic and social resources available for African American elderly because of restricted economic opportunities in their earlier life. African American elderly have less income and experience more poverty and more inadequate health care than do White elderly. In 2002, 23.8% of African American elderly lived below the poverty line compared with only 8.3% of White elderly (U.S. Census Bureau, 2003).

Within African American communities, informal care providers consisting of family, friends, and other unpaid help are responsible for providing a range of services for elders. These informal providers provide care and support that elders may not be able to receive through more formal health and social services. Thornton (1998) used national data collected by the Bureau of the Census to examine informal home health caregivers of various ethnic minority populations. The data were obtained on a representative sample of noninstitutionalized persons in the United States, 65 years and older, who received assistance with activities of daily living. Analysis reveals several patterns of home health care and how these patterns differ for African Americans and other ethnic groups. First, African American home health care providers spend considerably more time providing home health care than do Whites: Whereas African Americans spend an average of 29 hours per week, Whites spend 17 to 21 hours per week. African American health care providers spend an average of about 4 hours a day caring for an elderly person, oftentimes while working outside the home. Second, while home health care is most consistently provided by females, this is even more so among African American females. African American women spend approximately 32 hours a week in care, or about 9 to 12 hours more than White women. African American males spend about 20 hours per week in care.

Another interesting pattern is seen in caregiving to immediate family members versus nonimmediate family members who are elderly. Thornton found that African American caregivers spend more time caring for nonimmediate than immediate elderly family members: 30 versus 28 hours per week. This finding is consistent with the notion of extended family and fictive kin. The caring for and attachment to nonimmediate family members in a manner comparable to immediate family has policy implications. State and federal legislatures are examining family leave-of-absence policies that ensure job stability for family members who leave work to care for an elderly family member. If the family member is limited to an immediate family member, it will not capture the range of persons for whom African Americans provide informal care. Thornton notes that a failure to consider different systems of family care in family-leave policy would impose additional burdens on African American families, who often turn to members outside of the immediate family for support.

There may be no greater strain on the family unit than caring for a member with Alzheimer's disease. Loukissa, Farran, and Graham (1999) conducted a qualitative study to examine how family members experience caring for a family member with dementia. The authors conducted interviews and focus groups of care providers for African Americans and Caucasians with Alzheimer's disease. Overall, African American caregivers reported lower levels of burden and depression and higher levels of caregiver satisfaction compared with White caregivers. Also, African American caregivers reported using religion and spirituality to help them cope with stressors associated with caring for this family member. Family members were able to find positive experiences in providing care and reported that they had improved in their competence in providing care over time.

The Role of the Family in Adaptation to Disabilities

Among African Americans with disabilities, adjustment includes family as well as individual processes. The goal of treatment or intervention is to adjust the family system and, by doing so, affect the functionality of the person. The kinship network system may be used as a coping resource for African Americans with disabilities. This may include obtaining emotional support as well as direct involvement of extended family members in the treatment and rehabilitation process. In a study of African Americans and Whites with disabilities, Belgrave, Davis, and Vadja (1994) found that African Americans are more likely than Whites to report receiving support from kin or extended family members. However, they found no differences between African Americans and Whites in the number of immediate family members who provide support. This finding is consistent with other findings that have shown the importance of extended family in African American families. In this same study, African Americans reported more satisfaction with support from kin than did Whites.

African Americans with disabilities who receive support from the immediate and extended family tend to adapt better and achieve more positive outcomes. In a study of unemployed rehabilitation consumers, Walker, Belgrave, Jarama, Ukawuilulu, and Rackley (1995) investigated the relationship between social support and employment efficacy (defined as beliefs that employment could be found and maintained). The authors found that social support from family was linked to stronger employment efficacy. Social support from professionals was not linked to higher job efficacy among this sample. These findings and others suggest that the family is critical to successful functioning, coping, and adaptation. It helps to have family support when there are elderly family members and when a family member has a chronic illness or disability.

PARENTING ATTITUDES AND PRACTICES

African American parenting practices differ from those of other cultural groups. Some of these differences may be attributed to class differences insofar as many studies have used African American samples comprised of parents of low socioeconomic status. However, studies that have controlled for socioeconomic status suggest that some differences still exist between African American and White parents. Moreover, parenting practices and how the child adapts may differ for African Americans and Whites. Studies have traditionally examined differences in discipline, parental involvement or communication, parental attitudes, and child's behavior.

Discipline

African American parents are more likely than White parents to use punitive methods such as physical punishment and assertion of authority (Bradley, 1998). The use of more physical and authoritative discipline among African American parents has its origin in slavery. During slavery, the responsibility of the parent or slave family was to instill in children that they were to be compliant and subservient slaves. The method for maintaining docility and obedience was shown by the White slave masters' methods of disciplining slaves. Punishment was swift, harsh, and violent, no matter what the infraction (Lassiter, 1987). Consequently, African American parents used harsh discipline as a survival strategy. In order to teach children how to avoid violent punishment at the hands of the White slaveholder, adults had to use a less severe but still harsh form of punishment with children.

Enslavement also impacted how children reacted to adverse conditions. Enslaved parents socialized their children to behave in ways that were age inconsistent in order to keep them alive. For example, children were not allowed to cry out loud when they were hurt or in pain. Children were expected to assume adult responsibilities, including caring for younger children and doing chores in the house and in the field. Following slavery, the pattern of harsh and physical discipline continued as a mechanism for maintaining docility and compliance so that the child could survive in a racist society.

There is diversity in punitive disciplinary practices among African American parents. In a middle-class sample of African American parents, Bradley (1998) found that African American parents prefer to use non-physical forms of discipline. Parents in this sample only used the belt and spanking with the open hand as a means of physical punishment in severe situations. However, parents in the study were found to use the "order the child not to" disciplinary technique consistent with an authoritative approach. In other words, children are told (i.e., ordered) how to behave. Bradley suggests that parents may believe that demanding that their children obey authority is important for their survival. This finding is consistent with the importance attached to respecting elders and authority figures found among people of African descent. These values are needed to prepare African American youth to function well in society.

Firm and controlling discipline with African American youth, when augmented with a warm and supportive style, is related to better child behavior. Baldwin, Baldwin, and Cole (1990) found a positive association between good child outcomes and a parenting style that is vigilant and restrictive, yet also warm. Restrictive parenting styles are also associated with positive mental health among high-risk Black adolescents (Baldwin et al., 1993).

Deater-Deckard, Bates, Dodge, and Pettit (1996) asked whether or not differences in parental discipline and children's problem behaviors differ by ethnicity. An earlier study had found that authoritarian parenting is associated with more negative socioemotional outcomes for European American girls but not for African American girls. Deater-Deckard et al. tested the hypothesis that there are ethnic differences in the association between harsh parental discipline and child externalizing problems (i.e., aggression, acting out). They conducted a study using a sample of 585 African American and European American families and followed these children from kindergarten to third grade. Physical discipline was measured by interviewer rating, that is, by having parents respond to hypothetical vignettes, and by a questionnaire. Information about the child obtained from his or her mother, teachers, and peers to assess the child's externalizing behavior problem. The authors found that there was an association between harsh discipline style and externalizing behaviors such as aggression in the school setting for European American students only. There was no significant relationship between teacher and peer ratings of externalizing problems and physical discipline for African American children. The findings of this study suggest that a more authoritative harsh discipline style may not necessarily be associated with poorer child outcomes for African American youth, at least within the school setting. The authors caution that the ethnic group differences in the effects of harsh discipline on externalized outcomes is only true for nonabusive discipline. Harsh discipline that is physically abusive is a strong predictor of aggressive behavior among children irrespective of ethnicity.

The meaning of discipline may differ for African Americans and Whites. Among Whites, harsh discipline may be seen as parents being out of control, a non-child-centered household, or both. For African American parents, discipline may be viewed as a necessary component of one's role as a parent.

Parenting Attitudes and Involvement

Studies on parenting attitudes have looked at factors such as parental support for their children, warmth, acceptance, and expectations. In general, the literature reviewed by Magnus, Cowen, Wyman, Fagen, and Work (1999) suggests few differences between African American and White parents in parental attitudes. One exception is on the variable autonomy. African American parents are more likely than White parents to value and stress autonomy among their children. One positive implication of this is that children may be socialized to function independently, which may be useful when parents are not immediately available. However, parents who stress autonomy may be less likely to attend to minor distress signals from their children.

In summary, parenting practices of African American parents may include more discipline and punishment than parenting practices of other ethnic groups. These practices are viewed as necessary for successfully raising the African American child.

RACIAL SOCIALIZATION

The process of racial socialization is the process by which parents and families socialize African American children in how to function in this society. This process involves making children aware of their race and of themselves as Black or African American as opposed to simply being an American. Parents who racially socialize their children assume that their children will be in a hostile environment, at least at some times in their lives, and that they must be comfortable with being Black. Racial socialization includes specific messages and behaviors that families provide children about being African American, including group and personal identity, intergroup interactions, and their positions within the social hierarchy These messages are both implicit and explicit (Thornton, Chatters, Taylor, & Allen, 1990).

Certain demographic factors influence the extent of racial socialization (Thornton, 1998). Mothers socialize their children about race issues more than fathers do. This is attributed to general levels of maternal responsiveness of mothers to prepare children to function in the world. Parents with higher levels of education are more likely to socialize their children than those with lower levels of education.

According to Boykin and Toms (1985), the socialization process is related to identity. African Americans must be socialized through three experiences in order to acquire a racial identity. First, they must participate in mainstream American culture. In order to achieve this, Black parents teach their children that which is American. Within this context, parents teach their children necessary life skills, including personal qualities such as confidence, respect, and achievement. An example of this strategy is when parents teach children the importance of studying at school.

The second method of socialization used by African American parents is to teach their children about being an ethnic minority and to prepare them for an oppressive environment. African American parents prepare their children for what may be an unsupportive world by building their self-confidence and helping them learn how to cope with prejudice and discrimination. These parents also teach their children the value of a good education and that injustice may occur because of their skin color. The final strategy identified by Boykin and Toms (1985) is to socialize their children within the Black cultural experience. These parents socialize their children to value and identify with what is African centered. An example of this is when parents discuss historical events in their family's life or discuss famous Blacks and Africans. Racial socialization can serve a protective role for African American children because it provides support and affirmation for being Black in a racist world (Stevenson, Cameron, Herrero-Taylor, & Davis, 2002).

Impact of Oppression and Discriminatory Policies on African American Families

SLAVERY AND THE JIM CROW ERA

We discussed the impact of slavery on African American families earlier in this chapter. Families were not protected, as there were no legal unions between males and females, members could be sold at any time, and children could be taken away from parents.

The policies and laws of the Jim Crow era (from 1876 to 1954) and continued discrimination had an impact on family life. Males in particular had few employment opportunities and could only get jobs that were not desired by Whites. These jobs paid little and offered few advancement opportunities. African American women during this period tended to hold jobs that were in the service industry. Many continued to take care of White households and served as nannies, housekeepers, and cooks for long hours with little time off to take care of their own families. While the institution of slavery and Jim Crow laws had direct effects on the well-being of the African American family, other more contemporary institutional policies and practices have been subtler yet have also had an adverse impact on African American families.

CURRENT INSTITUTIONAL DISCRIMINATORY PRACTICES

African American family life has been affected by several societal factors that are discriminatory (Hill, 1998). These structurally discriminatory social policies have had a disproportionate negative impact on African American family life.

Age at Retirement

An institutional policy that discriminates against African Americans is retirement age. The increase in the eligible age for retirement with full benefits at 67 years of age by the year 2022 may be discriminatory to African Americans. This change was instituted in 1983 by Congress to benefit the Social Security Trust Fund. On the surface, this policy may not appear discriminatory, but it has differential consequences for Whites and African Americans. The African American male's current life expectancy is 68 years—much lower than for White males and Black females. This, in effect, means that many African American males will not live long enough to collect full benefits or will collect benefits for only a short period of time.

Adoption Policies

A second example of institutional bias can be found in the adoption regulations of many child welfare agencies. Many require adoptive parents to be husband-wife couples, younger than 45 years old, of middle class status, with no children of their own. Many African American prospective parents are not likely to meet these criteria and are screened out of the potential applicant pool. This contributes to a large number of African American children remaining in foster care or in African American families having to jump through additional hurdles to adopt a child, as they are not as likely to meet the standard criteria.

Historical Impact of the Welfare
System on the Role of the Male in the Family

Although the welfare system was originally designed to assist families who were living in poverty, it has not provided enough jobs, job training, or economic assistance to pull African American families out of poverty (Scott & Black, 1989). Scott and Black maintain that the "unemployment" system and the welfare system have combined to push African American men from the center to the periphery of family kin networks. Often, single African American males have become either part-time or floating members of other people's households. Many of these single males do not own or rent their own residences and from time to time must be housed, clothed, and fed by female heads of households. These females may include biological relatives or friends.

In short, the welfare system and institutional policies have not been supportive of African American males achieving economic parity such that they can function as contributing members of their households. When economic needs are not met through traditional sources, other, sometimes illegal avenues may be taken. The disproportionate number of African American males incarcerated is a strong indicator of poor economic options.

Methodological Issues

There are several methodological issues to consider when studying African American families. Many studies have examined African American families over a short period of time and have failed to consider historical perspectives when examining contemporary African American families (Hill, 1998). One cannot truly understand African American families without considering historical, cultural, social, economic, and political factors and institutional practices. In this chapter, we have examined historical, cultural, and economic patterns as they affect African American families. For example, understanding that enslaved African women were made to procreate early helps us to understand the earlier age of childbirth among contemporary African American females. Understanding economic conditions helps to explain marriage rates among African American men and women.

African American child-rearing practices have been compared either directly or indirectly with the child-rearing practices of European American parents, with European American child-rearing practices seen as the norm. African American child-rearing practices have been viewed as inferior and nonnormative (Bradley, 1998). However, as we have shown in this chapter, there are cultural as well as functional reasons for African American child-rearing practices. A more authoritarian parenting style may be functional for raising children who live under oppressive conditions.

Another methodological problem is that socioeconomic class has been confounded with ethnicity in studies of the African American family and child rearing (McLoyd, 1990b). Research has oversampled low-income African American families and generalized findings to all African American families. Among low socioeconomic status and single-parent family structures, physical punishment has been found to be associated with child externalizing problems (Huston, McLoyd, & Coll, 1994). However, there are several potential risk factors for problem behaviors among children from low-income families, regardless of ethnicity, including inadequate health care, discrimination and prejudice, and parental stress and lack of resources (Deater-Deckard et al., 1996). Socioeconomic status has been confounded with ethnicity. In summary, it is not possible to study the African American family without considering the myriad historical, social, cultural, and economic influences that have shaped the family.

Summary

The proverb at the beginning of this chapter, "The ruin of a nation begins in the homes of its people," conveys the message that families are important institutions. In this chapter, we have examined several aspects of African American families.

Hill defines the Black family as a household related by blood, marriage, or function that provides basic instrumental and expressive functions to its members. Much of the work on the Black family conducted during the first part of the 20th century viewed the Black family as disorganized and dysfunctional. Later, starting in the 1960s, family scholars wrote on the strengths of the Black family, noting that the flexible family patterns created natural support and resources for family members. Slavery had a long-lasting adverse impact on Black families due to the lack of legal recognition of unions between male and female slaves and the fact that children could be sold from their parents. Despite the fact that slavery had adverse effects on the African American family, it supported a flexible and extended family and kinship system that continues today.

Migration north and urbanization during the early 20th century contributed to many problems faced by African American families. These problems continue today. They include (a) higher levels of mother-headed households and a high percentage of poor African American children who reside in these households, (b) high unemployment and menial jobs for African American males that result in the residential separation of African American males from their families, and (c) social policies such as welfare and poverty programs that do not contribute to the economic viability of the African American family.

The African American family may be headed by a female. Children who live in mother-headed households are more likely to be poor than those who live in households with both parents. African American children are more likely than White children to live with their grandparents and to reside with someone other than a biological parent. African American parents, compared with White parents, are also more likely to be unwed as well as teen mothers. Marriage rates are lower for African Americans than for Whites, and African Americans are not as likely to remarry.

The African American extended family includes immediate family members, extended members, friends, neighbors, fictive kin, and church members. There is diversity in structural living arrangements. The extended family can serve as a resource for African American families, especially those who are coping with stressors. Grandmothers, in particular, serve an important role in extended family living.

African American fathers and husbands report satisfaction with those roles. However, given that many fathers may not be in the same residential setting as their children, alternative ways of thinking about their roles should be considered.

An African-centered perspective for understanding the behavioral value system of African American families incorporates the concept of spiritness that has allowed families to be supportive and to work together for collective survival.

African American families have been viewed from a strength perspective. Strengths among African American families have enabled the family to survive despite adversity. Family cohesion and support are associated with better outcomes for troubled youth. Families are also important in helping African Americans to cope with other stressful situations, such as chronic illness or the care of an elderly family member. African Americans spend considerably more time than Whites caring for elderly and infirm immediate and extended family members and report more satisfaction doing so.

The parenting practices of African Americans differ from those of other cultural groups. African American parents may engage in more punitive disciplinary practices than White parents. This practice has its origins in slavery, when slave children had to learn quickly the importance of following the rules and obeying authority. Physical punishment does not seem to be linked to problem behaviors among African American children to the extent that it is among White children. African American parents are also more likely than White parents to socialize their children to be autonomous.

African American parents engage in racial socialization to prepare their children to do well in a racist and discriminatory environment. Racial socialization involves making children aware of their race and of themselves as Black or African American.

Several public policies that discriminate against African American families have been identified. African Americans, especially males, are more likely to die before they are able to collect retirement benefits from social security. Adoption policies that favor two-parent households work against African American single-parent households. Finally, the welfare system has not provided the level of economic support and training necessary for African American males to contribute to household income.

There are methodological problems to consider when conducting research on the African American family. Often, research does not consider the historical, social, economic, and political context of African Americans, and this research may paint a pathological picture of the African American family. Often, low-income African Americans are included in research studies, and findings are generalized to all African Americans despite the fact that African Americans of different socioeconomic statuses differ.

4

Educational Systems

U.S. School Segregation Is at '69 Level

Jan. 18, 2004

By Michael Dobbs/*Washington Post*

WASHINGTON — Half a century after the Supreme Court ordered the desegregation of American education, schools are almost as segregated as they were when the Rev. Martin Luther King Jr. was assassinated, according to a report released Sunday by Harvard University researchers.

The study by the Harvard Civil Rights Project shows that progress toward school desegregation peaked in the late 1980s as courts concluded that the goals of the landmark 1954 Supreme Court decision *Brown v. Board of Education* largely had been achieved.

Over the past 15 years, the trend has been in the opposite direction, and most white students have "little contact" with minority students in many areas of the country, according to the report.

"We are celebrating a victory over segregation at a time when schools across the nation are becoming increasingly segregated," noted the report, which was issued on the eve of the holiday celebrating King's birthday.

Triggered by a civil rights case in Topeka, Kan., the Brown decision marked the start of three decades of intensive efforts by the federal government to integrate public schools, first through court orders that opened white schools to minority students and later through busing.

Its most dramatic impact was in Southern states, where the percentage of blacks attending predominantly white schools increased from zero in 1954 to 43 percent in 1988.

By 2001, according to the Harvard data, the figure had fallen to 30 percent, or about the level in 1969, the year after King's assassination.

"We are losing many of the gains of desegregation," said Harvard professor Gary Orfield, the primary author of the report.

"We are not back to where we were before Brown, but we are back to when King was assassinated."

Introduction and Overview of Chapter

From early educational experiences in the home and preschool through advanced vocational, professional, and graduate school, educational systems and experiences play an important role in individual development, cultural socialization, and the economic roles and opportunities to which Americans have access. Within the American context, academic experiences, achievement, and attainment have played a central role in African Americans' access to opportunities for economic, social, and career advancement. As a group, African Americans have historically experienced notable challenges and barriers to accessing quality and equitable educational resources. As described in the news article that opens the chapter, recent data suggest that historical efforts to desegregate schools within the United States as a strategy to support equal educational opportunity have had limited success. Research also has raised questions as to the benefits of desegregation.

Understanding the psychological role of education includes consideration of the educational settings and experiences that are relevant to African Americans, the role that education plays in the life course of African Americans, and what educational resources support the most positive outcomes for Black youth and adults. Several questions face us regarding education and African Americans: What resources and assets do African American parents and families use and contribute to support the learning of their children? What structural characteristics of schools and educational settings (e.g., school and classroom size, ethnic composition, access to resources) and educational processes (e.g., student-teacher relationships) play a role in the educational outcomes of African Americans? What role do specific educational outcomes play in the lives of African Americans? These outcomes include learning and mastery, grades and academic performance as measured by standardized test scores, and educational attainment (e.g., school dropout, high school completion or general equivalency diploma [GED] attainment, college, professional, or postgraduate degree completion).

In this chapter, we begin with a demographic portrait that helps us understand the current educational experiences of African Americans. Next, we provide overviews of historical and theoretical perspectives on the education of African Americans. We then review research, focusing on structural and process factors in the education of African Americans. Finally, we consider applied perspectives on the educational experiences of African Americans and end the chapter with a summary.

We find it important, in our discussion of the education of African Americans, to distinguish between various educational indicators and measures. Some research focuses on learning and cognition using tests or assessments such as intelligence tests, other cognitive assessments (e.g., SAT scores), or achievement tests. These indicators are most often *norm-referenced*; that is, measures that compare individuals to the average performance of others in their age-group. Other studies utilize *educational achievement,* employing indicators such as school grades that involve a subjective and social component. In addition, *educational attainment,* that is, how far a student continues in school (e.g., high school, college, or post-graduate degree completion), is used as an educational indicator. Educational attainment tends to show higher correlations with life outcomes (e.g., adult employment and income) than do grades or cognitive assessments.

A Demographic Portrait of the Educational Status of African Americans

To understand psychological factors in the education of African Americans, it is helpful to first examine the historical and current status of the education of Blacks. According to data from the U.S. Census Bureau (2001b) and the National Center for Education Statistics (NCES; 2001b, 2001c, 2002), African Americans have shown notable increases in educational attainment since the 1940s. Although only 39% of African Americans in the 25- to 29-year-old age-group had a high school diploma (or GED) in 1969, by 2000 86.8% of African Americans in this age-group had graduated high school. Educational attainment at this level was generally comparable between African American men and women. It is also notable that the gap between the high school attainment of more recent cohorts of African Americans and European Americans has narrowed such that U.S. census data from 1997 and 2000 show no statistical differences in high school completion rates.

In contrast to these data from the Current Population Survey and NCES, Orfield, Losen, Wald, and Swanson (2004) estimate that only 68% of youth from all ethnic groups who entered ninth grade in 2001 will complete high school with a diploma. Discrepancies between census data and the findings of Orfield et al. result from (a) states not counting students they cannot locate, including those who are incarcerated, institutionalized, or over mandatory age; or (b) surveys not distinguishing between GED completion and high school graduation.

For all African Americans, the overall rate of actual high school completion is 50.2%, with 56.2% of females and 42.8% of males graduating from high school. Orfield et al. (2004) report state graduation discrepancy rates between Whites and Blacks ranging from 0.0% (Alaska) to 41.3% (Wisconsin). New York (35.1%), Ohio (39.6%), Nevada (40.5%), and Florida (41.0%) have the lowest graduation rates for African Americans. Of the largest predominately Black school districts, Oakland (30.4%),

Atlanta (39.6%), Cleveland (30%), and Columbus (34.4%) have the lowest graduation rates. Beyond the effects of poverty, segregation is related to higher dropout rates. Orfield et al. raise concerns that recent educational testing policies appear to be exacerbating dropout problems among ethnic minority students (e.g., Haney et al., 2004), as school districts may have incentives to "push out" students who are perceived to bring down passing test score levels.

In 2000, of all African Americans over age 25, 78.5% had a high school diploma (compared with 88.4% of Whites), 6.4% had an associate's degree (compared with 8.1% of Whites), and approximately 10.9% had completed a bachelor's degree (compared with 18.5% of Whites). In 2000, 31% of Blacks aged 18 to 24 were enrolled in college as compared with 19% in 1980 (Hoffman & Llagas, 2003). Carey (2004) reports, however, that college completion rates remain problematic among African Americans, with almost 40% of colleges and universities graduating less than 30% of African American students who begin as freshmen. Almost 10% of colleges and universities graduate less that 10% of their Black students. With respect to advanced degrees, 5.1% of African Americans had advanced degrees in 2000, with 4.2% having master's degrees, 0.6% professional degrees, and 0.3% doctorates. In contrast, 9.5% of non-Hispanic Whites had advanced degrees, with 6.5% holding a master's degree, 1.7% having a professional degree, and 1.3% having a doctorate (Bauman & Graf, 2003).

One of the reasons educational attainment is important is that it is associated with employment and income, which often defines a person's access to resources such as housing, employment opportunities, and health care. Income is correlated with educational attainment; however, at the same level of educational attainment, income levels of males remain higher than for females and are higher for Whites as compared with Blacks. For example, in 2000, the average White male with a high school diploma working full-time year-round earned $39,067 on average, compared with $34,240 for the average Black male, $26,256 for a White female, and $24,044 for a Black female at the same educational and employment status (U.S. Census Bureau, 2001b).

SPECIAL EDUCATION

Although there have been notable increases in educational attainment over the past several decades, several concerns and challenges remain. Recent data suggest that although 17% of the school-aged population is African American, these children comprise 33% of those who receive labels of mental retardation (Office of Civil Rights, U.S. Department of Education, as cited in Losen & Orfield, 2002a), a rate three times that of European American students. Losen and Orfield point to a range of factors contributing to this disproportionate representation of Blacks among special education students, including unconscious racial bias, resource inequalities, and reliance on I.Q. tests. Blacks are overrepresented not only among students identified with mental retardation, but also among students labeled with learning disabilities and emotional disturbance (Parrish, 2002). In addition, when Black students are identified for special education, they are less likely to be mainstreamed (Fierros & Conroy, 2002).

Overplacement of African Americans in Special Education

Rates of identification for special education services vary by region, being highest in the South. In addition, although counterintuitive, rates of overidentification of Blacks for special education services occur most frequently in the wealthiest school districts (Losen & Orfield, 2002).

Problems with overidentification for services have often been tied to the role of assessment in the identification of students in need of special education. Problems appear to be linked not as much to test construction or cultural bias of test items as to the role of subjectivity in the processes by which students are identified and assessed. Court cases such as *Hobson v. Hansen* (1967/1969) challenged and limited the use of I.Q. testing in educational placement and tracking of African Americans. Cases such as *Larry P. v. Riles* (1972/1974) and *PASE v. Hannon* (1980) limited the use of I.Q. tests for placing African American students in classes for the mentally retarded (Hilliard, 1983). Legislation such as Public Law (P. L.) 94-142 (Education for All Handicapped Children Act, 1975) and its reauthorization as P. L. 101-476 (Individuals with Disabilities Education Act, 1990) protects students' rights to a free and appropriate education. P. L. 99-457 (1986), which extended this legal protection to children aged 3 to 5, and its reauthorization (P. L. 105-117, 1997) were based on many of the underlying tenets established by the earlier legal rulings. These laws require that student assessments for placement in special education services be based on multidisciplinary teams with expertise in the areas of the student's presumed deficits. They also require that assessment be culturally appropriate, that parents have the right to participation and due process in placement decisions, and that students be placed in the least restrictive educational environment possible.

Many educational and civil rights advocates are concerned with the apparent weakening of an individual's legal recourse under Title VI of the Civil Rights Act of 1964. In 2001, the decision rendered by the Supreme Court in *Alexander v. Savdoval* indicated that such cases should be pursued by the Office of Civil Rights and not by private individual action. The courts have played, and will continue to play, an important role in shaping the educational experiences of African Americans. Later in this chapter, we cover other roles that the courts and legislation have played in the educational experiences of African Americans.

Historical and Contemporary
Perspectives on the Education of Blacks

To understand current perspectives on educational systems and the experience of African Americans within them, it is useful to briefly consider historical perspectives. In 1831, Nat Turner led a rebellion to free slaves in Southampton County, Virginia. After this incident, many states enacted or began to more vigilantly enforce laws that made it illegal to teach African Americans to read and write. The fear was that education and the ability to read abolitionist writings would support the activities of slave rebellion. Prior to the Civil War, only 28 Blacks had received college degrees from a college or university in the United States. Free Blacks had established schools, many affiliated with churches, following the American Revolution. Following the Civil War, the Freedman's Bureau was established by the U.S. federal government in 1865 as a relief agency. Northern missionary societies also worked to increase access to educational opportunities for former slaves, and Blacks themselves spent over $1,000,000 on private education (Foner, 1988).

BOOKER T. WASHINGTON
AND W. E. B. DU BOIS PERSPECTIVES

Historical discourse on the educational needs of Blacks is illustrated in the tension between the perspectives of Booker T. Washington and W. E. B. Du Bois. Born in 1856 and having early childhood experiences as a slave in Virginia, Washington was educated at Hampton Institute and established Tuskegee Institute based on the principles of "thrift, economy and push" (Washington, 1896, p. 324) that prepared men and women for economic roles in industry, agriculture, and service. Washington felt that educational experiences should link practical applications with instruction of mathematics and the sciences. Washington's perspective emphasized the educational needs of Blacks in the "Black Belt" of the South, a context where wealth was based on agricultural production and land possession as opposed to manufacturing. In this setting, the practices of mortgaging crops had left many Blacks in debt. Washington believed that "friction between the races will pass away in proportion as the black man, by reason of his skill, intelligence, and character, can produce something that the white man wants or respects in the commercial world" (Washington, 1896, p. 326).

In contrast to Washington, Du Bois was born in 1868 in Massachusetts to free parents. Following his parents' separation, he attended school as a young child and eventually became the first African American to receive a Ph.D. from Harvard University. Du Bois felt that industrial education was not the final stage of educational development for Blacks. DuBois (1903) described popular beliefs about the education of Blacks in the statement "an education that encourages aspiration, that sets the loftiest of ideals and seeks as an end culture and character rather than bread-winning, is the privilege of white men and the danger and delusion of black." In contrast, Du Bois believed that for Blacks to truly progress, the community needed the "Talented Tenth," that is, the top 10% of Blacks, to pursue higher educational advancement to provide the African American community with teachers, ministers, lawyers, and doctors.

HISTORICAL AND MODERN CHALLENGES FOR EQUAL ACCESS

Blacks' access to educational opportunities continued to be an important issue in the African American community and was central among issues in the civil rights struggle. In challenging the legal principle of "separate but equal" public services and accommodations established by the 1896 *Plessy v. Fergusson* decision, Thurgood Marshall, in the 1954 *Brown v. Board of Education* case, used the doll research by Mamie and Kenneth Clark (1939, 1947) as evidence of the negative effects of segregation. (An overview of Clark and Clark's work is presented in Chapter 9.)

Although the Brown decision struck down the legality of the separate but equal doctrine, the decision was clearly not the end of the struggle for equitable access to educational opportunities for African Americans. For example, in Virginia, a political movement called Massive Resistance led to the closing of public schools in opposition to desegregation. The state legislature in 1958 passed a series of laws allowing local decisions in student placement, making public education optional, and cutting off state funding for schools that allowed Black and White students to attend the same schools. Although the effort was legally squelched in 1959, some schools in Virginia did not begin integration efforts until 1968. Whites in New Orleans boycotted integrated schools and governors in Arkansas, Mississippi, and Alabama attempted to block the entrance of Black students to White colleges and universities as late as 1963. Southern public school systems were notably slow to desegregate, and the courts frequently ordered school redistricting or busing to remedy unequal access to educational opportunity. The flight of Whites to suburbs in the 1950s led to the de facto segregation of most urban-suburban government jurisdictions. Later court decisions (e.g., *Freeman v. Pitts*, 1992; *Missouri v. Jenkins*, 1995; *Oklahoma v. Dowell*, 1991) released school systems from court supervision of their desegregation efforts and led to the return of school integration levels comparable to those of the late 1960s.

Several books and studies have examined changes in and the effects of desegregation efforts. Kain and Singleton (1996) document considerable racial disparity in students' access to equal opportunity in Texas schools. Their analysis provides an update to the 1966 Coleman report, which had unexpectedly found limited racial differences in students' access to resources in suburban versus inner city schools. Kain and Singleton found high levels of segregation in schools, but ultimately found relatively small differences in school inputs (e.g., indices of teacher experience and preparation and class size). They found that racial desegregation had decreased somewhat in Texas schools. However, low-income minority students' educational experiences were more likely characterized by larger classrooms, lower access to teachers with advanced degrees, and greater likelihood of being taught by a teacher who scored lower than other teachers on academic performance tests.

In his book *Savage Inequalities*, Jonathan Kozol (1991) provides an analysis of urban and suburban public schools in six metropolitan areas. He describes dramatic differences in access to resources and infrastructure between urban schools and their suburban counterparts. Kozol poignantly notes the urban students' awareness of the gross inferiority of their schools and school resources. He describes states' local property tax funding strategies that disadvantage urban school systems. These districts have higher proportions of nontaxable properties and higher numbers of students who may require costly special services. These services, when unavailable within the public school system, have to be paid for with public school funds. In some settings, upper-income individuals disproportionately access these services and resources such that public dollars are utilized to finance the special needs of middle and upper income children in private settings, further impoverishing public school districts.

From an international perspective, funding strategies that support the resource discrepancies between schools attended by African Americans versus European Americans are not universal. Darling-Hammond (1998) points out, "In contrast to European and Asian nations that fund schools centrally and equally, the wealthiest 10 percent of U. S. school districts spend nearly 10 times more than the poorest 10 percent, and spending ratios of 3 to 1 are common within states" (p. 28).

EDUCATIONAL ALTERNATIVES

Although research continues to document disparities in the educational resources and experiences available to African Americans, many Black students have access to high-quality educational opportunities and experiences. Many African American parents choose private schools such as independent Black institutions, Catholic schools, and private (predominately white) elite schools (Slaughter & Johnson, 1988). In "Dispelling the Myth Revisited," Jerald (2001) presents an analysis of almost 90,000 public schools in the United States in the year 2000. Findings reveal 4,577 high-poverty (at least 50% low-income) or high-minority (at least 50%

African American and Latino) enrollment in schools nationwide that had student reading and/or math scores in the top third of all schools within the state.

Recent data also suggest that increasing numbers of African American parents are choosing to homeschool their children. Although 1998 data from a study of homeschooling had fewer than 1% African Americans (Rudner, 1999), data from a 1999 NCES survey on homeschooling indicated that 9.9% of their sample was African American (NCES, 2001c). There is little existing research on the experiences and educational outcomes specific to African Americans who are homeschooled. However, a number of organizations, including the National Black Home Educators Resource Association, the Network of Black Homeschoolers, and the National African-American Homeschoolers Alliance (http://www.naaha .com) have developed networks and resources targeting African American families interested or involved in homeschooling.

Beyond traditional public and private schools, parents may choose to send their children to schools that specifically focus on the holistic education of children of African decent. The Council on Independent Black Institutions (CIBI) was established in 1972 as an umbrella organization for schools that are Afrikan centered and advocate Afrikan-centered education.

> CIBI defines Afrikan-centered education as the means by which Afrikan culture—including the knowledge, attitudes, values and skills needed to maintain and perpetuate it throughout the nation building process—is developed and advanced through practice. Its aim, therefore, is to build commitment and competency within present and future generations to support the struggle for liberation and nationhood. (CIBI, 1994)

Higher Education

HISTORICALLY BLACK COLLEGES AND UNIVERSITIES

At the college and university level, students and parents may also choose a Historically Black College or University (HBCU). Lincoln and Wilberforce were the only two private colleges for Blacks established prior to the Civil War. From schools supported by the Freedman's Bureau, northern churches, and post–Civil War Blacks, several teachers colleges emerged. By 1890, college courses and programs were being offered by 40 private colleges or universities for Blacks. Sixteen additional public HBCUs that still operate were established by 1890 (Roebuck & Murty, 1993). There are currently about 107 HBCUs. By the 1990s, HBCUs had provided the undergraduate education for over 75% of Blacks who held doctoral degrees. In 2000, 13.1% of African Americans in higher education were attending a HBCU (Hoffman & Llagas, 2003); however, approximately 25% of the degrees awarded to African Americans came from HBCUs.

In her book, *Blacks in College*, Flemming (1984) indicates that African Americans attending HBCUs have access to many important developmental experiences. They have opportunities for leadership and interactions that may support their future personal and career development, and these opportunities may be less available at predominately or traditionally White institutions. In comparing students attending a predominately White university with students attending a HBCU, Cheatham, Slaney, and Coleman (1990) found no statistical differences among African Americans on racial identity attitudes scales. However, African American students demonstrated greater emotional autonomy, that is, less reliance on the approval of others and greater trust in their own opinions and ideas. In addition, students at the HBCU reported lifestyles that promote greater well-being and health (e.g., engaging in good nutrition, avoiding alcohol and drug use).

RACE AS A FACTOR IN COLLEGE ADMISSIONS

Blacks' access to higher education is an issue that continues to be addressed in courts and legislation. The 1978 Supreme Court decision in the Bakke case (*Regents of the University of California v. Bakke*) supported the continuation of affirmative action in higher education, citing the educational benefits of diversity. In the 2003 cases of *Grutter v. Bollinger et al.* and *Gratz v. Bollinger et al.*, regarding admissions policies at the University of Michigan, the U.S. Supreme Court decided that race can be used in college and professional degree programs. Race cannot be used if it is based on explicit quotas or rigid procedures (e.g., adding a specific number of points to the admissions score of an individual from a particular ethnic or racial group). Colleges and universities continue to craft both admissions policies and procedures for the distribution of financial aid that meet these legal guidelines. Some states, such as California and Washington, do not allow race to be used as a factor in decisions such as university admissions, public employment, or the awarding of public contracts. Beyond arguments focusing on past discriminatory practices in higher education, these cases focused on the role of ethnic and cultural diversity in the educational environment.

Gurin, Dey, Hurtado, and Gurin (2002) analyzed data from 1,528 students who took part in the Michigan Student Survey and national data on 11,383 students attending 184 different colleges or universities from the Cooperative Institutional Research Program. Both data sets were collected during the late 1980s. The findings indicate that an ethnically diverse environment contributes positively to educational outcomes for all college students. Gurin et al. looked at indices such as the diversity of the institution, opportunities for informal interaction with students from diverse cultural backgrounds, and exposure to diversity in course content or activities. These indices were examined in relation to outcomes such as intellectual engagement, academic skills, perspective taking, and attitudes about cultural awareness and diversity. Results suggest that campus diversity supports educational outcomes, especially for European American students, and that these effects are achieved through student experiences.

Educational Theories and African Americans

Several conceptual and theoretical perspectives have been used to explain the educational experiences and needs of African Americans. In *The Miseducation of the Negro,* Carter G. Woodson (1933/1972) argues that neither practical (e.g., industrial) nor classical training (e.g., liberal arts education) was especially successful among Blacks during the late 19th and early 20th centuries. He strongly criticizes the lack of focus on the history, development, and experience of the Negro in the curricula and proposes that education for the Negro should support understanding of self, history, literature, and religion. Education should serve to uplift others of the same race who have not had access to resources or opportunities. Freire (1970/1989), in *Pedagogy of the Oppressed,* building on experiences as an educator in Latin America, similarly notes the importance of the cooperative role of teacher and student. He defines education as a collaborative, cooperative exchange between teacher and students in which both teach, learn, and construct the curricula.

Rosenthal and Jacobson (1968) examined the idea of the self-fulfilling prophecy and provided teachers with erroneous information about students in their classrooms. The researchers found that student performance conformed to teacher expectations; that is, if a teacher thought a student was smart and interacted with the student as if she or he was smart, then the student performed well. Although the study was controversial, additional research has established that teachers tend to pay less attention to students they perceive as low achievers, call on them less, criticize and interrupt them more, offer insincere praise, provide less feedback, and seat them farther from themselves (Good & Brophy, 1987). Teachers also tend to have lower expectations of Black students in contrast to White students (Baron, Tom, & Cooper, 1985), and research indicates that students are largely aware of these expectations. For example, in contrast to 54% of White males, only 20% of Black male seniors reported that their teachers "support me and care about my success in their class" (Noguera, 2003).

CULTURE IN THE CLASSROOM

As we emphasize throughout this book, African Americans are not a monolithic group, and African American parents vary in their ethnic identity, socialization beliefs, and cultural and child-rearing practices. As Black children transition from their homes and communities to school, they may encounter schools that are culturally congruent with their prior socialization and enculturation experiences, or they may face some level of cultural transition. Prior to desegregation and declines of infrastructure in some Black communities, schools were more frequently an integral part of the community infrastructure and largely shared the culture of the children. Currently, children may go to schools that vary in their sharing, acceptance, and tolerance of cultural differences in worldview and behavior.

Black English and the Ebonics Debate

One of the areas in education where cultural variants have been particularly apparent revolves around the use of Black English. African American Vernacular English (AAVE), Black English, or Ebonics has been identified as a rule-governed linguistic system with its own syntactic structure, lexicon, and phonology. In 1997, the Board of Directors of Teachers of English to Speakers of Other Languages (TESOL) stated that AAVE deserves "pedagogical recognition."

> Effective educational programs recognize and value the linguistic systems that children bring to school. There, programs use these linguistics systems as an aid and resource to facilitate the acquisition of Standard American English. Research and experience have shown that children learn best if teachers respect the home language and use it as a bridge in teaching the language of the school and wider society. Likewise, if the children's cultural and social backgrounds are valued, their self-respect and self-confidence are affirmed and new learning is facilitated. (http://www.cal.org/ebonics/tesolebo.html)

Despite strong reactions from a variety of detractors, a body of instructional research notes the relevance and positive contribution of teaching approaches that build on the use of AAVE. For example, Taylor (1989) used a contrast approach that supports African American youth in learning Standard English (SE) by making linguistic differences between the two language systems explicit and contrasting the syntax and phonics of SE and AAVE. Programs such as The Bridge (Simpkins & Simpkins, 1981) introduce reading in AAVE and later switch to SE. Teachers who respond to AAVE by interrupting, correcting, and rigidly treating differences in syntax, word use, and pronunciation as errors may unintentionally communicate to students that they have language deficiencies. The teacher behavior may also undermine the relational component of the student-teacher relationship. (See Chapter 7 for further discussion of African American language.)

Culturally Congruent Education

Beyond issues of dialect and language, Kunjufu (1984) and Akbar (1982) criticize mainstream educational curricula as those that "train" children as opposed to educating them. Training individuals, Kunjufu suggests, builds on skills of rote memorization and prepares young people for the role of employee in a job. In contrast, education supports students in learning to think in preparation for careers in which they serve as employers. In *Countering the Conspiracy to Destroy Black Boys*, Kunjufu (1985) presents the Fourth Grade Failure Syndrome, suggesting that this age-grade represents a pivotal point in the educational experiences of African American males. Kunjufu suggests that the academic performance of African American males drops off at this point, as Black boys see schools and their curricula as culturally and personally irrelevant. Kunjufu (1985) points to multiple contributors to the early disengagement of many Black males from educational settings. These include lack of relevant role models for youth in their early educational experiences, the transition from social-relational to competitive-individualistic classroom environments, parental apathy, and the increasing negative influence of peers and media.

Potts (2003) notes that schools also serve as the primary site for interventions to reduce developmental risks and promote the development of protective factors among African American children and youth. Potts presents a critical analysis of the schools in their roles in the reproduction of social and economic class hierarchies. Schools, according to Potts, provide person-centered and individualistic skill-based interventions that accept the status quo and do not challenge the structural inequity of schools and other social systems. Potts points to an alternative view of education, complementary to the educational perspectives of Paulo Freire and Carter G. Woodson, where the goals of education are to transform, empower, and uplift those who are being educated. Potts describes the contents of an emancipatory model of education, specifying the need to counter *maafa* (the majority system of domination, literally "disaster" in Kiswahili; Ani, 1994) through the teaching of the *nguzo saba* and *ntu* and *maat* principles and virtues.

Other aspects of learning style may be culturally important to African American children. Wimberly (2002) emphasizes the importance of school relationships between teachers and students. He notes that African American high school youth frequently do not have the types of social connections with teachers (e.g., contact in and out of classroom time) that may support their access to higher education. Shade (1982) suggests that in American schools, the cognitive style that supports academic achievement is sequential, analytical, and object-oriented. Her review of the literature describes the learning styles of African Americans, in contrast, as universalistic, intuitive, and relational. Boykin (1983, 1994) suggests that Black children prefer educational environments that are congruent with their cultural preferences for verve, and Hale-Benson (1990) suggests that Black children prefer relational learning settings and experiences. (For further discussion of cognitive style, see Chapter 7.)

MINORITY SOCIAL STATUS
AND STEREOTYPES IN EDUCATION

Ogbu and colleagues (e.g., Fordham & Ogbu, 1986) have proposed that some African Americans may reject education because it is identified with an economic and status attainment system linked to their oppression by European Americans. To identify with and pursue achievement within this status system is to identify with and buy into a system that is established and controlled by a group who has historically oppressed African Americans. Consequently, African Americans may adopt an oppositional cultural frame of reference and perceive educational attainment as "acting White." Within their conceptualization, Fordham and Ogbu suggest that there are three different types of American minorities. *Immigrant minorities* are cultural or ethnic groups that chose to come to the United States because of political or economic opportunities. *Autonomous minorities* are social groups with voluntary membership based on personal and individual preference, which, relative to the American context, are a numerical minority (e.g., Mormons). Autonomous minority groups are more frequently assimilated or integrated into mainstream middle-class American social culture. In contrast, *subordinate or "castelike" minorities* have come to the United States either through slave trade or political or economic duress and most often have physical markers (skin color or physical morphology) that signal their membership in these stigmatized groups. Within the status attainment system, these groups experience blocked opportunities for advancement (e.g., a glass ceiling) and perceive bias in their efforts for full and equal participation in the status attainment system. It is these subordinate minorities that are more likely to experience the conflict between their cultural identities and participation in the American educational system. This disidentification with the educational arena is implicated in the lower educational performance of African American students. There have been recent conceptual and empirical challenges to this hypothesis (e.g., Spencer, Cross, Harpalani, & Goss, 2003). (See Chapter 9 for more discussion of these issues.)

Claude Steele presents an alternative role that one's ethnicity may play in academic performance. Based on a series of studies (e.g., Steele, 1992;

Steele & Aronson, 1995), Steele and his colleagues suggest that Blacks and members of other groups classified as numerical minorities may be subject to "stereotype threat" or "stereotype vulnerability." This vulnerability refers to the pressure experienced by a member of a stereotyped group in a performance situation where he or she is at risk of confirming a negative or pejorative stereotype. For African Americans, academic performance situations increase concerns about confirming or being judged based on beliefs regarding the intellectual abilities of their racial group. This impaired performance is reflected in what Steele describes as the overprediction phenomenon. In these situations, even when African Americans are academically capable, as reflected in aptitude scores (e.g., SAT or ACT scores) that are comparable to their European American peers, they demonstrate lower academic performance. Steele argues that this lower performance may be due to processes associated with the priming of racial stereotypes about academic performance.

In one study (Steele & Aronson, 1995), Steele and colleagues gave both Black and White college students an academic performance measure. In one condition, respondents were asked to complete a questionnaire that asked general questions about their background (e.g., age, gender, major) prior to undertaking the performance measure. In the second condition, participants completed a similar questionnaire that ended with a question asking their race (race prime condition). African American students in the race prime condition showed lower performance than both African American students in the control condition and White students in either condition. Beyond these internal processes, Steele (1992) also raises questions as to whether subtle clues in the social environment (e.g., the manner in which instructors ask or respond to different students in their classes) communicate performance expectations and membership or inclusion within the specific learning community.

In contrast to Steele's perspective, Crocker and Major (1989) propose that membership in a stigmatized group may lead individuals to devalue the self domains in which they demonstrate lower performance. For example, research on African American adolescents indicates that academic competence is less central to their overall self-esteem than their social competence with peers; in contrast, academic competence was of greater centrality or importance to the self-concept of European American adolescents.

Work in the late 1970s at Berkeley by Uri Treisman suggests that support, expectations, and preparation strategies may be altered to support the academic performance of African American students. Triesman conducted an ethnographic study of African American and Chinese students and found that the Chinese students had peer networks that involved studying and discussing academic experiences (e.g., how to talk with faculty or get information from administrative offices). In contrast, African American students tended to study in isolation and have peer networks that were separated from their academic experiences. Rejecting remedial approaches to achievement challenges, the mathematics workshop program at Berkeley was developed and built on the strategies of successful students. The program was designed to work with students in small groups on assignments that complemented students' current course materials but also prepared them for future courses. African American students who participated in the program demonstrated very positive results. For example, 21% of Black students earned a B– or better in first-year calculus, 56% of Black students in the workshop achieved at this level. Even taking into account MSAT scores, Black students with higher MSAT scores who were not part of the workshops performed at a lower level than Black students who had entered college with lower MSAT scores but were part of the workshop (Treisman, 1992).

School Structures and Processes: Research Lessons

Considerable research has been conducted examining the educational experiences of African Americans. In the following section, we examine (a) research on the characteristics of the settings and structures within which African Americans are educated and the impact of these structures on educational outcomes and (b) research that assists us in understanding the transactions, processes, or experiences that African Americans have within education, home, and community settings that are related to educational outcomes.

THE STRUCTURE OF AFRICAN AMERICAN EXPERIENCES IN SCHOOL

Early Childhood Educational Experiences

Experience with structured, out-of-home educational settings begins relatively early for African American children. Black children aged 3 to 5 are more likely to be enrolled in an early childhood care center or educational program than either their White or Hispanic peers. For example, in 2001, 60.1% of Black children living below the poverty level and 66.2% of Black children at or above the poverty level were in some type of structured day care program. In contrast, 46.1% of White children aged 3 to 5 living below the poverty level and 60.8% of White children at or above the poverty level were in some type of structured day care program (U.S. Department of Education, 2002).

Quality early childhood experiences have been demonstrated to support later educational outcomes among low-income children. For example, from 1958 to 1962, the Perry Preschool Project in Ypsilanti, Michigan, provided 30 hours of weekly high-quality active learning experiences for 123 low-income children aged 3 to 4 at risk for school failure. The long-term benefits of participation in such a program were found to included fewer special education placements, greater school attainment, lower adult arrest rates, and higher incomes (Schweinhart, Barnes, & Weikart, 1993). While early evaluations of Head Start, (i.e. such as the Westinghouse in 1969), suggested that cognitive outcomes such as I.Q. gains were time limited, additional research suggests that students who attend Head Start are less likely to be held back in grade and less likely to be placed in special educational services (Zigler, Taussig, & Black, 1992). There is considerable ongoing work aimed at fully understanding the benefits of participation in Head Start and other early educational programming.

Testing and Accountability

With the enactment of legislation, such as the No Child Left Behind Act in 2001, there has been continued interest in the role and effect of high stakes testing (e.g., school tests that are required for receiving a high school diploma) and accountability efforts in public education. Based on a quali-tative study of Chicago's experience with high stakes testing and account-ability in educational reform, Lipman (2002) suggests that these policy efforts continue to promote and even exacerbate unequal educational access. Lipman describes extensive focus on test preparation in schools with low scores. This preparation includes redirecting resources from arts pro-grams to purchase test preparation booklets, pep rallies, and announcements supporting student performance on the Iowa Test. These efforts to improve test performance result in an overall narrowing of the educational opportu-nities available to students in lower-performing schools as schools increase their focus on test performance. In these settings, young teachers who are initially enthusiastic about learning are lost as the school focus turns to test preparation. In addition, school system workshops advise teachers to reduce their focus on both students who will clearly pass tests and students with little potential to help the school achieve its goals in test performance. In contrast, at higher-performing schools, teachers are described as focusing on developing richer curricula and promoting the value and love of learning.

Role of Race in School Selection

Research has also shown that race plays an important role in shaping students' access to educational opportunities and experiences. When schools use ability grouping or tracking, African American students are more likely to be placed in lower tracks. Some research has suggested that African American and Latino students with comparable test scores are less likely to be placed in advanced courses than their White or Asian peers

(Oakes, 1995). In a survey of 1,391 charter and 529 public school parents, Tedin and Weiher (2004) found that although school academic performance was the most important predictor of parental school choice, the racial composition of the school also played a role in parental selection of educational setting. Giles (1978) suggests that once a school's enrollment reaches 30% African American, European American parents begin to move their children out of the school at an exponential rate. Further research suggests that European Americans leave schools completely once they have student enrollments greater than 80% African American (Clotfelter, 1976).

Role of Race in Gifted and Talented Programs

Work by Ford (Ford, 1996; Ford, Harris, Tyson, & Frazier Trotman, 2002) and Worrell (2003) underlines another domain in which African Americans face challenges within American educational systems: educational opportunities for the gifted and talented (GT). D. Y. Ford et al. (2002) suggest that African Americans are underrepresented in gifted programs by 50%. The authors note that biased beliefs about the cognitive abilities of African Americans, and the use of intelligence tests as the primary method of identifying youth for participation in gifted and talented programs, places these youth at a disadvantage. The singular use of I.Q. tests may be particularly inappropriate as I.Q. scores predict only half of the variance in performance. In addition, standardized tests have less predictive validity in relation to the academic performance and outcomes of African Americans. More comprehensive analysis of capabilities and use of assessments based on multidimensional models of intellectual capacity may be warranted.

In addition, Worrell (2003) notes that potential biases in recruitment processes may play a role in the underidentification of African American youth for GT programs. Worrell also raises the question as to whether Steele's stereotype vulnerability may place African American GT youth at risk of academic underachievement. In his study of participants in a summer program for GT students, Worrell notes that gifted African American youth may come from homes that are less affluent and this raises questions as to whether youth and families are aware of opportunities for GT students. Ford also raises questions as to what types of educational experiences are engaging for, relevant to, and support the retention of GT African American students and what training is needed to support GT teachers and program designers in developing and using appropriate assessment, recruitment, and retention strategies.

Family and Neighborhood Structure

Structural factors in families and neighborhoods also shape educational experiences and outcomes for African Americans. Delaying childbearing increases the likelihood of college attendance among African American females. Among African American teen mothers, delaying the birth of a second child and having familial or educational supports may enhance the likelihood of educational attainment. Research further suggests that European American adolescents' cognitive outcomes appear to benefit more from having higher-income neighbors than cognitive outcomes of African American adolescents do. Several cognitive and academic indicators (e.g., school achievement, graduation rates, college attendance) suggest that affluent neighbors and ethnically diverse neighborhoods benefit African American males (Duncan, 1994; Ensminger, Lamkin, & Jacobson, 1996; Halpern-Felsher et al., 1997). Neighborhood cohesion also affects academic outcomes. In recent research, Plybon, Edwards, Butler, Belgrave, and Allison (2003) found that positive perceptions of neighborhood cohesion were positively associated with school self-efficacy and self-reported grades among a sample of 84 urban African American adolescent females.

PARENT AND TEACHER RELATIONSHIPS AND THE EDUCATION OF AFRICAN AMERICANS

Parenting Expectations, Practices, and Education

Exchanges between children and their parents, their teachers, and other members of their social environment are important to their educational experiences and outcomes. Research has continued to underline the importance of early stimulation in the brain development of infants and children that supports later cognitive development and academic achievement. Lower-income families and families with teen mothers may provide lower levels of stimulation, and African American children are more likely than their White peers to be born into low-income families or to teen moms.

Research has also found authoritative or democratic parenting (characterized by high parental warmth and control) to have a positive effect on the academic performance of White and Latino adolescents but less impact on the educational outcomes of African and Asian American youth (Steinberg, Dornbusch, & Brown, 1992). In addition, African American youth may have less peer group support for achievement (Steinberg et al., 1992). Smith-Maddox (1999) indicates that parental involvement in school activities is important to African American students' educational aspirations.

Expectations of parents, teachers, and students themselves are important and can have an impact on students' educational outcomes. In a longitudinal study of 1,242 African American first graders, Ensminger and Slusarcick (1992) found that for males, low academic expectations, aggression, and poor grades predicted higher risk of dropping out of high school.

Boys with lower grades or boys who had low educational expectations were more likely to graduate if their mother had finished high school. Boys whose mothers had not completed high school were especially likely to graduate if they received high marks in first grade or if they had high expectations about school. Early aggression predicted dropout for non-poor boys but not for poor boys. For girls, high expectations for themselves and from their mothers, stricter parental rules regarding school, and perceptions of teachers' satisfaction with their performance predicted graduation. In addition, graduation rates were higher for nonpoor girls with A's or B's in first grade than nonpoor girls with C's and D's. Grades made very little difference in the graduation rates of poor girls. It is troubling that half of this urban sample who provided data at follow-up did not graduate.

Mickelson's (1990) research assists us in better understanding the role of expectations among African American youth and families. Research has often found a discrepancy between the educational aspirations and the actual educational performance or attainment of African American adolescents. Many African American youth have very high educational or occupational aspirations, but low achievement. According to Mickelson, there are two sets of beliefs: (a) abstract attitudes about education, which include highly valuing education, and (b) seeing education as an important factor in occupational, social, and economic success. In contrast to abstract values, concrete attitudes are based in the proximal realities of an individual's experiences and the "probable returns" on an individual's personal educational investments. Results from Mickelson's (1990) research on 1,193 African and European American public high school students in the Los Angeles area indicate that African American youth hold stronger beliefs in the importance of education for social mobility than do European American youth. However, there is a significant discrepancy between the abstract and concrete educational attitudes of African American youth, with concrete attitudes predicting their academic achievement.

Disciplinary Actions and Treatment in Schools

African American males are disproportionately represented among students receiving disciplinary actions, including expulsions. Townsend (2000) reminds us that expulsions result in more limited access to learning opportunities. She links the higher levels of disciplinary actions to cultural conflicts including lack of cultural knowledge among instructors (e.g., focusing on strict, hierarchical compliance to the teacher's desire for students' posture as opposed to focusing on the primacy of the learning task). Townsend proposes a range of potential factors that may contribute to the improvement of these disciplinary problems, including greater focus on building relationships and cultural bridges, and linking schools to families and communities. With the enactment of zero tolerance policies, additional concerns have been raised regarding the inequitable enforcement of these disciplinary guidelines (e.g., Polakow-Suransky, 1999).

Applications

Research, theory, leadership, and vision are important resources to support educational outcomes for African Americans. Schools such as Westside Preparatory School, founded by Marva Collins in 1975 in Chicago, and the current Marva Collins Preparatory School are examples of the rich educational opportunities available to African American students. Schools that promote strong connections between parents and the schools have also shown great promise in supporting the educational outcomes of African American students. Some school districts that have enacted the Comer School Development Program (SDP) model also show great promise in providing effective educational experiences for African Americans students, especially in low-resource communities. The SDP model focuses on supporting six developmental pathways, that is, the physical, psychological, language, social, ethical, and cognitive pathways. The program provides school structures to support

- School planning teams involving administrators, teachers, and parents
- Student and staff support teams that work to facilitate relationships and communication
- Parent teams that are based on no-fault problem solving, consensus decision making, and collaboration

Operational processes that support schools in the SDP model are

- Comprehensive planning based on an understanding of child development
- Staff development based on the comprehensive plan
- Assessment and modification

According to Millsap et al. (2000), students in schools that more effectively implement the Comer model and who remain in those schools for longer periods of time show higher educational gains.

For psychologists, especially school and educational psychologists, several issues regarding the school experiences of African American children and youth must be considered. For example, what is the role of culture and multiculturalism in the educational arena? How should cultural preferences and identities be addressed in schools? What is the role of culture in the educational assessment process? What are the potential benefits of gender-segregated schools for Blacks, especially for Black males?

Debates will likely continue over these and other issues. In addition, research findings will likely continue to impact court actions that affect educational experiences and opportunities for African Americans.

Summary

Educational opportunities are important resources for individual development, as well as individual economic and career achievement, with clear implications for the broader economic development of the African American community. With both positive attitudinal values toward and significant historical investments in education, a long-term historical perspective shows that African Americans have made notable educational strides over the past 140 years despite considerable barriers. Many of these barriers persist, and African American students, especially students in low-income communities, continue to face great disparities in access to equitable educational resources. African American children are more likely to be placed in special education and less likely to be identified for gifted education. The courts have played—and continue to play—a significant role in arbitrating access to equitable educational opportunities.

Beyond access to equal structural resources, theoretical perspectives underline the important role that culture plays in the educational experience, through shaping curricula or educational processes that use culture and language to support positive educational outcomes. A range of traditional and culturally based academic opportunities are available to African American learners. Educational policy and related structural factors shape and constrain the educational opportunities available to many Black children. Family support and neighborhood context support positive educational outcomes for African Americans, especially for African American males. Research makes it clear that many African American students face processes and social interactions in the school context that may affect their school experience. The African American community and psychologists working on educational issues will continue to face important questions about the education of African Americans. What structures are most effective in supporting positive educational outcomes for African Americans? To what extent do current curricular content and educational processes "train" as opposed to "educate" African American students? What does it mean to effectively educate an African American at the start of the 21st century?

The role of education has and will continue to play a crucial role in the African American community. The African proverb indicating that "He who learns, teaches" is consistent with Woodson's and Friere's perspectives on education, implicating both the important role of cultural education for African Americans and the collaborative communal dynamics of education. African Americans may have important roles in shaping the educational experiences of their community and may not be able to rely on mainstream American culture and educational structures to understand, acknowledge, or address these educational needs.

Neighborhoods and Communities 5

I am because we are and we are because I am.

—Xhosa proverb

Wide Strategy Could Reduce Local Impact

Court ruling seen opening way for regional strategy; Wide reach reduces local impact

Baltimore Sun

By Eric Siegel

Jan. 7, 2005

Local and national public policy advocates expressed the hope Friday that a judge's decision that the federal government should have taken a regional approach to desegregating Baltimore's public housing could be the catalyst for the development of an area-wide housing strategy.

"The big picture is we've got a housing crisis in this region," said Michael A. Sarbanes, executive director of the Citizens Planning and Housing Association, which is working on a plan it hopes to unveil by the fall. "This decision is a piece of solving it. To the extent it can garner federal resources to help solve it, it can be a key step."

Yet lawyers still must struggle through another phase in the courts. While it's not clear what the remedies will be, nothing in this 10-year-old case has come easily. And at least one substantive effort in the early 1990s to move some city public housing residents to the suburbs engendered fierce political and community opposition.

David Rusk, a Washington-based urban policy consultant and author, pointed out that Montgomery County for the past three decades has had a model inclusionary zoning law that sets aside up to 15 percent of newly constructed housing units for low- and very-low-income households. It has become more racially diverse while continuing to be one of the country's wealthiest jurisdictions.

"If a Montgomery County policy was in effect in this region for a 20-year period, the problem addressed by the ruling would be substantially resolved," said Rusk, who has studied the metropolitan area extensively.

107

"People ought to view the decision as taking the region by the shoulders and saying, 'Look, folks, you've got a problem you don't have to have,'" he said.

On Thursday, U.S. District Court Judge Marvin J. Garbis said that the U.S. Department of Housing and Urban Development violated federal fair housing law by failing to look beyond the city's boundaries for ways to disperse the concentration of public housing residents.

Ruling on a civil rights case brought by the American Civil Liberties Union on behalf of African-American public housing residents, Garbis said he would schedule a conference soon to discuss possible remedies and said he would invite representatives of the region's counties.

In a 322-page decision, Garbis wrote, "HUD has failed adequately to consider regionalization over the past half-century and, absent judicial compulsion, appears most unlikely to do so in the foreseeable future."

As an example, he cited the agency's failure to prod the city of Annapolis and several counties to agree to a report two years ago by the Maryland Center for Community Development proposing a regional fair housing action plan.

Becky Sherblom, executive director of the statewide nonprofit that seeks to spur neighborhood investment in affordable housing and economic development, said Friday that the report's proposals included joint negotiations with lenders and creation of a single, region-wide waiting list for federally subsidized Section 8 housing vouchers. "As far as I know, nothing's been done," she said.

Sherblom said she hoped Garbis's decision "can bring us all together and not finger-point but say, 'What can we do?'"

"It may be the impetus that gives us the political will that didn't exist two years ago," she said.

Rusk suggested that one way to make any solution more palatable to suburban jurisdictions would be to give a preference for any new units that are created within a given jurisdiction to public housing residents who work in that jurisdiction.

"People shouldn't see the judge's decision as somehow unleashing welfare queens and their drug-dealing boyfriends," he said. "That's not who they are. They are hard-working folks. They're just not earning a lot of money. This is the nursing home aide taking care of your elderly parent, the clerk at the laundry you've been taking your cleaning to for years."

Introduction and Definitions

Whether in a high-rise apartment building in a bustling urban neighborhood, a farmhouse in a small rural community, or a house in a suburban development, we live in the context of a physical and social community. Race, historical forces, and social policy have shaped the racial composition of neighborhoods and communities, and the availability of other resources, such as housing, schools, libraries, and stores. As described in the news article that opens this chapter, cities and communities continue to struggle with policy and issues of race that shape where people live. But a community is more than the houses or apartments in which people live. How are communities important to the psychology of African Americans?

In considering the construct of community relative to African Americans, we face a definitional challenge. What is the "Black community"? Are we talking about the predominately African American neighborhoods and geographic areas in southeast Washington, D.C., Harlem, Compton and Watts, and the Southside of Chicago? Or are we speaking instead of a national community of Americans of African descent who are joined by a sense of common peoplehood, history, heritage, and sociopolitical experience and challenge. How does community make a difference to African Americans? Does it really matter where Blacks live? What does community provide? In this chapter, we address these questions. We begin with definitions of community and neighborhood. Then, we provide a description of African American communities, including historical perspectives on the communities within which African Americans live and to which they move. We examine theories that help us understand how neighborhoods are relevant to the psychology of African Americans, and we present lessons learned about the role that neighborhood and community play in the lives of African Americans. We provide an overview of strategies that have been used to study neighborhoods and community, and we close with a summary of the material covered in this chapter.

DEFINITIONS

Definitions of Community

German sociologist Ferdinand Tonnies (1855–1936) provides some support in helping us define the African American community. He uses the terms *Gemeinschaft* and *Gesellschaft* to describe the development of modern communities. For Tonnies, Gemeinschaft reflects our traditional, preindustrial sense of community that is defined as association based on family and kinship relationships, neighborhood, and friendship. These social ties are linked through loyalty, affection, love, and closeness and are reflected in social structures of family households, villages, and small towns. In these settings, we think of individuals who know and care about one another and depend on each other not only for shelter, food, and clothing, but also for relationships. Current manifestations of Gemeinschaft would include close-knit neighborhoods and areas that have retained their small-town qualities. As industrialization began to change our sense of social connection, communities were organized and linked based on the structures of a civil society. The term Gesellschaft reflects the sense of community based on social interaction for the structured exchange of resources. This type of community is more typical of industrial society and the development of cities. Modern cities and professional associations would be reflections of Gesellschaft. Within these social structures, the roles that individuals play are specialized, and there may be a greater risk of social isolation.

Chaskin and Richman (1992) define *community* as

> the local context in which people live. It is referred to by its geographic identity, but its place on the map is only one of its attributes. It is a place of reference and belonging, and the community includes dimensions of space, place, and sentiment as well as of action. It is defined by a dynamic network of associations that binds (albeit loosely) individuals, families, institutions, and organizations into a web of interconnections and interaction. (p. 113)

The local community is a functional unit in which goods and services are provided and consumed, interpersonal relationships are created and maintained, participation in activities is shared, and commonality exists among local residents. This definition of community is not necessarily dependent on clear geographic boundaries (e.g., different residents may have slightly different conceptions of where the neighborhood begins and ends), but it does assume that the community's residents hold in common a range of mutual experiences and circumstances and share access to an array of organizations, institutions, services, and activities.

These definitions emphasize that when we speak of community, we are not simply talking about a geographical location, but a sense of social connection and belonging. McMillan and Chavis (1986) describe this perception as one's "psychological sense of community"; "a feeling that members have of belonging, a feeling that members matter to one another and to the group, and a shared faith that members' needs will be met through their commitment to be together" (p. 9). It also involves a sense of membership, influence, integration, needs fulfillment, and emotional connection.

Definitions of Neighborhood

Similar to definitions of community, definitions of neighborhood vary across a range of professions and disciplines, and from within and outside of the neighborhood. Chaskin (1998) notes that neighborhoods have been defined "as a social unit, neighborhoods as a spatial unit and the neighborhood as networks of relationships, associations and patterns of use" (p. 1). Boundary designations of these areas have included *politically defined neighborhoods*, based in the community or residents' civic organizations designed for the legitimate representation of community residents and their goals within the local political sphere; *social neighborhoods*, which reflect external boundary assessments for marketing, analytic, or programmatic efforts; and *physical neighborhoods*, which are based on designated bounded geographical areas for government administrative use

(Chaskin, 1998). African Americans are more likely to define neighborhood based on social relationships than on location (Lee & Campbell, 1990).

Although Tonnies (1925) considers ethnic communities to be reflections of Gesellschaft (society), not Gemeinschaft (community), the African American experience can be captured by both. Historical experiences and continued structural supports of racial segregation in the United States have led to the continuation, formation, and concentration of a considerable number of African Americans in small or circumscribed neighborhoods and communities that vary widely in their resources and infrastructure. However, for many African Americans, their personal sense of identity includes a strong sense of membership in the Black community, regardless of the racial composition of the neighborhood within which they currently reside.

Community "Capacity" and Why Neighborhoods Are Important to Study

Communities and neighborhoods vary in the extent to which they are able to provide resources or contain the infrastructure to meet the needs of their members and residents. Iscoe (1974) defines a competent community as "one that utilizes, develops, or obtains resources so that members of the community may make reasoned decisions about issues confronting them" (p. 607). Cottrell explains:

> A competent community is one in which its various parts are able to: (1) Collaborate effectively in identifying the problems and needs of a community; (2) Achieve a workable consensus on goals and priorities; (3) Agree on ways and means to implement the agreed-upon goal; and (4) Collaborate effectively in the required activity. (quoted in Mattessich & Roy, 1997, p. 63)

One of the reasons that it is important to better understand neighborhoods and community is because of the impact that neighborhood and community factors have on the well-being of African Americans. LaVeist (2003) matched data from the National Survey of Black Americans, a national multistage probability sample of 2,107 African Americans, with the National Death Index. The author found that racial segregation predicted mortality even after controlling for age, health status, sex, marital status, and level of educational attainment. Earlier research (LaVeist, 1993) found racial segregation to predict differences in Black and White infant mortality rates. That neighborhood racial composition predicts these health outcomes underlines the importance of examining neighborhood context in understanding the psychology of African Americans.

Describing the African American Community

In understanding the African American community, it is useful to consider where African Americans live and the geographical areas within which they reside. Historical perspectives on African American neighborhoods and communities provide a foundation for understanding contemporary issues.

WHERE AFRICAN AMERICANS LIVE

According to the 2000 U.S. Census, African Americans comprised 12.9% of the total U.S. population, and 86.5% of Blacks lived in metropolitan communities (Iceland, Weinberg, & Steinmetz, 2002), with approximately 53% living in central cities and an increasing number living in suburbs (34.9% in 2000, up from 27% in 1990). Although racial residential segregation declined for African Americans between 1980 and 2000, African Americans remain the most segregated ethnic group in the United States. Larger cities and metropolitan areas (with populations of one million or more) showed higher levels of racial segregation than smaller cities. Although the majority of metropolitan areas showed some level of reduction in Black-White segregation between 1980 and 2000, areas in the Rust Belt[1] have demonstrated the lowest levels of change in racial segregation (Lewis Mumford Center, 2001). Using national averages, the typical Black lives in a neighborhood that is 51.4% Black, 33% White, 11.4% Hispanic, and 3.3% Asian. In contrast, the typical White lives in a neighborhood that is 80.2% White, 6.7% Black, 7.9% Hispanic, and 3.9% Asian (Lewis Mumford Center, 2001).

POVERTY AND AFRICAN AMERICAN COMMUNITIES

Recent census data also suggest that the concentration of poverty in many urban, predominately African American communities is declining. The number of census tracts characterized as poor, where more than 60% of residents were African American, dropped from 48% in 1980 to 39% in 2000 (Kingsley & Pettit, 2003). This reflects a decline from 4.8 million African Americans living in high-poverty neighborhoods in 1980 to 3.1 million in 2002, further indicating a reversal of trends from the prior 20 years of increased concentration of urban poverty (Jargowsky, 1997). These historical trends in segregation are based on a range of documented causes including discriminatory housing practices, zoning laws that support economic segregation, and economic disparities (Frey & Myers, 2002). Although higher-income African Americans tend to live in more integrated neighborhoods, this difference tends to be minimal, and the neighbors of middle-class Blacks tend to be of lower economic status than the neighbors of their White peers at the same income level (Alba, Logan, & Stults, 2000). In addition, when African Americans own homes, the value of their residences is 35% lower than the homes of their European American counterparts (National Urban League, 2004).

RESIDENTIAL MOBILITY

African Americans experienced decreases in their rates of residential mobility over the second half of the 20th century. However, residential mobility tended to remain stable or even to increase among those more economically challenged (Fischer, 2002). This may be due in part to lower overall rates of homeownership among African Americans (less than 50% as compared with more than 70% for European Americans). Homeownership for African Americans is linked to rates of loan denials for home mortgages and home improvement that are twice those of Whites. Residential mobility presents challenges to communities: Neighbors may not develop strong social connections or neighborhood-based support, and children may move from school to school.

Wilson (1987) suggests that the sense of social connection and community within many predominately African American urban neighborhoods has declined significantly over the past decades, and the loss of these social connections results in many individual- and community-level challenges.

Historical Perspectives on African American Communities

COMMUNITIES DURING SLAVERY

In our look at community, it is important to consider the historical role of community for African Americans. Several factors in the early American enslavement experience worked to undermine a sense of community and social connection among Americans of African descent. The history of slavery in West Africa was built in part on the selling of prisoners from intertribal conflict and warfare into slavery, separating individuals from their families and tribes. Slave traders and owners mixed members of different tribal groups so that there would be no common language and so that communication that might support rebellion could be undermined. Breakup and dispersion of families and of biologically based kinship networks through slave trade were common practices that further disrupted social connections among slaves. Despite these efforts and forces, historical narratives describe rich and complex social connections among members of many slave communities. Separations from blood kin supported the construction of social networks not bound by biological relationship. We see such connections today among fictive kin (see Chapter 3 for further discussion). In addition, communities of free blacks demonstrated the building of neighborhood capacity through the development of community infrastructures, frequently organized around religious institutions (Horton & Horton, 1997).

MIGRATION PATTERNS

After the Civil War, a trend toward northern migration began, based in part on southern hostility, Jim Crow laws, economic crises in the South, and perceived employment opportunities in the North. Northern migration slowed with the Great Depression, but expanded between the 1940s and the 1950s and continued through the 1970s. Beginning in the 1970s, the migration of Blacks out of the South began to reverse, with population growth occurring in both metropolitan and nonmetropolitan areas. Overall, these residential transitions resulted in greater geographic dispersion of Blacks in the Northeast and Southwest and greater urbanization. For example, in 1860, when 85% of American Blacks were enslaved, 90% lived in the rural South. In contrast, U.S. census estimates from 2000 showed that 55% of African Americans reside in the South and 52% live in the central city of a metropolitan area (U.S. Census Bureau, 2002a). The patterns of racial residential mobility and government policies that have supported ethnic variations and segregation in residence continue to play an important role in the experience of community by African Americans.

Theoretical Perspectives on Communities

There are important theories and research that can support our understanding of the role of neighborhood and community. We consider these in our examination of trends in neighborhood composition and the effects of neighborhood on African Americans.

EUROCENTRIC AND TRADITIONAL WESTERN PERSPECTIVES ON COMMUNITIES

Africentric theory suggests that community, social connections, and relationships may be particularly important for African Americans. Some

Western theoretical perspectives have also emphasized the importance of a sense of connection to the psychological functioning of individuals. Jung's descriptions of the collective unconscious expanded Freud's ideas of the unconscious and depicted a deeper structural layer of the unconscious that is based on ancestral memory traces containing archetypes (i.e., patterns, themes, or dynamics). This collective unconscious is shared by all of humanity because of our common ancestral heritage, and it reflects the universality of themes and struggles experienced by humans. Examples of these common archetypes are seen in cultural roles reflected in art, literature, and personal dynamics (e.g., roles of the Innocent, the Orphan, the Warrior, the Caregiver, the Seeker, the Destroyer, the Lover, the Creator, the Ruler, the Magician, the Sage, and the Fool; Pearson, 1991). Other theory and research that emphasizes social connections, community environments, and neighborhood include work on the collective sense of self (e.g., Crocker, Luhtanen, Blaine, & Broadnax, 1994; also see discussions in Chapter 9 on self and identity); Bronfenbrenner's (1979) ecological theory underlining the role of context in development (described in Chapter 10); and Emile Durkheim's (1897/1951) sociological analyses of anomie and suicide. Durkheim's analysis addresses the consequences of the lack of community.

SOCIAL DISORGANIZATION THEORY

Much of the recent theoretical work examining the effects of neighborhood contexts on psychological outcomes traces its origins to the work of the Chicago School of Sociology's social disorganization theory (Shaw & McKay, 1969). Social disorganization theory makes the assumption that criminality is linked to limitations in a community's social resources and capacity to meet the needs of its residents. This results in an erosion of social controls. Factors such as limited community-level economic resources, ethnic heterogeneity, and high rates of residential mobility reflect community social disorganization. Sampson, Raudenbush, and Earls (1997), working on the Project on Human Development in Chicago Neighborhoods (PHDCN), have found a negative relationship between community violence and residents' sense of collective efficacy, that is, neighborhood resident's beliefs that they can effectively have an impact on behavior within their communities. The PHDCN has provided a rich source of information on neighborhood factors that affect children and families (for additional information, see http://www.hms.harvard.edu/chase/projects/chicago/about/).

Related work has identified the physical environment as a potential focus for interventions. The "broken windows" theory suggests that crime is more likely to occur in areas where the physical environment is disorganized and unkempt (Wilson & Kelling, 1982). The theory suggests that the disorganization of the physical space in a neighborhood sends a message to potential criminals that residents do not care about their neighborhood. Although healthy and safe housing and neighborhoods are important to our physical, emotional, and social well-being, community interventions that only address "broken windows" may not be adequate to address the full range of supports and resources needed by community residents. Research by Sampson and Raudenbush (1999) suggests that the community's sense of collective efficacy may be more important to indicators such as neighborhood crime than the upkeep of the physical environment.

OTHER THEORIES OF NEIGHBORHOOD

Another conceptual perspective on neighborhood effects comes from Jencks and Mayer's (1990) analysis of conceptual pathways through which neighborhoods may affect individual-level outcomes. The five models articulated by Jencks and Mayer include *contagion (epidemic) models*, which suggest that community residents influence the behavior of their peers based on the level of residents' susceptibility to risk. *Collective socialization models* suggest that neighborhood adults serve as role models who monitor and socialize children and youth in the community. *Institutional models* emphasize the role of community-level infrastructure and institutional resources (e.g., quality schools, libraries, recreational facilities, and police), whereas *social competition models* suggest that community residents may compete for limited environmental resources. In contrast, *relative deprivation models* suggest that individuals engage in social comparison and evaluate their status relative to peers within the community.

Kupersmidt, Greisler, DeRosier, Patterson, and Davis (1995) offer an alternative set of neighborhood models. These include *risk models* that suggest that children growing up in high-risk neighborhoods are at greater risk of negative outcomes (e.g., social and behavioral problems) than youth living in low-risk settings. *Protective models* predict that low-risk communities may protect youth living in high-risk families, and *potentiator models* predict that living in low-risk environments may positively enhance the development of children in low-risk families. Finally, a *person-environment fit model* suggests that the lack of match between individuals and their environmental context may result in adaptive challenges.

SOCIAL CAPITAL

"Social capital" (Coleman, 1988; Putnam, 1993) is an additional theoretical perspective that can assist us in understanding the value and contribution of social relationships within neighborhood and community contexts. According to Coleman (1988), social capital involves three primary components: (a) obligation and expectations involving reciprocity,

(b) information channels based in relationships, and (3) shared norms and values with effective sanctions.

In contrast to Coleman's emphasis on social capital as the relations among people, other conceptualizations of social capital have emphasized macro-level and political science perspectives that link social capital to organized community structures and processes such as civic engagement and democratic participation (Putnam, 1993). This civic-democratic construction of community social capital is argued to facilitate "coordinated actions" and "enable participants to act together more effectively to pursue shared objectives" (Putnam, 1995, pp. 664–665).

Portney and Berry (1997) examined social capital among different ethnic groups in Birmingham, Dayton, Portland (Oregon), St. Paul, and San Antonio. They found that African Americans show higher levels of participation in civic or neighborhood associations in contrast to issue-based groups such as crime watch organizations, or self-help/service organizations.

ENVIRONMENTAL HEALTH RISKS

There are environmental health risks to which African Americans may be disproportionately exposed because of their places of residence. African Americans in low-income communities are more likely to reside near transportation routes, industrial sites, and toxic waste sites that increase their exposure to airborne and other toxins (United Church of Christ Commission for Racial Justice, 1987). These toxins and other environmental pollutants may play a role in the high rates of asthma experienced by African Americans. Due to the aging housing stock and limitations in the comprehensive implementation of lead abatement programs, African American children have disproportionately higher rates of lead exposure, which can lead to a range of negative cognitive and behavioral effects and even death (Centers for Disease Control and Prevention, 1997).

COMMUNITY PSYCHOLOGY
AND AFRICENTRIC PSYCHOLOGY

Within the field of psychology, community psychology has emerged as an area of specialization that focuses explicitly on the role of psychology in the community. Brookins (1999) provides a useful comparison of community psychology to African psychology, noting both similarities and unique features of each paradigm. Brookins's analysis notes that both community and African perspectives emphasize an ecological perspective that sees the individual within his or her broader social context. However, the conceptual foundations of an African psychology also emphasize African philosophy, spirituality, and a liberation ideology. Both perspectives also operate from a humanitarian values orientation; however, the African perspective underlines the importance of integrating theory and research and the "lived experience" of African Americans. Social change strategies within community psychology include prevention, empowerment, advocacy, and self-help. African perspectives also view empowerment as an important change strategy, but emphasize empowerment as a vehicle for the development of "race consciousness and self-actualization" (Brookins, 1999, p. 40). Brookins criticizes community psychology for its traditional focus on supporting an individual's skills in coping with a challenging community as opposed to attempting to reduce the risk and challenge that African Americans experience within their communities. In general, research within African psychology more strongly emphasizes community experience, participation, and dissemination. Brookins's analysis underlines the need for ongoing community change and the development of long-term perspectives on change for African Americans and their communities.

Lessons From Research on African American Communities

Research examining the role of neighborhood contexts in the lives of African Americans has expanded over the past 20 years. First we discuss W. J. Wilson's work in this regard, and then we present research on the link between neighborhood characteristics and indicators of well-being (or lack thereof) for African Americans, especially children.

DISADVANTAGED NEIGHBORHOODS

William Julius Wilson (1987, 1997) argues in *The Truly Disadvantaged* and *When Work Disappears* that the concentration of poverty and correlates (e.g., out-of-wedlock births and murder rates) in poor urban neighborhoods result from the loss of community resources, including the out-migration of higher socioeconomic status groups, that is, working-class and middle-class African Americans, from the urban core. Wilson proposes that these historical transitions in urban poor communities are linked to neighborhood structures and processes that support limited access to employment, social resources, and infrastructure.

Wilson rejects the culture of poverty hypothesis that focuses on individual-level dysfunction. Wilson describes the increasing inaccessibility of jobs in many inner-city neighborhoods. The loss of jobs near urban cores has been linked historically to the suburbanization of manufacturing, increased educational requirements for jobs because of technological advances, and automation that has reduced the number of industrial jobs. With working- and middle-class African American families moving to suburban neighborhoods, the resulting depletion of community infra-structure and resources resulted in social isolation and concentration of poverty in these urban neighborhoods. Wilson notes that more recent census data suggest that urban poverty is being dispersed over larger geographic areas with lower population density, resulting in more aban-doned housing and greater opportunities for neighborhood drug traffick-ing, drug use, and related crime.

Narratives from community residents illustrate the impact of historical community changes on the depletion of community resources and infra-structure. One resident described changes in her urban neighborhood in Chicago:

> I've been here since March 21, 1953. When I moved in, the neighborhood was intact. It was intact with homes, beautiful homes, mini mansions, with stores, Laundromats, with cleaners, with Chinese [cleaners]. We had drug stores. We had hotels. We had doctors over on Thirty-ninths Street [sic]. . . . We had the middle and upper class. It has gone from affluent to where it is today. And I would like to see it come back, that we can have some of the things we had. (Wilson, 1997, p. 3)

This conceptual analysis that emphasizes limited access to employment and increased neighborhood-level risk helps explain the complex interplay of neighborhood-level changes in murder rates, out-of-wedlock births, and unemployment. In contrast to the oft-quoted proverb "It takes a vil-lage to raise a child," the decline of these urban neighborhoods reflects the loss or destruction of "the village" and its social connections and supports.

Effects of employment challenges for urban community residents have been documented by the Gautreaux Project, a quasi-experimental study where fam-ilies moved to other residential areas in the city or to suburban areas follow-ing a federal court decision finding discriminatory practices in the Chicago Housing Authority. Adolescents within families who moved to the suburbs had higher rates of employment than peers who remained in the city (Kaufman & Rosenbaum, 1992; Popkin, Rosenbaum, & Meaden, 1993; Rosenbaum, Kulieke, & Rubinowitz, 1988; Rosenbaum & Popkin, 1991).

CHILD FUNCTIONING AND PARENTING WITHIN HIGH-RISK NEIGHBORHOODS

Parenting Strategies

Despite the challenges presented by high-risk neighborhoods, many parents are effective in using a "community bridging" parenting style. This style encompasses three types of strategies: youth monitoring, resource seeking, and in-home learning (Jarrett, 1999). Youth monitoring works to protect teens from neighborhood risks through the close parental supervision of the youth's whereabouts and the management of peer relationships. Monitoring may also involve chaperonage. When more extreme measures are deemed necessary to protect a child, the child may be removed from the neighborhood and sent to live with relatives. Resource-seeking strategies involve parents promoting their children's development by identifying and accessing available institutional supports both within and outside of their residential neighborhoods, sometimes through the utilization of extended kinship ties. In-home learning strategies involve the social reinforcement of desired behaviors and promotion of academic skills and competence. "Inner city neighborhoods with limited social, economic, and institutional resources demand that parents be 'super-parents' to ensure conventional development for their adolescents" (Jarrett, 1999, p. 49).

In contrast to Jarrett, Anderson (1994) suggests that the overwhelming negative influences and despair in many urban poor communities has "spawned an oppositional culture," a street culture that emphasizes respect and deference. Anderson describes this as a cultural adaptation to a lack of faith in the police and judicial system. Families who accept street culture may aggressively socialize and inconsistently discipline children; provide limited supervision; suffer from addiction or other types of maladaptive coping; value toughness and dominance; and utilize external objects to support their self-image and status in contrast to "decent" families who value hard work and self-reliance.

With respect to the effect of neighborhoods on early parenting, Crane (1991) found that levels of professional and managerial workers at the neighborhood level predicted adolescent childbearing and that these effects were stronger for Black adolescent females than for Whites.

NEIGHBORHOOD AND CHILD DEVELOPMENTAL OUTCOMES

Leventhal and Brooks-Gunn (2000) conducted an extensive literature review examining neighborhood effects on child development. Their analysis suggests that neighborhood may affect young children and adolescents across a range of developmental outcomes, but that these effects may vary by race. For example, there were fewer cognitive benefits (measured using I.Q. scores) for young African American children (aged 0–6) of having higher-income neighbors as compared with European American children (Brooks-Gunn, Duncan, Klebanov, & Sealand, 1993; Chase-Lansdale & Gordon, 1996; Chase-Lansdale, Gordon, Brooks-Gunn, & Klebanov, 1997; Duncan, Brooks-Gunn, & Klebanov, 1994). However, several academic performance indicators suggest that affluent neighbors and ethnically diverse neighborhoods benefit African American males (Duncan, 1994; Ensminger, Lamkin, & Jacobson, 1996; Halpern-Felsher et al., 1997). Affluent neighbors and ethnically diverse neighborhoods are correlated with higher academic achievement among African American males. In a related study, Plybon, Edwards, Butler, Belgrave, and Allison (2003) found that positive perceptions of neighborhood cohesion were related to school self-efficacy and self-reported grades among a sample of 84 urban African American adolescent females.

Residence in middle-income and ethnically diverse neighborhoods (as compared with low-income and more racially segregated communities) has been associated with lower rates of peer aggression and internalizing behavior problems for African American children (Chase-Lansdale et al., 1997). Within a community sample of 12- to 17-year-olds in Los Angeles, conduct disorders were highest among adolescents living in low-income, predominately African American neighborhoods, but oppositional defiant disorder was lowest in these same neighborhoods (Aneshensel & Sucoff, 1996).

According to Leventhal and Brooks-Gunn (2000), the benefit of high socioeconomic status neighborhoods may be more important for European American than for African American youth. Citing the work of Sampson, Morenoff and Earls (1999), Leventhal and Brook-Gunn (2000) attribute this "to the fact that African American children who reside in affluent neighborhoods are more likely to be living in closer geographic proximity to less affluent neighborhoods (i.e., larger environments that are more disadvantaged), in contrast to their European American peers, who, although residing in similarly affluent neighborhoods, are in closer geographic proximity to other affluent neighborhoods (i.e., larger environments that are more disadvantaged, p. 328).

Based on their review and analysis, Leventhal and Brooks-Gunn (2000) offer the following explanations for neighborhood effects:

1. Institutional resources: The availability, accessibility, affordability, and quality of learning, social, and recreational activities, child care, schools, medical facilities, and employment opportunities present in the community

2. Relationships: Parental characteristics (mental health, irritability, coping skills, efficacy, and physical health), support networks available to parents, parental behavior (responsivity/warmth, harshness/control, and supervision/monitoring), and the quality and structure of the home environment

3. Norms/collective efficacy: The extent to which community-level formal and informal institutions exist to supervise and monitor the behavior of residents, particularly youth's activities (deviant and antisocial peer-group behavior) and the presence of physical risk (violence and victimization and harmful substances) to residents, especially children and youth. (p. 322)

The effects of racial differences in the neighborhoods within which Black and White children grow up is that the influence of neighborhood characteristics, such as high SES may have less impact on the well-being of African American children than on that of European American children. (Leventhal & Brooks-Gunn, 2000, p. 328)

Methodological and Applied Perspectives on African American Communities and Neighborhoods

MEASURES OF NEIGHBORHOOD

When conducting research on neighborhood and community, researchers have several options. From an Africentric perspective, researchers can utilize the communalism scale developed by Boykin, Jagers, Ellison, and Albury (1997). This 31-item scale was developed using four samples of college students and assesses interdependence and individuals' sense of social obligation with items such as, "I believe that a person has to work cooperatively with family and friends." The measure has good reliability and validity. Another available measure includes collective efficacy and neighborhood cohesion used by Sampson and Earls in the PHDCN studies (Sampson et al., 1997). Neighborhood cohesion assesses the perceptions of community residents with respect to trust (e.g., "People around here are willing to help their neighbors"). Collective efficacy is an index of residents' sense of control and influence reflected in their ratings of items such as whether they would intervene if children were engaging in behavior such as showing disrespect to an adult. These measures are reliable. A scale is also available to assess an individual's sense of community index (Chavis, Hogge, McMillan, & Wandersman, 1986). This index is composed of three subscales that measure connection (8 items, e.g., "People on this block know each other"), support (4 items, e.g., "People on this block watch out for each other"), and belonging (4 items, e.g., "People on this block think of themselves as a community").

STUDYING NEIGHBORHOOD EFFECTS

Leventhal and Brooks-Gunn (2000) note that researchers use a variety of strategies to study neighborhood effects, including national databases, city and regional studies, neighborhood-level studies, and experimental designs. Units of analysis vary, and data are taken from the U.S. census, boundaries and administrative districts set by local governments, government administration (e.g., police, local housing), and participant ratings of their perceptions of neighborhood characteristics.

Windshield surveys are also used as objective assessments of neighborhoods. For example, the Neighborhood Assessment of Community Characteristics (Burton, Price-Spratlen, & Spencer, 1997; Spencer, Cole, Jones, & Swanson 1997; Spencer, McDermott, Burton, & Kochman, 1997) is a windshield survey of social (e.g., presence of children playing, visibility of police, gender and ages of community members) and physical characteristics (e.g., housing stock, playgrounds and parks, churches) of neighborhoods. The survey was developed by Margaret Spencer and subsequently adapted by Linda Burton and Kevin Allison. Different versions of the measure allow trained evaluators or trained community residents to drive or walk through discrete neighborhood sectors and rate them.

PRACTICAL IMPLICATIONS

The research on the effects of neighborhood has a wide range of intervention and policy implications. Powell (1999) argues that racism and federal housing and transportation policies have supported urban sprawl and subsidized white flight while simultaneously reducing investments in increasingly poor urban neighborhoods. Government and banking policies including *redlining* (i.e., refusing to lend in an area because of race) have persisted. Some believe redlining grew worse in the 1980s because the federal government decreased enforcement of fair-lending laws and the Fair Housing Act of 1968. Several factors continue to support the concentration of poverty in low-income neighborhoods within which African Americans are overrepresented. These include rising urban housing costs and displacement of lower-income residents by the gentrification of many urban neighborhoods, the development of new rings of poverty in many older suburban neighborhoods, and the lack of effective regional cooperation in most large metropolitan areas. Despite many of the problems of residential segregation of African Americans, many of their political gains have been based on the concentration of African Americans within specific voting districts. There are ongoing struggles to achieve and maintain voting districts that allow fair representation of African American communities.

A number of efforts to address community challenges take place within the policy arena. Strategies such as community empowerment and community organization can be used to build on community assets (e.g., Kretzmann & McKnight, 1993). Young-Laing's (2003) analysis of community development and organizing strategies provides a historical analysis of community building efforts within the Black community. She discusses the roles of the Universal Negro Improvement Association, the Southern Christian Leadership Conference, and the Black Panther Party in community change. In her analysis, Young-Laing points to three primary strategies currently used by African Americans to promote community change. These include political and social action (with the focus being on changing social policy through protest, political effort, and media); resource and capacity development (where individuals work to build local community resource access and capacity); and cultural empowerment (emphasizing cultural education, raising cultural consciousness, and using culture as a form of resistance). This work is consistent with the earlier Progressive Era strategies of figures such as Ida B. Wells-Barnett and Lugenia Burns Hope, who organized and provided services and resources to individuals and families within challenged African American communities during the late 1800s and early 1900s (O'Donnell, 1996). Recent neighborhood interventions, such as the Annie E. Casey Foundation's Plain Talk strategies (http://www .aecf.org/initiatives/plaintalk/index.htm), similarly work with community residents to provide door-to-door outreach, bringing resource information to their neighbors. The "Plain Talk" intervention has been used to address adolescent pregnancy. The program works to create a shared view of community prevention needs, increase community skills to communicate about and intervene regarding the specific prevention issue, and improve youth access to adult and other resources specific to the target behavior. Psychology has not been closely aligned with many of these grassroots and broader community development interventions. However, there are many opportunities to learn from and collaborate with community-level efforts of philanthropy, urban studies and planning, social work, and public health (Brookins, 1999).

Interventions have focused on work with individuals and groups at the community level to increase individual-level coping, reduce neighborhood risk, and increase community capacity. Several capacity-building efforts have begun to emphasize the role that the community plays in shaping its own destiny. For example, the Urban Institute's National Neighborhood Indicators Partnership involves several groups that work to "democratize data" (i.e., make data about the community easily accessible) so that communities can more effectively plan and advocate for the change they want in their communities. For example, groups can monitor where crimes occur and work with police to address their concerns, or they can examine the availability of public resources and advocate for new initiatives. These efforts provide hope that many neighborhoods can more effectively address the challenges that result in neighborhood-level risk.

Summary

African Americans live in multiple-layered communities that include being members of the group of Americans of African descent as well as being members of diverse sets of neighborhoods. Important sociopolitical factors, including structural racism, have historically shaped—and continue to shape—the places where African Americans live and the sets of social and infrastructural resources available in those communities. This has included the impact of the northern migration of Blacks during the late 1800s and early 1900s and the concentration of urban poverty linked to changes in job access, the impact of suburban development and job relocation, and housing and banking policies. Several theories help us to understand the role of community in the psychology of African Americans, including the important role of communalism from an Africentric perspective. The sense of connection among African Americans is theorized to be an important component of our cultural heritage, and initial research suggests that this communalism functions to protect individuals and communities. African American parents may develop specific strategies to support the adaptive development of their children when they grow up in challenged communities. Select educational achievement outcomes may be linked to neighborhood characteristics for African American males.

There are several ways of measuring community, including windshield surveys and the use of census data. Other disciplines have a lot to offer in support of our understanding of ways to build community. Efforts at "rebuilding the village" will require a long-term perspective and a shift from individual-level interventions that support African Americans in coping with challenges, to interventions that work to reduce the risk in these neighborhoods. Building on the assets and strengths of African American communities is crucial to the availability of resources within these communities.

The Xhosa proverb "I am because we are and we are because I am" underlines the importance of the sense of social connection, sense of belonging, and sense of self based on community. Whether in neighborhoods, in social or political groups, or from one's sense of self, the African American community is core. This sense is reflected in an excerpt from Martin Luther King Jr.'s "Letter From a Birmingham Jail": "We are caught in an inescapable network of mutuality, tied in a single garment of destiny. Whatever affects one directly, affects all indirectly" (King, 1963, p. 290).

Note

1. The Rust Belt refers to areas in the northeastern and midwestern sections of the United States that experienced declines in their industrial manufacturing during the 1970s.

Section III

Individual and Developmental Processes

Interpersonal and Close Relationships 6

One finger cannot lift up a thing.

—African proverb

Washington Post, March 29, 2004

To Have and to Uphold Black Marriages

Courtland Milloy

The second annual Black Marriage Day on Saturday included workshops and the renewal of wedding vows in about 70 cities throughout the United States.

One elementary school class in Atlantic City marked the occasion by staging a wedding, according to Nisa Muhammad, president of the Wedding Bliss Foundation and founder of Black Marriage Day. "The teacher had asked her students to raise their hands if they'd ever been to a wedding," Muhammad told me. "No one raised their hand. Then she asked if they knew anybody who was married. And they all said no." So while the students took on such roles as bride, groom, bridesmaids and best men, the teacher became the preacher and explained how being married requires a moral center made up of trust, commitment and fidelity—"that's what separates husbands and wives from playas and girlfriends, she said. "We have not shared with this generation what it takes to have a healthy marriage," Muhammad said. "It takes an understanding of the sweetness of surrender and the joy in giving up the 'I' for the 'we'."

At the Everlasting Life Complex in Largo, dozens of singles and couples showed up for workshops that had such titles as "Breathing New Life Into Your Relationship" and "Finding Your Soul Mate." The bottom line: Appreciate your mate for the flawed human being that you both are, not as a consumer product to be discarded at the first signs of imperfection; learn to forgive and how to seek forgiveness.

To help promote Black Marriage Day activities, Muhammad teamed with Diann Dawson, director of the African American healthy marriage initiative at the U.S. Department of Health and Human Services. The initiative is part of a plan by the Bush administration to spend $1.5 billion to promote "healthy marriages." According to the 2000 Census and 2003 National Center for Health Statistics: African Americans still have the lowest marriage rates and the highest divorce rates of any group in the United States; the highest rate of households headed by single mothers; and the highest rate of births to unmarried mothers, who constitute the majority of childbearing black women. "What we have now is an opportunity to find out what makes marriage so problematic for us," Dawson said. "Why is this phenomenon occurring, whether the black woman is educated or not?" More education and training are necessary to teach the importance of marriage, and also—in the absence of role models—how to build foundations for healthy ones.

Introduction, Definitions, and Historical Perspectives

The news story highlights the eroding institution of marriage among African Americans. The workshops discussed in the article address ways to reverse this trend. We discuss several factors that account for marriage among African Americans in this chapter. These factors are influenced by historical events (e.g., enslavement) as well as by contemporary factors (e.g., higher rates of incarceration of African American men). Marriage and other close relationships are the focus of this chapter.

All humans have a need to belong, to affiliate, and to be in relationships with others. Friendships and meaningful relationships with others are essential (Berscheid, 1985). We form relationships to have fun, to share intimacies, and to get our goals met. In this chapter, we examine interpersonal and close relationships from the perspective of African Americans.

We begin this chapter with an overview of the nature of relationships and follow it with a discussion of relationships among Africans. We discuss close relationships, including family relationships, friendships, and romantic relationships including marriage. We comment on factors that affect mate selection among African Americans. We then discuss interpersonal attraction and review influences on our choice of friends and partners. Along with proximity and similarity, physical attraction is a factor in our relationship choices. We discuss beauty, skin color, and other physical attributes as they relate to African Americans. Interracial relationships, including friendships and intimate relationships (e.g., dating and marriage), and also gay and lesbian relationships are discussed next. Methodological issues are identified, and a summary is are provided.

THE NATURE OF RELATIONSHIPS

A relationship is a "particular type of connection existing between people related to or having dealings with each other" (*American Heritage*

Dictionary, 2004). Relationships exist for varying reasons and operate in many ways. Relationships are voluntary and involuntary. Relationships with one's family are involuntary. A relationship with a romantic partner is voluntary. Some relationships are oriented toward getting one's needs and goals met. Other relationships exist because they are fulfilling for partners involved. Still other relationships exist because one person feels responsible for the other, as in a parent-child relationship. One useful distinction in understanding relationships is the distinction between communal and exchange relationships (see discussion of this topic following the section "Equitable Relationships").

Equitable Relationships

One norm-governing relationship is equity (Deutsch, 1985). In general, people want their relationships to be equitable. This means that we want out of a relationship as much as we put into it. An assumption of equity theory is that people want to maximize their outcomes in a relationship. When people perceive that a relationship is inequitable, they feel distressed. The greater the inequity there is, the greater the distress we feel. We feel distress even if on the receiving end of the relationship. In other words, we want to get out of a relationship as much as we put in, but we don't want the benefits from a relationship to greatly exceed our inputs. When people are in an inequitable relationship, they will try to restore equity, or they will leave the relationship. However, all relationships do not operate based on equity theory. Some research suggests that relationships among people of African descent are not based on equity. Exchange and communal relationships help to explain these relationships.

Exchange and Communal Relationships

In both exchange and communal relationships there are exchanges, but the rules that govern them differ (Clark & Mills, 1979). In exchange relationships people give benefits with the expectation that they will soon receive comparable benefits. This is akin to what we think of as an equitable relationship. Communal relationships are those in which the person feels responsible for the well-being of the other person. Communal relationships usually occur between family members, friends, and romantic partners. Exchange relationships may be between employees and employers, coworkers, neighbors, and, in some cases, friends.

In communal relationships, the person benefits the partner without an expectation of benefits in return. People are more attentive to the needs of a partner in a communal than in an exchange relationship. People in communal relationships prefer to talk about emotional and intimate topics, such as likes and dislikes. People in an exchange relationship prefer to talk about nonemotional topics, such as an activity or a hobby. Because of values that are oriented toward relationships, many people of African descent have communal relationships.

RELATIONSHIPS AMONG AFRICANS

As discussed in Chapter 2, a core value among people of African descent is interpersonal relationships. Other terms used to describe this value include *communalism, relationship orientation, collective orientation,* and *relational.* This relationship orientation includes sensitivity to the emotional state of others and an orientation that considers others in one's thoughts and activities (see Chapter 2). Relationships are less hierarchical and are based on genuine concern for others' needs.

On the topic of African core values, the scholar Gyekye (1996) writes,

> The communal structure of African society has created a sense of community that characterizes social relationships among individual members of the African society. Communal values consider the importance of the community and include mutual aid, caring for others, interdependence, solidarity, reciprocal obligation, and social harmony. Interpersonal relations are what makes up a community. (p. 35)

A community is a group of persons tied together by interpersonal relationships, which are not necessarily biological; these people share common values, interests, and goals. Community exists for the benefit of the individual member. The communalistic orientation is also seen among contemporary African Americans. The extended family is one such example of communalistic relationships. Another example is involvement with and practices of the church and other places of worship.

Close Relationships

Close relationships, also referred to as intimate relationships, have three features: (a) emotional attachment; (b) need fulfillment; and (c) interdependence (Brehm, 1992). Emotional attachment is affection and positive feelings toward another person. Need fulfillment means that physical and psychological needs of people in the relationship are met. Interdependence means that there is mutual influence and involvement of persons in each other's activities and lives. Close relationships involve family members, close friends, and romantic partners. These will be discussed, first generally, and then more specifically with regard to African Americans.

FAMILIAL RELATIONSHIPS

Family relationships are the first relationship a child encounters. Family relationships affect our conceptualization of who we are and who we desire to be. The first type of relationship that an infant acquires with his or her primary care provider is attachment.

Attachment

Attachment is the infant's positive response to the caregiver. The infant feels better when the caregiver is close and seeks out the caregiver when frightened (Bowlby, 1982). Early interactions between the primary caregiver (usually the mother) and the infant may result in different types of attachment styles. Attachment style is a temperamental orientation that comes from an infant's emotional response to early interactions with the primary care provider. Three attachment styles have been described as secure, avoidant, and ambivalent. Within Western culture, it is believed that sensitive, responsible parenting during the child's first year leads to a secure attachment style. A secure attachment style is characterized by the infant's ability to love and to trust others. Avoidant attachment occurs when the primary care provider is unresponsive to the needs of the infant. This results in the infant's detachment from the primary care provider. An ambivalent attachment style occurs when the primary care provider does not respond consistently to the infant's needs and/or if the primary care provider is anxious.

Attachment styles developed during infancy contribute to the type of interpersonal relationships that an adult has within and outside the family (Morgan & Shaver, 1999). The attachment style affects one's relationships with family members, friends, coworkers, and romantic partners. Secure individuals seek closeness, are comfortable in having to depend on their partner, and do not worry about losing the partner. Avoidant individuals are not comfortable with intimacy and do not trust other people. The ambivalent person both wants and fears a relationship. This individual may perceive the partner as unloving and may fear that the partner will break off the relationship. Attachment theory has been widely accepted in Western culture. However, as will be discussed next, the applicability of attachment theory for African Americans may vary.

Cultural Differences in Attachment Style. The universality of attachment styles has been questioned, as has the way of assessing attachment style among different cultural groups. Attachment theory was developed to describe the relationship that formed between infant and mother to protect the infant from environmental dangers. It is assumed that attachment is adaptive for both infant and mother in that it functions to promote the infant's survival (Lamb et al., 1985).

The Strange Situation Test was designed by Ainsworth (1979) to measure attachment style. In this test, one observes the reaction of the mother and the infant at varying stages of being together (i.e., first infant left alone and then infant left alone with a stranger). The reactions of the infant to the reunion with the mother after being left alone are used to define the child's attachment style. The Strange Situation Test was developed for and seems to work well with middle-class White Americans.

However, the applicability of this test may be questionable for some people of African descent. For example, within African and some African American households there may be more than one primary care provider. Two or even three generations of mothers and other family members may live together and assume joint care of the child. The concept of the extended family is discussed in Chapter 3. Grandparents, aunts, uncles, other relatives, and unrelated people may be included in the extended family (Wilson et al., 1995). Because some African American infants are used to being cared for by others and to being in different environments, the Strange Situation Test may not be novel to them. Therefore, the reactions and the resulting attachment style of African Americans may not be completely described by reactions to this test. Clearly the culture and context that African American infants/children live in must be considered when generalizing about their attachment styles.

Close Friendships

Close friendships can be very rewarding. Friends provide support, intimacy, a confidant, and an activity partner. Some differences in male and female friendships will be discussed next. This will be followed by a discussion of African American adolescent, female, and male friendships.

GENDER DIFFERENCES IN FRIENDSHIPS

Close friendships can occur with opposite sex members, but generally, close friends are of the same gender. The nature of close friendships differs for men and women (Floyd, 1995). Women rate their friendships more positively than men do, and these friendships are more intimate. Male friends bond by participating in common activities whereas female friends bond by sharing feelings and emotions. Both men and women are more likely to self-disclose to women friends. And men are more likely to name their wives as friends than vice versa. Women's relationships are more spontaneous and personal than men's. Differences between African American male and female friendships are similar to those of other ethnic groups. Some exceptions will be discussed.

AFRICAN AMERICAN ADOLESCENT FRIENDSHIPS

Friendships are important for adolescents, and there are several benefits of friendships, including psychological and social well-being (Way, 1996). The nature and quality of friendship vary based on cultural and social context. In a study that compared three ethnic groups, Mexican Americans, African Americans, and European Americans, African American males were more likely than males from the other two ethnic groups to reveal their personal thoughts and feelings to their male friends (Jones, Costin, & Ricard, 1994). Dolcini and colleagues (2004) examined the content and quality of adolescent friendships in an urban African American neighborhood. The study looked at cliques. Cliques were defined as small, close-knit groups ranging in size from 3 to 10 and composed of peers who are similar with respect to age, gender, and race. The researchers conducted interviews with 113 friends whose ages ranged from 13 to 21. The study found that half of the respondents were in cliques, and about one fifth were in dyads only; the others were not linked with friends. The average clique consisted of four youth of the same gender and ethnicity. The friendships were relatively long-term with a mean friendship length of over 5 years. The trust levels of the friendships were high, and friends provided each other with instrumental support (e.g., lending money). Levels of emotional support and intimacy were not as high as instrumental support. This study shows that friendships serve essential functions for African American adolescents.

AFRICAN AMERICAN ADOLESCENT MALE FRIENDSHIPS

Peer friendships are likely to affect how one presents him- or herself to others. In a study of peer friendships among African American adolescent males, Cunningham and Meunier (2004) looked at how relationships with peers influence the bravado attitudes that are sometimes seen among African American youth, especially those from high-risk neighborhoods. Bravado is a hypermasculine or macho identity that individuals who live in high-risk environments develop as a reactive style (Cunningham & Meunier, 2004). Peer relationships and bravado were examined in a sample of 356 adolescent African American boys in an urban southeastern U.S. city. The authors found that poor attitudes toward and relationships with peers, including alienation from peers, discomfort speaking to peers, and the experience of neighborhood gang or turf problems were related to bravado attitudes. It appears that bravado attitudes may in part be related to the lack of positive peer experiences among African American adolescent males. The authors recommend that helping males to develop positive peer relationships should be the focus of prevention and intervention programs.

AFRICAN AMERICAN ADOLESCENT FEMALE RELATIONSHIPS

The authors of this book and colleagues have implemented several programs that focus on strengthening relationships among African American adolescent females (Belgrave, 2002; Belgrave et al., 2004). In these programs, we have emphasized the importance of peer relationships. We assume that positive peer relationships are important for self-worth and success across many life domains for girls. Relationships are central to females and to people of African descent, so positive and fulfilling relationships are expected to be critical to the African American female's identity and self-worth.

Our programs involve creating an environment whereby positive sister relationships can be facilitated among these girls. This program is described in a curriculum called *Sisters of Nia*. This curriculum identifies several strategies to facilitate positive relationships. The first two sessions of the curriculum are devoted to the development of positive relationships among girls and with the female facilitators; activities are structured so that girls engage in activities to increase bonding and cohesion. Girls meet in small groups to problem solve and to develop life skills. The groups are structured so that achievement and rewards are interdependent. That is, the success of the group is dependent on the cooperative work of all members. Girls are discouraged from talking negatively about others girl, and they are rewarded for being kind and considerate to each other. Evaluations of this program show that girls improve in several ways. Girls who participated in the Sisters of Nia program had higher feelings of self-worth and ethnic identity after participation. After participation, they were also less likely to engage in relational aggression (i.e., being mean, gossiping, and excluding other girls).

AFRICAN AMERICAN ADULT FEMALE FRIENDSHIPS

There is relatively little research on African American female friendships in spite of everyday exposure to these relationships via the media. The book and movie *Waiting to Exhale*, by Terry McMillan, tell the story of the bond between African American women who provide support for each other through financial, family, male, and other challenges. Other more recent television programs, such as "Girlfriends," focus on the supportive relationships young Black women have with each other.

The importance and benefits of female friendships are also addressed by bell hooks. Her book *Sisters of the Yam* provides strategies for affirmation of self through Black women nurturing each other. The word *yam* symbolizes life-sustaining Black kin and community. Sisters of the Yam is the name of a women's support group to which hooks belongs. There is an increase in sister circles, that is, groups of African American women who regularly get together for friendship and support. These groups engage in book clubs, church and spiritual activities, or just friendly get-togethers. Whatever the situation, strong female friendships are being created. In fact, these relationships have led Hallmark to create a new line of greeting cards under the Mahogany brand called "Sister to Sister" (see http://pressroom .hallmark.com/mahogany_sister_to_sister.html). These cards are designed for African American female friends.

AFRICAN AMERICAN ADULT MALE FRIENDSHIPS

The literature on African American male relationships is also limited. Like the friendships of White men, African American male friendships tend to be centered on activities and specific tasks. However, there are some differences. One interesting study examined friendships among lower- and working-class and middle-class Black men (Franklin, 1992). Franklin interviewed 30 African American men in these three socioeconomic classes. He observed that friendships were different for working- and lower-class and middle-class Black men.

Friendships among working- and lower-class Black men may serve as a buffer against what they perceive to be a hostile environment. Their relationships promote a brotherhood consciousness that is seen in their gestures and conversations. Salient within these friendships is their shared experience of oppression and victimization in American society. This is seen, for example, in the greeting and response "yo, bro" "hey, home." These greetings convey the message, "I share your experience and know what you are going through. However, in spite of the struggle, I am proud to be a Black man." Franklin sees these communications not as mere greetings but as political statements that show togetherness and survival.

The men Franklin interviewed reported that when they talk to their friends, their friends know what they are saying without them having to say it. This is not the case when conversing with White men and bourgie (high-class) Black men. Conversations held with Black men on street corners, in barbershops, and in other gathering places reveal that these men's friendships are warmer and more intimate than the relationships of upwardly mobile Black men.

However, the relationships among poor and working-class Black men are not without problems. Expectations from same-sex friendships are high and include loyalty, altruism, and closeness. Given these high expectations, it is not uncommon to see unexpected violence when one of the friends perceives a violation of these expectations. Notably, some of the Black-on-Black male crime within poor and working-class communities may be due to violations of friendship expectations. When a Black male feels that his friend is disloyal, lying, cheating, or untrustworthy, the high friendship expectations may lead to violence. In fact, the males Franklin interviewed told him that they would be enraged if their friends violated their friendship, and that this would call for some type of retaliation.

Franklin describes the friendships of Black men of higher socio-economic status as being different, but in some ways similar, to those of lower- and working-class Black men. Both groups receive messages that emphasize the need for trust, empathy, warmth, and altruism, along with messages of threats to Black men from the larger society. Both also receive messages that the larger society will block their efforts to succeed. However, upwardly mobile Black men do not see discrimination as an impediment to their own successes to the extent that lower- and working-class Black men do. These men talk about the need to be the best in spite of prejudice, the need to be competent, and the need to "play the game" well. These men are more likely to feel that they have to maintain a certain distance from others in order to be successful.

For middle-class and upwardly mobile Black men, the quantity and quality of same-sex relationships are lowered. Many indicated that they really did not have time to cultivate deeper relationships, because they spent most of their time trying to get ahead. Males moving up the social ladder in the United States are expected to portray a masculine style of competitiveness, aggressiveness, coolness, and rationality. In fact, if a man does not have these traits, it may be hard for him to move up the ladder. One man Franklin interviewed indicated that upwardly mobile Black men form relationships with others on the basis of the financial profitability of those relationships.

However, a few of the middle-class Black men indicated that they did feel friendship and connection to all Black men. Nonverbal cues such as simple glances, brief acknowledgments, and the like give them a feeling of unity when they are around other Black men.

Romantic Relationships

A romantic partner is that one person in the world to whom you feel clos-est (Berscheid, Snyder, & Omoto, 1989). An intense close relationship may be described as love. There are different types of love, and there are cultural differences in how love is conceptualized.

WHAT IS LOVE?

Love is difficult to define, as it is a subjective experience. It differs from liking and is not limited to intimate relationships. Most scholars agree that there are two types of love, companionate love and passionate love. Companionate love is the feeling of intimacy and affection that does not include physiological arousal, passion, and desire (Hatfield & Walster, 1978). Passionate love involves intense feelings and physiological arousal for another. Companionate love is seen in close friendships. Companionate love may also be present in passionate love relationships. A relationship in Western culture typically starts with passionate love and then is replaced with companionate love. Passionate love develops quickly, whereas companionate love develops gradually. Passionate love is more intense and includes both positive and negative emotions.

Love in Individualistic and Collective Cultures

Research on passionate and companionate love, specifically among African Americans, is scarce. However, cross-cultural research has looked at love among those in individualistic cultures (like the United States) and collective cultures (like Africa).

When the United States and a collective culture, such as China, are compared, the findings show that Americans value passionate love more than Chinese people do, and Chinese people value companionate love more than Americans do. Africans are likely to endorse the concept of both companionate and passionate love. For example, the Tiaya African people consider the best love to be a combination of passionate and companionate love (Bell, 1995).

MATE AVAILABILITY, FEASIBILITY, AND DESIRABILITY

Finding a desirable dating partner and mate depends on many factors. Males and females with similar lifestyles and characteristics are not distributed proportionally. We next discuss mate availability, feasibility, and desirability generally and then specifically for African Americans.

Mate Availability

Mate availability is dependent on two concepts, marriage squeeze and sex-ratio imbalance (Tucker & Mitchell-Kernan, 1999). Marriage squeeze is the decrease in the availability of marriage partners among female baby boomers. This shortage of partners is because of an increase in the number of women born relative to men.

Sex-ratio imbalance is defined as the imbalance of the ratio of men to women. Sex ratio is expressed as the number of males to females. This ratio varies by geographic region, urbanicity, socioeconomic level, and age. The sex ratio for both African Americans and Whites has been less than

1.00 since 1950. In 1990, the sex ratio was 89.6% for African Americans and 95.4% for Whites. This means that there were 89.6 African American males for every 100 African American females. If one considers other mate selection factors (to be discussed), this ratio is even lower among African Americans.

Economic Feasibility

The relationship between economic stability and marriage has been examined for African Americans. There is a decline in marriage among African Americans, and compared with Whites, more African Americans end up not married. One perspective on the decline in African American marriage is that it is due to the decline in economic viability (low employment and unemployment) among African American men (Tucker & Mitchell-Kernan, 1999). Over the past several decades, the increasing economic marginality of African American males has made them less desirable as potential husbands. Also, African American males may not be as interested in becoming husbands because they are constrained in their ability to perform the provider role in marriage.

Marriage Desirability and Cohabitation

African Americans still view marriage as highly desirable and do not differ from other ethnic groups regarding whether or not it is desirable to marry (Tucker & Mitchell-Kernan, 1999). Given the decline in marriages among African Americans, one question is whether cohabitation is a factor in that decline.

Cohabitation may be an alternative to marriage. Cohabitation can be considered advanced courtship or a stage between dating and marriage. Sexual freedom, effective contraception, increased financial independence among women, and changes in gender roles have led to more cohabitation (Tucker & Mitchell-Kernan, 1999). Tanfer (1987) conducted a study using a national sample of 20- to 29-year-old women and found that African American women were less likely than White women to cohabit. White women were one and one half times more likely than African American women to cohabit. Therefore, cohabitation is probably not the reason for the decline in marriage among African Americans.

MATE SELECTION

Socialization and cultural influences affect the process of mate selection. In the United States, we tend to marry someone who is similar in age, race, education, religion, and other demographic characteristics. This norm is known as homogamy (Kalmijn, 1991). Another norm is known as the marriage gradient. This is the tendency of men to marry women who are slightly younger, smaller, and lower in status, and of women to marry men who are slightly older, larger, and higher in status. This norm affects partner choice by limiting the number of potential mates for women, especially as women get older. On the other hand, this norm provides more options to men. However, it also affects men if they cannot find women of lower status or women of the same or higher status who would want to marry them. As will be discussed, these norms may not be as applicable to African Americans.

Another norm in the United States is that men are more likely to prefer and marry mates who are more physically attractive, whereas women are more likely to prefer and marry men with higher levels of education and income potential. This norm is grounded in social exchange theory. According to social exchange theory, a relationship will exist if it benefits both partners. One attribute is exchanged for another. In this case, social status from the male partner is exchanged for physical attractiveness from the female partner.

Homogamy and social exchange norms may not operate in the same way for African Americans as for other ethnic groups. Africentric beliefs among some African Americans may emphasize relationships and character over attributes such as material wealth and education. Hence, social exchange norms may not operate in the same way in relationships among African Americans.

There are other reasons why African Americans may not subscribe to social exchange norms. Partner choice is more limited for African American women. African American females tend to be better educated and more upwardly mobile than African American males. More African American women than men attend college. Also, a substantial percentage of African American males in the marriageable age category (20s to 30s) are involved in some way in the criminal justice system. Finally, African American women have a longer life expectancy than Black men. Therefore, many African American females will either have to marry down, postpone marriage, marry someone from another race, or marry someone who is much older or younger.

Mate Selection Among African Americans

What are some of the characteristics affecting mate selection for African Americans? One study addressed this question. Parmer (1998) examined factors most important in mate selection for African American male and female college students attending a historically Black college in the southeastern United States. The author was interested in how gender and year in college interacted with other variables to influence mate selection. The other variables were (a) social stratification variables (i.e., good financial prospects, similar religious and educational backgrounds, similar political background; (b) personality variables (i.e., dependable character, mutual attraction, refinement/neatness, emotional stability, desire for home and children); and (c) physical characteristics (i.e., good health, good sex, good looks, same race, athletic). The effect of gender and year in college along with social stratification, personality, and physical characteristics on the ratings of mate selection were examined.

The findings differed from what has been seen in the general literature regarding the importance of social stratification variables for men and women. Although the literature has shown that social stratification variables are more important for women than for men, such was not the case in this study. Among women, social stratification variables were only important for freshmen and sophomores, not for juniors and seniors. Among men, social stratification variables were important for juniors, seniors, and graduate students. One possible explanation for the decreasing importance of social stratification variables for women is that as the female students approach finishing their degree, the importance of social stratification changes. This change is in a direction opposite that of White society. The author speculates that perhaps African American women go to college with the traditional expectation of finding a mate but find out that the pool of eligible mates has either shrunk or never existed. Also, African American women are socialized to be independent and to believe that they are capable of taking care of themselves, so perhaps the social stratification factors of income and education are less important to them. Upper-level college women may be willing to compromise with regard to their expectations, perhaps settling for more primary needs, such as love and marriage, over social status.

Among African American men, the findings were that social stratification variables are important. This may suggest some degree of economic insecurity among African American men. Given the higher level of economic instability for African American men (compared with women), perhaps they want a mate who will carry her own financial weight.

Personality variables such as sense of mutual attraction and good character were important to both men and women. There were no differences between men and women in their rating of personality variables. This finding differs from that of studies done with White samples. Studies with White samples have shown that personality variables such as industriousness and dependability were more important as mate selection characteristics for women than for men.

Regarding physical characteristics, the findings were consistent with studies of gender differences in attractiveness in other ethnic groups. African American men favored physical characteristics more than African American women did.

Physical Appearance and Mate Selection

One of the physical characteristics that affect mate selection is skin color. Historically, being light skinned has been a favored status. Studies conducted during the 1940s through the 1960s indicated that skin tone was a predictor of socioeconomic status, employment, and mate selection among Blacks. Lighter-complexioned persons had better employment opportunities, higher income, and higher occupational status. Light-skinned Blacks were favored more than dark-complexioned Blacks by Whites, because they were closer in appearance to Whites. Skin color was a source of status among African Americans and became a factor in mate selection (Goode, 1982). A premium was placed on light-skinned African American women, and skin color was considered an asset for marriage (Zack, 1995).

Today, there is less but still some discrimination among African Americans based on skin color (Bond & Cash, 1992). Ross (1997) looked at how gender and socioeconomic status affected the preference to date and marry light-skinned African Americans. The author also examined how gender and socioeconomic status affected willingness to date and marry down and preference to date and marry someone who is upwardly mobile. Participants were college students attending two historically Black universities located in the southeastern United States. Ross found that 16.4% of the women and 38.3% of the men preferred to marry a person with light skin.

Males were more likely than females to prefer dating light-skinned persons and marrying a person with light skin, and they were also more willing to marry a person from a lower social class than their own. Females were more likely than males to prefer to marry someone with more material wealth than themselves and to agree that having a good time and getting along with their mates was more important than being attractive. Note the findings from this study differ from the finding reported by Parmer (1998), who found that African American male college students rated social status as more desirable than did African American females. Another finding was that the higher the minority percentage in the neighborhood that the participants came from, the less the preference for lighter skin. Also, the higher the minority percentage in the neighborhood students came from, the more willing they were to date persons with lower levels of education. The findings suggest that exposure to diversity decreases preference for light skin color and increases willingness to marry someone of a lower socioeconomic status.

MARRIAGE

African Americans are less likely to be married than Whites and other ethnic groups (U.S. Census Bureau, 2000; also see Chapter 3). When the 2000 census was taken, 42% of African American males were married, and 31% of African American women were married. This is the lowest proportion of women married in any racial or ethnic group. Also, the 11% difference in the percentage of African American men and women who were married was the largest difference between men and women in any ethnic group.

Factors that contribute to the difference in marriage rates for African American men and women include higher mortality and incarceration among males. Also, African American men tend to marry non-African American women more often than African American women marry non-African American males. All of these factors result in a larger population of potential spouses for African American men.

Both male and female African Americans are more likely than other ethnic groups to have never married; 41.6% of African American men (aged 15 and over) have never married compared with 27.3% for White men. There are similar differences for women; 39.7% of African American women have never married compared with 20.8% of White women. All in all, the statistics suggest that both African American men and women are less likely than members of other ethnic groups to be married or to have ever been married.

ENDING INTIMATE RELATIONSHIPS

Marital Satisfaction and Dissatisfaction

Psychological factors play a role in marital satisfaction. People who know how to express their emotions report being happier in marriages than those who are not able to express emotions. Women who have more feminine gender role beliefs and who are more expressive and nurturing report higher levels of marriage satisfaction than those with less feminine role beliefs (Langis, Sabourin, Lussier, & Mathieu, 1994). There has been limited research on marriage satisfaction among African Americans, so these findings may not apply.

Problems arise in a marriage when partners begin to discover that they are dissimilar. The dissimilarity is not a problem during dating but may become a conflict later on. This may be why those of dissimilar ethnic groups and religious beliefs have higher divorce rates. Disagreements and conflicts lead to negative emotions that erode marital satisfaction. Finally, sex is associated with marital well-being or discord (Henderson-King & Veroff, 1994). In spite of the high rate of divorce, many marriages do succeed. Ingredients for successful marriages seem to be friendship, similarity, commitment, and positive emotions.

DIVORCE

Each year, many marriages end in divorce. Divorce is the end stage of a large number of complex factors that contribute to the breakup of a marriage. Some demographic factors are related to whether a couple will divorce. Marriages are more likely to end in divorce when the partners are younger; when they have a child prior to marrying; when they have had previous marriages; and when they have stepchildren. Money and economic problems are often major factors in divorce. People of different ethnic and religious backgrounds have a higher probability of divorce than those of the same religious and ethnic background (Bird & Melville, 1994; Bumpass, Martin, & Sweet, 1991).

Social and psychological variables also predict who will divorce and who will remain married. Partners who are similar in how they cope with stress are more satisfied with their relationship and less likely to divorce than those whose coping strategies differ (Ptacek & Dodge, 1995).

African Americans and Whites divorce at similar rates (U.S. Census Bureau, 2000). About 9% of White males are divorced compared with 9.5% of African American males, and 10.9% of White females are divorced compared with 12.8% of African American females. However, African Americans are more likely than Whites to be separated: 1.4% of White males are separated compared with 4.4% of African American males; 1.8% of White females are separated compared with 5.9% of African American females. Because African Americans are less likely to remarry, they may be separated longer without divorcing.

Interpersonal Attraction and Relationships

In this section we discuss interpersonal attraction, including some of the factors that affect whether we are attracted to others. We discuss physical features, including skin color and body weight, and how these affect self- and other-perception of attractiveness among African Americans.

ANTECEDENTS TO INTERPERSONAL ATTRACTION

One of the most influential determinants of whether we are attracted to others is proximity. The people we are most attracted to tend to be people that we live close to. In a study conducted in 1950, Festinger, Schachter, and Back (1950) investigated friendship formation among couples who lived in different apartment buildings. Residents were assigned to apartments at random as vacancies occurred. However, when they were asked to name their three closest friends in the entire housing project, 65% of the friends they named lived in the same building, although the other buildings were close by.

Patterns of friendships within a building also demonstrated the influence of proximity. Residents tended to like those who lived closest to them within the building. Forty-one percent of next-door neighbors said they were close friends, 22% of those who lived two doors apart said they were close friends, and 10% of those who lived on opposite ends of the hall said they were close friends. Proximity increases attraction because of familiarity and exposure. The more exposed we are to something, the more we come to like it (Aronson, Wilson, & Akert, 2002).

Another antecedent of interpersonal attraction is similarity. We tend to like and to be attracted to people who are demographically similar to us in terms of socioeconomic status, education, and religion. We also are attracted to those who have values and opinions that are similar to ours (Berscheid, 1985).

Similarity increases interpersonal attraction in three ways. First, we think that people who are similar to us will also like us. Second, people who are similar to us provide us with some validation of our beliefs and values. Third, we tend to be more negative toward people who are not similar to us in values and beliefs and ascribe more negative values to these people.

We also like those who like us. When a person communicates either verbal or nonverbal liking for us, we are more likely to return the affection than when they do not communicate liking for us. This is in part because of the self-fulfilling prophecy. When we think another person likes us, our behavior will be consistent with the expectation we feel the person has of us.

Finally, we tend to like more physically attractive persons. Physical attraction is especially a factor in initial attraction. This is true for both men and women. However, men tend to value physical attractiveness more than women do (Feingold, 1990). The importance of physical attractiveness is not limited to heterosexual relationships; it is also seen in homosexual relationships.

WHAT IS ATTRACTIVE?

There are some universal opinions of what is beautiful. A meta-analysis (a comparison of many studies) found agreement across many cultures as to what constitutes an attractive face (Cunningham, Barbee, & Pike, 1990). Students from different ethnic groups, including Asian, Latino, Black, and White, rated the appearance of women from all of these ethnic groups. Overall, the ratings were consistent in that they all shared agreement as to what was attractive.

College students rated the pictures of individuals from class yearbooks for attractiveness and found that high attractiveness ratings were associated with faces with large eyes, a small nose, a small chin, prominent cheekbones and narrow cheeks, high eyebrows, large pupils, and a big smile (Cunningham, 1986). In another study, women rated men and found that large eyes, prominent cheekbones, a large chin, and a big smile were considered attractive.

Other dimensions used in the evaluation of physical attractiveness are body type, hair, and skin color. There are racial differences in how physical characteristics are valued. The attractiveness rating of individuals with variations of these features is discussed next.

SKIN COLOR, HAIR TEXTURE, AND BODY WEIGHT

Skin color, hair texture, and body weight are attributes in which African Americans physically differ from other ethnic groups. There is also a great deal of variability among African Americans in these physical characteristics.

Skin Color

As discussed previously, historically, African Americans with fair skin have been considered more attractive than those who are darker skinned. Fair-skinned African Americans were the offspring of slave masters and enslaved women and were treated better than those who were dark skinned. They were given more household duties as opposed to field duties and had better living conditions. Free blacks were more likely to be fair than dark (Wade, 1996). Skin color became a criterion for success and prestige in the African American community. African Americans along with Whites considered fair skin, White facial features, and straight hair to be more attractive than dark skin, Black features, and curly hair. This bias for white features is less prevalent today than in the past, but it still exists to some degree.

As recently as 1990, a report on the advantages of skin color showed that fair-skinned African Americans do better than dark-skinned African Americans economically, vocationally, and educationally (Hughes & Hertel, 1990). Family income of fair-skinned African Americans was 50% greater than that of dark-skinned African Americans, and their personal income was 65% greater than that of dark-skinned African Americans (Keith & Herring, 1991). Fair-skinned African Americans were more likely to be employed in professional and technical positions and to have more education.

There are gender differences in skin-color bias. Compared with Black males, Black females have been affected more by their skin color, hair texture, and facial features. Fair-skinned females are considered more attractive and are preferred by dark-skinned males, and fair-skinned males are preferred by dark-skinned females. Bond and Cash (1992) examined how skin color was related to body image among African American college women. College women were classified into three skin color categories: light, medium, and dark. They were then asked questions about satisfaction with skin color and the ideal skin tone for Black women. Eighty-nine percent of the women reported moderate to high levels of satisfaction with their skin color. But when asked if they would change their skin color if they could, only 47% said they would remain their own skin color. Thirty-six percent said they wanted to be lighter and 17% said they wanted to be darker in skin tone. Seventy percent believed that Black men found light-skinned Black women more attractive than dark-skinned women (Bond & Cash, 1992).

Skin Color and the Media

Preference for light-skinned females is evident when we see that successful Black males often marry women lighter skinned than themselves. Movies and television often cast light-skinned women in the leading love role, whereas dark-skinned women play the mammy or the comedian. A disproportionate number of television programs and advertisements and popular music (particularly rap) videos feature light-skinned and light-eyed women (Perkins, 1996). These women are presented as desirable and beautiful. In contrast, when darker skinned women with more African features are presented, they are portrayed as maternal, belligerent, and lacking sensuality. These media images may have an adverse impact on Black females' self-perception.

Hair Texture

Historically, curly and nappy hair has been considered "bad" hair, and long, straight hair has been considered "good" hair. However, this trend is changing somewhat as reflected in the title of a popular children's book, *Happy to Be Nappy* (hooks, 1999). Today, there is more acceptance of the diversity of hair styles that include straight, curly, twists, braids, locs, Afros, extensions, and weaves.

A good hair "do" is important to the self-presentation of many African American women. And African American women spend the necessary time and money on their hair. This includes long hours at the beauty salon, purchase of hair care products, and purchase of synthetic and human hair. The versatility of African American hair and the availability of diverse styles and products allow African American women an opportunity to be creative in hairstyle. A good hairstyle is essential to looking good. African American men also appreciate a good haircut and style, and there is wide diversity in their hairstyles also.

Body Weight

In the United States, thinness is considered attractive. Being thin demonstrates access to high-protein and low-fat foods. However, in areas of the world where there is famine and disease, body fat indicates health and attractiveness. In examining preference for female body size in 54 cultures, the authors found that heavy women were judged to be more attractive than slender women in places where food is in short supply (Anderson, Crawford, Nadeau, & Lindberg, 1992). The same may be true within cultural groups in the United States, as African American culture differs from White culture in standards of attractiveness regarding body weight. Black women weigh more on average than White women. Also relative to White women, Black women have less concern about being overweight.

Cunningham, Roberts, Wu, Barbee, and Druen (1995) examined African Americans' and Whites' differences in ratings of body preferences and in ratings of facial attractiveness. The authors presented 63 African American and White male students with stimuli showing the head and shoulders of Black college- age women to assess facial attractiveness. To assess body preferences, two poster boards were used for the presentation of physiques. Each displayed a full body silhouette, differing only in lower body size, with one depicting 7% larger buttocks. Participants were asked to choose the silhouette with the most attractive figure and to rate the attractiveness of each silhouette on a 9-point scale. They were also asked to report the height and weight of their ideal woman.

Black and White ratings were similar on judgments of the attractiveness of the face. Regarding body weight, Blacks gave a heavier weight than did Whites for their ideal figure but did not differ in their ideal height. Blacks were more likely than Whites to select the larger of the two silhouettes as being more attractive (60% vs. 35%), and Blacks tended to rate the larger silhouette more positively. This finding is consistent with the idea that Black men prefer a heavier female physique and larger buttocks than do White men. Blacks and Whites were both similarly likely to mention buttocks as a source of attraction (41% and 29%), but Blacks were more likely to use the adjectives "big" or "large" and Whites were more likely to use adjectives such as "firm" or "small." Among Blacks, 24% indicated large buttocks as the feature they found most attractive in a woman, whereas no Whites gave this response. Whites were three times more likely than Blacks to mention a dislike of large buttocks (21% vs. 7% respectively). Whites were also more likely to have a general dislike of overweight women compared with Blacks (41% vs. 7%).

Reactions to overweight and obese persons also differ between African Americans and Whites. Hebl and Heatherton (1998) conducted a study to examine African American and White reaction to the stigma of obesity. Black and White college students rated photographs of professional models dressed in fashionable clothing. The photographs were of thin, average, and large Black and White women.

They found greater stigmatization of obesity among White women than among Black women. White women rated large White targets as lower in attractiveness, intelligence, popularity, happiness, relationship success, and job success. They also rated the large White women as less likely to hold prestigious occupations than their thinner counterparts. Black women rated large Black women lower in attractiveness but not in the other attributes, suggesting very little stigma for obesity. In fact, Black participants rated the large Black targets as more popular than the average and thin targets. In summary, Blacks are more likely than Whites to see a larger body as ideal and to not stigmatize larger persons.

Interracial Attitudes, Friendships, and Relationships

The United States is a diverse society. But how often do people of different ethnic and cultural groups interact in friendships and intimate relationships? How do African Americans and Whites feel about interracial dating and marriage? We address these and related questions next.

INTERRACIAL FRIENDSHIPS

Investigators in a study on interracial youth friendships collected data between 1975 and 1995 (Tuch, Sigelman, & MacDonald, 1999). Youth were asked about the ethnicity of their friends. Fewer African Americans tended to have all or almost all same-race friends than did Whites. About 52% of African Americans had almost all same-race friends compared with 62% of Whites. This may be due to the fact that African Americans are more likely to live in predominately White neighborhoods than vice versa. African Americans had an increase in cross-race friendships during the late 1970s and early 1980s, but this reversed in the early 1990s. By the mid-1990s, the percentage of African Americans with all or almost all same-race friends had increased. The percentage in the 1990's was similar to that of the mid 1970's.

Tuch and colleagues (1999) reviewed several studies that examined the percentage of interracial friendships among African Americans. These researchers found, across different studies, that the percentages of interracial friendships were 18%, 20%, 24.7%, 30.1%, and 82%. The reason the percentage was a high 82% in one study is that youth in this study were asked if they had any cross-race friends. The other studies asked youth if they had any cross-race "best friends." The data suggests that about one-fourth of African American youth have cross-race best friends.

What are some of the factors that are associated with interracial friendships among children and adolescents? School environment is one factor. Students who attend small, demographically diverse schools tend to have more interracial friends than those who attend larger schools with more homogeneous student populations. Students in the smaller, diverse schools have more opportunities to interact with each other (Slavin, 1995).

Cooperative learning teams in schools in which students are rewarded for group success and not for individual success also seem to encourage cross-race friendships. Studies of cooperative learning teams among school-children show increases in both the quantity and quality of students' inter-racial friendships.

Some interpersonal skills relate to whether there are cross-racial friend-ships. More popular children are more likely than less popular children to initiate cross-racial friendship (Hallinan & Teixiera, 1987). Children with interracial friendships have more social skills and multicultural sensitivity than those without such friendships.

Similarly to children, adults who participate in cooperative learning teams and work ventures tend to have more interracial friends. Business environments that reward team and group achievement instead of individ-ual achievement foster more interaction and more interracial friendships.

INTERRACIAL ROMANCE

Favorable attitudes toward interracial dating and marriage have increased steadily over the past few decades, although there are still some negative attitudes. Interracial dating and marriage vary demographically and geo-graphically. People who live in California and other states on the West Coast are more likely than persons who live in other parts of the country to date and marry interracially.

Interracial Dating

Studies have shown that African Americans are more accepting than Whites of interracial dating (Rosenblatt, Karis, & Powell, 1995). Knox, Zusman, Buffington and Hemphill (2000) conducted a study on interracial dating attitudes and behaviors among a sample of 620 college students attending college in North Carolina. The majority of the students were White (87%), followed by African American (8.5%). When students were asked if they were open to involvement in an interracial relationship and if they had dated someone of another race, fifty percent of the students said they were open to an interracial relationship. African Americans were twice as likely as Whites (83% vs. 43%) to be open to an interracial relationship.

Almost a fourth (24.2%) of the African American students said they had dated someone of another race. There are several reasons why African Americans may be more accepting than Whites of interracial dating. African Americans may perceive that there is more of a social benefit to dating Whites than vice versa. There are more Whites available for dating African Americans than vice versa. And African American parents have differing expectations about interracial dating and are likely to be more accepting of interracial dating than White parents are.

Parenting roles and expectations influence whether or not interracial dating is a choice for children. In many African American families, it is the mother who plays the key role in accepting or not accepting an interracial relationship. In White families, the father is the key parent and sets expectations and norms about relationships, including interracial dating. Women may be more open than men to the relationship choices of their sons and daughters. Because the primary African American parent is more likely to be the mother, one would see more acceptance of interracial dating among African Americans (Rosenblatt et al., 1995).

Gender is also a factor in interracial attitudes and behavior. Men are more likely than women to date interracially. In a study in California in 2000, 81% of White men were willing to date outside their race (Fiebert, Karamol, & Kasdan, 2000). Seventy-five percent of African American men were willing to date outside of their race. Both African American and White women have less positive attitudes toward interracial dating. This is in part fueled by concerns about marriage compatibility.

One explanation for African American men dating White women is based on social exchange theory discussed previously. According to this theory, White women will only date African American men (or other ethnic minority men) if they have other beneficial qualities such as money, physical attractiveness, or social power. In turn, African American men date White women to gain social status (Warren, 2002).

One study compared attitudes of African Americans and other ethnic minority groups on interracial dating (Fiebert et al., 2000). Participants were unmarried African Americans, Asian Americans, Euro-Americans, and Latinos. They were asked if they would consider being romantically involved with an African American, Asian American, Euro-American, and Latino(a) of the opposite sex.

Dating preferences varied by ethnicity. Latinos and Euro-Americans were more likely to be desired dates than were African Americans and Asian Americans. Latinos and Euro-Americans were also preferred as romantic partners. As shown in other studies, African Americans reported greater willingness to date other ethnic and racial groups than these groups reported willingness to date them. Thirty-three percent of African Americans indicated a willingness to date Whites, whereas 25% of Whites reported a willingness to date African Americans. Forty percent of African Americans said they would date Latinos, whereas 28% of Latinos said they would date African Americans. Twenty-one percent of African Americans indicated that they would date Asian Americans, and 16% of Asian Americans indicated they would date African Americans. African Americans were the ethnic group that all other ethnic groups were least willing to date.

Interracial Marriages

Until as recently as 1967, interracial marriage in the United States was a felony (Porterfield, 1982). Despite the greater acceptability of interracial dating, the rate of interracial marriages is still low. In general, Whites and African Americans were much less likely than Hispanic Americans and Americans of other races to cohabit with or to marry an interracial partner. This may be due to more negative societal attitudes toward African American and White unions. Among African Americans who are married, 5.8% are married to a person of another race (U.S. Census Bureau, 2000). White male-Black female marriages have traditionally been one of the least common of all possible interracial combinations and were almost nonexistent prior to the 1970s.

About 10.3% of African Americans who are unmarried but cohabiting have an interracial partner. For Whites, the percentages for marriage and for cohabiting are 3.2% and 6.8%, respectively. For Hispanic Americans the percentage for interracial marriage is 15.5% and 25.2% for cohabitation.

Perception of Interracial Couples

Despite increases in interracial marriage, it is still viewed unfavorably by some. Both African Americans and Whites have expressed objections to interracial marriage on the grounds that it destroys family traditions and that the children from these marriages will have more problems. Although this last point is unfounded, this remains the perception of some.

Interracial couples may violate perceivers' beliefs about "goodness of fit"—that is, who should be paired with whom. Consequently, interracial couples may not be perceived as couples at all but as separate and mismatched individuals (Lewandowski & Jackson, 2001).

Prejudice also contributes to negative perceptions of interracial couples. African American male and White female pairing, although most common, is also seen as most problematic. A study was conducted to identify perceptions of interracial and intraracial (same race) couples who were White and African American and White and Asian (Lewandowski & Jackson, 2001). Participants were White students at a large midwestern university. Participants read descriptions of interracial or intraracial couples and rated the couple on compatibility. Participants also rated their degree of comfort with the couple. Interracial couples were perceived as less compatible than intraracial couples. Marrying outside of one's race was seen as a professional liability for men. White men who married African American or Asian women were perceived as less likely to be professionally successful than men in same-race marriages. White and African American couples were viewed as less compatible than White and Asian couples. The White sample also found it more difficult to imagine being married to an African American than to an Asian American. When African American couples were composed of same-race partners, the degree of liking and perceived compatibility of African American and Asian couples was about the same as for White couples. In other words, when the couples were of the same race, they were accepted more than when they were not of the same race. The findings may have differed if the participants in the study were African American. As noted previously, ethnic minorities, including African Americans, are more accepting than Whites of interracial relationships. Although Whites' attitudes toward interracial friendships are neutral, if not somewhat positive, they are much less accepting when it comes to interracial dating and marriage (Baldwin, Day, & Hecht, 2000).

Gay and Lesbian Relationships

Writings on gay and lesbian relationships within psychology have been fairly limited. And there has been even less written on African American gay and lesbian relationships. A book titled *American Couples* (Blumstein & Schwartz, 1983) provided some of the first authoritative work on the topic of gay and lesbian relationships. The authors surveyed over 12,000 couples via questionnaires and conducted more than 300 interviews with gay, lesbian, married heterosexual, and cohabiting heterosexual couples. Questions about money, work, power, and sex were asked. Similar patterns in gay and lesbian and heterosexual relationships were found with some differences noted.

QUALITY OF GAY AND LESBIAN RELATIONSHIPS

One myth is that gay men and lesbians are not involved in long-term, stable relationships. In fact, surveys of gay men show that between 40% and 60% are currently involved in a steady relationship (Harry, 1993). The percentage of lesbians in steady relationships is higher; between 45% and 80% of lesbians report being in a steady relationship.

Other studies have looked at the quality of the relationship and have compared relationship quality among gay and lesbian couples and heterosexual couples. In general, these studies have shown that when homosexual and heterosexual couples are matched on age and other relevant background characteristics, they do not differ in reported affection, love, satisfaction, or adjustment (Peplau, Cochran, & Mays, 1997). Moreover, the things that lead to good relationship quality in heterosexual relationships lead to good relationship quality in gay and lesbian relationships.

However, some differences in gay and lesbian and heterosexual relationships have been reported in more recent studies. Kurdek (1998) examined ways in which heterosexual and homosexual relationships are similar and different and found that gay and lesbian relationships operate similarly to heterosexual relationships with a few exceptions. One exception is that there are fewer barriers to leaving in gay and lesbian relationships. Gay and lesbian relationships also emphasize autonomy more than heterosexual relationships do. Compared with married couples, lesbian couples reported more intimacy in their relationships and more autonomy, as well as more equality. However, there were more frequent breakups (Gottman et al., 2003).

GAY AND LESBIAN RELATIONSHIPS AND RESPONSE TO CONFLICT

How a couple handles conflict is a predictor of relationship quality, satisfaction, and ultimately whether the couple will remain in the relationship. Gottman et al. (2003) conducted an observational study to examine how gay and lesbian and heterosexual couples respond to conflict. Participants were 40 heterosexual and gay and lesbian couples who had been in committed relationships for at least 2 years. Participants were told to discuss a topic in a conflict area in the relationship. The partner who initiated and presented the conflict relationship issue was called the *Initiator* and the other person was called the *Partner*.

The couples' discussions of the relationship conflict topic were observed and recorded. The findings showed that the way in which an issue is presented and received in a conflict interaction is positive for homosexual couples and negative for heterosexual couples. Homosexual initiators were less belligerent and less domineering than heterosexual initiators. The partner in the homosexual couple also showed less belligerence, less dominance, and less fear and tension than the partner in the heterosexual couple. The responses of gay and lesbian couples to conflict suggest that equity and fairness is of greater concern in homosexual than in heterosexual relationships. There is less fear, tension, and sadness among homosexual initiators than among heterosexual initiators. The observations also indicated that the homosexual initiators of the conflict had more positive emotions when compared with the heterosexual initiators. They displayed more affection, more humor, and more joy. The homosexual partners also showed more humor than the heterosexual partners. After the issue had been presented, gay and lesbian couples were more likely to maintain a positive state than were heterosexual couples.

All in all, this is an important study, as it suggests that gay and lesbian relationships may operate on different principles than heterosexual relationships with respect to power and emotions. Homosexual couples were more positive and less negative overall in how they responded and recouped from the conflict situation. One reason for these differences might be that gay and lesbian couples value equality more than heterosexual couples do. Because there are fewer barriers to leaving homosexual relationships than to leaving heterosexual relationships, the perception of equity is important. Gay and lesbian relationships do not have the status differences often seen in heterosexual relationships. The status differences between men and women may promote hostility, particularly from women who tend to have less power than men and who also typically initiate conflict issues in the relationship. Because there are fewer barriers to leaving homosexual relationships, homosexual couples may be more careful in the way they accept influence from one another and perhaps in the way they resolve conflicts. This may be the glue that holds these relationships together. This study did not indicate whether African Americans were included in the sample, and it would be interesting to see if there are differences in how African Americans respond to conflict.

AFRICAN AMERICAN GAY AND LESBIAN RELATIONSHIPS

African American gay and lesbian couples have similar relationships and face similar issues as do non-Black and White gay and lesbian couples. However, there are some issues that are unique because of race and sometimes class.

Homophobia, double and triple minority status, and fear of disclosure are issues affecting African American gays and lesbians. Homophobia is the "fear of or contempt for lesbians and gay men" (*American Heritage Dictionary*, 2004). Research suggests that African Americans tend to be more homophobic than Whites (Greene, 2000). The Church has been a contributor to homophobia in the African American community. Ministers and other leaders may teach that gay and lesbian relationships are sinful and against "God's" will. Therefore, African American gays and lesbians are less likely than White gays and lesbians to disclose their sexual orientation.

The relationships of African American gays and lesbians are not typically supported outside of the gay and lesbian community (Greene, 2000). When families are supportive, it is generally dependent on the relationship being invisible.

COPING WITH HETEROSEXISM

Two of the challenges facing gays and lesbians are homophobia and heterosexism. Heterosexism is institutionalized negative beliefs about and systematic discrimination against people who are not heterosexual (Wilson & Miller, 2002). African Americans may use some of the same strategies for coping with heterosexism as they use for coping with racism.

Some people cope with heterosexism by monitoring self-presentation to prevent disclosure of sexual orientation to avoid stigma (Peterson & Marin, 1988). Peterson and Marin (1988) suggest that African American gay and bisexual men deal with heterosexism by using some of the same types of strategies that are used for racism. They interviewed 37 gay African American men about strategies they use to cope with heterosexism. Five strategies for managing their homosexual status were identified. Four of the strategies were used in non-gay friendly contexts. Non-gay friendly places were those that were intolerant of homosexuality. These might include work sites, neighborhoods, churches, and schools. One strategy used by the majority of the men was "role flexing." Men who role flexed changed their behaviors, dress, and mannerisms in non-gay friendly settings. This strategy kept their gay and heterosexual worlds separate and distinct. Some of these men also would assert their manliness in order to eliminate suspicions about being gay. Other men engaged in role flexing by covering up, that is, using deceit to conceal their sexual identity from others, such as by lying about hanging out in gay clubs and being discreet about sexual relationships. A second strategy was "keeping the faith." Men who used this strategy used their faith and their relationship with God as a coping strategy. These men sought the advice of ministers at gay Christian organizations and attended and participated in Church activities. A third strategy was termed "standing your ground." These men openly confronted those who spoke negatively of gays. The fourth strategy was changing sexual behavior. These men abstained from homosexual behaviors altogether.

Gay friendly contexts involved those situations in which the individual was with gay or gay friendly individuals. These included gay clubs, gay areas of town, or places were people were gay friendly. Self-acceptance was the strategy used in this context. Men who used this strategy loved and accepted themselves for who they were. These men saw heterosexism as a form of oppression and did not act differently in non-gay friendly contexts, despite the possibility of hostility.

Peterson and Marin report similarities between coping with heterosexism and coping with racism. Two strategies that have been used to cope with racism include mental colonization and social change. Mental colonization occurs when the individual accepts his fate in a racist society and does not make any effort toward social change. Role flexing, keeping the faith, and changing sexual behaviors are examples of mental colonization. Two strategies, standing your ground and self-acceptance, are similar to those used by Black Pride advocates. The men stood up for themselves and accepted themselves for who they are.

Methodological Issues

There are some methodological issues to consider when studying interpersonal relationships among African Americans. These revolve around (a) the lack of research conducted with African Americans on this topic and (b) conceptualizing and measuring relationship constructs that may not be universally meaningful.

LACK OF RESEARCH

Although interpersonal relationships are central to well-being, there has been fairly limited research conducted with African Americans. The research that has been done has been sporadic and isolated. In reviewing literature and research for this book, it was often the case that only one or two studies or articles could be identified for any given topic. For example, on the topic of African American gay and lesbian relationships, there was little or no published literature. Similarly, the literature on friendship patterns among African American youth revealed only a few studies in the psychological literature. Given the importance of relationships, there is a need for more study of African American relationships. This research should consider both historical and contemporary factors that affect family, intimate, and other types of African American relationships.

CONCEPTUALIZATION AND MEASUREMENT

Like so many other topics in psychology, methods used to assess relationships may or may not be as relevant to African Americans. For example, the Strange Situation Test that is used to assess infant and provider attachment may be less appropriate to use in households in which there are multiple care providers.

As we have seen in this chapter, variables that are correlated with mate selection, attractiveness, and other aspects of interpersonal relationships also vary across ethnic groups. These variables are important when considering theories of interpersonal attraction. For example, as noted previously, partner selection among African Americans is influenced by contextual factors (e.g., community, employment) and institutional policies (e.g., higher incarceration of African American men) as well as personal preferences (e.g., preference for lighter skin color).

Summary

The proverb "One finger cannot lift up a thing" illustrates the need for others in our lives. Relationships with others, including family and friends, have been the focus of this chapter.

All humans have a need to belong, to affiliate, and to be in relationships with others. Relationships can be exchange or communal. In exchange relationships people give benefits with the expectation that they will receive comparable benefits in return. Communal relationships are those in which the person feels responsible for the well-being of the other person.

Relationships among Africans may be described as communal. Communal relationships consider the importance of the community and include mutual aid, caring for others, interdependence, solidarity, reciprocal obligation, and social harmony.

Close relationships are intimate relationships and involve family members, close friends, and romantic partners. The very first relationship is the one the infant has with his or her caregiver and is called attachment. The attachment style developed during this period affects subsequent interpersonal relationships. However, the conceptualization and measurement of attachment style may differ cross-culturally.

Close friendships are rewarding with many benefits. Women's friendships tend to be more intimate than men's. Men's friendships tend to center more on activities than feelings. Friendships are important to African American youth's just as they are to members of other ethnic groups.

A romantic partner is that one person in the world to whom you feel closest. An intense close relationship may be described as love. There are two main types of love, passionate and companionate love. There are cultural differences in how love is conceptualized, with the Western conceptualization of love as more passionate than companionate love. African American women have fewer mates from which to select than do African American men and White women. African Americans do not subscribe to the same norms as Whites for mate selection. African Americans are less likely to be married than are Whites. Forty-two percent of African American males are married, and 31% of African American women are married (U.S. Census Bureau Census, 2000).

We are attracted to individuals who are in close proximity to us, who are similar to us demographically, and who have similar values and beliefs. We also like people who are physically attractive. There is agreement across cultures as to what constitutes an attractive face.

Historically, African Americans with fair skin have been considered more attractive than those who are darker skinned. There are ethnic differences in ideal body weight. African Americans are more likely to endorse a heavier ideal body weight and less likely to stigmatize overweight persons.

African Americans tend to have more interracial friends than Whites have. Despite increases in interracial marriages, they are still viewed unfavorably by some. In general, studies have shown that relationship quality of homosexual and heterosexual couples do not differ for the most part. One difference is in how conflict is handled. Gay and lesbian couples tend to handle conflict in a more positive way. African American gay and lesbian couples have similar relationships and face similar issues as non-Black and White gay and lesbian couples. However, some issues are unique because of race and sometimes class. Homophobia, double and triple minority status, and fear of disclosure are issues affecting African American gays and lesbians. More research is needed on the topic of interpersonal relationships among African Americans.

Cognition, Learning, and Language

Knowledge kept to oneself is as useless as a candle burning in a pot.

—Oromo proverb

N.C. Linguists Trying to Quantify Ebonics

By Catherine Clabby, *The News & Observer of Raleigh*

RALEIGH, N.C. (April 25, 2002)

Rural African-Americans increasingly speak the urban-sounding dialect called Ebonics, even when their grandparents sound like their white neighbors. That helps explain how the distinctive tongue is spreading nationwide, two N.C. State University linguists say.

N.C. State researchers Walt Wolfram and Erik Thomas analyzed interviews with working-class blacks and whites born in the state's coastal Hyde County, where regional speech long has reigned. Two generations back, members of both groups shared the distinctive Pamlico Sound dialect that calls a "high tide" a "hoi toide," the linguists found.

But as younger black men and women are exposed by travel, television and pop music to a wider African-American culture, they sound less like their rural Hyde neighbors and more like strangers reared in New York or Los Angeles. Their talk is peppered with Ebonic verb structures such as "she be" or "we wasn't." "Listening to older African-Americans in Hyde County can tell you what black speech was like," said Wolfram, a sociolinguist and professor of English. "Listening to younger African-Americans can tell you where it's going."

Wolfram and Thomas recognize Ebonics as a legitimate dialect, a form of English developed by a dynamic minority. In their new book, *The Development of African American English*, the linguists say that the dialect's growing popularity might stem from African-Americans' trying to bond more closely with one another. "If you want to be embedded in your own culture," Wolfram said, "you don't want to talk white." Wolfram and Thomas analyzed the speech of 50 black and white residents of Hyde County, including as many as five generations from the same family. The linguists found only subtle differences between black and white speech among old-timers in Hyde County, where blacks made up 33 percent of the population in both 1740 and 2000. Older black residents skip s's on some verbs ("she sing" rather than "she sings") and drop some consonants ("wes'en" for "west end"), traits that can be traced to West African languages, the linguists found. But mostly they sounded like white locals.

In fact, only 10 percent of people who listened to recordings of older Black Hyde County residents recognized the speakers as African-American. "That made his daddy mad cause I beat him. He was taking up for the boy but he weren't taking up for me," is the way a black man born in 1910 described a fistfight from his past.

But 90 percent of listeners could identify the ethnic background of younger blacks whose interviews were analyzed for this research. The younger speakers tend to abandon local phrases such as "he weren't." They make liberal use of "he be."

The N.C. State findings are expected to have a lasting impact because the researchers used scientific instruments to break down and compare elements of black and white speech, said John Singler, a New York University linguist. The North Carolina scholars detected convincing differences, especially with tone, that previously have been hard to analyze.

Reprinted with permission of *The News & Observer* of Raleigh, North Carolina.

Introduction, Definitions, and Historical Perspectives

The news story describes the language of older and younger African Americans in one southern county. It also illustrates the value of Black language for the younger group. Black English and Ebonics are discussed in this chapter along with cognition and language. Learning, cognition, and language are products of one's socialization. The socialization experiences of African Americans are influenced by both African and American cultures. The acculturation process of enslaved Africans left its indelible mark on current language structures—as in the case of Black English and its modern-day counterpart, Ebonics, both of which are based on English and African language structures. Common patterns of learning, cognition, and language among African Americans are not genetically predetermined, but they are influenced by culture and the socialization process.

Differences between African Americans and Whites in learning, cognitive patterns, and language should not be interpreted as deficits in either group. For example, Black English and Ebonics are often negatively contrasted with Standard English. Ebonics may be associated with low socioeconomic status or being uneducated. Some consider it a "ghetto" language. Yet, the unique features of Ebonics have evolved from legitimate language structures used by speakers from both Africa and the United States. Ebonics is the language of communication among many African Americans in the United States. In this chapter, we review the unique features of African American language, cognition, and learning and examine how they interact. Because cognitive patterns and language begin at an early age, much of the research on cognition and language has been conducted on children; thus, most of the studies referenced in this chapter focus on children. Methodological issues are also considered. First, we analyze the relevant terms and historical perspectives on the study of cognition and learning among African Americans.

DEFINITIONS

Cognition is the process of thinking or mentally processing information. Information may take the form of images, concepts, words, rules, or symbols (Coon, 1997). Cognitive functions include attention, perception, thinking, judging, decision making, problem solving, memory, and linguistic ability (Gall, Beins, & Feldman, 1996). Learning is the process through which experience causes permanent change in knowledge or behavior (Woolfolk, 1998). Simply put, learning is the cognitive process of acquiring knowledge (Colman, 1994). Language is a fundamental learning tool. Language is a collection of words and/or symbols and rules of use that allow for thinking and communicating (Coon, 1997).

AFRICAN AMERICAN COGNITION: HISTORICAL PERSPECTIVES

Historically, in psychology, the study of cognition among African Americans has examined cognitive and intellectual differences between African Americans and Whites. Many of the studies conducted in psychology in the 19th and 20th centuries focused on these differences. For the most part, studies found that African Americans were inferior to Whites in their performance of many cognitive tasks, including general intelligence and perceptual fluency, as well as in analysis and synthesis of information. A study discussed in Chapter 1 is representative of the type of research done during this period. Peterson (1923) tested White and "Negro" children on group intelligence tests and individual learning tests. He found significant race differences: White 8-year-old children scored higher than Negro 10-year-old children on both group and individual tests. Peterson concluded that these differences pointed to inferior intellect rather than socioeconomic status among the Negro children because 60% of the White 8-year-olds came from poor sections of the city, while 97% of the Negro 10-year-olds came from one of the best Negro schools in the city.

He reported that about 83% of the Whites were smarter than the Negroes, and that only 15% to 18% of the Negroes were as smart as the Whites. According to Peterson, differences between the two groups were most notable on tasks that required abstract and logical thinking. Based on the finding that Negroes did not possess abstract and logical thinking, he recommended that there be less of this type of education for Negro children. Peterson did not consider that although the Negro children may have been at one of the best Negro schools in town, there were still substantially fewer resources at these Black schools than there were at the poor White schools.

More recent work has shown that there are differences, not deficits, between the two groups. Though most work continues to exclude comparisons with, or considerations of, African Americans and other cultural groups in the United States (e.g., Asian Americans, Latinos, and Middle Eastern Americans), some progress has been made in methods used for studying differences between Blacks and Whites. This work has also focused on evaluating the unique features of African American language and cognition. The unique features of cognition among African Americans affect how knowledge is acquired and used, and thus affect the group's learning styles. These unique features are discussed next.

THE ACQUISITION OF KNOWLEDGE

The acquisition of knowledge and how knowledge is used vary according to culture. Myers (1988) contrasts a Eurocentric view with an Africentric view of knowledge acquisition. According to Myers, the Eurocentric view of knowledge assumes that external, or "objective," knowledge is the basis of all knowledge. From this perspective, knowledge is acquired by observing the external environment. Counting and measuring are ways of acquiring this type of knowledge. The process by which learning goals are met focuses on that which is measurable, repeatable, and reproducible. From this perspective, learning goals rely heavily on some form of technology or established social or scientific system of evaluation. The cultural system that supports this type of knowledge acquisition is more likely to link self-worth and value to extrinsic criteria that are measurable, such as the amount of money one makes, the level of education one has attained, and the affluence of the neighborhood in which one lives.

In contrast to a Eurocentric approach to knowledge acquisition, an Africentric framework places the origins of knowledge within an intrapersonal and social context (see Chapter 2). From an Africentric view, self-knowledge is the basis of all knowledge. Recognition of one's own perceptions, values, and feelings is necessary for knowledge acquisition. Knowledge is subjective and based on the perspective of the person.

Knowledge acquisition from a Eurocentric perspective would consider as valid and true knowledge that is derived from measuring, counting, and quantifying information. Knowledge derived this way is considered valid if it is considered objective. From an Africentric framework, knowledge that is derived from individuals with whom one has positive interpersonal relationships has value over and beyond knowledge that is generated by experts or published in established media. Making meaning of the world clearly means two different things in the Eurocentric and Africentric frameworks.

Kochman discusses how differences in perceptions of knowledge acquisition can create conflict between African Americans and Whites. In his book *Black and White Styles in Conflict,* Kochman (1981) discusses differences in how Black and White students view the truth and authority of an idea. As a college professor, Kochman observed that White students were likely to regard information as true or authoritative if it had been published or put forth by an expert. Furthermore, White students were likely to present their ideas in an impersonal way. For these students, the merits of the idea and the credibility of its original source established its authenticity. White students did not see themselves as personally responsible for the idea, and their obligations were limited to the presentation of the idea. The merits of the ideas were independent of who was presenting the idea. On the other hand, among Black students, attention was focused on who in the classroom presented the idea. Kochman's Black students considered it important to have a personal opinion on an issue; they believed that the value and truth of the idea presented was linked to the presenter. Black students wanted to know that the presenter cared about the idea enough to have a personal opinion. Thus, if the presenter was passionate about the idea, more weight was given to its validity than if the presenter was neutral. Along the same lines, if the presenter had positive interpersonal relationships with class members, more weight was given to the idea.

Kochman (1981) further observed that differences in establishing the authority of information often produced conflict between Black and White students. For example, White students would make statements they believed to be true because of who said them and where they were published. Black students would view these statements in light of their own personal opinions and would challenge White students to either agree or disagree with the statements. Because White students did not feel that they had to agree or disagree, they were seen by Black students as copping out and not being willing to give their own opinions. White students, on the other hand, saw Black students as being too personally involved and not able to give an objective opinion of the idea.

Bell (1994) identifies two features of a cultural model of knowledge acquisition among African Americans. Her cultural model assumes that attention is paid to both affect and symbolism. The affect dimension captures the preference for social, personal, and spiritual aspects of knowledge acquisition. Knowledge is acquired within the context of social and personal relationships. One's spiritual beliefs also play a role in knowledge acquisition.

Here, learning is linked to one's belief that there is a spiritual significance to acquiring knowledge.

The other dimension of knowledge acquisition is the symbolic dimension. This dimension captures the conceptual organization of information for the learner. This dimension is rational. It recognizes that the analytical approach to knowledge acquisition co-occurs with the affective approach.

The work by Kochman, Myers, and Bell suggests that there are variations among African Americans and Whites in how knowledge is acquired. These variations are likely to affect learning.

Cognitive Styles

Cultural variations in cognitive style assume that individuals attend to and process information from the environment in ways consistent with their cultural group (Hilliard, 1992; Watkins, 2002).

Barbara Shade (1991) has written about the unique ways in which African Americans process and analyze information in their environment. Her analyses of cognitive patterns among African American youth address the type of stimuli that are attended to, the sensory channels that are used, and how information is integrated and applied. Given the voluminous amount of stimuli within our environment, it is not possible to attend to all or most of it, so we select the information most relevant to us. Culture and socialization determine what is relevant. Studies show that African Americans and Whites attend to dissimilar types of stimulus information. Some of the work of Shade and colleagues is reviewed next.

ATTENTION TO SOCIAL AND INTERPERSONAL STIMULI

African American children's perception of their environment shows that they usually attend more to social and interpersonal aspects than to physical aspects of their environment. In a classroom setting, African American children are more likely to attend to the teacher or to each other than to aspects of the physical environment such as desks, blackboard, and chairs. A preference for the social over the physical environment may be socioculturally determined. This preference may be due, in part, to living in an urban environment, home to a large percentage of African Americans (Shade & Edwards, 1987).

Stimuli are overabundant in urban environments, so one must choose that to which one will attend. Social stimuli, in contrast to physical stimuli, are more likely to be personally relevant. Rewards and punishments can be received from others, who can either help us to achieve or prevent us from achieving our goals. Another reason for the preference among African

Americans for social stimuli over physical stimuli is that African Americans tend to place value on communalism and relationships (see Chapter 2).

Whether or not one is extroverted or introverted is associated with preference for social stimuli. Introverted people orient themselves away from others and extroverted people orient themselves toward others. In a study of African American and European American children, Shade and Edwards (1987) found that most high-achieving African American children are oriented to extroversion, whereas their European American counterparts are oriented to introversion.

Because of communal and interpersonal orientations, being a member of the group as shown through extroversion may be of higher value and more functional for African Americans than Whites. High-achieving African American children may be seen as "selling out," and these children may need to reassert themselves as members of the group through extroverted activities. In fact, observations of high-achieving African American children show that extroversion is one way they manage to be successful and still remain respected members of their social groups.

People who are more in tune with their social environment are more likely to be sensitive to facial expressions and the emotions they convey. Sensitivity to emotions expressed nonverbally has a functional origin for African Americans in the United States and around the world. Under oppressive and discriminatory conditions, the ability to detect emotional and social states was beneficial. During slavery in particular, sensitivity to nonverbal cues was helpful to slaves who could not communicate verbally with Whites. African Americans have been found to be better than European Americans in reading facial emotions (Shade & Edwards, 1987).

SENSORY PREFERENCE

African Americans differ from Whites not only in what is attended to in the physical environment, but also in their preference of certain sensory channels. Within the United States, most information is transmitted via the visual channel. However, the visual channel may not be the only preferred modality for African Americans (Shade, 1991). Studies suggest that African Americans may prefer auditory (hearing) and tactile (touching) channels when receiving information. We will return to this when we discuss the concept of verve as a preference for multiple stimuli in learning styles (Cunningham & Boykin, 2004). Consequently, presenting information in auditory as well as other sensory modes may lead to more effective learning for African Americans.

African Americans appear to use kinesics or movement more than other ethnic groups. Later in the chapter, we discuss studies of movement and rhythm among African American children and the implications of movement and rhythm on learning.

HOLISTIC APPROACH TO INFORMATION ORGANIZATION AND ANALYSIS

There are also preferences among African Americans for the manner in which information is organized and analyzed. To better understand these preferences, a distinction is made between a holistic approach and an elemental approach to how information is organized and analyzed.

A holistic approach organizes information relationally, that is, by how bits of information belong together or by the connection that stimuli have to each other. An elemental approach to organizing information considers the commonality of stimuli. For example, consider the following social stimuli in which a decision has to be made as to which two of the three stimuli belong together: a student, a teacher, and a principal. An elemental approach to organizing this information might pair the teacher with the principal because they are both adults and school staff. A holistic approach to organizing this information might link the student with the teacher since the teacher is responsible for teaching the student. Some African Americans demonstrate a preference for integrating information using a relational approach rather than an elemental, piecemeal approach. In the next section we discuss analytical and relational learning styles, which parallel the contrasts between the elemental and holistic approaches.

In summary, African American children relative to White children are more likely to attend to social stimuli rather than physical stimuli. They are more likely to prefer receiving information via auditory and tactile channels along with visual channels. And they are more likely to organize information holistically rather than in a piecemeal fashion.

Learning Styles

As noted previously, the process by which information is acquired is culturally determined. Self and relational considerations influence the ways in which African Americans learn most effectively.

Bell (1994) contrasts two learning styles—the analytical learning style and the relational learning style. The analytical learning style is similar to the elemental way of organizing information, and the relational learning style is linked to the holistic style for integrating information. African Americans have learning styles that are more relational and European Americans have learning styles that are more analytical. Because analytical learning is more Western and reflects the learning style of the majority, some may view relational learning as inferior to analytical learning. Differences in learning styles have implications for how students are taught, how they perform, and whether or not they are successful in educational settings. However, these different styles should not be considered better or worse, but simply different.

ANALYTICAL LEARNING STYLE

In Western culture, knowledge is acquired through rational and analytical methods. A set of rules by which information is attended to and organized is used. Stimulus centeredness, field independence, and reflectivity are chief components of the analytical learning style.

Stimulus Centeredness

Stimulus centeredness means that the attributes of a stimulus object, rather than personal social features, determine how knowledge is acquired about that object. For example, a child might learn that a cat is an animal by looking at a picture of a cat while repeating a number of times that the cat is an animal.

The focus on stimulus features over personal or social features is associated with an emotional or affective distancing or objectivity from the stimulus object. A person using an analytical learning style can acquire knowledge without attending to the social context. This kind of learning separates or inhibits feelings when information is processed. Technologies like distance and Internet learning, which do not include an interpersonal aspect, would be appropriate for those with this learning preference.

Attention and concentration in problem-solving situations may be facilitated when one is centered on the stimulus object rather than the social context. When a person is completely focused on the stimulus material, he or she is more able to pay attention and to recall more details, gaining a fuller understanding.

Field Independence

Field independence is another aspect of the analytical learning style. Learners who are field independent focus on the parts rather than the whole when information is processed. For example, a classroom is seen as individual components (e.g., students, teacher, books, and desks) rather than globally as a classroom. When this learning style is used, attention to any one aspect of the environment is facilitated.

Reflectivity

Another aspect of the analytical learning style is reflectivity. Those with a reflective learning style spend more time and energy reflecting and processing information; they do this in a sustained and systematic way. Only after a process of reflection and evaluation will these learners make a decision or integrate the information. Analytical learners may make fewer mistakes when problem solving because of the cautious manner in which they process information.

There may also be a higher tolerance of stimulus repetitiveness among analytical learners. For example, a point could be repeated several times for an analytical learner without the message disinteresting the learner. Much of the learning that takes place within educational institutions in this country is based on analytical learning. Students are encouraged to be independent learners, and a goal of education is to have students learn how to access and use information on their own. Students are taught to be objective processors of information and not to let their personal feelings influence what they learn. Furthermore, they are taught to process information reflectively by carefully considering the information prior to making a decision. For African American students, this environment may not always be conducive to learning.

RELATIONAL LEARNING STYLE

The relational style is characterized as holistic processing of information. There is a preference for field self-centeredness (rather than stimulus centeredness), field dependence (rather than field independence), and spontaneity (rather than reflectivity; Bell, 1994).

Self-Centeredness

Self-centeredness is an orientation toward social and personal cues in learning situations in which social features of the environment are used to process information. To put it another way, the relational learner who relies on self-centeredness is more interested in people than nonpeople. Here, the relationship that a person (e.g., a student) has with the information provider (e.g., a teacher) may influence whether or not the individual listens and learns. This is akin to what Kochman (1981) observed among his Black students. The credibility of information presented was linked to the presenter.

A self-centered learner is more motivated to acquire knowledge that can be applied to addressing or solving social problems than learning simply for the sake of knowledge. For example, if a self-centered learner is learning about theories of poverty, information on ways in which poverty might be solved will help these learners to master the materials.

Field Dependence

Field dependence is characterized by the tendency to perceive and process stimulus material holistically. Stimulus material and problems are processed by attending to features of the stimulus materials in an integrated way. Using the previous example, a discussion of theories of poverty, devoid of solutions to poverty, would not be useful for the field dependent learner. Field dependent learners are aware of what is going on in the social context in which they acquire knowledge.

Spontaneity

Spontaneity is a preference for responding to the obvious and prominent aspects of stimulus material. This response style compared with the reflective response style is more immediate and not constrained by an in-depth evaluation of the stimulus material. In a problem-solving situation, a spontaneous learner might more quickly make a decision about a course of action.

In summary, people with a relational learning style prefer learning within a social environment, through affective means, and have a higher tolerance for stimulus variety and change. Relational learners are also more likely to value learning for its social value. In the United States, a learning style that is self-centered, field dependent, and spontaneous may disadvantage African Americans who attend school and work in environments that reward stimulus centeredness, field independence, and reflectivity. Other learning preferences among African Americans are discussed next.

COMMUNAL LEARNING STYLE

A communal learning situation recognizes the interconnections among people. Sharing information is encouraged because it emphasizes the importance of social interconnectedness (Cunningham & Boykin, 2004). Communal learning is contrasted with independent learning whereby each individual is responsible for his or her own learning. Several studies have examined the effects of communal learning contexts on the cognitive performance of children.

Albury (1998) conducted a study with low-income African American and European American children in the fourth grade. The purpose of the study was to examine the effects of group versus individual learning contexts on vocabulary. Students were given a pretest to determine initial vocabulary skills. They were then assigned to one of four learning conditions. The first condition was the individual condition: Three children worked at the same table and were given separate study materials. They were told that any one of them achieving 18 out of 25 on a posttest would receive a reward. The second condition was the interpersonal competition condition: Three children sitting at a table were given separate materials and told that the one receiving the highest score would receive a reward.

In the group competition condition, three participants at a table were given one set of materials and were told that they were competing against other groups to receive a reward. In the communal condition, three students were at a table and were told the importance of sharing information. Participants in all groups were given 20 minutes to study the material. In each of the learning groups, children were of the same ethnicity.

Results showed that European American children learned most in the individual study condition and least in the communal condition. African American children learned the most under the communal condition and the next highest amount under the group competition condition. They gained the fewest points in the individual condition. African American children in the communal condition not only scored higher at posttest but also had the highest learning gains of all groups in the study. African American children reported that they liked the group study conditions best, whereas European American children liked the individual study condition best.

The findings from several other studies are consistent with those of the Albury (1998) study (Coleman, 1998; Cunningham & Boykin, 2004). These studies have found that when African American children are in communal learning contexts (in contrast to individualistic learning contexts), the quality and quantity of learning are enhanced.

VERVE, RHYTHM, AND LEARNING

Verve and Rhythm

Other cultural dimensions seen among African Americans are the orientation toward verve and rhythm. These orientations affect learning style. *Verve* is a term coined by Boykin and colleagues to describe an improvisational style expressed as rhythmic and creative. This behavior can be seen in movement, posture, speech patterns, and behavior (Boykin, 1983; Cunningham & Boykin, 2004). Verve arises out of the contextual environment in which many African Americans live. When the home and neighborhood environments of African Americans are examined, much physical intensity and variation are seen. The immediate sensory environment of African Americans lends itself to receptiveness to heightened variability and intensity of stimulation. Accordingly, incorporating this heightened level of sensory stimulation can lead to enhanced performance for African American children.

Within the learning environment, the presence of verve would suggest a preference for several stimuli rather than one repetitive stimulus. There is also a preference for stimulus change, a higher energy level, and faster pace. According to Boykin, verve is important in terms of how children learn. The didactic "teacher talks and students listen" mode of learning may not work as well with African American children as it does with European American children.

Rhythm is the regular repetition of weak and strong elements, often silence and sound, in speech and music, art and everyday life. Rhythm is expressed in one's movement and other activities of daily living. The cultural orientation by which the environment is experienced through rhythm may affect cognitive and learning processes. In a series of studies, Boykin and colleagues have shown that learning among African American children is enhanced under conditions of rhythm and verve (Cunningham & Boykin, 2004). The study described next is illustrative of this research.

Tuck and Boykin (1989) assessed the performance of low-income African American and European American fourth- and sixth-grade students in problem-solving tasks, including color matching, listening, dot pattern reproducing, and letter scanning. The tasks were presented in a low verve condition and a high verve condition. In the low verve condition, five examples of each of the four task types were presented in a blocked sequential format such that all five examples of a task type were presented together. In the high verve condition, the four task types were presented in a randomized order regardless of task type. Also, children provided their impression of the level of stimulation in their homes by answering questions about the amount of time music was played or the television was on. Children were also asked about the level of physical stimulation they preferred. Finally, the teacher rated each child on his or her academic standing and motivation.

Findings indicated that (a) the African American children rated their homes higher in stimulation and had a higher preference for physical stimulation and task variety than did the European American children, (b) European American children performed significantly better than African American children under low verve conditions, and (c) the higher the degree of sensory stimulation in the homes of the African American children, the more they preferred physical stimulation in the school.

Movement

Movement is another dimension that is salient in the lives of African Americans. Learning contexts that provide opportunities for movement expression facilitate the learning performance of African American children (Allen & Butler, 1996; Cunningham, 1997; Cunningham & Boykin, 2004). In general, African American students perform better under conditions where there is movement and music, and White students perform better under conditions devoid of music and movement. Findings from a study conducted by Allen and Butler (1996) illustrate the role of movement and music in performance.

Allen and Butler (1996) investigated whether or not music and the opportunity to move facilitated cognitive processing in African American and White third graders. Children's performance on reasoning tasks was measured under two conditions: high-movement expressive (HME) and low-movement expressive (LME). In the HME condition, the children could move around while a rhythmic tune was playing; they were told that they could dance or clap if they wanted, as they listened to a story being read. In the LME condition, children were told to sit or stand, but not to move, in front of the person who was reading the story.

A reasoning task was used to assess three types of processes: encoding, inferring, and mapping. Encoding tasks required children to identify names, events, and actions in the story. Inferring tasks required children to understand the relationship between characters and events. Mapping tasks required children to understand the relationship between separate events.

The findings showed that African American children's performance was slightly better under the HME condition than the LME condition and White children's performance was significantly better under the LME condition. African American children performed at the same level as the White children despite the fact that the White children were from middle-class backgrounds and the African American children were from low-income backgrounds. The performance of the African American children defied expectations and the norm. This finding is important and suggests that African American children can perform at levels comparable to other academically successful ethnic groups when they are taught under culturally congruent conditions.

The finding that movement facilitates learning among African American children is not surprising. Earlier studies have noted differences in movement between African Americans and Whites. Guttentag (1972) examined differences in movement among African American and European American 4-year-olds. African American children displayed more movement variety and responses than did European American children. This suggests that African Americans' propensity toward movement and improvisation speaks of a more open and receptive state that can enrich the learning process.

Learning Preferences and Misdiagnoses

As discussed, spontaneous behaviors, use of body language, movement, and the like might indicate verve and rhythm and movement preferences. However, sometimes these forms of self-expression and receptivity to the social environment are seen as an indicator of attention deficit disorder. Or the child may be viewed as acting out and not paying attention to the teacher. An incorrect diagnosis of a child may lead to inappropriate placement in special education classes. In addition, these labels may create a negative self-fulfilling expectation. Diagnostic assessment of a child should consider culturally specific ways of learning. In summary, the homes of African American children are filled with higher levels of sensory stimulation leading to an orientation labeled "verve." Learning environments that capture the preference of African American children's propensity for verve, rhythm, and movement may be culturally conducive to learning.

Language

WHAT IS BLACK ENGLISH?

Coon (1997) defines language as a collection of words or symbols and rules for combining them that facilitates thinking and communication. Language spoken by African Americans has been referred to as African American English, Black Language, Black English, and Ebonics. African American English is a systematic, rule-governed linguistic system that is spoken by many, but not all, African Americans in the United States (Washington, 1996). It is estimated that at least 80% of African Americans speak some form of African American English (Hollie, 2001). Robert Williams coined the term *Ebonics* in 1973. The term came from the words *ebony*, which means black, and *phonics*, which refers to speech sounds (Williams, 1997). He defined Ebonics as "the linguistic and paralinguistic features that represent the communicative competence of West Africa, the Caribbean and the United States" (Williams, 1997).

Both the academic and lay communities have extensively discussed Black language. Two landmark cases spoke directly to the consideration of Black language (Smitherman, 2004). The first case, *King v. Ann Arbor* (1979), was filed on behalf of 15 Black children who attended school in Ann Arbor, Michigan. The children lived in a low-income community. The judge ruled that the Ann Arbor school district had to consider Black English in its educational process. It also acknowledged the responsibility of schools to teach Black children standard English. This case was significant because it recognized the legitimacy of Black English and laid the foundation for Black English to be recognized in the educational process.

Almost 20 years later, in December 1996, the Oakland California School Board adopted the position that in order to achieve Standard American English (SAE) proficiency, the unique language of African Americans must be recognized. This position generated a lot of controversy. Opponents of this position felt that it encouraged inferior education for Blacks. Some thought that by recognizing as legitimate a language that was not SAE, African Americans would not be able to compete in the real world where SAE is the norm. Supporters of the new policy argued that the recognition of Black English as a language would help develop language strengths in students by building on Black English in the classroom. For example, SAE could be reinforced if teachers were familiar with the language students used. Rather than always correcting students for using Black English, teachers could allow students to communicate using this language while teaching them SAE. Opponents felt that using Ebonics would promote another educational handicap for African Americans.

Dialect or Language?

Whether or not Black English is a language or a dialect has been heavily debated. According to Smitherman (2004), whether or not a language is defined as such depends on who has the power to define. Because Blacks have less power than the majority Whites in this country, they alone cannot define Black English as a language. Validation and recognition from the majority culture is necessary for Black English to be recognized as a language. Smitherman further notes that the language of Blacks has been considered inferior and consequently has been used to justify the discrimination and exclusion of Black people from major social, political, and economic institutions. Because Black English has been stigmatized, many middle-class African Americans have rejected it, feeling that those most likely to speak it belong to a lower class. These middle-class African Americans would rather not risk being stigmatized, though some do speak Black English at home.

Williams (1997) rejects the notion that Black English is not a language. He discusses two theories on the origins of Ebonics: (a) the pidgin/creole theory and the (b) African retention theory. According to the pidgin/creole theory, Africans who were brought to the United States from Africa spoke many languages. Pidgin is a simplified version of the language of different slave groups. The children of slaves acquired as their language the pidgin their parents spoke and the new language that the slaves' children spoke was called creole. Eventually a process referred to as Englishization began. The speaker maintained the original communication style, some lexical items, and the ability to code switch. During the Englishization process, enslaved Africans and their descendents began to speak some Standard English.

The second theory on the origin of Ebonics is that it is the retention of features of African languages that represents the deep structure of Ebonics. Some West African languages such as Ibo, Twi, Ful, Yoruba, and Wolof are relatives of Ebonics.

FEATURES OF BLACK ENGLISH

Black English has many unique features. It is derived from European American English (called Standard English), West African languages, and African American pidgins and creoles spoken at different times and in different regions of the United States. Some of the unique features of Black English as summarized by Smitherman (2004) and Washington (1996) are described next.

Use of the Verb *Be* to Express Habitual Action

The use of *be* is derived from a verb structure that is found in many African languages, in the Caribbean, and in West African Pidgin English. The verb *be* in this context is used to convey a qualitative nature and consistency of an action over time. "He be playing" is qualitatively different from "He is playing." The SAE version would be "He is playing all the time" or "He is constantly playing."

Zero Copula

A unique feature of African American English is the absence of the copula. The complete sentence can be a noun or pronoun followed by an adjective, adverb, verb, or noun, for example, "He fast" or "She my sister." SAE, on the other hand, requires a form of the *be* verb to complete a sentence (e.g., "He is fast" or "She is my sister"). Zero copula is more likely to follow pronouns than full noun subjects (Wyatt, 1995), for example, "He strong" as opposed to "He is strong." This aspect of Black English is found in West African languages.

Use of the Word *Been* With Stress to Convey the Remote Past

This language pattern gives weight to events and actions that occurred in the distance past by stressing the word *been* in conversation. For example, "She had been finished cleaning the room." "We had been home." The stress on the word *been* indicates that this action occurred some time ago. The SAE equivalent to the first example would be, "She had finished cleaning her room a long time ago."

Turning a Word Into Its Opposite

Words that are traditionally thought of as negative may be given a positive connotation. This is especially seen in Black slang. For example, the word *bomb* is used to denote something that is really good. "She is the bomb" may be used to denote an attractive woman rather than something dangerous such as an explosion.

Using a Pronoun to Repeat the Subject for Emphasis

Subjects are repeated in a pronoun form when the speaker wants to emphasize a point about the subject. For example, "John, he left two hours ago." "The baby, she is learning to walk." This feature of speech is seen in some West African languages.

Showing Possession by Context and/or Juxtaposition

In Black English, there is no standard rule for how possession is shown. For example, "My sister name is Shanita" or "She live near my sister house." In SAE, possession is shown by the letter "s" preceded by an apostrophe.

Lack of Subject-Verb Agreement

In African American English, subject and verb may differ in number or person, for example, "What do this mean?" instead of "What does this mean?"

Multiple Negation

Two or more negative markers in one sentence may be used in African American English. This may be used to emphasize a point: "I don't got no money" may be used instead of "I don't have any money."

Zero Past Tense

In African American English, -ed is not always used to convey regular past constructions, or the present tense form is used in place of the irregular past form. "Her dress was stain" instead of "Her dress was stained."

MEANING OF SPEECH FOR AFRICAN AMERICANS

One's social and cultural meaning is conveyed in how one talks. Ogbu (1999) studied the patterns of African Americans in a speech community (i.e., a population that shares the same language and a common theory of speaking) to understand the social meaning and context of their speech. Ogbu observed and interviewed students, parents, grandparents, and other adults in a Black speech community in Oakland, California. The study revealed the following findings.

1. Participants knew that there were two English dialects in the community, slang English and proper English.

2. The community perceived that White people spoke correct or proper English and that Black people spoke slang English. Black and White people's English differed in vocabulary, accent, and attitude. The same statements could be interpreted differently when spoken by a Black or a White person.

3. Black English was regarded as more appropriate for speaking in the community and proper English was regarded as more appropriate for school.

4. Students switched between slang and proper English in the school, speaking slang in the hallways and proper English in the classroom.

5. Children learned slang before they learned proper English. Because slang was learned within the family and community, children felt more comfortable with it.

6. Parents and children recognized that slang dialect might cause problems at school.

Participants in Ogbu's study believed that proper English was necessary for school and employment success. On the other hand, they felt that proper English could threaten their identity within their community. Speaking proper English was regarded by some as trying to be White and thinking that you are superior to Black people. Some residents felt that speaking proper English was "putting on airs" by not talking in what was assumed to be one's natural way of speaking. Furthermore, they felt that White people forced proper English on Black people, resulting in a loss of slang language and thus, the loss of an element of Black culture.

PERCEPTIONS OF BLACK ENGLISH

Language is not only a means of communication but also is used to form initial impressions of others (Koch & Gross, 1997). Findings from studies suggest that as African Americans move in mainstream society, Standard English may be seen as more desirable and speakers of Black English may be seen as not competent (Doss & Gross, 1992).

Doss and Gross (1992) tested the effects of Black English on interpersonal perceptions or how people perceive others. In this study, audiotapes were made of an African American male who spoke either Standard English or Black English. Participants were African American college students. They listened to the tape and then evaluated the speaker on interpersonal characteristics. They rated the Standard English speaker as more likable and competent than the Black English speaker. Participants also indicated that they would like to get to know and work with the Standard English speaker more than they would with the Black English speaker. Participants in this study were all adult college students and findings might differ with a population of non-college students.

In fact, a study on perception of speakers of Standard English and Black English with a younger population revealed a different finding. Koch and Gross (1997) examined African American junior high students' perceptions of an African American speaking Black English or Standard English. They then rated the speaker on several characteristics. Students rated the person who spoke Black English more positively than the person who spoke Standard English. The authors speculated that children in the age range of 10 to 14 might prefer the language of their culture and view this as a way of creating identity and view the use of Standard English as selling out.

In general, the studies suggest that as African Americans get older and move into the mainstream, they may prefer speakers of Standard English to speakers of Black English. However, as the newspaper article at the beginning of this chapter points out, younger African Americans are more likely to speak Black English, and they are more likely to prefer speakers of Black English than of Standard English.

Implications for Educating African Americans

One of the reasons African Americans do not do as well as Whites on academic and achievement tests is that the educational system does not support alternate learning styles. Learners who are analytical and elemental in their approach tend to do better than those who are relational and holistic. Attending to cultural differences specifically in learning activities should improve learning and subsequently test scores for African Americans. On this topic, Asa Hilliard (1992), an expert on cultural issues in education, writes, "All students have an incredible capacity for developing the ability to use multiple learning styles, in much the same way that multiple language competency can be accomplished" (p. 373). On the other hand, African Americans have to function and compete in many environments that are not supportive of their unique learning style. Learning when and how to modulate one's learning preference might be another strategy when the environment is nonresponsive to the African American learner.

A related question is, what is the best language to use when educating African American children? According to Smitherman (2004), educational and institutional policies should recognize the legitimacy of Black English. Black English could be a language of co-instruction, especially among children who live in environments where it is spoken. The distinctive language patterns and other aspects of Black English should not be viewed as dysfunctional and inferior, but as a unique style that can aid in instruction in and outside of the school system. Black English is functional for most Black people and is a valid means of communication.

At the same time, language policy must also emphasize the need for Standard English competency among African Americans. Standard English is oftentimes rejected or not fully accepted by Blacks because it is associated with White English. Rejection of Standard English may be linked to ethnic identity, especially among African Americans. However, when there is acceptance and respect of one's native language, there is less reluctance to accept Standard English. The acceptance of both languages would greatly benefit African American children and adults.

Methodological Issues

One methodological issue is that knowledge acquisition and differences in learning styles might in part account for the lower performance of African Americans compared with Whites on standardized tests. If one group is disadvantaged by the way tests are designed and administered, the question arises as to whether or not the test is valid for that group. According to Bell (1994), people who have more analytical problem-solving strategies tend to do better on intelligence tests. These tests are designed such that when a rational and analytical method is used to solve a problem, the answer tends to be intended or "correct." On the other hand, the attributes that characterize African Americans' way of learning and problem solving may not be reflected on the intelligence test. When the test taker uses relational methods to solve the problem, he or she may choose the unintended or "wrong" answer. According to Bell, learning environments that facilitate self- centeredness, field dependence, and holistic orientations should facilitate more effective learning and problem-solving skills among African Americans. African Americans should perform best when these aspects are reflected on tests and in other assessment situations. These considerations have implications for the way in which intelligence and other related attributes are assessed. African Americans will most likely achieve lower test scores given these differences in learning styles. (See Chapter 4 for a more detailed discussion of intelligence testing among African American students.)

Summary

The proverb at the beginning of the chapter states, "Knowledge kept to oneself is as useless as a candle burning in a pot." One feature of learning for African Americans is the utility or practicality of knowledge. Learning will be facilitated to the extent that the knowledge gained can be used to solve problems. This and other culturally congruent aspects of cognition, learning, and language have been discussed in this chapter.

African American culture influences learning, cognition, and language. Cognition is the process of thinking or mentally processing information. Learning is the acquisition of knowledge and is a cognitive process. Language is the collection of words and/or symbols and rules of use that allow for thinking and communication. The acquisition of knowledge and how knowledge is used vary across cultural groups. According to Myers (1988), the Eurocentric view of knowledge acquisition assumes that external, or "objective," knowledge is the basis of all knowledge. From an Africentric perspective, knowledge acquisition occurs within social and interpersonal contexts.

Cognitive patterns also differ among cultural groups. African American children's perception of their environment shows that they attend more to social and interpersonal aspects than to physical aspects of their environment. They also prefer to receive information from multiple channels, including auditory and tactile along with visual channels. African American learners are likely to process information using a holistic rather than an elemental approach.

African American children are more likely to use a relational than an analytical learning style. The relational learning style focuses on social rather than nonsocial aspects of the learning environment, uses a gestalt or relational approach to learning, and uses spontaneity when processing information.

A communal learning environment is preferred over an independent learning environment. African American children tend to perform better when communal methods are used. Achievement and performance are also enhanced in learning environments that include verve, rhythm, and movement. Understanding the learning style of African American children should facilitate their performance on intelligence tests and other tests.

Black English has several unique features. It is derived from Standard English, West African languages, and African American pidgins and creoles spoken at different times and in different regions of the United States. It is a legitimate language with structure and rules of use. A consideration of the cognitive styles and language of African Americans should facilitate learning and achievement.

8

Religion and Spirituality

God drives away the insects from the tailless animal.

—Akan proverb

Transformed by Violence: Churches Hit Hard by Lost Connection

First in an occasional series

January 2, 2005

By Ervin Dyer, *Pittsburgh Post-Gazette*

Evelyn Stanton is among the 22 souls who show up on Wednesday nights for Bible study at Lighthouse Cathedral, a soaring name for a high-spirited church that meets in a tent in one of Arlington's roughest neighborhoods. That doesn't matter for Stanton, a mother of seven and a former crack user and dealer. Wednesday is a mid-week chance to keep finding her way back to God. She is led by Bishop Maurice Trent Jr., a boyish-looking minister with an Afro and a special mission. Though now happily married for 20 years, Trent wants to use his personal testimony—he was once an alcoholic and a wife-beater—and stern sermons to bring the "unchurched" back to faith.

He's already touched Stanton, 39. She's given up drugs and is now considered an evangelist. A supervisor at a South Side sandwich shop, Stanton used to make her tithes when she was out of work by cleaning the church toilets. In helping to restore Stanton to God, Trent has reconnected her to one of the oldest, most influential institutions in the black community: the church.

Famed sociologist W.E.B. Du Bois, in his 1899 study of blacks in Philadelphia, observed that the black church was poised to become "a centre of social intercourse to a degree unknown in white churches. . . . Consequently all movements for social betterment are apt to centre in the churches."

Almost 100 years later, in their ground-breaking 1990 book, *The Black Church in the African-American Experience*, Eric Lincoln and Lawrence Mamiya found Du Bois' work prophetic.

In a survey of nearly 2,000 black ministers and churches, the authors concluded that black churches, on the whole, are more socially active than white churches and tend to participate in a greater range of community programs.

In one sense, the results are not surprising. Black Americans are among the most religious people in the country. Polls say some 82 percent of blacks (versus 67 percent of whites) are church members; 82 percent of blacks (versus 55 percent of whites) say religion is very important in their lives.

Those same studies show that black people pray more often, read more religious material and use religion and prayer to cope with stress and illness. This "faith factor" influences many to make positive choices that keep them off the streets, which in the more impoverished pockets of Pittsburgh remain deadly.

For two generations now, though, more people of all races have grown up unchurched. As many as 29 million Americans claim no religious identity. They are called "nones," and their numbers have doubled in the past decade, making them third behind Catholics and Baptists.

In urban communities, especially those that suffer from lack of jobs, lack of individual responsibility and broken families, the consequences from the churches' lost connection can be dire, said the Rev. Eric Gerard Pearman, an Atlanta theology professor.

Introduction, Definitions, and Background

The news story that opens this chapter illustrates the positive benefits of Church on the life of one African American woman. Religiosity and spiritual beliefs are practices and behaviors central to most African Americans. Spiritual and religious beliefs are interwoven in all aspects of African American life. They influence family and social relationships, choice of romantic partners, employment and educational decisions, and community involvement. Religion and spirituality also influence one's political beliefs and participation in political activities. Physical and psychological well-being and coping mechanisms are affected by religious and spiritual beliefs (Mattis, 2000).

In the first section of this chapter, we provide definitions and information on religious groups, practices, and activities among African Americans. We go on to discuss historical influences, particularly the West African perspective on spirituality; religion and spirituality in early America; and some African American religious experiences. Then we discuss some unique features of the African American Church and review findings on the links between spirituality, religion, and mental and physical well-being; we also examine the role of the Church in liberation and salvation. Methodological issues related to conceptualizing and measuring spirituality and religion are considered, and finally a chapter summary is offered.

African Americans are of diverse faiths and yet the majority are Christian. Therefore, our discussions of the religious experiences and activities of contemporary African Americans mostly stem from the Christian perspective.

DEFINITIONS

Religion differs from spirituality although the terms have been applied interchangeably. People generally report themselves to be more spiritual than religious. Spirituality comes from the Latin word *spiritus* (spirit). Spirituality has been defined as the belief in a sacred force that exists in all things (Potts, 1991). Spirituality is not dependent on any doctrine, organization, or culture but on individual beliefs. To be spiritual implies something other than the body or that which is material. Meraviglia (1999) defines spirituality as "experiences and expressions of one's spirit in a unique and dynamic process reflecting faith in God or a supreme being; connectedness with oneself, others, nature, or God; and an integration of the dimensions of mind, body, and spirit" (p. 29).

Religion comes from the Latin word *religio* (good faith ritual). Religion is a "system of beliefs and practices that nurture the relationship with the Supreme Being" (Meraviglia, 1999, p. 25). Religion involves universal life experiences and the meaning that is attached to these experiences. The universal experiences include all the ways in which humans make sense of the world including birth, death, joy, sorrow, knowledge, ignorance, success, failure, love, hate, suffering, relief, body, and spirit (Musser & Price, 1992).

Mattis (2000) studied the differences in the meaning of spirituality and religion in an African American sample. Respondents defined spirituality as a connection to a higher power. They considered spirituality the internalization and expression of key values, such as goodness, in daily life. Spirituality was conceptualized as one's relationship with a higher power or with transcendent forces, including nature. Religion was seen as the mechanism for achieving spirituality.

Newlin, Knafl, and Melkus (2002) conducted a concept analysis of the meaning of spirituality for African Americans. They reviewed 20 qualitative and quantitative studies from the fields of nursing, psychology, and sociology on African American spirituality. A main finding is that there is consistency across the disciplines in how the antecedents, attributes, and consequences of spirituality are described for African Americans. The antecedents of spirituality include cultural influences, life adversities, faith in God, and a belief in a divine intervention. The authors describe one attribute of African American spirituality as a central quintessential dimension as seen by benevolence, omniscience, omnipotence, and transcendence. A second attribute is expressed as a personal caring and intimate relationship with God or a higher power. A third attribute is the interpersonal and supportive connections with others. The fourth spiritual attribute, called consoling, is described as a liberating source of peace, compassion, comfort, and love. And the fifth attribute, called transformation, is a source of healing, strength, and personal growth.

Table 8.1   Religious and Spiritual Beliefs and Activities of African Americans and Whites

Type of Activity	% African American	% White
Prayed during past 7 days	93	80
Read Bible during past 7 days	52	35
Attend church on Sunday	43	42
Do not affiliate with a regular church	21	32
Religious faith is important	83	66
Feel responsible for telling others about religious beliefs	46	33

Source: Barna Group, 2005

Newlin and colleagues also identify four consequences of spirituality for African Americans. One consequence, divine reciprocity, is faith and love and gratitude for God. A second consequence, heightened interpersonal connectedness, is reflected in positive interpersonal relationships and increased love for others. A third consequence, emotional equilibrium, is a sense of perceived support and peace of mind, as well as absence of stress. The fourth consequence, empowering change, comprises active coping, positive interpretation of life events, and better physical health.

RELIGIOUS ACTIVITY

Data from the National Survey of Black Americans (NSBA) show high levels of religious and spiritual activity among African Americans; for example, 38% reported that they read religious materials, and 36% said they listen to religious broadcasts at least once a week (Chatters, Taylor, & Lincoln, 1999). The Monitoring the Future survey indicates that among African American high school seniors, 45% consider religion to be very important in their lives. Furthermore, 52% of African Americans attend religious services at least two or three times per month (Chatters et al., 1999). As shown in Table 8.1, African Americans are more likely, compared with Whites, to have prayed and read the Bible over the past 7 days and attended Church on Sunday. They are less likely than Whites to be without a home Church. African Americans report that religious faith is important to them and feel a responsibility to tell others about their beliefs (Barna Group, 2005).

Church attendance is an important Sunday ritual in many African American households. The typical Sunday service for African Americans is 70% longer than that attended by Whites. The typical Black Church has more people in attendance than the typical White Church, with attendance about 50% greater in Black Churches than in White Churches (Barna Group, 2005). The pastor is an influential person, and 65% of African

Americans report that pastors of Black Churches are important leaders in the African American community.

Religious Groups

African Americans belong to many different denominations, including Baptist, African Methodist Episcopal, Jehovah's Witnesses, Church of God in Christ, Seventh-Day Adventist, Nation of Islam, Presbyterian, Lutheran, Episcopal, Roman Catholic, and many others. Baptist and African Methodist Episcopal have the largest percentages of Black members.

Surveys show at least half of African Americans—from 49% to 60%—are Baptist (Chatters et al., 1999). The percentage of African Americans who report being Methodist ranges from 6% to 14%, and the Catholic percentage ranges from 5% to 10%. Those without a specific denominational affiliation range from 4% to 8%.

African Americans are overrepresented in certain religious groups. That is, they account for a larger percentage than would be expected given their percentage in the overall population of the United States. Although African Americans compose about 12% of the general population, they account for 37% of Jehovah's Witnesses, 29% of Baptists, 27% of Muslims, 26% of Seventh-Day Adventists, and 22% of Pentecostals (Mayer, Kosmin, & Keysar, 2001). African Americans are underrepresented (8%) in the group that claims no religion.

Demographic Factors Associated With Religious Activity

African American religious participation varies by demographic variables. Women attend religious services more frequently than men, and older persons attend more frequently than younger ones. Married persons attend religious services more frequently than persons who are not married. Those with more years of education attend services on a more frequent basis than those with fewer years of education. Income does not affect participation in religious activities (Chatters et al., 1999).

There are also regional differences in Church attendance. Southerners have higher rates of religious service attendance than persons in other regions of the United States. Whether or not one resides in an urban, rural, or suburban area does not affect religious service attendance.

Demographic differences are also seen in prayer. Older individuals pray more than younger individuals. In a study of four age cohorts (18–30, 31–40, 41–60, and 61 and higher), Levin and Taylor (1997) found that prayer is more frequent in successively older cohorts. The findings from this study also show that African Americans pray more frequently than Whites and females more frequently than males.

Historical Influences

RELIGION AND SPIRITUALITY IN TRADITIONAL AFRICAN CULTURE

Spirituality and religion permeate every aspect of the African's life from birth to death, regardless of life circumstances. There are many religious practices by people of African descent. These include Ifa (Yoruba faith), Vodou, Santeria, and other African-derived religions, especially those practiced in countries with large populations of African descent people such as Brazil, Haiti, and Cuba. Our discussion here, however, centers on African religion and spirituality experiences in West Africa.

Within traditional African society, the person is immersed in religious experiences that start before birth and continue after death. In fact, African religion may be better thought of as a philosophy of life. Names of people have religious meaning; rocks and streams are not just objects, but religious objects; the sound of the drum conveys a religious tune (Mbiti, 1970). Within social, economic, and political systems, the influence of religion is seen. In politics, the people believe that the king or chief is divine. In economics, many traditional Africans believe that malevolent forces cause crop failure. In the social world, there is the belief that supernatural forces cause success. In the moral arena, many Africans fear instant retribution by divinities.

The African explains the world around him in religious terms. In all that is undertaken, whether it is cultivating, sowing, harvesting, eating, or traveling, religion is at work. An individual cannot separate himself from the community's religion. This implies that in traditional African society there are no atheists or agnostics.

Although many Africans are Christians or Muslims, traditional African religion is the basis for religious activities for many Africans in past and contemporary times. According to the Ghanaian scholar Gyekye (1996), there is no religion that has been misunderstood or misrepresented more than Traditional African Religion. Traditional African Religion has been referred to as primitivism, animism, paganism, and fetishism. When the European missionaries came to Africa, they did not need to convince Africans to believe in God or life after death. In fact, Traditional African Religion shares three basic beliefs with other religions: (a) belief in a Creator who is in control of the universe, (b) belief that man's bond to his Creator and his later separation from the Creator is due to his own fault, and (c) belief that man will attempt to reconcile himself with his Creator and that this reconciliation will lead to his salvation.

FEATURES OF TRADITIONAL AFRICAN RELIGION

Each community in Africa has its own system of religious beliefs and practices. However, despite the different religious systems, there are many practices, beliefs, and rituals that are common to all. None of these religions are "revealed," like those of Christianity, Islam, or Buddhism. A revealed religion is one in which divine truth is believed to be revealed to one person who becomes the founder (i.e., Jesus Christ, Muhammad, or the Buddha). Because Traditional African Religion is not a revealed religion, it is difficult to point to a specific time in history when it was founded. Traditional African Religion operates beyond any such notion.

One feature common to all Traditional African religious communities is the belief in mystical power, a belief in the existence of mystical forces or powers in the universe that can be tapped by those human beings who have the knowledge to do so for good or ill. Because these experiences cannot be given scientific explanations, some scholars have associated African religion with the practice of magic. In Traditional African Religion, God (though not the Christian God) is the Supreme Being but not the object of direct "worship." Worship is directed at nature—trees, rivers, mountains, and rocks. This does not mean that African religion is nature worship but that objects of nature are inhabited by spiritual beings who exist as intermediaries between God and humans but who cannot be seen by the human eye. Worship is toward these spiritual beings and not the object itself. Thus, objects of nature take on spiritual meaning and respect.

The major beliefs of Traditional African Religion are described below (Gyekye, 1996; Quarcoopome, 1987):

1. **Belief in a Supreme Being.** There is a supreme being who is a God who created all things. Through one's experience in the world, one comes to know that God exists. Africans refer to God as Creator, the Great One, Omnipotent, Omnipresent, and the Great Spirit.

God is believed to be everywhere but God is also believed to be far away, beyond the reach of humans. There is nothing greater than God, and humans should humble themselves before God. An Akan proverb states, "If you want to say something to God, say it to the wind." The wind is everywhere and blows in all directions. Even through the wind is intangible, its effects are felt everywhere just as God. Daily spiritual acts such as prayer, offering, and sacrifices are presented to God. One is completely dependent on God.

2. **God Is Good.** God is identified with goodness. The goodness of God is seen in the satisfaction of human needs, including supplying rain, averting disasters, and healing diseases. God is compassionate, generous, and kind. God is fair and rewards those who are good and punishes those who are evil. . Humans are expected to exercise free will for good rather than evil and so the human being, not God, is held responsible for all acts of good or evil.

3. **Belief in Divinities.** The divinities stand next in relation to God and are God's children. They are ministers of God who have derived powers and act as intermediaries between God and man. They are nature spirits and dwell in objects in nature such as rivers, lakes, trees, mountains, and so forth. God is worshipped indirectly though them. The divinities are therefore worshiped daily, weekly, and annually.

4. **Belief in Spirit Beings.** After God and the divinities come the spirit beings. These spirits may be good or bad, but they are usually good. Spirits are immaterial but can assume dimensions when they wish to be seen. Ghost spirits are spirits of those who die cursed death or bad deaths, that is, by hanging, drowning, or disease. Sometimes these spirits may enter into animals or birds to destroy or harm people. These spirits are bad spirits.

5. **Beliefs in Ancestors.** The ancestors are the heroes and heroines from various tribes. Ancestors are believed to have special powers in the afterlife and, through these powers, intervene in the lives of the living. They also act as intermediaries between God and divinities and men. Ancestors are the unseen members at family or tribal meetings and serve as guardians. The ancestors are respected and honored and are remembered especially at annual festivals.

6. **Belief in the Practice of Magic and Medicine.** Magic is the attempt to influence people and events by supernatural means. Magical objects like charms, talismans, and amulets are used as protection against evil forces such as witchcraft and sorcery and to achieve success. Some may use magic to harm others or to gain an advantage. Medicine is the art of restoring and preserving health. An African belief is that medicine is closely associated with religion. The Divine Healer (i.e., God) dispenses medicine though the divinities and to spirits who in turn provide the knowledge to priests, medicine men, and traditional healers.

7. **The Soul Is Immortal.** Traditional African religious views on death and immortality are complex. There is the common view that the soul is an immortal part of the human being that survives death, and in an afterlife this soul will give an account of its physical life to God. Because the soul returns to God when the person dies, the soul is immortal. This immortal soul enters the world of the spirits, that which is beyond this world. This belief implies that a person is immortal.

8. **Little Concern With Afterlife.** While there is belief in an afterlife, Traditional African Religions do not concern themselves with what kind of life will be led by the immortal soul. For example, there are no beliefs about heaven or hell, a better life, or resurrection. In contrast to an emphasis on a better life after death as in many Christian religions, more focus is placed on the attainment of human fulfillment in this world. Religion is considered essential in attaining the needs and happiness of human beings in this life. Prayers often request that God provide comforts and the things necessary for a happy, satisfying life. This belief emphasizes that religion must have a social value. Religious faith is perceived as useful and practical, rather than as a means for salvation.

The functional perspective of Traditional African Religion is seen in the lives of Africans who convert to Christianity and Islam. Even though the main focus of Christianity is on the redemption of the human soul, many African converts continue to consult traditional African religious leaders in times of need. We see this practice of getting advice from pastors in times of need among contemporary African Americans in the United States. Religion must have immediate relevance in coping with the various problems of life.

9. **Communalism.** Traditional African Religion is communal and supports the values of social solidarity, harmony, and cooperation. Traditional African Religion is not primarily useful for the individual but for the community to which the individual belongs. Community celebration and rites, with public drumming, dancing, and singing have religious meanings. They are important occasions for the collective affirmation of communal values and strengths, bonding members of the community together.

10. **Provides a Moral Code.** Traditional African Religion provides sanctions for the moral obligations and responsibilities of the community members. The enforcement of these sanctions is often done by the traditional religious leader. Misfortunes that befall individuals or communities are often interpreted as punishment for bad behavior or failure to fulfill moral obligations to kinsfolk and the community. Good fortunes are seen as rewards for meeting the community moral obligations.

Religion as experienced by contemporary African Americans shares some commonalities with Traditional African Religion and provides a mechanism to support the political, educational, health, and social needs of community members. The "Church" historically has provided the moral dictates of how individuals within the Church should behave. The head of the Church is a leader not only in the Church but also within the community.

HISTORICAL PERSPECTIVES ON AFRICAN AMERICAN RELIGION

In the 1700s and 1800s, slave owners used Christianity as a means of social control to keep enslaved Africans compliant and docile. Slave owners and clergy taught slaves that Christianity would save their souls and provide them with a good afterlife if they were obedient to their masters. This emphasis on afterlife was one difference seen in religious beliefs among Africans and enslaved Africans in America.

Although many enslaved Africans adopted Christian beliefs, they adapted the religion to their native spirituality. Enslaved Africans began organizing their own worship services, and met at prearranged times in secret places for singing, preaching, and praying. Jesus Christ became a liberating figure for enslaved Africans as they identified with his persecution, were strengthened by his perseverance, and found hope in his resurrection (Lincoln & Mamiya, 1990). Enslaved Africans found hope and comfort in the presence of God, in meetings to support each other, and in music and dance. Within the Church, they felt respected and in control of their destiny. The Church remains today a place where Blacks can achieve status and influence regardless of socioeconomic standing.

In the latter part of the 18th century, independent congregations and Churches for African Americans were formed. Due to segregation, African Americans could not worship with Whites, so they formed their own congregations (Phelps, 1990). These independent Churches allowed African Americans to emphasize aspects of Christianity that spoke to their unique experiences in America. For example, emphasis was placed on slaves being "children of God" rather than three fifths of a person.

The theme of liberation and control continues to echo in Churches today. The freedom to be all that God intended has been a key theme in civil rights and equality messages. The message of liberation and freedom is consistent with messages that preach against the negative self-images of African Americans brought about by internalized racism.

During the 20th century, many African Americans converted to the Islamic faith as a result of the perceived view that White Christianity was oppressive. The physical images of a White Jesus made many African Americans turn to the teachings of The Honorable Elijah Muhammad and the Black Muslim faith.

Along with messages of liberation and empowerment came messages about the responsibility of the Black Church to provide social, economic, psychological, and educational support to its people. The African American Church has been described as the only institution within the African American community that is owned and controlled solely by African Americans (Cook, 1993).

STOREFRONT CHURCH
MINISTRY OF THE URBAN NORTH

The storefront Church is a central institution for African Americans in urban areas. It is an example of an institution that was developed by African Americans to meet their special needs. These Churches are named storefront Churches because they are often located in an abandoned storefront building. The storefront Church grew out of the migration of African Americans from the rural South to the urban North. During the Great Migration of the 1930s and 1940s, large numbers of African Americans migrated to northern cities to find jobs in industry and government (Boyd, 1998).

When African Americans migrated from the South to the North, they brought with them a preference for religious worship services similar to those in the rural South. The Churches in the urban northern communities did not meet the Southerners' preferences for a Church that was emotional and intimate (Boyd, 1998). Church services in the urban North were more formal and less intimate. These Churches were viewed by Southerners as cold and ritualistic, and the pastors' sermons were seen as too scholarly and impersonal. Southerners were used to services where there was improvisational singing, shouting, and other forms of active participation. The emigrants from the South generally had belonged to small rural Churches in which everyone knew each other and felt like family. Many felt alienated and anonymous in the larger northern Churches. Therefore, many of the African American emigrants organized their own Churches and the storefront Church was born. Pastors were identified and hired, many of them brought up from the rural South. The urban storefront Church provided social and psychological benefits and became an important institution in the community that continues today.

Contemporary African American Churches

African Americans belong to diverse religious denominations and worship in diverse places (i.e., mosque, hall, temple, Church). However, the majority worship within the Church, and so the Church is the focus of this discussion. Among African Americans, the Church is second in importance only to the family. Following slavery, the Church became the institution for civic, art, economic, business, education, and political activities (Calhoun-Brown, 1998), which continue today. The Church serves several purposes for its members. It is the place to receive spiritual renewal, religious education, family and community connections, and reinforcements and rewards for positive behaviors and service to the community.

FEATURES OF AFRICAN AMERICAN CHURCHES

Although there is a great deal of diversity within and between African American Churches, there are some features common to most African American (Christian) Churches. These features, as described by Cook and Wiley (2000), are discussed next.

Community Fellowship

Churches provide an opportunity for people in a community to belong. Many individuals are born into a Church and remain within the Church until they die (Cook & Wiley, 2000). The Church becomes part of the extended family, and Church life is often intermixed with family life. The concept of the Church family is relevant to most African Americans and describes the overarching involvement of the Church in its members' lives. The Church provides stability, affirmation, connection to others, recreational activity, and opportunities for educational and learning experiences. Finding a Church home becomes important when African American families move (Boyd-Franklin, 1989). Some continue as members of their previous Church; others seek out a new Church, usually with a similar ministry, closer to their new residence. Most African Americans participate in activities and services outside of routine Sunday worship services. Children participate in activities such as Sunday school and vacation Bible school. Adults participate in Sunday school, Bible study, choir, and special interest groups (i.e., women's ministry, couples ministry, prison ministry, etc.).

Often resources available to Church members are extended to those outside the congregation. Support groups, educational and tutoring programs, and health programs are some examples of such resources. Larger Churches may offer programs to support community residents, including school and child care facilities, clothing and housing, support for incarcerated individuals, and counseling and support for individuals affected by substance abuse and HIV/AIDS.

There are many leadership and service positions, and ministries in African American Churches. Civil rights and political action activities are also undertaken by many Churches. Many of the civil rights activities of the 1950s and 1960s began in the Church. Contemporary Churches continue to support political positions and candidates.

Often the values, attitudes, and behavior of a Church stem from its members. While the Church is a positive force in most people's lives, it may also be a source of conflict, as when the Church's values are in conflict with individual values and beliefs. This may be especially the case with adolescents who may be influenced more by peers than by the Church. Also, members with alternative lifestyles, such as gay men, bisexuals, and lesbians, are not always accepted by the Church.

Women Are Followers

Traditionally, African American Churches have been led by men with congregations largely composed of women and children (Cook & Wiley, 2000). The leadership structure is usually men in the pulpit and women in the pew, men in power and women following their edicts. Many Christian Churches hold to the biblical writing that the man is the head of the household. Pastors may become the dominant male figure in a female-headed household. Women usually conduct most of the Church activities, from organizing fellowship dinners to laying out the clothes for a baptism.

However, women are gaining influence in leadership positions, and more women are becoming Church pastors.

Worship Practice Is Based on the Holy Trinity

As noted, the majority of African Americans are members of the Christian faith, including Baptist or other Protestant denominations. Therefore, many of the practices described next are rooted in these traditions. Worship practices in Christian African American Churches are based on belief in the Holy Trinity of God the Father, Jesus Christ the Son, and the Holy Spirit. African American Christians consider Jesus the One who liberates, reconciles, heals, and guides (Cook & Wiley, 2000).

Music, an important part of the Church service, provides an opportunity for people to relate to lyrics of joy, peace, and thoughts of a better time in the future, or the pain and sorrow of life. Clapping, dancing, testifying, and shouting provide other ways for African Americans to express themselves spiritually.

Congregations regularly engage in prayer, a crucial aspect of the worship service. Members share testimonials, or stories, that tell how God is working in their lives. Biblical scripture informs Church members of how God is available through the written word and how God's relationship with the people in the Bible is a meaningful experience. The preacher's sermon can be comforting, educational, and practical in that it may address what should and should not be done. There is the expectation that attending the service will change the people's lives in some way, that is, that they will be different when leaving than coming.

The Pastor Is Influential

The pastor typically has great influence both in the African American Church and in the larger community. As in African cultures, religious professionals are the link and the intermediaries between individuals and God (Lincoln & Mamiya, 1990). The values and beliefs of the pastor influence the beliefs, values, and behaviors of Church members. Pastors provide counseling to members, and they are called on in good times (weddings, house blessings) and bad times (funerals, times of sickness).

Funerals Support Grief

Funerals in African American Churches involve members of the Church coming together to grieve and celebrate the life of the one who has died. Funerals support the grief process and are viewed as "homegoing" celebrations. The deceased has passed from this life to a better life and has returned home to join God and previously departed loved ones (Cook & Wiley, 2000).

The funeral service provides support for the deceased's family and loved ones. Testimonials from friends and family speak of the good actions of the deceased while living and what that person may be doing in heaven. The pastor who delivers the eulogy may assure family and friends that the deceased will have a good and eternal life in heaven and that the he or she will be reunited with loved ones who have gone on.

When there is a notice of death, Church members are supportive to the family of the deceased. They may reach out with cards and gifts, and help those in grief with their daily routines by preparing meals and doing other household chores.

Spirituality, Religion, and Well-Being

The findings from several studies show that various dimensions of spirituality and religiosity increase subjective well-being, lower depression and distress, and reduce mortality and illness (Ellison, 1991).

SPIRITUALITY AND COPING WITH STRESSFUL EVENTS

Studies have shown spirituality to be an influential factor in helping African Americans cope with problems and stressful life events. Spirituality gives meaning to one's life and provides an alternative reason for lifes outcomes. A belief that one's final destiny is in God's hands provides hope and inspiration. These beliefs are especially adaptive for individuals who may have lived under harsh circumstances.

Several studies have shown that among diverse African American populations, spiritual and religious beliefs are an integral part of coping with adverse situations. The presence of spiritual beliefs is linked to positive and adaptive coping strategies like planning and organization. The absence of spiritual beliefs is associated with maladaptive coping strategies such as denial and use of alcohol and drugs (Mattis, 1996; Newlin et al., 2002).

Interviews conducted with caregivers of African American children with chronic illnesses (e.g., HIV/AIDS, nephritic syndrome; Armstrong, 1999) revealed that spirituality helped to reduce stress and increase positive coping among caregivers. One positive coping strategy among caregivers was positive reframing. For example, having a child with a chronic illness helped to bring the family closer together.

Belgrave (1998) found similar results in a study on coping strategies in a sample of African American mothers with children with cognitive, emotional, and physical disabilities. Many mothers dealt with the stressors of having a child with a disability by positively reframing the situation in which they found themselves. They felt that having a child with special needs was a blessing from God. They reported that this child provided them with an opportunity to realize their strengths and ability to overcome adversity. Having a child with a disability made them appreciative of all things, including the small accomplishments of their child.

Spirituality has also been linked to better coping outcomes among children who live in neighborhoods with increased violence and crime. Children who live in high-crime neighborhoods often display posttraumatic stress symptoms similar to those found among children who live in countries at war. Saunders (2000) examined posttraumatic stress disorder among 71 African American children between the ages of 9 and 11, selected from neighborhoods in high-crime, high-poverty communities in Houston, Texas. Those children who held high spiritual beliefs were protected from the effects of violence and showed fewer symptoms of posttraumatic stress than those without such beliefs.

Spirituality is also a factor in how individuals cope with HIV/AIDS. A study of over 200 African American urban low-income women living with HIV/AIDS in New York City indicated that they had high levels of spirituality and religiosity and used it to cope with HIV/AIDS-related problems (Prado et al., 2004). Religious activity was associated with the use of positive coping strategies and less distress.

Religious rituals and practices are a mechanism for achieving spirituality. For Christians, this is seen in a relationship with God through prayers and reading the Bible. Interviews with African American mothers of seriously ill children demonstrated that prayers were instrumental in helping the mothers maintain good mental health (Wilson & Miles, 2001). Prayers may include hope that God is in control, a focus on a personal relationship with God, and asking of support from others. In a national survey of African Americans, prayer was reported as the coping response most frequently used to deal with personal problems and adversity (Newlin et al., 2002).

SPIRITUALITY AND PSYCHOSOCIAL FUNCTIONING

Spirituality affects mental health both directly and indirectly. Indirectly, spirituality promotes better mental health by reducing stress through the adaptive coping strategies mentioned previously. Religious practices and spiritual beliefs in and of themselves are coping strategies that are linked to other positive coping strategies (i.e., better health care, less drug and alcohol use). Spirituality also has a direct connection to mental health outcomes.

In a study on spirituality among children attending elementary school, 249 children completed scales that measured racial identity, drug attitudes and use, and spirituality (Oler, 1996). Findings showed that higher levels of spirituality were associated with attitudes that disapproved of drug use. Also, spirituality was correlated positively with social and academic outcomes such as helping behavior, academic achievement, and life satisfaction.

Self-esteem and aggression among youth are linked to spirituality. Spirituality promotes higher self-esteem and less aggressive behavior. This effect is seen for youth who live in high-crime neighborhoods. In a study of African American youth, Walker (2000) found that more spiritual support was significantly associated with higher levels of self-esteem and lower levels of aggression. Youth with spiritual support who lived in high-violence environments scored higher on the self-esteem and lower on the aggressive beliefs scale than youth with less spiritual support who lived in the same neighborhoods.

SPIRITUALITY AND HEALTH

Other studies have examined the role of spirituality and religiosity on health and illness among African Americans. Spirituality and religiosity help to protect individuals from the effects of stress on physical health. Those with high religiosity and spirituality have better physical health and recover from illnesses more quickly than those with low spiritual beliefs. Spirituality is also linked to better overall health and less pain. Among more than 400 patients at a family practice clinic, those who reported being highly or moderately spiritual reported better overall health and less physical pain than those who reported low levels of spirituality (McBride, Arthur, Brooks, & Pilkington, 1998).

Individuals with higher levels of religious practice live longer than those without. Hummer, Rogers, Nam, and LeClere (1999) found that those who never attended Church lived to be about 75 years old whereas those who attended services one or more times a week lived to an average age of 83 years old. This study also found that the beneficial effects of attending Church were strongest for African Americans and females. Attending Church may provide increased social support and access to resources.

In a study of Black spiritual Churches and physical health, healing and prophecy were seen as "two gifts" of the spirit on which these Churches were built (Jacob, 1990). Religious activities directed toward healing the sick include collective prayers for the sick, collecting offerings for the sick, visiting the sick, testifying, reading the scriptures, group singing, preaching, laying on of hands, participating in holy communion, and being possessed by the Holy Ghost. These acts were all seen as vehicles for healing and supporting the sick (Potts, 1996).

Potts (1996) conducted interviews with African American cancer patients. Patients identified several themes related to spirituality and their coping with cancer. These patients saw healing as God's work and felt that the healing and recovery from cancer was part of God's will. Several spoke of God being the Doctor who has never lost a patient. Another theme identified by the cancer patients was that prayer was central in coping with cancer. Prayer was used to ask for a cure and to help patients gain peace of mind. Another theme was turning it over to the Lord. These patients had the theme of acceptance and faith in their outcome.

The link between religious beliefs and health may differ for African Americans and Whites. In one study, Steffen, McNeilly, Anderson, and Sherwood (2000) studied religious coping and blood pressure in a sample of African Americans and Whites. Religious coping involved praying and turning to God for support. They found that higher levels of religious coping were significantly related to lower blood pressure among African Americans but not among Whites. In the African American sample, higher levels of religious coping strategies were correlated with less depression, more social support, and less alcohol use.

HIV/AIDS, Spirituality, and Religion

Given the disproportionate prevalence of HIV/AIDS within the African American community, several studies have examined the role of religion, spirituality, and the Church in HIV/AIDS prevention and treatment. The research into the impact of spirituality and religion on persons who are living with HIV/AIDS shows mixed effects. Religion (but not necessarily spirituality) can have both positive and negative effects for persons living with HIV/AIDS (R. A. Jenkins, 1995). Some religious doctrines may show intolerance for persons living with HIV/AIDS because of the stereotypical association between HIV/AIDS and high-risk groups (e.g., homosexuals and intravenous drug users). Sometimes persons living with HIV/AIDS are alienated from organized religion because of teachings that seem punitive toward "stigmatized groups" associated with HIV/AIDS.

However, according to R. A. Jenkins (1995), religious organizations have served as vehicles for HIV/AIDS-related services, including support from parishioners and clergy. Jenkins conducted a study on 422 HIV seropositive military personnel, of whom 28.7% were African American, to examine the meaning of spirituality within their lives. The author found that many of the males renewed their religious faith as a consequence of learning they were HIV seropositive. Coping strategies included spiritually-based coping (e.g., accepting limits of personal control), good deeds (e.g., helping others), religious support (e.g., emotional support from Church leader or member), alienation from God, religious pleading (e.g., pleas for a miracle), and religious avoidance (e.g., activities that divert attention from problems, such as focusing on an afterlife). Individuals with more distress and depression used more alienation and pleading as a coping style.

Contemporary Topics

There are several contemporary issues that come to mind when discussing the Church and African Americans. One issue is what is the role of the

Church when considering how psychological and social problems such as depression and addiction are addressed. A second topic is how the conservative White Church affects policies that lead to social disadvantage for African Americans. And a third topic is the role of the African American Church in salvation and liberation. These contemporary issues are discussed next.

AFRICAN AMERICAN CHURCHES AND PSYCHOLOGICAL AND SOCIAL PROBLEMS

Many African American Churches, especially Christian ones, have traditionally held the view that counseling and mental health services are not needed and that all one needs is God. However, this is changing, and many Churches have added mental health and counseling components to their ministry. Mainline Protestant and Catholic denominations tend to be more open to counseling than Pentecostal and Holiness Churches, which may be more traditional. Cook and Wiley (2000) discuss ways in which some African American Churches handle psychological and social issues. These are reviewed next.

Depression

Depression is an issue that must be considered in light of the client's spirituality. One of the symptoms of depression may be a cessation of spiritual activities that could be helpful in treatment. Individuals may stop praying, reading the Bible, attending Church, or seeking out other Church members. They may feel embarrassed to ask the Church for help. Some may be reluctant to take medication, especially if they feel that the Church's view is that taking medication reflects doubt in God's ability to heal. Hence, depressed persons may view symptoms not as depression but as lacking spiritual connection to God. Depressed clients may need support and education to help them benefit from therapy. In addition, they may need to be supported and reminded of the benefits of engaging in routine spiritual activities (Cook & Wiley, 2000).

Addictions

Addiction is another issue that should be considered in light of spiritual beliefs. There is diverse opinion within African American Churches on how individuals with addictions should be treated. Some Churches prohibit the use of alcohol and drugs, thereby discouraging individuals from admitting that they have a problem and seeking help. Other Churches recognize the extent of addictive diseases in the African American community and offer support groups like Alcoholics Anonymous. Church members (and sometimes pastors) may offer testimonies of how God delivered them from their addictions and imply that this is all that is needed for treatment. While these testimonials are encouraging for some, they may be discouraging to others if they do not feel similarly healed (Cook & Wiley, 2000).

For some individuals, religion may be another type of addiction. These individuals may move from being addicted to drugs to becoming overly involved in Church activities, or by becoming inflexible about spiritual doctrines. Therapists may want to explore clients' positive and negative addictive behaviors and how the Church's practices support these behaviors.

Homosexuality

In general, although there are exceptions, homosexuality is either admonished or neglected in African American Churches. Conservative Churches may speak out about the evils of homosexuality and see homosexuality as a choice that an individual makes to be immoral. In extreme doctrine, Churches have claimed HIV/AIDS to be God's punishment for homosexuality.

Churches with more liberal views are more accepting of homosexual individuals. However, there is often no open discussion of homosexuality as an alternative lifestyle, nor are Church services and practices geared for homosexual members. For example, few Churches perform union ceremonies for gays and lesbians. And many gay and lesbian members of African American Churches are closeted about their lifestyles.

THE CHURCH AND OPPRESSION, LIBERATION, AND SALVATION

The Church is an institution that has been used for both oppression and liberation of African Americans. Some African American Churches see empowerment and liberation as central missions. These Churches typically have ministries that are actively involved in political action, social services, and economic empowerment. Others focus on salvation or the afterlife as a central mission.

The Role of the Church in Oppression and Discrimination

During the 1700s and 1800s in this country, Church doctrine was used by slave owners to justify the exploitation and domination of Africans in America. Africans were believed to be lesser humans in the eyes of God and therefore deserving of the treatment they got. Christian slave owners, who permitted Blacks to go to Church, believed their religion to be superior to the Traditional African Religion that Africans brought with them. Christian slave owners considered the Africans' religion to be primitive and magical. Enslaved Africans were able to blend their native religious practices with Christianity and make it work for them.

Religion and Inequality

In contemporary times, religion has been used to justify the status quo and the social position of African Americans in the United States. In one study of white conservative Protestants, Emerson, Smith, and Sikkink (1999) looked at how religious beliefs helped this group to justify racial inequalities. White conservative Protestants believe that one's life opportunities are due not to social and situational factors but to an individual's free will. In other words, each person is accountable for his or her own actions. This view minimizes societal influences on one's behavior.

According to Emerson et al. (1999), the belief that individuals have free will is grounded in theological doctrine. This view assumes that humans are free to determine, choose, and effect their own salvation. If humans are free, then they can be held responsible for their acts. In this study, the authors found that Whites holding these theological beliefs were more likely to explain the Black-White socioeconomic gap in more individualistic, and less structural terms. That is, Blacks were perceived to have lower socioeconomic standings because they chose not to engage in behaviors and actions that would promote a higher standard of living.

White conservative Protestants also felt that African Americans engaged in dysfunctional relationships and that this contributed to racial inequality (Emerson et al., 1999). These Protestants believed that Blacks do not do well economically because their families do not have strong bonds and because significant others do not help them to make the right choices. Some of the respondents in this study indicated that one reason for the poor outcomes of African Americans was the breakup of the family. Others indicated that African Americans had not been responsible when it came to raising their children. The significance of this study is that it suggests that this group of White conservative Protestants will likely oppose policies and programs aimed at reducing racial inequality.

The Role of the Church in Liberation and Salvation

Many clergy and laypersons have debated whether the Church should seek to liberate or save people. Religious practices within the Church can promote a sense of well-being that contributes to pride, self-worth, and independence. Further, many Christians believe that God must be present to strengthen the Black race. On the other hand, salvation is a basic doctrine of Christianity, and many consider that the primary responsibility of the Church is to serve as a vehicle for salvation. Churches that focus on salvation concentrate their efforts on saving souls and guiding people toward a life that will be rewarded in heaven. These Churches typically have a strict interpretation of biblical doctrine. Churches that focus on liberation strive to help individuals achieve what is necessary to attain the best possible quality of life on this earth. These Churches may have active programs that support civic, economic, and educational activities. Most Churches attempt to promote both salvation and liberation.

Methodological Issues

For people of African descent, central questions are "What is spirituality?" and "What does it means to be spiritual?" A related question is "How can religion and spirituality be measured?"

CONCEPTUALIZING SPIRITUALITY FROM AN AFRICENTRIC PERSPECTIVE

From an Africentric perspective, spirituality is intricately linked to all aspects of one's life and cannot be viewed as a separate dimension. It would be difficult, if not impossible, to isolate spiritual beliefs and practices from other life domains. For example, one's physical health is linked to one's higher power, as is one's economic success (or lack thereof). While African Americans' spiritual beliefs differ from those found in traditional Africa, there are some parallels. The labeling of an event or practice as spiritual may depend on the spiritual interpretation of its meaning. For example, success at a job could be viewed as an act of God. The birth of a child may be seen as a spiritual act. One's recovery from an illness can be is seen as faith and God's will. These interpretations are not unique to African Americans but may be found among other spiritual believers.

MEASURING RELIGIOSITY AND SPIRITUALITY

There are several measures of religion, spirituality, and related constructs (i.e., purpose in life, values, belief in God, etc.; Hill & Hood, 1999). Because the development of these measures has not typically involved African American participants, it is not clear how valid they are when used with African American populations.

Measures of religion include measures of religious beliefs and practices, religious attitudes, religious orientation, religious morals and values, religious coping and problem solving, and relationship with God scales. As noted previously, these scales may not consider the meaning of spirituality and religion from an African-centered perspective.

One good measure of religious practices that has been used with African American populations comes from the National Survey of Black Americans (Chatters et al., 1999). This survey asks about prayer frequency, watching religious television, listening to the radio, reading religious books and materials, and requesting prayer from others (Levin, 1999).

Summary

The proverb at the beginning of this chapter, "God drives away the insects from the tailless animal," symbolizes God's relationship with people of African descent. Beliefs about God, religious practices, and spiritual beliefs influence all aspects of life among African Americans.

Religion and spirituality are interwoven into all aspects of African American life. Religion differs from spirituality in that religion comprises practices and rituals and spirituality is one's relationship with a higher being. African Americans attend Church more often, engage in more religious practices, and hold stronger religious and spiritual beliefs than do Whites. There is diversity among African Americans in religious affiliation, but the majority are Christian and members of a Baptist denomination. Older persons, females, and Southerners attend Church and pray more often than younger individuals, males, and people who live outside of the South.

Spirituality and religion provide the moral code for a community. Traditional African Religion shares some similarities with Christian religions but also differs in many respects.

Research has shown that religious and spiritual beliefs are associated with better coping and better mental and physical health. Religion has been used to both oppress and liberate African Americans. During slavery, Christian doctrine was used to justify slavery and oppression. However, enslaved Africans could relate to Christian messages by identifying with the liberation of Jesus Christ, who was a persecuted and oppressed figure. African American Churches are institutions of both liberation and salvation. Most measures of religion and spirituality have not been developed with African American samples and should be used cautiously. The religious measure from the National Survey of Black Americans is an exception.

9

Self-Attributes and Racial Identity

The fowl does not act like the goat.

—Ghana proverb

The Self-Esteem Fraud: Feel-Good Education Does Not Lead to Academic Success

Nina H. Shokraii
USA Today, January 1998

Self-esteem theory made its first dramatic impact upon American schools in 1954, when the Supreme Court accepted that school segregation damaged the self-esteem of African-American children in its Brown v. Board of Education ruling. Low self-esteem, the Court said, "affects the motivation of a child to learn, and has a tendency to retard children's educational and mental development." According to author Barbara Lemer, this proposition makes three questionable assumptions about Blacks: Low self-esteem is the major cause of low academic achievement; Blacks have a lower self-esteem than Whites; and changing White attitudes toward Blacks will raise Black self-esteem. Taken together, these notions provide the reasoning behind the current repudiation of high standards and expectations in the public schools.

In reality, research reveals that Black children at the same grade level and in the same school system as White children display a higher sense of self-esteem. African-Americans usually report slightly higher levels of agreement with statements about taking a positive attitude toward oneself, judging oneself to be a person "of worth," and being generally satisfied with oneself.

Studies show that, like Whites, enhancement of global self-concept is not a potent intervention for academic improvement for African-American adolescents. Stanley Rothman and his colleagues at Smith College's Center for the Study of Social and Political Change found that, while the self-esteem levels of Blacks now are at least as high as those of Whites, the average academic attainment among African-American students still is below that of Whites. They conclude that the evidence "appears to show quite conclusively that the low self-esteem hypothesis is neither a necessary nor sufficient explanation of African-American achievement levels."

Introduction, Definitions, and Conceptual Framework

As illustrated in Shokraii's article, the study of self-esteem and self-concept has played an important role in the history of African Americans. Although the popular notion that African Americans, because of their history of oppression, suffer from low self-esteem has not been supported, self-attributes such as self-esteem, self-concept, and racial identity have been studied more than any other topic in African American psychology. Not only are these self-attributes interesting to study in their own right, but perhaps more important is the study of the relations between these constructs and the well-being and functioning of African Americans across several domains, including academic and vocational achievement, interpersonal and social relations, and mental and physical health.

We begin this chapter by considering conceptualizations and definitions of the self and identity, with attention to cultural differences therein. Historical and contemporary models of self-concept among African Americans are then discussed. Identity development and change are discussed next, as theory and research show that identity is not static across the life span. We also describe models of racial identity, and we review the research on variables related to high and low levels of racial and ethnic identity. We show that racial socialization and acculturation are cultural constructs that, like racial identity, impact the functioning and well-being of African Americans. Methodological issues related to measuring identity and related constructs are examined, and we end the chapter with a summary.

DEFINING SELF-ESTEEM AND SELF-CONCEPT

The self has been studied extensively in psychology. Many of the early studies in African American psychology were on the topics of self-concept and self-esteem (Clark & Clark, 1939).

Self-concept involves beliefs and knowledge about the self. Our self-concept organizes and manages information about how we see ourselves (Baumeister, 1999). The self-concept is a component of our self-schema. A *self-schema* is a cognitive representation of the self. It organizes how we process information about the self and others (Fiske & Taylor, 1991). A question one may ask relevant to self-concept is, "Can I accomplish a particular task?" In contrast, *self-esteem* is one's affective reaction toward and feeling about oneself that is also evaluative. The question, "Do I like myself?" is a question relevant to self-esteem.

CULTURAL DIFFERENCES IN SELF-CONCEPTUALIZATION

Conceptualization of the self depends on culture and socialization. Cultures can be categorized as *collective,* where people have an interdependent view of the self, or *individualistic,* where people hold an independent view of the self. Interdependent cultures include many from Africa, Asia, and Latin American countries. Independent cultures include the cultures of Europe and the United States. Differences in self-attributes among members of interdependent and independent cultures have been observed (Markus & Kitayama, 1999). Many of these self-attributes are described throughout this book. People of African descent are likely to have interdependent conceptualizations of the self, as are many women, and members of Latino, Asian, and Native American cultural groups.

In interdependent cultures, the self is seen as interdependent with the surrounding social context, and the self is considered in relation to others. This means that one's thinking and acting are influenced by the relevant others in one's social context. For example, if I am a member of an interdependent culture, I cannot make a decision about employment without considering members of my family. Fitting in, attentiveness to others, and harmonious relationships are important.

In individualistic cultures, emphasis is placed on the uniqueness of the self. If I am a member of an individualistic culture, my self-interest and well-being are more likely to direct my thoughts and actions than the well-being of others. In addition, I will be less likely to care about the consequences of my actions for others. I will want to stand out as an individual and not be like other people. An example of cultural differences in self-attributes can be found in commercial advertisements found in interdependent and individualistic cultures. In individualistic cultures, an ad might show how a product can be used to make a person "stand out from the crowd." This ad would appeal to one's need to be separate from others and to be unique. In interdependent cultures, an advertisement might emphasize that others use this product and that the use of this product would make one "fit in."

In interdependent cultures, relationships are important, and maintaining a connection to others means being constantly aware of others' needs, desires, and goals. The assumption here is that one needs to consider the goal of others in order to meet one's own goal.

In summary, one's beliefs and feelings about the self may be linked to one's social group for those from interdependent cultures and less so for those from independent cultures.

SOCIAL IDENTITY

Social identity is that part of an individual's self-concept which is derived from his or her membership in a social group and adherence to the values associated with that group (Tajfel, 1981). Identity may be thought of as an adaptation to a social context (Baumeister & Muraven, 1996). Identity focuses on self-ascribed definitions that include social roles, reputation, values, and possibilities. Social identity may include one's self-concept with relation to nationality, religion, gender, sexual orientation, age, health status, and racial and ethnic identity. The latter two types of identity have been studied extensively among African Americans because of the physical salience of race in the American context.

Conceptualization of identity along racial lines can be contrasted with conceptualization of identity among other salient personal attributes. Racial identity models have most often emphasized that race is the key defining feature of one's social reference group. Salience models assume that race is only one of several other types of referent factors that may determine salience of one's social identity group. Other factors might include ethnicity, religion, sexual orientation, or gender. Whether or not one's identity is based on race or some other attribute, it is likely to be influenced by contextual factors. For example, race is likely to be salient for a lone Black person in a White group, whereas gender is likely to be salient for a lone female in an all-male group.

There is a difference of opinion regarding the terminology that best describes the identity of African Americans. Some scholars prefer the term *racial identity* because race is seen as the single most important aspect of the person's social identity (Helms, 1990). Others prefer the term *ethnic identity* because of the lack of clarity regarding what constitutes a race. Ethnicity is culturally prescribed, whereas race is biologically prescribed.

RACIAL IDENTITY AND ETHNIC IDENTITY

Racial identity is based on the perception of a shared racial history. Helms (1990) defines racial identity as "a sense of group or collective identity based on one's perception that he or she shares a common racial heritage with a particular racial group" (p. 3). Racial group orientation is the psychological attachment to the social category that designates the racial group to which one is a member (Helms, 1990).

Ethnic identity is defined by involvement in the cultural practices and activities of a particular ethnic group and by positive attitudes toward, attachment to, and feelings of belonging to that group (Phinney, 1995).

In this chapter, the usage of one term over the other (i.e., racial identity vs. ethnic identity) corresponds to that of the particular author and literature being cited.

OTHER RELATED CONSTRUCTS

Other constructs are kin to and sometimes confused with racial and ethnic identity. These include acculturation, racial socialization, and

Africentric values. *Acculturation* refers to both individual and group-level changes in behaviors, attitudes, and values that take place over time as two or more cultural groups come into contact (Berry, 1990). *Racial socialization* is a process involving messages and behaviors about race that parents or other members of a person's social context transmit to children and adolescents (Stevenson, 1995). *Africentric values* are the beliefs, attitudes, and worldview that come from people of African descent. Acculturation and racial socialization are discussed later in this chapter. (See Chapter 2 for a discussion of the Africentric worldview.)

Self-Concept Among African Americans

HISTORICAL PERSPECTIVE ON BLACK SELF-CONCEPT

Historically, Blacks in the United States have been described as having a negative self-concept and self-denigration as a result of inferior status in this country. Kardiner and Ovesey (1951, 1962) wrote about the impact of oppression on the self-concept of Blacks. Their classic work, *The Mark of Oppression*, makes the point that Blacks have a negative self-concept because of oppression, discrimination, and inferior status. In another early book on the Negro self-concept, Jean Grambs (1965) explains why "Negroes" perceive themselves as inferior and have negative self-concepts. "The self-concept of the Negro is contaminated by the central fact that it is based on a color-caste complex" (p. 13). "The self-esteem of the Negro is damaged by the overwhelming fact that the world he lives in says, 'White is right; Black is bad'" (p. 15). The author goes on to cite instances of the manifestation of low self-concept including increased Black-on-Black crime, aggression, low levels of educational achievement, and instable household and parenting practices.

A central premise in the landmark *Brown v. Board of Education* (1954) case, which outlawed school segregation, was that Blacks who attended Black schools not only suffered educationally but socially and psychologically from low self-concept; the findings from the "doll" studies conducted by Mamie and Kenneth Clark were cited as evidence of this. Clark and Clark (1939) conducted studies with African American preschool children using dolls as stimulus materials. Children were asked to choose the doll that they would like to play with, the doll that was the prettiest, the doll that was the smartest, and the doll that most looked like them. Children were more likely to select the White doll as the one that they would most like to play with and the one that was the prettiest. A conclusion from this study was that the historical context of separatism and racism had affected the self-esteem and racial identity of Black children.

There were several methodological concerns with this study that later replications have addressed and these later studies have yielded different results concerning Black self-concept. One concern was that asking children to select a doll that is most like them did not taken into account the diversity of complexion among African American children. Lighter complexioned children may see themselves as more similar to the White doll than to the Black doll. Another problem was that the Black dolls were very similar in appearance to the White dolls and only differed in skin color. Additional research (e.g., Cross, 1991; Spencer 1982) has further clarified the distinction between young children's feelings of self-worth and their racial self-awareness and knowledge of cultural biases. Although young children understand racial categories and biases by the time they are of school age, their self-esteem is not directly linked to this awareness and they do not necessarily feel negatively toward themselves.

CONTEMPORARY MODELS OF BLACK SELF-CONCEPT

More affirming models of Black self-concept do not assume that minority status results in negative self-concept. Wade Nobles's (1991) model of the extended self and Adelbert Jenkins's (1995) model of self as an agent of change are two such examples of more affirming models.

According to Nobles, people of African descent have an extended sense of self. The extended self-concept is derived through identification with people of African descent. This self-concept encompasses others that are significant to the individual. One's personal well-being is intricately linked to the well-being of others in the group. The saying "I am because we are, and because we are, I am," (Mbiti, 1991, p. 106) exemplifies this conceptualization of the self. For African Americans, one's self-concept is closely aligned with racial identity and one's sense of connection and identification with members of the group. Using Nobles's model of the self, self-concept will only be high if racial identity is high. In fact, some recent studies have shown this to be the case: High self-concept is associated with high racial identity among adolescents (Townsend & Belgrave, 2000).

Adelbert Jenkins's (1995) model does not centrally consider others key to the self-concept, as does Nobles's (1991). A primary assumption of Jenkins's model is that the self is an active agent. By agent, he means we recognize ourselves as persons who can take action, initiate, and make decisions. The self is a way of talking about our ability to make choices and to shape the course of our lives. This view of the self is a humanistic and empowering view, as it considers the active role that the person plays in shaping and carrying out his or her own destiny. The humanistic model of the self conveys that even under conditions of oppression and discrimination, African Americans are active in shaping their own destiny.

It is possible to consider Jenkins's and Nobles's perspectives as complementary. For example, African Americans may have a sense of being collectively agentic, feeling positive about themselves as members of a group working actively on their own behalf. It is also possible that these perspectives may emphasize specific dimensional aspects of African American personality, with some individuals having a more collective orientation and some having a more agentic emphasis. It might also be possible for individuals to be high (or low) on both dimensions.

Identity Development and Change

The development of identity is a process that involves personal insight and observation of oneself in a social context. The observation might make one realize that members of one's ethnic group are treated differently than members of other ethnic groups. The self-observation may also point out how the behavior of one's ethnic group differs from the behavior of other ethnic groups. As we discuss next, ethnic identity is important and serves many functions. Ethnic identity is not static; it changes throughout the life span.

IDENTITY DEVELOPMENT

Identify formation begins at birth and continues throughout the life course. Early understanding by children of ethnicity and race is mainly derived from the family and the community (Spencer & Markstrom-Adams, 1990). Research and theory suggest that children's understanding of self, ethnicity, and ethnic identity changes developmentally. As children's social cognitive development progresses, they move from understanding and describing themselves based on individual external characteristics to increasingly emphasizing more internal, multidimensional, psychological, and situational factors (Damon & Hart, 1982). American children develop an understanding of racial categories, their group membership, and the broad cultural ascriptions and biases associated with race and ethnicity during their preschool years, and this appears to be shaped in part by their general social cognitive development (Spencer, 1982).

It is during the adolescent years that identity formation is emphasized, as explained by the psychosocial stage theory of Erik Erikson (1963, 1968). With developmental increases in cognitive ability, dramatic physical changes in adolescence, and the impending transition to adulthood, the question of "Who am I?" becomes increasingly important. Identity development is dependent on prior experiences, developmental context, and historical period.

Building on Erikson's perspective of adolescence identity exploration and commitment, Marcia (1966, 1980) articulated four identity statuses for adolescents: achievement, moratorium, foreclosure, and diffusion. African Americans' experiences of these statuses may differ from those of majority youth.

- *Identity achievement* is the status reflecting the exploration of and commitment to an identity. At this stage, adolescents understand and accept who they are in terms of their racial and ethnic background. For example, individuals may refer to themselves as Black and be committed to being African American.

- *Identity moratorium* occurs when there has been or there is an ongoing exploration of identity, but no commitment has been made to a specific identity. Individuals may have some confusion about their ethnicity during this stage. They may know that they are African American but may not necessarily feel committed to this as part of their identity and subsequently may not participate in activities of their ethnic group.

- *Identity foreclosure* is when individuals have clarity about their ethnicity but have not explored their identity. Feelings about their ethnicity may be positive or negative depending on the socialization process. Individuals in this status may be clear that they are African American, but they do not think deeply about what it means to be African American.

- *Identity diffusion* is a status in which the individual has neither explored his or her identity nor developed a clear understanding of identity-related issues. An individual in this stage has not thought about or experienced aspects of being African American.

ETHNIC IDENTITY CHANGE

Situational and environmental factors have an impact on one's ethnic identity. Identity change may occur if an individual moves into a new situation or a new environment, or has a change in life circumstances such as relocation, marriage, new job, new school, and so on. When a new situation is encountered, the individual is prompted to search for a new source of support. The new support may move the individual into another context in which he involves himself in activities and organizations that support that new identity. For example, students starting college previously may have had support for their identity within their community or church environment. However, once in college, they may find support for their identity through greater involvement in Black clubs and organizations. This may especially be the case if they attend a predominately White college. In fact, research has shown that ethnic minority students' feelings of belonging to a group and commitment to their ethnic group increase when they go from a predominately minority community to a predominately White college (Saylor & Aries, 1999).

INCREASING ETHNIC IDENTITY

Ethnic identity serves many functions. Identity (a) provides a sense of group belonging and affiliation; (b) acts as a buffer against stress that may arise from prejudice, racism, and discrimination; and (c) serves as a link to a larger social group. Being part of a group that shares one's history, perspectives, and values is important in developing a positive sense of one's self-worth.

Some of the beneficial aspects of having a positive ethnic identity include higher academic achievement, less drug use and violence, better peer relationships, better coping skills, and higher self-esteem. Because of the positive associations with ethnic identity, there has been a growing movement for programs to increase ethnic identity among ethnic minority youth. These programs seek to increase or improve ethnic identity using culturally appropriate methods and topics.

Rites of Passage Programs

Rites of passage programs have been used as a vehicle for promoting positive identity. Rites of passage have been used in both historical and contemporary times as a mechanism for encouraging youth to develop the attitudes and behaviors necessary for productive citizenship. Many of the rites of passage programs for African Americans are modeled after those in Africa. For example, in some traditional African cultures, male youth are taken away from the village to learn skills that contribute to the survival of the village, for example, hunting and food gathering. Contemporary rites of passage programs do this symbolically by asking parents for permission to take their youth away from their community environment. Generally this is done in a weekend or overnight retreat. Often the youth participants are taken to naturalistic environments outside of their home environment (e.g., farm settings, peaceful retreat, etc.).

In contemporary times, rites of passage programs have been used to provide the structure to promote a change in the lives of participants. Rites of passage programs may help African American youth to clearly define their gender roles, and they may be used to initiate males and females into adult social roles and responsibilities. Rites of passage can be viewed as a developmental progression that separates individuals from their previous identity and facilitates their transition into a new identity that incorporates their new role, responsibilities, and status.

Brookins (1996) describes four stages in a rites of passage program called the Adolescent Developmental Pathway Paradigm (ADPP).

- The first stage is the *preparation and awareness* stage, in which individuals are encouraged to become aware of their personal and ethnic characteristics. There is an initial ceremony that provides information on what is involved in the rites of passage process. During this stage, the beginner is introduced to community members who will serve as adult role models and be responsible for guiding youth through the process.

- The second stage is one of *separation*. During this stage, individuals are provided with opportunities to increase their awareness of the need to develop a new identity. The formal beginning of the transition process begins during this stage. The youth are urged to evaluate previous beliefs, roles, and responsibilities. There may be some anxiety during this stage, as youth are encountering new values and behaviors that may be foreign to them. There are activities designed to help them understand their fear and to begin the official training in the roles and responsibilities for adulthood. Genealogical and ancestral information may be discussed in terms of how it relates to the youth's current situation and their hopes and possibilities for the future. Life-management training sessions may focus on skills, knowledge, and values associated with responsible adulthood, such as careers and social success. Group-based community service projects may be carried out in order to help individuals develop an understanding of the social and political factors within their environment.

- The third stage is the *transition* stage. It is during this stage that adolescents may begin to adapt to new ways of thinking and behaving. They begin to understand their abilities and future possibilities in the vocational, academic, and personal realms. Attitudes and feelings toward their own and other ethnic groups become more salient. During this period, adolescents begin to develop psychological resistance strategies. These strategies are developed through an understanding of the historical struggle of African people and the culturally derived means by which African people have counteracted oppression. These strategies are useful to help African American youth deal with experiences of prejudice and discrimination.

- *Reincorporation* is the final stage, in which the individual and the community acknowledge that the old identity and peer group have been abandoned, and a new identity has developed along with a new support group. During this stage, the community is recognized formally as important and influential to the adolescent.

In summary, rites of passage programs have proven effective in enhancing identity and other positive values and beliefs among African American youth.

Nigrescence Models of Racial Identity

Most racial identity models assume that people progress through phases or stages of identity. Individuals in a particular stage have certain attitudes, beliefs, and behaviors that are distinct from those that emerge within other stages. Nigrescence models of racial identity have been widely studied, although new perspectives on racial identity are emerging.

Nigrescence models take in account the process by which Blacks become aware of being Black in this country. *Nigrescence,* a French term, means "to become Black." Nigrescence models have been developed by African American psychologists, including Charles Thomas, William Cross, Janet Helms, and Thomas Parham. These models provide a template of what happens during each of the stages that African Americans go through to reach racial awareness. Each of these stages is characterized by certain affective, cognitive, and behavioral features. A description of the stages follows (Helms, 1990).

STAGE 1: PRE-ENCOUNTER

In the pre-encounter stage, there is an orientation toward White culture and away from Black culture. People in this stage may feel ashamed and embarrassed about being Black and may hold the values of the White culture. These individuals may feel that Blacks are responsible for their own oppression and fate. Correspondingly, they may hold individualistic views about opportunities, seeing the individual and not the environment as responsible for what happens to people. Individuals in this stage may believe that Blacks who do not do well are responsible for their lack of success and that the historical background of slavery and discrimination are not relevant factors. Individuals in this stage are likely to engage in activities with Whites or activities that they assume are culturally White.

Emotional reactions during this stage may be defensiveness, avoidance, and anxiety. The individual in this stage is looking for acceptance among Whites, which may or may not be available. Compliance and conformity to societal norms are also seen in this stage.

Individuals in this stage may hold beliefs and behaviors that are not overtly anti-Black and pro-White (especially if they want to be seen as politically correct) but which may be inferred from unobtrusive and indirect indicators. This may be seen, for example, when individuals prefer to buy from White merchants over Black merchants and rationalize that the product, the service, or both are better.

STAGE 2: DISSONANCE

During the dissonance or encounter stage, individuals encounter an event or series of events that shatter the perception of themselves or the perception of the conditions of Blacks in America. This experience described as "pulling the rug from under one's feet" (Cross, Parham, & Helms, 1998, p. 9), makes salient the consequences of being Black. An example might be when a person realizes that he cannot buy a house in a certain neighborhood because of his race. Dissonance may also be experienced when an individual is transitioning from one environment to another. This might occur when a person leaves a predominately Black high school to attend a predominately White school. In the transition process, his race becomes salient to himself and to others.

During the dissonance stage, the person begins to wonder what it might be like to have an identity as a Black person. This person may begin reading and seeking out information about Blacks and may begin to question what he had previously believed to be true about Blacks and Whites. The emotional state associated with this stage is one of vigilance and anxiety. The person in this stage is motivated to learn about Blacks and actively seeks out information about being Black. He may begin to read magazines and listen to Black-oriented television shows.

STAGE 3: IMMERSION AND EMERSION

The immersion and emersion stage is characterized by a new way of thinking and a new identity that incorporates being Black. Immersion is the beginning phase and emersion the end phase of this stage. Individuals in this stage may have a glorified perception of the goodness of being Black. Dichotomous thinking comes to the fore: For example, Black is good and White is bad. Persons in this stage want to affiliate only with other Blacks and participate in organizations that are Black. These individuals also attend events and participate in activities that affirm and support the Black identity. The first part of this stage has been described as total immersion into Blackness, with individuals experiencing the emotions of energy and elation. During the second part of this stage, called emersion, there is some leveling off of this energy and elation.

STAGE 4: INTERNALIZATION

During this stage, the individual has internalized a new identity. The conflicts between the old and the new identity have been resolved and the anxiety, emotionality, and defensiveness of the prior stages are gone. The individual feels more calm and secure. This person knows who he is, and he does not have to display his Blackness in order to prove that he is Black. Blacks are still seen as the primary reference group, but friendships and interactions with Whites are possible. Furthermore, persons in the internalization stage do not participate in Black organizations exclusively. Their thinking is more flexible, and they are more tolerant of people from other cultural groups.

STAGE 5: INTERNALIZATION-COMMITMENT

At the fifth stage, called internalization-commitment, the individual possesses all of the characteristics of those in the internalization stage. However, not only does she have a firm self-identity about what it means to be Black, but she also is likely to work for the liberation of all oppressed people. For example, a person in the internalization-commitment stage might work to support the civil rights of other oppressed groups (e.g., gays and lesbians).

ADAPTATIONS AND REFINEMENTS OF NIGRESCENCE THEORY

The Nigrescence theory of racial identity has been modified since its original conceptualization over a quarter of a century ago. These modifications more accurately reflect identity among contemporary African Americans.

Lifespan Development Perspective

Parham (1992a) modified the Nigrescence theory to include a lifespan perspective on racial identity. His adaptation addresses how the stages of racial identity are manifested in three phases of life: (a) late adolescence/early adulthood, (b) midlife, and (c) late adulthood. Each of these phases has a central theme that relates to a particular stage of racial identity. Parham's adaptation of the model accounts for how one would experience Nigrescence during the three developmental periods.

During childhood and late adolescence, parents and the immediate environmental context (e.g., schools, neighborhoods, churches, etc.) have greater influence than during later developmental stages. This means that individuals might be more likely to progress through stages during adolescence and early adulthood. For example, leaving home during late adolescence and going to a new school environment might trigger the dissonance stage. One's immediate sociocontextual environment, close contact and collaborations with other Blacks might also encourage the emersion-immersion stage.

A lifespan approach to identity also recognizes that *recycling* occurs. In recycling, the individual goes back to an earlier completed stage. Parham (1992a) defines recycling as the reinstatement of the racial identity struggle and resolution after having achieved it at an earlier time in one's life.

During midlife, changes and transitions might cause one to reevaluate racial attitudes and return to an earlier stage and/or move forward to another stage. Events such as child rearing, marriage, and new or changing jobs may serve as catalysts for a particular attitude.

The lifespan perspective also assumes that a person's initial identity can be at any of the stages and that it does not always have to begin at the pre-encounter stage. For example, if a child is immersed in a culture of pro-Black activities and beliefs based on his parents and other socialization influences, he may never have held pre-encounter attitudes.

The lifespan perspective on Nigrescence holds that identity resolution can occur in one of three ways: (a) stagnation or failure to move beyond one initial identity stage, (b) through the sequential linear stage progression described previously, and (c) by recycling.

Multidimensional Model of Racial Identity

In contrast to stage or developmental models, Sellers and colleagues (Sellers, Rowley, Chavous, Shelton, & Smith, 1997) have developed a model that emphasizes the multidimensional nature of racial identity. The multidimensional model of racial identity (MMRI) builds on symbolic interactionism and outlines four primary dimensions of racial identity: salience, centrality, ideology, and regard. *Salience* involves the extent to which individuals emphasize race as an important dimension of their self-concept at a specific point in time. Sellers and colleagues note that the salience of racial identity may vary over time and from situation to situation. *Centrality* refers to the extent that race is core to individuals' self-concept and how they normally define themselves. *Ideology* is the third dimension of the MMRI and describes four different sets of beliefs and attitudes: (a) nationalist, (b) oppressed minority, (c) assimilationist, and (d) humanist. The nationalist perspective emphasizes "the importance and uniqueness of being of African descent." The oppressed minority ideology focuses on oppression and commonalities with other oppressed groups. The assimilationist perspective emphasizes "commonalities between African Americans and the rest of American society." Finally, the humanist perspective underlines "the commonalities of all humans." The fourth dimension of identity, *regard*, involves both the individuals' feeling about group membership (private regard) and their sense of others' evaluations and feelings about their group (public regard). This model seeks to address a variety of research and conceptual issues on racial identity. We discuss the Multidimensional Inventory of Black Identity (MIBI), which is based on the MMRI, later in the chapter.

Correlates of Self-Concept and Racial Identity

There are causes and effects of having high and low self-concept and racial identity. We discuss next the relationship between racial identity and own-group preference and then the relationship between racial and ethnic identity and other variables.

RACIAL IDENTITY AND OWN-GROUP PREFERENCES

Individuals in the pre-encounter stage compared with the other stages are more likely to have anti-Black attitudes. These individuals are more likely to be mistrusting of other Blacks, to affiliate less with other Blacks, and to blame Blacks for their predicament. Blacks in the pre-encounter stage also have a stronger desire to assimilate within White cultures than do Blacks in other stages (Helms, 1990).

A study found that racial identity attitudes are related to Africentric values such as harmony with nature and positive social relations (Carter & Helms, 1987). Racial identity attitudes are not related to Eurocentric values such as mastery over natural forces and individualism. Immersion/emersion and internalization are associated with group-oriented beliefs and social relations. Internalization attitudes are associated with a belief in harmony and nature. Persons with pre-encounter and internalization attitudes are less anti-White while high immersion/emersion attitudes show more hostility and anti-White attitudes.

Persons in the transitional immersion/emersion stage have been found to engage in behaviors that separate themselves from the White world. Individuals with these attitudes show an outward presentation of Blackness. Their outward presentation includes hairstyles, clothing, speech patterns, value system, and self-designation (e.g., changing one's name to an African name). Individuals high in the immersion/emersion stage are rejecting of White colleges and institutions but accepting of all Black colleges and institutions (Helms, 1990).

RACIAL IDENTITY AND RACIAL SELF-DESIGNATION

Racial self-designation is one's preferred self-referent, or the name with which one labels oneself. African Americans have been labeled colored, Negro, black, Black, Afro-American, and African American. Does an individual's racial consciousness relate to how she defines her racial group? Speight, Vera, and Derrickson (1996) addressed this question using a community and college student sample. The authors examined the relationship between racial identity attitudes, self-esteem, and racial self-designation. The age of the sample ranged from 17 to 32 years old. The majority, 49%, preferred the label *Black*, followed by 30% who favored *African American*. Sixteen percent chose the term *Afro-American* and 6.5% the term *American*. Five percent chose other terms (3% *Other*, 1.3% *Negro*, and 0.9% *African*). Those who chose the term *Black* did not have a particular reason or value for this preference. Those who preferred the term *African American* appeared to do so for symbolic reasons. *African American* tended to be chosen as a term that showed a sign of empowerment and political consciousness. Respondents who chose the term *Afro-American* did so primarily because of heritage. The term *American* was selected to de-emphasize race and to reflect an American heritage.

Racial identity attitudes were related to racial self-designation. Persons with higher pre-encounter attitudes were more likely to use labels such as *Other, American,* and *Black.* Speight et al. (1996) speculated that individuals with pre-encounter attitudes would be reluctant to embrace the label *African American* because being Black is not salient to their identity and also because they do not want to emphasize the connection with Africa. Individuals with high immersion/emersion scores were more likely to choose the term *African American* because of the relevance of African descent to their identity.

RACIAL IDENTITY STAGES AND DEMOGRAPHIC VARIABLES

Several studies have examined the Nigrescence stages of racial identity (described previously) and their correlations with demographic variables. One question is whether or not certain demographic factors are more likely to be found among persons in a specific racial identity status. A study that used data from the National Survey of Black Americans (NSBA) and the National Election Panel Study (NEPS) addressed this question (Hyers, 2001). The authors found that some demographic variables correlated with different identity stages. Respondents were classified into one of three racial identity types—pre-encounter, immersion, or internalization—based on their responses to questions on the NSBA and the NEPS. Persons were classified into the pre-encounter stage if they answered yes to a question such as, "Do you think what happens generally to Black people in this country will have something to do with what happens in your life?" An immersion-type question was, "How much say or power do you think Black people have in American life and in politics?" A question aimed at internalization was, "How close do you feel in your ideals and feelings to White people in this country?" The study found that most of the respondents (80% in the NEPS and 84% in the NSBA) could be classified into the pre-encounter, immersion, and internalization stages. The percentage categorized as pre-encounter in the NEPS survey was 44% and in the NSBA survey 35%. Immersion types represented 16% of the NEPS sample and 21% of the NSBA sample. The internalization types represented 40% of the NEPS sample and 28% of the NSBA sample.

The findings indicated that socioeconomic status is a predictor of identity status. Less educated and lower income respondents were more likely to be in the pre-encounter than the immersion stage. In addition, respondents in the NEPS from urban areas were more likely to be in the pre-encounter than in the immersion stage. Data from the NEPS showed that men and older participants were more likely to be in the internalization than in the immersion stage.

Individuals classified in the pre-encounter stage were the least likely to blame the system for the problems Black people had, most likely to have White friends, and least likely to self-label as Black. Those in the pre-encounter stage, compared with those in the immersion and internalization stages, were least likely to report experiencing racism or having a family member who had experienced racism, and were least likely to report feeling discriminated against in hiring and other situations. Regarding psychological well-being, individuals in pre-encounter were the most satisfied, those in internalization were the second most satisfied, and individuals classified within immersion were the least satisfied with their lives. While pre-encounter types reported high psychological well-being, they had the lowest level of global self-esteem. This may be because self-esteem has been linked to high ethnic identity. Internalization types had the highest level of global self-esteem.

RACIAL IDENTITY STAGES AND MORAL REASONING

Stages of racial identity functioning also seem to be related to moral reasoning. Moral reasoning is the evaluation of the "goodness" or the "rightness" of a particular behavior or choice. It helps to explain why some people behave as they do. Moreland and Leach (2001) administered the Defining Issues Text (a measure of morality) and the Racial Identity Attitude Scale to African American college students. They found that less mature racial identity attitudes (i.e., pre-encounter attitudes) were related to less mature moral reasoning. Persons with more developed racial identity attitudes (i.e., internalization attitudes) had more highly developed moral reasoning. Immersion attitudes were also associated with less mature moral reasoning. Immersion attitudes glorify Black values and standards and reject beliefs and values perceived to be White. These individuals would selectively perceive their environment and may therefore be less likely to make objective moral decisions.

ETHNIC IDENTITY AND ACADEMIC ACHIEVEMENT

Findings regarding the relationship between ethnic identity and school achievement are mixed. On the one hand, high ethnic identity should foster achievement-related activities, such as studying and affiliating with peers who have high academic success. On the other hand, Fordham and Ogbu (1986) note that high achievement among African American youth may be viewed as "acting White" by their peers. For some, high achievement may be seen as selling out the Black culture. This occurs when students do not see academic achievement as a core-defining attribute for themselves and their peers; consequently, high academic achievement is not a positive accomplishment. Research findings and conceptual perspectives on this issue have varied.

This purported devaluing of educational achievement has a historical context. Historically, White America has doubted Blacks' capabilities to perform well, and some Blacks subsequently bought into this, doubting their own capabilities. In order to maintain self-esteem, Blacks have thereby defined success for Whites as school achievement and defined success for Blacks based on other attributes. From this perspective, students who are strongly connected to their culture and who have high racial identity may not be successful in school.

This finding was confirmed in a study that found that high school students with high dissonance and immersion attitudes had a lower grade point average. Involving oneself strongly in the Black culture is a central feature of the immersion attitudes. Some Black students may fear that successful academic achievement associated with White behavior (Witherspoon, Speight, & Thomas, 1997). This may be especially so for males, who are more likely to have immersion attitudes than are females. The reaction of teachers and others in the learning environment that Black males are hostile may also be a contributor to the association between immersion attitudes and not valuing academic success.

In contrast, Spencer, Noll, Stolzfus, and Harpalani (2001) found African American youth who scored high on Eurocentric identity to have lower academic achievement and those higher in Africentric identity to have higher achievement. Spencer and colleagues challenged the "acting White" hypothesis, noting empirical and conceptual work in several areas that challenge this hypothesis. These include important individual differences among African Americans in their conceptions of identity, the role of biculturality and code switching in negotiating American culture, and positive youth and parental values on education among African Americans.

The relationship between ethnic identity and academic achievement for males and females may also be better understood by examining the unique components of ethnic identity (Oyserman, Harrison, & Bybee, 2001). Separating the components of ethnic identity helps to explain how ethnic identity relates to academic achievement among males and females. One component of ethnic identity includes positive in-group identification that involves having a positive sense of connection to the common fate of Black people. This component makes salient group norms and practices. A second component is the awareness of negative out-group perception. This component involves being aware that others are likely to see Blacks as members of a negatively valued group. This component of ethnic identity may help by providing a framework for understanding others' negative responses but can also have a negative impact on academic self-efficacy by making salient others' negative expectations. For some youth, this may be a component that adds to stereotype vulnerability, that is, the greater risk of having lower performance in performance situations where racial stereotypes regarding achievement are made salient (Steele, 1992). The third component, labeled "viewing academic achievement as part of one's ethnic identity," focuses on the extent to which one's academic achievement is seen as important to or embedded in one's racial-ethnic group. This component may focus attention and motivation on doing well and succeeding. There are gender differences in how these components of ethnic identity relate to academic achievement. The achievement component of ethnic identity might be more salient for females because having beliefs that academic achievement is important to Blacks may serve as a buffer even when the awareness of racism is high. On the other hand, the connectedness component of racial identity might be most beneficial for helping males to achieve academically.

ETHNIC IDENTITY AND PROBLEM BEHAVIORS

Several studies have examined ethnic identity in relation to problem behaviors including drug use, risky sexual activity, juvenile delinquency, and violence. Much of this research has been conducted with adolescents. These studies have generally found ethnic identity to be a protective factor for youth. Ethnic identity provides an alternative to poor behaviors and a more appropriate way of resisting negative forces that lead to problem behaviors.

There are several other ways in which positive ethnic identity protects against problem behaviors (Brook, Balka, Brook, Win, & Gursen, 1998). One way is that a positive ethnic identity may support adolescents' identification with their parents. Identification with parents in turn leads to better problem-solving skills. Rather than seeking approval from deviant peers, adolescents seek and receive support from parents. This support may also include socialization in culturally sanctioned, prosocial coping strategies.

Another way that high ethnic identity protects against problem behaviors is that high ethnic identity buffers against poor self-esteem that could be a risk factor for drug use and other problem behaviors. Youth with high ethnic identity are not likely to have poor self-esteem and feelings of incompetence, which lead to problem behaviors.

Acculturation and Racial Socialization

ACCULTURATION

Acculturation refers to the extent to which ethnic minorities participate in the cultural traditions, values, beliefs, and practices of their own culture versus the mainstream White culture (Landrine & Klonoff, 1996a). Ethnic minorities function on an acculturation continuum, with *traditional* on one end and *acculturated* on the other end. In the middle are those who are bicultural. Traditional individuals retain the values, beliefs, and practices of their indigenous cultural group. Individuals who are highly acculturated have assimilated the beliefs and behaviors of the majority White culture. Bicultural individuals hold the beliefs and practice the behaviors of their traditional culture but have also assimilated White beliefs and practices.

In a series of studies, Landrine and Klonoff (1996a) investigated the relationship between acculturation and mental health, physical health, and other variables among African Americans. They report that acculturation is associated with the amount of racism experienced, with more traditional African Americans experiencing more racism than more acculturated African Americans. Racism in turn predicts health-related problems such as smoking and hypertension.

In looking at the relationship between acculturation and mental health problems, Landrine and Klonoff (1996a) found that predictors of poor mental health (i.e., depression, anxiety, obsession-compulsion) differed for acculturated and traditional persons. Acculturated persons tended to blame themselves and to take responsibility for their problems, whereas traditional people tended to deny and avoid their problems. Acculturated persons also tended to appraise their everyday stress at higher levels. In general, mental health symptoms among acculturated African Americans are related to self-blaming and ordinary stressors, whereas symptoms among traditional African Americans are associated with denial of problems.

RACIAL SOCIALIZATION

One process that supports ethnic identity development is racial socialization. Racial socialization involves messages and practices that provide information concerning one's race as it relates to (a) personal and group identity, (b) intergroup and interindividual relationships, and (c) position in the social hierarchy (Thornton, Chatters, Taylor, & Allen, 1990). Racial socialization is the process by which messages are communicated to children to bolster their sense of identity in light of the fact that their life experiences may include racially hostile encounters (Stevenson, 1995). Racial socialization messages are more likely communicated by mothers than by fathers and by married parents than by never-married parents. Also, older and more educated parents provide more racial socialization messages than do younger and less educated parents. Those who live in more racially mixed neighborhoods are more likely to provide racial socialization messages than those who live in predominately African American neighborhoods.

What are the types of socialization that parents provide? Parents socialize their children in several ways. Parents may socialize their children into the mainstream of American society, they socialize them as to their minority status in the country, and they socialize them to their Black culture (Thornton, 1997).

Different types of socialization experiences promote different messages. When parents socialize their children regarding minority status, they may socialize them to, for example, "Accept your color." Mainstream socialization messages might say something like, "Hard work will pay off in a good life." Parents who provide socialization messages related to the Black experience might convey to their children, "It is important to study Black culture and history."

These socialization experiences affect children's psychosocial and academic development. For example, children who are aware of racism and racial barriers may perform better than those who are not. Sanders (1997) found that students who have a strong awareness of racism show increased academic motivation and effort.

In general, children of parents who report higher ethnic socialization are more likely to have a racial identity that questions the majority standards and values. These children are more likely to value being African American and participate in African American experiences and activities. In addition, they are more prepared for and less likely to be adversely affected by racist and discriminatory practices.

There are some gender differences in the racial socialization messages parents provide to their children. Parents tend to emphasize racial pride for girls and racial barriers for boys (Thomas & Speight, 1999).

Parents want girls to be proud of being Black. They want their boys to understand that they will be discriminated against. Gender differences in socialization messages may be due in part to realistic barriers for African American males.

Methodological Issues

Methodological issues center on the conceptualization and measurement of self and identity constructs. One issue is clarification of the components of the self that are important to the well-being of African Americans. The importance of measuring certain components of the self is discussed in this section. A second issue is clarity regarding racial and ethnic identity constructs. Although the terms *racial identity* and *ethnic identity* are often used interchangeably, they are different constructs and require different measures. In this section, we review measures of both racial identity and ethnic identity, along with measures of racial socialization and acculturation.

COMPLEXITY AND MEASUREMENT OF SELF-CONCEPT

Findings from studies that have investigated the relationship between self-concept and other variables have been mixed. Some studies have found that self-concept is not related to academic performance, mental health, and problem behaviors (e.g., violence, drug use), whereas others have found positive relationships. Closer examination of how self-concept is measured shows that global measures of self-concept are not correlated with these variables, but domain-specific measures of self-concept are. For example, in a study using a sample of African American youth, global self-concept was not related to risky drug attitudes and behavior but self-concept in the social and interpersonal domain was (Townsend & Belgrave, 2000). High self-concept in the social and interpersonal domains was related to less risky drug behavior. Other studies have similarly shown that social and physical (e.g., athletic) aspects of self-concept are correlated with social and psychological well-being for African American youth, especially males (Whaley, 1993). In general, what the literature suggests is that measures of self-concept for African Americans should be domain specific and not global.

MEASURES OF RACIAL AND ETHNIC IDENTITY

Several good measures of racial and ethnic identity and related constructs exist for both adolescent and adult populations.

The Racial Attitudes Identity Scale (RAIS), developed by Janet Helms (1990), is the most widely used racial identity scale for adults. There are four subscales of the RAIS that correspond to the racial identity attitudes described previously. An example of a pre-encounter item is "I feel very uncomfortable around Black people." A dissonance item is "I find myself reading a lot of Black literature and thinking about being Black." An immersion item is "I believe that everything Black is good, and consequently, limit myself to Black activities." An internalization item is "People, regardless of their race, have strengths and limitations." The 50-item scale uses a Likert format whereby respondents indicate the degree of agreement from 1 = *strongly disagree* to 5 = *strongly agree.*

The Multi-Ethnic Identity Measure (MEIM) is a measure of ethnic identity and not racial identity. The MEIM was developed to measure ethnic identity in ethnically diverse populations. It has been extensively used with several ethnic minority adolescent populations. The measure assesses young people's identification with unique characteristics of their ethnic group (Phinney, 1992).

The three subscales of the MEIM include (a) affirmation and belonging, (b) ethnic identity achievement, and (c) ethnic behaviors. There are

14 items on a 4-point scale that goes from *strongly agree* to *strongly disagree*. An example of an item that measures affirmation and belonging is "I am happy to be a member of the group I belong to." An item that measures ethnic identity achievement is "In order to learn more about my ethnic background, I have often talked to other people about my ethnic group." An ethnic behaviors item is "I am active in organizations or social groups that include mostly members of my own ethnic group." Respondents are also asked to indicate their ethnicity and the ethnicity of their mother and father.

Smith and Brookins (1997) developed a measure of ethnic identity specifically for African American youth. The Multi-Construct African American Identity Questionnaire (MCAIQ) is used with youth from 11 to 18 years of age. Four components of ethnic identity are included in the measure. The social orientation subscale assesses the youths' affinity toward socializing with their own or other racial and ethnic groups. An item from this subscale is "I prefer White friends." The appearance orientation subscale assesses the values regarding physical characteristics ("Black is beautiful"). The attitudinal subscale assesses the degree to which respondents accept or reject stereotypical portrayals of African Americans ("Blacks can do anything if they try"). The other group orientation subscale assesses preferences for working with people other than Blacks ("I like working with other people better").

The Multidimensional Inventory of Black Identity (MIBI) is based on the Multidimensional Model of Racial Identity (MMRI) and has 56 items assessing three stable dimensions of racial identity: centrality, ideology, and regard (Sellers et al., 1997). Centrality is measured with 8 items (e.g., "Being Black is important to my self-image"). Regard is measured using two subscales: a 6-item scale for Private Regard (e.g, "I feel good about Black people") and a 6-item scale measuring Public Regard (e.g., "Overall, Blacks are considered good by others"). There are four scales, each with 9 items, examining Ideology. These subscales include Assimilation (e.g., "Blacks should try to work within the system to achieve their political and economic goals"), Humanism (e.g., "Blacks would be better off if they were more concerned with problems facing all people than just focusing on Black people"), Minority (e.g., "The same forces that have led to the oppression of Blacks have led to the oppression of other groups"), and Nationalism (e.g., "White people can never be trusted where Blacks are concerned").

The African Self-Consciousness Scale (ASC) is an Africentric measure of Black self-concept. While it is generally considered a measure of Black personality, it also measures racial identity. The ASC has 42 items and uses an 8-point Likert scale. There are four subscales that correspond to the four components of African self-consciousness identified by Kambon (1998): (a) awareness and recognition of one's African identity and heritage; (b) general beliefs and activity priorities for African survival, liberation, self-knowledge, and affirmation; (c) collective African survival through the practices of

Africentric values and customs; and (d) a position of resistance toward anti-African and anti-Black forces. (For more details, see Chapter 2.)

MEASURES OF OTHER CULTURAL CONSTRUCTS

Acculturation Measure

The African American Acculturation Scale is a widely used scale that measures acculturation among African Americans (Landrine & Klonoff, 1994). The 74-item scale has several subscales:

1. Preference for African American Things ("I try to watch all the Black shows on TV")

2. Traditional Family Practices and Values ("I often lend money or give other types of support to members of my family")

3. Traditional Health Beliefs, Practices, and Folk Disorders ("Some people in my family use Epsom salts")

4. Traditional Socialization ("When I was young, I was a member of a Black Church")

5. Traditional Foods and Food Practices ("I eat a lot of fried foods")

6. Religious Beliefs and Practices ("I like gospel music")

7. Interracial Attitudes ("Whites don't understand Blacks")

8. Superstitions ("What goes around comes around")

A shorter version of the scale, with 33 items, also exists (Landrine & Klonoff, 1995).

Racial Socialization Measure

Racial socialization has been studied by asking adolescents what messages they have received from parents and grandparents. Stevenson (1995) developed a 45-item Racial Socialization Scale that measures these processes. The scale is used with adolescents and has four components. The spiritual and religious coping component includes items about messages that recognize spirituality and religion as helpful to surviving life's experiences. A second component is extended family care. These items express attitudes and interactions that promote the role of extended and immediate family as serving a child-rearing and caring function. A third component is teaching of African American history, culture, and pride to children. This component is called cultural pride reinforcement. The fourth component is racism awareness teaching. These items focus on messages and attitudes that promote cautious and preparatory views regarding the presence of racism in society. In addition to the adolescent scale, there is a recently developed parental racial socialization scale.

Summary

The study of self-attributes such as self-esteem, self-concept, and racial and ethnic identity has a long-standing history in African American psychology. Aspects of the self relate to well-being and functioning across several domains.

Self-concept is knowledge about and beliefs about the self, and self-esteem is one's evaluation of the self. Conceptualization of the self depends on culture and socialization experiences. Racial identity is group or collective identity based on one's perception that he or she shares a common racial heritage with a particular racial group. Ethnic identity is defined by involvement in the cultural practices and activities of one's ethnic group and by positive attitudes toward, attachment to, and feelings of belonging to one's group. Acculturation refers to both individual and group-level changes in behaviors, attitudes, and values that take place over time as two or more cultural groups come into contact. Racial socialization involves messages and behaviors about race that parents and others transmit to children.

Historically, Blacks in this country were described as having a negative self-concept and were believed to engage in self-denigration as a result of inferior status in this country. However, more contemporary models of Black self-concept are affirming and indicate that the self-concept of African Americans is not negative. Both Nobles's (1991) model of the extended self and A. H. Jenkins's (1995) model of the self as an agent of change convey positive conceptualizations of the self-concept of African Americans. The development of identity is a process that involves personal insight and observation of oneself in a social context. Nigrescence models are the most common models of racial identity. Nigrescence models account for what happens during each of the stages through which African Americans go through to reach racial awareness. New models emphasize that there are multiple dimensions important to understanding racial identity. In general, studies have found that high ethnic identity is associated with better self-concept, better mental health, higher achievement, and fewer problem behaviors.

There are several good measures of racial and ethnic identity as well as acculturation and racial socialization.

The African proverb "The fowl does not act like the goat" implies important lessons about what it means to be African American in our commonality, in our uniqueness, and with our individual differences.

Lifespan
Development 10

One is born, one dies: the land increases.

—Ethiopian proverb

Death Toll for Black Children Perplexing
Premature Births Boost County Rate

By Matt Leingang
The Cincinnati Enquirer

Friday, May 14, 2004

Premature births among African-Americans drove up the number of child fatalities in Hamilton County last year, according to a report to be released today.

A total of 145 children in the county died in 2003, up from 138 in 2002 and the second-highest total since the report began eight years ago. The record is 153 in 1998. While the report did not specifically look at child deaths in other Ohio metropolitan areas last year, Hamilton County's overall infant mortality rate for African-Americans is believed to be among the highest in the state.

Experts continue to struggle to understand why. The Hamilton County Child Fatality Review Team documents the cause of death of all children in the county 17 or younger. The goal is to identify causes that may be preventable.

The majority of child deaths in 2003—75 percent—were from natural causes, a category that includes prematurity, medical disorders and infection. But prematurity is where the story lies. Of the 64 infants dying prematurely, 56 percent were African-American. This is disproportionate to the percentage of African-Americans in the county's overall population (23 percent).

"There are a lot of programs in Hamilton County that do outreach and provide prenatal care and other support services, but we never seem to make a dent in this. It's really disconcerting," said Patricia Eber, executive director of the Family and Children First Council and chair of the fatality review team.

Racial disparity in childhood deaths has been an issue nationwide. But data from the Ohio Department of Health shows how severe the local problem is. For example, the overall infant mortality rate for African-Americans in Hamilton County was 19.5 per 1,000 live births in 2001, the latest data available. For Cuyahoga and Franklin counties, it was 13.2. "Those cities (Cleveland and Columbus) have the same risk factors that we do, and it's just amazing that our problem is so much worse," Eber said. Risk factors include poverty, lack of prenatal care, maternal smoking, substance abuse and poor nutrition.

In terms of deaths that could have been prevented, the fatality team reviewed 53 cases where the cause of death was unintentional injury, homicide, suicide or undetermined. Of these, 51 percent were deemed preventable. For example, inappropriate sleeping arrangements were linked to 12 infant deaths last year. Eber said infants should always be placed in cribs and not in adult beds or couches, where loose blankets or pillows can suffocate children.

Other preventable deaths were linked to traffic accidents, drownings, poisonings and a handgun.

The team emphasized the importance of:

- Wearing seat belts.
- Close supervision of toddlers and infants.
- Taking seriously threats of teen suicide or violence.

The team includes representatives of the Cincinnati Health Department, the county coroner's office, the Cincinnati Fire Department, and Children's Hospital.

Used with permission from the *Cincinatti Enquirer* and Matt Leinlgang.

Introduction and Definitions

When we look at newborns, hear their first cries, count their fingers and toes, and check the color of their ears, we can imagine with hope and wonder who these little persons will become. All too soon, they will crawl, stand, talk, walk, run, ride a bike, and learn to read. They will go to school and be asked, "What do you want to be when you grow up?" Their world will grow from that of their families to the neighborhood and peers, and with technology, they may gain a sense of their place in the global community. They will grow larger and larger and will increasingly learn who they are and who they want to be. They will rely less and less on parents and form increasingly important friendships. They will face many choices. Should I go to college? What kind of career should I have? Should I get married? Have kids? As adults, who have this little people become, and as they enter their maturity and as they look at their lives, how will they assess them? How will the community use and respect their knowledge as elders and care and support them as they age?

Developmental psychology is the study of the physical, emotional, cognitive, and behavioral changes in humans, beginning at conception and continuing through death. This field of study describes and explains the processes and phenomena that shape our behavior and experience across our lives. Over the past two and a half decades, developmental psychology has increasingly moved from a primary focus on development during childhood and adolescence to include a *lifespan* perspective. That is, to examine developmental changes that occur across the entire life course, ranging from prenatal influences through older age.

In considering the development of African Americans, we seek to understand the unique features of their developmental experience. How do culture, history, and social forces shape the contexts in which African Americans live, grow, and develop? What roles do family, school, and neighborhood play in the development of African Americans? What challenges are faced, and how do we define positive developmental outcomes? As illustrated in the news article that opens this chapter, we are concerned with how well African American infants, children, adults, and seniors fare at each age of development.

In this chapter, we first define key concepts in lifespan development and then describe the population of African Americans from a demographic perspective. Next, we discuss theories that can help us to understand the development of Americans of African descent, and we provide a snapshot of African Americans at different developmental periods. We raise methodological issues to consider in reviewing or conducting research with African Americans and end the chapter with a summary.

On some level, we can consider most of this book to be an examination of the development of African Americans. When we consider development, we often look at the contexts within which an individual develops. Many of these settings, such as family, schools, peer relationships, and religious institutions, are addressed in detail within other chapters in this book.

Developmental psychology is also interested in the processes that are important in understanding change, stability, and growth. These processes may include learning and cognitive development, gaining a sense of self and identity, developing the capacity for intimacy and entering relationships, and achieving at school or in the workplace. We can also expand our understanding of development by considering a range of positive and negative developmental outcomes, such as well-being or compromises in health, or engagement in destructive behavior such as violence or drug use.

We cover many of these issues—including education, family, neighborhood context, identity development and adjustment—in other chapters. In this chapter, we provide a select overview of important developmental issues for African Americans in infancy, middle childhood, and adolescence and among older adults.

DEFINITIONS AND KEY CONCEPTS

Within a developmental perspective, several processes are central. For example, *maturation* is the genetically directed set of biologically sequenced changes that shape our physical and behavioral development and our movement from embryo to mature adult. *Ontogeny* similarly refers to the development and unfolding of an individual's life. Developmental psychology has struggled with nature versus nurture questions and has focused considerable attention on understanding both genetic and environmental contributions to individual development. This work attempts to understand how much our genetic makeup (i.e., *genotype*) contributes to our actual *phenotype,* that is the unique person we become.

The study of developmental psychology involves our attempt to understand humans' physical development and the impact of social contexts (such as families, peers, communities) on that development. It studies how our emotional, cognitive, and social capacities develop and shape the direction of our lives. This direction can be toward positive outcomes (e.g., good physical health, school achievement, successful employment) or it can be toward more challenges (e.g., problems with drugs and alcohol, school failure, and mental health challenges).

African Americans are an incredibly diverse group. Male, female. Young, old. Baptist, Muslim, Atheist, and Buddhist. Rich, middle class, and poor. The study of the development of African Americans can assist us in understanding the development of subgroups. However, much of the available literature is based on between-group comparisons that help us see, on average, how African Americans compare in developmental processes and outcomes with members of other groups. We must take care to understand that taking an average for over 30 million people does not capture the diversity within the African American community, but it allows us to make broad comparisons between ethnic groups.

Demographics

To assist us in understanding the development of African Americans, we will provide a demographic portrait of African Americans in different age-groups. Demography is the descriptive study of human populations, including change over time and distribution. It uses a range of indicators (e.g., income, educational achievement, health data) to allow us to understand how various groups compare on these various indicators. Differences across groups can help us to understand where there may be particular challenges, the need for intervention or the direction of resources, or the need for additional study to further our understanding of these differences.

LIFE EXPECTANCY AND AGE OF THE AFRICAN AMERICAN POPULATION

Of U.S. residents counted in the 2000 U. S. Census, 12.9 % (or 34.9 million) indicate that they are African American or African American in combination with one or more other races (McKinnon, 2001).

Table 10.1   Percentages of the Population by Age and Ethnic Group

Age	% Black Males	% White Males	% Black Females	% White Females
Under 5	9.1	6.5	8.0	5.9
5–9	10.3	6.9	8.5	6.3
10–19	19.4	14.0	16.7	12.7
20–29	14.3	12.5	15.4	12.1
30–44	23.1	23.9	23.8	23.0
45–64	17.2	23.9	18.9	24.1
65 and Up	6.6	12.2	8.8	15.8

Source: U.S. Census Bureau (2001).

For an African American infant born in 2002, life expectancy is 72.5 years, compared with a life expectancy of 77.8 years for a White infant born at the same time (Kochanek & Smith, 2004).

The African American population tends to be younger than non-Hispanic Whites although somewhat older than members of other racial groups combined (e.g., Asians, Hispanics, and Native Americans). For example, as illustrated in Table 10.1, whereas approximately a third of African American males and females are 19 years old or younger, only a quarter or less of European American males and females are in this age-group. In contrast, although over a third of European American males and females are 45 or older, approximately a quarter or less of African American males and females are in this age-group. What factors may account for these variations?

In later sections of this chapter, we consider factors such as reproductive, birth, and death rates among different age-groups that can help us better understand these ethnic variations in age-group composition. These variations are also important in considering the developmental function of different age-groups within a community. What are the advantages and disadvantages of having an overall younger population? What are the implications for the survival of the group? What are the implications for the demands placed on adults raising a relatively large cohort of youth? What are the losses from having fewer seniors available to support and provide wisdom and guidance to the community?

CHILDBIRTHS

Demographic data can help us understand reproductive trends among African Americans. We can consider a range of questions: Are Blacks having more or fewer children? How old do Blacks tend to be when they become parents? Are there changes in the number of African American births?

Demographic data indicate that the number of births among African American women declined from 95.5 per 1,000 in 1970 to 77.0 per 1,000 in 1985. There was an increase in the birthrate during the early 1990s (with a rate of 90.5 births per 1,000 in 1990) and a reduction continuing through 2001 (68.2 births per 1,000 in 2001). Nonmarital births across this same time period showed an increase from 37.5 per 1,000 in 1970 to 69.9 per 1,000 by 1995 and remaining relatively stable through 2001 (68.4 per 1,000). Teen pregnancy rates dropped 29% for African American adolescent females aged 15 to 19 between 1992 and 2000 after peaking in the United States at 116 per 1,000 for African American adolescents in 1991. Still the rate of teen pregnancy among African American adolescent females (153 per 1,000 aged 15 to 19 years old in 2000) is almost triple that of non-Hispanic Whites (55 per 1,000; Alan Guttmacher Institute, 2004).

In 1997, 40.6 out of 1,000 African Americans aged 15 to 17 years old and 96.7 out of 1,000 of those aged 18 to 19 years old ended their pregnancies through abortions, rates lower than those reported in 1990 (57.7 and 117.4, respectively). In comparison in 1997, rates of abortion among non-Hispanic White women aged 15 to 17 were 11.6 per 1,000 and 28.4 per 1,000 for 18- to 19-year-olds (Ventura, Mosher, Curtin, Abma, & Henshaw, 2001).

The high rate of births among unmarried parents and earlier timing of births among African Americans have negative effects on both the educational outcome for the mother (Klepinger, Lundberg, & Plotnick, 1995) and developmental outcome for the infant (Levine, Pollack, & Comfort, 2001; Mathews, Curtin, & MacDorman, 2000; Moore, Morrison, & Greene, 1997). These earlier births and higher rates of single-parent families among African Americans can also have important implications for the extended family and result in higher rates of intergenerational caregiving and child rearing. Various reasons for the earlier timing of childbearing have been offered, including young women's concerns about their health and capacity to reproduce if they delay childbearing (Geronimus, 1991, 1996).

INFANT MORTALITY

Although infant mortality rates have declined for African Americans over the past 20 years (from 22.2 per 1,000 pregnancies in 1980 to 14.0 per 1,000 pregnancies in 2000), the rate for African Americans still remains over twice that for Whites (5.9 per 1,000; Centers for Disease Control and Prevention [CDC], 2002b).

Infant mortality rates are disproportionately high in urban communities. A study of the 60 largest U.S. cities indicates that higher rates of infant mortality are associated with higher proportions of births to African American mothers, higher rates of teenage birth, lack of or delayed prenatal care, and racial segregation (Anderson & Smith, 2003). African American infants are born with low birth weight (LBW [i.e., less than 2,500 grams]) twice as often (13.0 LBW per 1,000) as White infants (6.5 per

1,000 live births; CDC, 2002b). LBW rates among African Americans raise concerns about access to quality prenatal care, resources, and knowledge within the African American community.

POVERTY

Understanding African Americans' access to income and resources is important, as socioeconomic status is associated with a range of positive or negative developmental outcomes. The federal poverty threshold for a two-parent family of four in 2001 was $17,960. In contrast to 34% of White children, 57% of African American children live in low-income families. In 2001, nearly 1 million of the almost 11 million African American children under age 18 (8.4% of African American children) lived in extreme poverty (one half the after-tax income), the highest level in 23 years (Children's Defense Fund, 2003). One third of African American children live in poverty, compared with 9.3% of non-Hispanic White children (Annie E. Casey Foundation, 2003).

EARLY DEATHS, INCARCERATION, AND SUICIDE

African American males have a disproportionately high death rate in the 15- to 19-year-old age category, with rates of 130.4 deaths per 100,000 versus 88.3 for White males, 40.8 for Black females, and 38.5 for White females (Anderson & Smith, 2003). Among African American males aged 15 to 19, the leading cause of death in 2001 was assault (58.2 per 100,000). Assault was also the leading cause of death for African American males in the age-groups 20 to 24 and 25 to 35 years old (116.3 and 78.8 per 100,000, respectively). In contrast, assault is the third leading cause of deaths for White males in the 15 to 19, 20 to 24, and 25 to 34-year-old age groupings (7.9, 14.5, and 12.3 per 100,000, respectively; Anderson & Smith, 2003).

African Americans have a higher rate of incarceration than European Americans. Based on 1991 rates, African American men have a 28.5% lifetime chance of incarceration, compared with a lifetime probability of 16.2% for European American men, 3.6% for African American women, and 0.5% for European American women (Bureau of Justice Statistics, 1997).

The suicide rate of African Americans is half that of Whites; however, the suicide rate among African Americans aged 10 to 14 years old increased 233% between 1980 and 1995. Suicide attempts among high school–age African American males (5.3%) are almost as high as those of their White male counterparts (7.5%; CDC, 1998). These data underline the particularly precarious developmental risks and challenges faced by African American males. Although we must be careful not to ignore the positive developmental outcomes achieved by the majority of African American males, these data clearly point to the need to address developmental challenges that negatively affect outcomes for Black males.

EMPLOYMENT AND EDUCATION

In 2000, the rate of unemployment for African Americans was 10.5%, in contrast to 5.1% for Whites. Data show that African Americans complete high school at a rate somewhat higher than the national average (National Center for Education Statistics, 2001a). In 2002, 79% of African Americans aged 25 or over had at least a high school diploma, and the rate of high school completion among African Americans 25 to 29 was 87%. Among African Americans aged 25 or older in 2002, 17% held at least a bachelor's degree, and 46% had completed their college education within 6 years of enrollment. In addition, 18.4% of African American males and 17.4% of African-American females had completed their college degrees within 4 years of initial full-time enrollment (Mortenson Research Seminar on Public Policy Analysis of Opportunity for Postsecondary Education, 2002).

SENIORS

Among American seniors, there are ethnic variations in educational achievement levels, with 51% of African Americans over age 65 having completed high school in 2001, compared with 74% of Whites and 35% of Hispanics (U.S. Census Bureau, 2001a). Historical factors (e.g., segregation, lack of educational access, and lack of family economic resources) underlie these ethnic differences. Compared with older Whites (26%), older African Americans (41.6%) more frequently rate their health as fair or poor (Administration on Aging [AOA], 2002). With the aging of the baby boomers, the percentage of seniors in the American population is projected to grow.

By 2030, there will be about 70 million older persons, more than twice their number in 2000. People 65 years and older represented 12.4% of the population in the year 2000 but are expected to grow to be 20% of the population by 2030. Minority populations are projected to represent 25.4% of the elderly population in 2030, up from 16.4% in 2000 (AOA, 2003, p. 3).

Between 1999 and 2030, the African American population over age 65 is projected to increase by 131%, compared with 81% for European Americans. Compared with European American seniors, African American seniors have more limited access to economic resources. Whereas 21.9% of elderly African Americans have incomes below the poverty level, only 8.9% of older European Americans live below the poverty level (AOA, 2002).

CHALLENGES AND STRENGTHS

This demographic portrait presents a picture that is both positive and challenging. Many poor African American infants are clearly at higher developmental risk than their White counterparts, and overall, African Americans are at greater risk for a range of negative health outcomes. To the extent that development is linked to access to economic resources, despite historical gains, African Americans (especially African American children and elders) have more limited access to economic and related health resources. This comparative analysis, however, focuses only on traditional indicators of outcomes, uses middle-class Whites as the normative comparison group, and may not capture many developmental outcomes that are important from the cultural perspective of many African Americans.

For example, Burton, Allison, and Obeidallah (1995) note adaptations among African American adolescents in inner cities with limited access to resources and opportunities to support middle-class outcomes. These include adaptation of "traditional" developmental goals (e.g., revising the American Dream) to focus on accessing short-term, attainable symbols of middle-class success and achieving adult status through varied pathways to economic independence. Among these are a sense of spiritual well-being (often accompanied by engagement with a religious organization), expression of creative talents and abilities, and serving as a community and family resource. In describing the success of a 19-year-old man who had dropped out of school, one community leader said,

> Anthony may not have finished high school and he may not have a job, but he is the treasure of our community. He helps the young mothers around the neighborhood with their kids. He does the grocery shopping for some of the old folks around here who can't get out. And he keeps the peace between rival street gangs in the community. (Burton et al., 1995, p. 133)

It is important for our research to clarify and help us understand culturally and contextually relevant indicators of developmental "success." Having a well-paying job does not always mean happiness. For example, well-being among African Americans is linked to spirituality and social connections (e.g., Edwards, 1999). These may be particularly important to consider as developmental outcomes.

Theories

Several theoretical perspectives have been used to shape and further our understanding of developmental phenomena. Sigmund Freud and Anna Freud's stage model emphasized sequential stages in the description of psychosexual stages of development (Muus, 1988). These theoretical perspectives focused on the sequential resolution of stage-based developmental issues to shape subsequent development. In contrast, the behavioral, learning, or social learning theories, of B. F. Skinner, Watson, and Bandura, have also been used in supporting the understanding of development. These perspectives emphasize the individual learning episodes that shape an individual's ongoing development and articulate no specific sequence of developmental tasks or stages (Muus, 1988).

Whether considering more stage, dynamic, or learning perspectives on development, these theories tend to emphasize a universal perspective on human development. That is, regardless of the context or population, developmental processes or progression are believed to occur in a similar fashion for all humans regardless of context or culture. Anthropologist Franz Boas and his students, Ruth Benedict and Margaret Meade, challenged these universal perspectives and proposed that development may be shaped by more proximal cultural and contextual forces. This perspective is called *cultural relativism*. Several more recent developmental perspectives emphasize the role of culture and context in development. These include Vygotsky's social cognitive theory and Bronfenbrenner's ecological model.

VYGOTSKY'S THEORY

Vygtosky's (1934/1978) work in social cognition and learning emphasized the role of culture in development and posited that

> every function in the child's cultural development appears twice: first, on the social level, and later, on the individual level; first, between people (interpsychological) and then inside the child (intrapsychological). This applies equally to voluntary attention, to logical memory, and to the formation of concepts. All the higher functions originate as actual relationships between individuals. (p. 57)

Vygotsky suggested that culture often shapes not only the content of a child's cognitions (i.e., what a child thinks) but also the process (how a child thinks). Several researchers and theorists have suggested that the cultural and developmental contexts of African American children support the development of a learning style that emphasizes (a) relationships, social interactions, and emotional expressiveness; (b) verve, rhythm, movement, and kinesthetics; and (c) oral, verbal, and auditory modes (Boykin 1978; Hale-Benson, 1986; Shade, 1991; Townsend, 2000; see also Chapter 7).

A strong oral tradition that uses social interactions and that integrates physical movement into everyday activities from jump rope and patty-cake to walking and dance characterizes of the rich cultural environment experienced by African American children. These are important when considering the cultural implications for teaching and education (Townsend, 2000). Vygotsky's analysis also notes that culture supports the content of our learning and cognitions. As an illustration, consider hip-hop and rap, music forms that are clearly grounded in a Black history of oral tradition with an emphasis on rhythm and a highly varied content of messages. However, some hip-hop and rap include blatant misogyny and negative messages strongly reminiscent of Azibo's (1996) perspective on mentacide (the imposition and destruction of a group's cultural resources through their experience of oppression; see Chapter 12 for further discussion). From Vygotsky's perspective, the content of these negative messages may shape developing cognitions and understandings of the social world and illustrate the tension between Africentric perspectives on culture and the sequelae of racism.

BRONFENBRENNER'S THEORY

A second model that emphasizes the role of context is Bronfenbrenner's (1977) ecological theory. Ecological theory suggests that development is shaped by the interaction between the person, the contexts within which the person develops, and the types of exchanges that take place in the interaction between the individual and his or her context. Person factors include characteristics of the individual (e.g., age, gender, ethnicity or race, temperament, personality) or the individual's specific competencies (e.g., social skills, academic ability). Context includes factors such as residence in an urban or rural community, family structure, and neighborhood characteristics. Processes involve exchanges such as parental monitoring, teaching style, and dating behaviors. Bronfenbrenner believed that developmental outcomes are a function of the specific individual, his or her unique developmental context, and the specific developmental processes involving the individual.

Bronfenbrenner described a series of contexts that may affect development. These include the *microsystem*, that is, the social relationships in which the individual is directly involved (e.g., peers, family, and teachers); the *mesosystem*, that is, the next level of context that encompasses the connections between different microsystems (e.g., linkages between home and school, or family and peers); the *exosystem*, that is, the social settings that may indirectly affect development but where the individual does not have direct contact (e.g., school boards that set educational and school policy or the supervisors at a parent's place of employment); and the *macrosystem*, which is the broader context that involves the social structure, including media, culture, and government. To these systems, Bronfenbrenner (1986) added the need to consider the *chronosystem*, or the set of historical changes that may affect development and alter the settings, contexts, and characteristics of the individual.

We can consider Bronfenbrenner's ecological theory of development for African Americans. Questions at the person level might ask whether there are specific group characteristics inherent to African Americans that play a role in shaping developmental outcomes. In the process domain, questions might focus on whether developmental processes (e.g., socialization processes) are similar or different for African Americans and other cultural groups and how these shape development. In the contextual domain, we might examine how the contexts in which African Americans develop shape their emotions, thinking, and behavior. Finally, we can also consider how changes in contexts, processes, and people over time shape developmental outcomes for African Americans.

Taking the intersection of the last two dimensions of Bronfenbrenner's ecological model (i.e., context and chrono systems), we can briefly illustrate how developmental contexts for African Americans have seen an amazing transition over the past 75 years. Most recent demographic data indicate that African Americans more frequently live in the South and in urban areas in the Northeast, Midwest, and West (see Chapter 5 on neighborhood and community for a fuller description). Historians note that northern migration based on the combination of Jim Crow laws in the South and employment opportunities in the North and Midwest resulted in a large movement of African Americans between the end of the Civil War and 1970. In addition, the move of industry's to the suburbs with limited access to transportation, and the concurrent movement of middle-class African Americans to the suburbs resulted in the concentration of poor African Americans in many urban cores (Wilson, 1987, 1997). Poor families had support from Aid to Families with Dependent Children, established in 1935, but families were eligible only if one parent was absent or incapacitated. It was not until 1968 that "man-in-the-house" rules were struck down by the Supreme Court (*King v. Smith*, 392 U.S. 309, 1968). Many suggest that these policies limited child and family access to male parents and role models for cohorts of poor urban youth. With *Brown v. Board of Education* (347 U.S. 483, 1954) and the civil rights movement came the growth of a significant African American middle class.

Currently, media and technology, increasing cultural diversity and globalization, and hip-hop culture are critically important factors in the developmental contexts of African Americans. When we consider developmental outcomes such as educational attainment, personal adjustment, and family creation, it is important to set our understanding within the dramatic historical changes in the social contexts within which African Americans develop. For example, how are variations in the family formation strategies of African Americans linked to the changes in historical opportunities? How are historical changes in the community contexts of urban African

American communities linked to changes in suicide and adolescent incarceration rates?

Phenomenological Variant of Ecological Systems Theory

Spencer, Dupree, and Hartmann (1997) offer an expansion of Bronfenbrenner's ecological model that explicitly considers the experience of African Americans. In their phenomenological variant of ecological systems theory (PVEST), Spencer et al. suggest that the processes and outcomes linked to any specific phenomenon are shaped by the individual's meaning making and the developmental, sociocultural, and contextual influences that shape that meaning making. The PVEST is reciprocal and suggests that for African Americans, contributions to risk include social-cognitively based social and self-appraisals linked to race, gender, socioeconomic status, physical status, and biological characteristics.

For example, it is possible that social and cultural meaning attributed to being a large, dark-skinned male adolescent as opposed to a small, light-skinned female adolescent may shape both interpersonal and intrapersonal perceptions and result in variation in risk linked to self-cognitions. These risks, in turn, influence and are influenced by an individual's immediate experience of stress, and this stress is shaped by factors such as neighborhood dangers, access and utilization of social support, and daily hassles. Stress experiences are linked to coping methods involving either adaptive (e.g., self-acceptance) or maladaptive (e.g., male bravado) problem-solving strategies. These more event-dependent coping reactions are also reciprocally tied to more stable coping styles and identities (e.g., personal and cultural goals and perceptions related to personally and contextually available means to achieve these goals). These identities influence and are influenced by developmentally specific productive (e.g., competence) and adverse (e.g., deviance) life stage outcomes, which in turn are linked back to risk contributions.

Snapshots of African American Development

Within the scope of this chapter, it is impossible to provide a complete review of the developmental literature on infants, toddlers, preschoolers, middle childhood, early adolescence, young adulthood, and the elderly. In addition, as noted in the introduction, several other chapters in this book address important core issues in development in detail (e.g., family, identity, education, community, and adjustment). In this section, we provide an overview of some key findings relevant to African Americans in four specific developmental periods: infancy and early childhood, adolescence, adulthood, and older adulthood.

INFANCY AND EARLY CHILDHOOD

Although data suggest that African Americans may be at higher risk for LBW and infant death (largely linked with limited income), lower rates of prenatal care, and younger age of mother, some research has raised questions as to whether infants of African parentage show some level of precocity in early development.

Precocity Among African Infants

Some research suggests that the physical and social settings in which African infants develop frequently involve greater physical proximity to parents and physical stimulation, more frequent feeding, and briefer periods of sleep. These social and environmental influences may result in the early development of certain capacities (i.e., precocity), particularly in the areas of motor development for infants in Africa (Super, 1987; Super & Harkness, 1986; Warren, 1972). However, Konner's (1991) literature review on African infant precocity indicated that available research does not support this hypothesis. It is also important to note that seeing one child's development as "early" or "precocious" implies that the developmental norms or standards are based on children from other groups.

African American Children's Socialization and Parenting

Within African American families and among African American children, research has suggested that there is less rigid gender role socialization (Lewis, 1975; Peterson, Bodman, Rush, & Madden-Derdich, 2000). Family roles are more flexible and African American fathers, when they are available to their families, have shown higher levels of involvement but less warmth than their White or Hispanic peers (e.g., Hofferth, 2003).

African American children also seem to be somewhat more relationship oriented than their White counterparts especially compared with their White male peers (DuBois & Hirsch, 1990). These studies of social networks show that African American males and females and White females report higher levels of intimacy in their peer relationships than do White males.

Other research has suggested that parenting may differentially affect African Americans as opposed to children from other ethnic groups. For example, Dornbusch, Ritter, and Steinberg (1991) and Steinberg, Mounts, and Lamborn (1991) found that although parenting style (i.e., the extent to which parents can be characterized as warm or hostile, or the extent to which they are highly permissive or controlling) was predictive of the educational outcomes for most children, parenting style was not a strong predictor of the academic achievement of African American youth. In contrast, work by Radziszewska, Richardson, Dent, and Flay (1996) and

Attaway and Bry (2004) utilized larger samples of African American adolescents and found relationships between parenting style and educational outcomes. For example, Attaway and Bry (2004) found stronger parental beliefs about control to be associated with lower grade point average.

ADOLESCENCE

African American adolescents, especially those youth growing up in resource-poor communities, face a range of challenges in the transition to adulthood. In the words of Chestang (1972), these youth face character development in a hostile environment, have limited access to employment opportunities, and show early expectations of and transitions to markers of adult role attainment.

Physical Development

African American female adolescents, despite having a similar age at menarche to that of their White female counterparts, show earlier physical development. Earlier research and reviews by Tanner (Eveleth & Tanner, 1976) noted that African American children and youth show markers of faster physical maturity and larger size than their European American peers. With the continued impact of the secular trend (i.e., the historical trend toward earlier physical maturation among preadolescents and adolescents documented since the 1800s), researchers have questioned whether this earlier physical development among American youth is in general linked to exposure to specific hormones and chemicals or to the high rates of obesity among American children, especially African American and poor children.

Roles, Developmental Tasks, and Expectations

As described previously, on average, African American youth begin sexual intimacy at earlier ages and experience higher rates of adolescent childbearing than their White peers. In urban, low-resource communities, researchers have discussed issues of age condensation in African American families where adolescents and parents (particularly when these parents were young parents themselves) may be engaging in similar developmental life tasks (e.g., completing or continuing education, dating, seeking employment; Burton et al., 1995).

African American youth in families with limited economic resources may face a discrepancy in the role expectations they face. At school, they may be expected to act as children and respond to the authority of the adult, whereas in their homes and communities they may take on important adult financial and child care roles. The challenges many African American youth face, particularly in low-resource communities and in the face of higher risk of experiencing violence and death, may lead to individual- and community-based socialization that pushes youth to skip childhood and adolescence and transition earlier into adult roles.

Socialization

Over the past 20 years, there has been growing interest in work to explicitly socialize African American youth and to better understand what has been lost from practices that support the enculturation of youth, that is, the explicit cultural socialization of youth into the values, practices, beliefs, and behaviors needed to function in adult social roles. A range of rites of passage programs based on African cultural traditions have supported the transition of youth from childhood by officially marking their entrance into adult status within the community. Research indicates that participation in these cultural programs may provide access to cultural knowledge and support the development of beliefs that counter drug use and other negative behaviors (Belgrave, Brome, & Hampton, 2000; Belgrave, Townsend, Cherry, & Cunningham, 1997). (For a broader discussion of these programs, see Chapter 9 on self-conceptualization and identity.)

Intervention Programs

Our review has underlined that because of the overrepresentation of African American children and youth growing up in contexts that have limited resources and high levels of risk, they may face high levels of developmental challenge. A range of intervention programs have been developed to support successful development and to provide youth with a range of skills that assist them in coping with the risks, dangers, and lack of opportunities that are part of their developmental contexts. CDC's *Best Practices of Youth Violence Prevention: A Sourcebook for Community Action*, available at http://www.cdc.gov/ncipc/dvp/bestpractices.htm, is one guide to these programs. Although programs for delaying pregnancy, increasing prenatal care, and providing early childhood interventions have shown success, it is notable that many of these programs focus on enhancing the skills of youth, rather than reducing the explicit risks and lack of community resources. In the face of this dilemma, Wilcox (1999) raised the challenge to stop creating "Teflon kids" and begin providing children and youth with healthy communities and neighborhoods within which to develop.

ADULTHOOD

So, what have you become, now that you're all grown up? What's your job? Married? Got kids? The lives of adults are not just the developmental time between becoming an adult and "getting old." Much of our understanding of adult development is linked to our cultural ideas as to the social roles that adults fulfill within their communities. Our development during childhood and adolescence prepares us to make successful transitions into work, relationship, and community roles.

Influences on African American Women's Developmental Experiences

Building on Levinson's (1978) model of adult development, Ruffin (1989) proposes that African American women may experience variations in their developmental experiences and that these variations may be shaped in part by the timing of marriage, parenthood, and career. Based on a study of men between ages 35 and 45, Levinson's (1978) original model suggests that after adolescence, we go through a transition period (around age 17 to 18) to early adulthood that lasts from our early 20s until our early 40s. Next we begin a transition to middle adulthood, which lasts from our mid-40s until our early 60s. We then transition into late adulthood during our mid-60s. In Ruffin's qualitative study of eight working African American women, she divided her sample into three groups. The first group married early and began childrearing during their early to mid-20s. The second group had never married or had divorced by their early 30s. The third group either remained unmarried or married late. Findings from her study underline the importance of the historical context in which the women grew up and developed. These historical and developmental contexts shape the resources, opportunities, available social support, and conceptions of female social roles. For example, few of the women in Ruffin's study had access to mentors to support career development and transitions, and for those who had mentors, they were African American. Racial identity and related coping styles were a central theme in Ruffin's analysis, and life events linked to subjects' social networks also shaped life course decisions and trajectories.

Influences on African American Men's Developmental Experiences

Focusing on the early adulthood of African American males, Gooden (1989) also built on Levinson's work and interviewed a sample of 10 African American men, half of whom were employed as teachers or administrators in the public school system and half of whom he identified as "street men" because of their participation "in street corner society" (p. 64). The experiences of the school sample reflect a developmental course that evidenced the limited availability of adult male support but the presence of support from female family members. These men had stable occupational transitions but generally did not achieve their highest career aspirations, due in part to resource constraints, challenging life events, and social network demands. These men were also involved in the life of the broader community. The majority had married and experienced some level of marital conflict but relatively low levels of marital disruption.

The street group also reported a lack of support from older males as mentors and had work lives marked by instability, with few opportunities for advancement. They tended to start families early, and they experienced high levels of disruption of intimate relationships. These relationship challenges were linked to fear of intimacy, extramarital relationships, and inability to handle conflicts within their relationships. Some men in this group had established stable long-term employment, but many experienced difficulty in making a successful transition to well-paying, long-term jobs. Both groups reported financial concerns as part of marital conflict, but street men reported more limited economic resources, and thus their relationships may have suffered more from this additional financial strain.

Gooden's (1989) and Ruffin's (1989) work illustrates only a part of the variability in the life course trajectories and developmental experiences of adults. Their work illustrates the significance of developmental tasks linked to work, family, and community and underlines the role that historical and environmental factors play in shaping and sometimes constraining the development of African American adults.

OLDER ADULTHOOD

Our earlier demographic portrait noted that African Americans have a shorter life expectancy and that once they reach this level of maturity, many African American elders face both economic and health challenges. The cohorts of African American elders over age 65 were born before the 1940s. Many were children during the northern migration and the Great Depression, and experienced the rigid segregation and overt discrimination of the pre–civil rights era.

Despite these challenges, many African American elders continue to play crucial roles in their communities. Research has documented the important role of African American grandparents as primary care providers for their grandchildren, especially when parents have challenges with drug dependency (Burton, 1992; see also Chapter 3 on family and kinship). These parenting demands may place additional stress on these adults, which contributes to an increase in depression and decreases in effective parenting (Rodgers-Farmer, 1999). For support and coping, African American elders frequently rely on spirituality as a means of coping (Krause, 2003).

As this cohort ages, many African Americans note the importance of capturing the oral history and wisdom of this age group of African American seniors as reflected in efforts such as Renee Poussaint and Camille Cosby's (2003) book, *A Wealth of Wisdom: Legendary African American Elders Speak.* From an African perspective, elders are respected and revered members of the community, and even beyond their life span, as ancestors they remain ongoing members of the community.

Research and Methodological Issues

McLoyd's (1991) review and analysis of research on the study of African American children notes a range of historical and ongoing concerns regarding the methods used in studies of child development. These concerns include the role of the experimenter's race in the performance of African American children within an experimental or assessment context, the utilization of measures developed for and normed on Whites, and the emphasis on race-comparative versus race-homogeneous studies. We discuss some of these and related issues next.

RACE-COMPARATIVE STUDIES

Race-comparative studies compare children of different racial groups on a set of measures or indicators, whereas race-homogeneous studies descriptively examine factors within a single racial group to describe how members of a specific racial group behave and develop. McLoyd and others note that a considerable number of research studies of African American children utilized the race-comparative model, although she reports a reduction in this model across the period 1935 to 1980.

Sue (1983) suggests that historically, the literature examining ethnic minority groups has moved away from inferiority models, which hypothesize that African Americans and other non-European ethnic groups are inherently inferior to Whites. Subsequent to the use of inferiority models was the use of deficit models, which did not lay blame on ethnic minority groups for lower performance on specific indicators, but which used comparative analyses to document the effects of external factors on performance. Researchers relying on the deficit perspective often ignored the strengths of ethnic communities and did not seek to understand cultural factors relevant to the psychology of the group. Cross-cultural models utilize more "value-free" analyses of cross-cultural differences, and bicultural models consider the dual status of ethnic groups. These models are often used by researchers who are members of the focal ethnic group to support the use of appropriate methodologies and interpretations.

INCLUSION AND REPRESENTATIVENESS OF SAMPLE

Another crucial consideration in research is inclusion and representativeness of African Americans in research samples. Many studies lack specificity in the description of the sample of African Americans involved in the study, their residence, and their access to economic resources. Given the cultural, residential, educational, and economic diversity among African Americans, it is important to locate the sample used in any study, such that a reader can critically examine whether research that is used to describe African Americans as a whole (i.e., as an entire population of people) is actually representative of the entire range of experiences and performance of all African Americans. For example, a considerable proportion of the developmental literature on African Americans focuses on lower-income and urban samples as opposed to rural or middle-class African American samples. This raises the question of to which group or groups of African Americans the findings are generalizable.

LONGITUDINAL AND CROSS-SECTIONAL DESIGNS

Developmental researchers sometimes use a longitudinal research design, in which the same research participants are followed across time, and changes and continuities in their development are examined. Cross-sectional studies take a "snapshot" approach and might compare different age-groups at the same point in time. In contrast to longitudinal studies, cross-sectional studies do not allow researchers to make statements about change. For example, they cannot say whether differences between the younger and older members of the sample are due to normative developmental changes that occur for an individual across time or due to historical effects. When longitudinal designs are used, issues of attrition, that is, the extent to which research participants are retained in the study across time become very important. Factors that impact the lives of many lower-income African Americans (e.g., residential mobility, lack of financial and other social resources) may make it difficult for researchers to keep research participants engaged over time. Several investigators have developed a series of strategies to support African American and other ethnic research participant engagement over time (e.g., Dilworth-Anderson & Williams, 2004). Useful strategies have included interviewer consistency across time, training project staff in issues relevant to African American families, access to project staff through toll-free phone numbers, and flexibility in the scheduling and rescheduling of research tasks and contacts.

There are also cultural assumptions in some research that may reflect an ethnocentric and often Eurocentric bias. In some developmental research, standardized measures are used that examine age norms for performance on a specific measure or the presence, absence, or level of a descriptive indicator.

Many measures have historically been normed on middle-class White samples. When African Americans or other ethnic groups are included, they are only included in a stratified sample based on their representation within the broader American demographic context. Although this inclusion allows comparisons to be made between individuals and the overall American norms for all children, considering the diversity within and between cultural groups, it is often difficult to fully understand the implications of comparisons of individual African Americans to overall national norms.

For example, what does it mean if an African American child scores lower than the American norm on a particular index? What support does the index provide in understanding the contributions of the individual's experience with similar test situations or stimuli, the contribution of the individual's abilities, and the individual's access to environments, social resources, and opportunities relevant to the specific index? How does the use and interpretation of the index inform our understanding of what work is needed for knowledge development, intervention or prevention, and policy?

Summary

In this chapter, we reviewed a demographic portrait examining the lives of African Americans. Although individually diverse, African Americans as a group have a younger mean age and tend to have children when they are younger. African Americans also have shorter life expectancies than other ethnic groups.

Several theoretical perspectives including Vygtosky's theory, Bronfenbrenner's ecological theory, and Spencer and colleagues' phenomenological variant of ecological systems theory help us understand the role of context and culture and support our understanding of the development of African Americans.

Because of fewer resources and higher levels of environmental risk, some young children and adolescents (especially those living in areas of concentrated poverty) may be at risk of compromise. Despite these challenges, African American youth are relational and connected.

Adults rise to the developmental challenges of work, family, and community shaped by their historical and sociocultural context. Elders continue to play important support functions within the community, especially as a resource for children; their wisdom and contributions are important to acknowledge.

Overall, research and theory suggest that understanding the ways in which African Americans grow and develop requires the consideration of a range of historical and cultural factors that have influenced the development of individuals and historical cohorts of African Americans.

In conducting developmental research, careful identification and specification of the target population and care with generalizations are warranted because of the overrepresentation of lower-income urban African Americans in the existing research literature. From an African perspective, life is cyclical. The Ethiopian proverb "One is born, one dies: the land increases" acknowledges the contributions of all members of the community, the cyclical nature of life, and the forward progression of individuals and the community along the paths of their development and growth. Despite challenges, African Americans continue to make progress from generation to generation.

Section IV

Adjustment and Adaptation

Health, Illness, and Disability

11

He who conceals his disease cannot expect to be cured.

—Ethiopian proverb

Racial Disparities Played Down

Washington Post, January 14, 2004

Shankar Vedantam

A federal report on racial disparities in health care was revised at the behest of top administration officials, and a comparison with an earlier draft shows that the version released in December played down the imbalances and was less critical of the lack of equality.

Government officials acknowledged and defended the changes yesterday, even as critics charged that the Department of Health and Human Services rewrote what was to be a scientific road map for change to put a positive spin on a public health crisis: Minorities receive less care, and less high-quality care, than whites, across a broad range of diseases.

The earlier draft of the report's executive summary, for example, described in detail the problems faced by minorities and the societal costs of the disparities, and it called such gaps "national problems."

The final report's executive summary interspersed examples of disparities with success stories and emphasized the role of geography and socioeconomic factors— rather than just race—in producing different outcomes. It dropped the reference to "national problems."

Government officials agreed that the tone of the report had been changed, saying the revisions reflected HHS Secretary Tommy G. Thompson's strategy of triggering improvement by focusing on the positive.

The National Healthcare Disparities Report was intended by HHS to be a comprehensive look at the scope and reasons for inequalities in health care. A number of studies have shown that even among people with identical diseases and the same income level, minorities are less likely to be diagnosed promptly and more likely to receive sub-optimal care. Documented disparities exist in the diagnosis and treatment of cancer, heart disease, AIDS, diabetes, pediatric illness, mental disorders and other conditions. They also exist in surgical procedures and nursing home services.

An IOM (Institute of Medicine) report suggested last year that widespread racial differences in health care "are rooted in historic and contemporary inequities" and asserted that stereotyping and bias by doctors, hospitals and other care providers may be at fault—a much stronger critique than the HHS report.

The earlier version of the executive summary defined "disparity" and mentioned it 30 times in the "key findings" section, Waxman said. The final version mentioned the word only twice in that section and left it undefined.

In what they called "a case study in politics and science," Waxman and four other members of Congress said the final version "drops findings on the societal costs of disparities, and replaces them with a discussion of 'successes'."

Introduction and Definitions

In this chapter, we discuss reasons for and consequences of the disparities in health care for African Americans. We also discuss factors that promote good health and well-being for African Americans. Cultural values and beliefs have a pervasive impact on health, illness, and disability outcomes among African Americans. Socioeconomic status, racism, and oppression also contribute to health outcomes. In this chapter, we review factors that contribute to the physical health of African Americans. Mental health is discussed in Chapter 12.

Physical health is a function of biological, psychological, social, and environmental factors. We begin with definitions and a model of the role of cultural factors on health outcomes. The health status of African Americans is discussed next. Western models of health behavior and culturally based health models for African Americans follow. The chapter ends with a review of cultural considerations of four health conditions that disproportionately affect African Americans.

DEFINITIONS

Health psychology is the field of psychology that studies psychological influences on how people stay healthy, why they become ill, and how they respond to illness (Taylor, 1991). Health psychologists are concerned with health promotion and illness prevention behaviors, as well as with how people experience illnesses and disabilities.

Illness is the condition of being in poor health (Neufeldt & Guralnik, 1996). Disease is an impairment of the normal state of the body that interrupts or modifies the performance of vital functions and is a response to environmental factors, specific agents, or inherent defects of the organism (Merriam-Webster, 1997). A chronic disease is one that lasts a long time or is recurring (Neufeldt & Guralnik, 1996). Although chronic diseases typically cannot be cured, they can be managed. A disability is a limitation in performing certain roles and tasks that society expects of an individual (Institute of Medicine, 1991).

FACTORS AFFECTING THE HEALTH OF AFRICAN AMERICANS

African Americans have poorer health outcomes than any other major racial or ethnic group in the United States. The disparities are especially noteworthy when comparisons are made with Whites. Socioeconomic factors such as employment, income, and education affect access to health and medical services, and lack of access to such services contributes to poor health outcomes. African Americans have high unemployment rates and underemployment, both of which contribute to less access to health and medical services. However, we should not assume that all African Americans face poor health outcomes, as there is a great deal of diversity among African Americans. Differences in health outcomes among African Americans may be due to socioeconomic status, lifestyle risk factors (such as cigarette smoking), and geographical residence (urban, rural, suburban).

Lower socioeconomic status for African Americans has been viewed as a primary reason for poor health outcomes. However, socioeconomic factors do not account for all of the health disparities between African Americans and Whites (Belgrave, 1998). Cultural beliefs along with institutional policies within health care institutions also contribute to poorer health outcomes for African Americans. Also, health care providers who are not knowledgeable of and sensitive to African American culture may contribute to the underutilization of health care systems by African Americans.

Morbidity, Mortality, and Disability Among African Americans

Morbidity is the rate of disease or proportion of disease in a given locality or nation, whereas *mortality* is the incidence of death (Neufeldt & Guralnik, 1996). A number of conditions account for morbidity disparities between

Table 11.1   Life Expectancy by Race and Sex in the United States, 2001

Specified Age and Year	White Males	Black Males	White Females	Black Females
At birth	75.0	68.6	80.2	75.5
At 65 years	16.5	14.4	19.5	17.9
At 75 years	10.2	9.3	12.3	11.7

Source: Arias, Anderson, Kung, Murphy, and Kochanek (2003, p. 133).

African Americans and Whites. These conditions also contribute to excess deaths among African Americans. Excess deaths are the number or incidence of deaths from a certain risk factor in a population that is over and above the number in the unexposed group (U.S. Department of Health and Human Services, 1985). Excess deaths among African Americans are due to cancer, heart disease and stroke, homicide and unintentional injuries, infant mortality, diabetes, and HIV/ AIDS (Freid, Prager, MacKay, & Xia, 2003).

DIFFERENTIALS IN LIFE EXPECTANCY

Life expectancy discrepancy between African Americans and Whites is especially noteworthy for males. Table 11.1 shows that African American males born in 2001 have a life expectancy of 68.6 years, and White males born in the same year have a life expectancy of 75.0 years. Similarly, White females have a higher life expectancy (80.2 years) than African American females (75.5 years). Note that the racial discrepancy between Black and White females is not as great as it is for males. The life expectancy for both African American and White females is greater than that for African American males (Freid et al., 2003).

PREVALENCE OF HEALTH CONDITIONS

The prevalence of selected health conditions among African Americans and Whites is shown in Table 11.2. African Americans have higher morbidity than Whites across all selected conditions. Across these conditions, the mortality rate for African Americans is 1,101.2 out of 100,000 and for Whites it is 836.5 out of 100,000. The mortality rates for African Americans range from a few to several times the rates for Whites. For example, mortality from diabetes is over twice as high for African Americans as it is for Whites. Mortality from HIV/AIDS is about eight times higher and mortality from homicide is four times higher for African Americans than for Whites.

Table 11.2   Age-Adjusted Death Rates by Cause and Race in the United
States, 2001 (Deaths per 100,000)

Cause of Death	Black	White
All Causes	1,101.2	836.5
Natural Causes		
Diseases of heart	316.9	243.5
Ischemic heart disease	211.6	176.5
Cerebrovascular diseases	78.8	55.8
Malignant neoplasm	243.1	193.9
Respiratory system	62.5	55.6
Colorectal	27.6	19.6
Prostate	66.1	26.6
Breast	34.4	25.5
Chronic lower respiratory diseases	30.9	45.6
Pneumonia and influenza	24.1	21.7
Chronic liver disease and cirrhosis	9.3	9.6
Diabetes mellitus	49.2	23.0
HIV/AIDS	22.8	2.6
External Causes		
Unintentional injuries	37.6	36.0
Motor vehicle–related injuries	15.4	15.6
Suicide	5.5	11.7
Homicide	21.2	4.9

Source: Arias et al. (2003, Table C).

Cardiovascular disease is a leading cause of death in the United States.
Rates for all forms of heart disease are 68% higher for African Americans
than for Whites (Freid et al., 2003). While historically, African Americans
have had lower suicide rates than Whites, these rates are steadily increasing
with 5.5 of 100,000 deaths accounted for by African Americans and 11.7 out
of 100,000 for Whites (Freid et al., 2003; Washington & McCarley, 1998).

DISABILITY AMONG AFRICAN AMERICANS

African Americans compared with Whites report higher levels of
disability and impairment in carrying out the activities of daily living.
Limitations in activity of daily living affect one's ability to carry out routine
activities and to function within the home, community, and workplace. In
2001, 15.6% of African Americans were limited in some activity compared
with 11.8% of Whites who were limited in some activity (Freid et al.,
2003).

Health Promotion, Disease Prevention, and Health Care Utilization

African Americans are less likely than Whites to engage in health promotion and disease prevention activities (Belgrave, 1998). Regular preventive checkups and visits to health care providers could decrease the amount and severity of long-term and chronic health and disability problems. Positive health behaviors, such as eating nutritious foods and exercising regularly, can help prevent many health problems.

African American women are more likely to be satisfied with a larger body size than White women (Jordan, 1999; Thompson, Sargent, & Kemper, 1996), and African American girls report greater body satisfaction (Gluck & Geliebter, 2002). While a more favorable body image may reduce the incidence of eating disorders in African American females, the acceptance of larger body size may also contribute to less exercise and excess food consumption. Studies show that African American women are less inclined than White women to participate in physical activity and exercise (Wilcox, Bopp, Oberrecht, Kammermann, & McElmurray, 2003). They are also more likely to be overweight and obese (Harrell & Gore, 1998). In 1999–2000, 50% of African American women aged 20 to 74 were overweight enough to be classified as obese (Freid et al., 2003).

HEALTH CARE UTILIZATION PATTERNS

Morbidity, mortality, disability, and activity limitations are affected by health care utilization patterns. The extent to which African Americans receive regular and routine preventive medical care affects long-term health status. African Americans are less likely than Whites to have physician contacts and more likely to have longer periods of hospitalizations (Bernstein et al., 2003). Longer hospitalizations suggest that African Americans who are hospitalized are sicker when admitted to the hospital.

Access Factors

Access factors include whether or not health and medical care and rehabilitation services are affordable and available when needed. Another access factor is whether facilities are convenient to the consumer, whether the operating hours are convenient, and whether there is accessible transportation to the treatment facility.

Affordability is a factor that can either facilitate or impede access. African Americans are less likely than Whites to make routine office visits to a primary care physician. Many minority women and children who are eligible for medical treatment, medicine, and hospitalization and other low-cost or affordable health care do not have access to preventive care due to financial or insurance reasons (U.S. Department of Health and Human Services, 2003). In 2001, more than 50% of African Americans were considered poor or near poor (Alliance for Health Reform, 2004).

The problem of medical coverage is most likely to affect the working poor. These are the people who work typically at minimal wage jobs and whose employer does not provide medical coverage. However, because they work, they no longer qualify for low-cost or free medical coverage.

As noted previously, the absence of routine and preventive health care contributes to overutilization of emergency room services and ultimately longer hospitalizations. Moreover, African Americans who are enrolled in managed care plans are one and a half times more likely to be refused authorization than Whites (Alliance for Health Reform, 2004). Overall, the lack of health and medical insurance is linked to employment opportunities and barriers for African Americans.

Another access barrier is lack of transportation to medical facilities. In a study on rehabilitation service utilization patterns among African Americans and European Americans, more European Americans than African Americans reported owning or having access to a private car or vehicle to transport them to rehabilitation appointments. African Americans were more likely to report that they used public transportation to attend medical and rehabilitation appointments (Belgrave & Walker, 1991).

A related access problem is location of the treatment facility. Clinics, hospitals, social service agencies, rehabilitation agencies, and other facilities are often not located within urban communities or in close proximity to where African Americans live. Consequently, travel to and from facilities may require time and economic resources that may not be available.

Other Barriers Affecting Health Care Utilization

There are nonsocioeconomic access factors that contribute to lower utilization of health and medical services by African Americans. Racism and stereotyping may play a subtle but influential role in keeping African Americans from needed medical services. African Americans are often viewed as the less desirable patients, lacking the ability to understand their medical condition and follow through with medical recommendations. Suspected drug and alcohol use among African American clients contributes further to stereotyping (Alliance for Health Reform, 2004). Still other African Americans may not trust the health care system. A graphic example of this is what occurred with the Tuskegee study.

The Tuskegee Syphilis Experiment

Even today some African Americans remain suspicious of the motives and intent of the health care system because of the Tuskegee study (Byrd &

Clayton, 2001). Between 1932 and 1972, the U.S. Public Health Service conducted an experiment on 399 Black men in the late stages of syphilis. These men were for the most part uneducated and poor. They were not told they had syphilis, but were informed that they were being treated for "bad blood." With the disease untreated, these men were left to degenerate and acquire many of the effects of advanced syphilis, including heart disease, paralysis, blindness, insanity, and death.

Even when, by 1943, penicillin was used to treat syphilis, these men were denied access to treatment. By the end of the experiment, 28 of the men had died directly of syphilis, 100 were dead of related complications, 40 of their wives had been infected, and 19 of their children had been born with congenital syphilis. These men and their families were sacrificed in the name of science. In spite of the Henderson Act of 1943, a public health law that required testing and treatment for venereal disease, and despite the World Health Organization's specification that "informed consent" was needed for experiments involving human beings, the Tuskegee experiment continued. The suspicion and fear generated by the Tuskegee study remain among some African Americans today. The results of a 1999 survey showed that 27% of African Americans believed that the U.S. government created HIV/AIDS as a plot to exterminate Blacks, and another 23% of African Americans could not rule out the possibility that this might be true (Landrine & Klonoff, 1999).

Divergent Values and Communication

When the health care provider is not familiar with or does not acknowledge differences in cultural values, attitudes, and communication patterns, the exchange between the professional and the consumer may be negative or nonproductive. Under these conditions, the consumer may not return for needed health and medical services.

To illustrate a cultural difference between African Americans and Whites, a colleague who works in a hospital recounts the communication exchange between African American consumers and White health care specialists (e.g., physical therapists, occupational therapists, nurses). These health care professionals refer to African American consumers informally by their first names instead of more formally as, for example, Mr. Smith or Mrs. Jones. Although this may be how the White health care professional communicates with White consumers (using informality to promote an interpersonal relationship), the African American consumer may, in fact, view this lack of formality as being talked down to and may find such language offensive. African Americans may perceive being called by one's first name as disrespectful, especially older men who were historically addressed by White persons using their first names as a way to keep them in their place.

Another example of how cultural values affect communication and subsequently health care utilization is derived from an understanding of the communal and relationship orientation of African Americans. The communal orientation stresses and places a positive value on the person's ability to connect with and to establish a harmonious interpersonal relationship with others. From this perspective, the ability of the health care provider to establish an interpersonal relationship with the consumer should facilitate health care utilization. If the African American consumer "likes" or "connects" with the health care professional, health and medical utilization patterns should be facilitated. It is important for the provider to convey sincerity and genuineness when dealing with the consumer. This orientation may be contrasted with a more Eurocentric orientation whereby perceived expertise and competency, rather than interpersonal relationship, may be more valued. For African American consumers, the health provider's expertise and skill may not be enough, and compliance to recommendations is likely to be influenced by how well the consumer likes, trusts, and respects the professional.

Spirituality is another example of how African American cultural values can affect the relationship between the health care professional and consumer. For example, when an African American or a member of his or her family acquires a chronic illness or disabling condition, there may be a positive reinterpretation of this event. In a study of parents with children with disabilities, Belgrave and Walker (1991) found that African American parents were likely to report the use of positive reinterpretation as a coping strategy. In interviews with these parents, several reported positive outcomes derived from having a child with a disabling condition. For example, parents reported that they became stronger, that the experience had strengthened their faith, and that the experience had made them grow stronger as a family. These alternative coping strategies should be recognized by health care professionals and integrated in treatment approaches when appropriate.

Another potential conflict is when health and medical professionals speak in professional or technical jargon—minimizing the consumer's ability to understand the message. Twenty-three percent of African Americans reported difficulty with communication with health care providers (Alliance for Health Reform, 2004). Unanswered questions may remain unanswered, and the opportunity to inform and educate is lost.

Models of Health and Illness Behaviors

SOCIAL AND PSYCHOLOGICAL MODELS

Several social and psychological models have been developed to help explain and predict health behaviors. In this section, we give an overview of three health models—the health belief model, the theory of planned behavior, and the self-efficacy theory—and provide a critique of the usefulness and the limitations of these models for understanding health and illness behaviors in African Americans.

The Health Belief Model

The health belief model is one of the oldest health models (Wallston & Wallston, 1984). The health belief model was developed to explain public participation in screening programs and has been used to predict a variety of health and illness behaviors (e.g., exercise, diet, getting breast exams, taking medication, keeping appointments, HIV/AIDS protective behaviors).

According to the model, people who perceive a severe health threat or feel susceptible to a particular disease are motivated to make behavioral changes if they perceive that the benefits of risk reduction behaviors outweigh the costs of performing the behaviors. Readiness to take a health action is determined by a person's perceived likelihood of susceptibility to the illness and by personal perception of the severity of the consequences of getting the disease. Together these make up the person's vulnerability. The potential benefits of a given behavior are weighed against the potential barriers to or costs of action. A cue to action, whether an internal cue such as a symptom or an external cue such as a prevention message, is necessary to trigger a health behavior. The health belief model is depicted below.

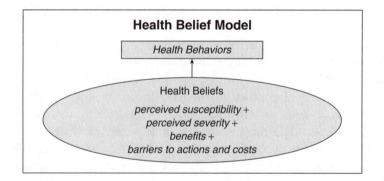

An example will show how components of the health belief model can be used to explain whether or not an individual engages in an HIV/AIDS protective behavior such as condom use. First, a person must perceive that she is susceptible to acquiring HIV/AIDS and second that HIV/AIDS is a severe disease. Assuming this is the case, then the benefits of wearing a condom (e.g., less worry about contracting HIV/AIDS) are weighed against the barriers and costs of condom use (e.g., less pleasure, embarrassment, partner may not want to use condom, etc.). The four beliefs depicted in the box determine whether or not a condom is used.

The health beliefs of African Americans may differ from those of Whites. Glanz, Resch, Lerman, and Rimer (1996) found that African American women were more likely than Whites to underestimate their cancer risk and to fear radiation, and less likely to have a doctor advise them to get mammograms. These beliefs suggest a lower level of perceived susceptibility to cancer and a higher degree of perceived barriers for engaging in preventive health behaviors to reduce the risk of cancer (Lyna, McBride, Samsa, & Pollak, 2002).

African Americans' cultural values, which emphasize present and past time relative to future time, may also interact with health belief components found in the health belief model. Brown and Segal (1998) found that more present-oriented respondents perceived themselves to be less susceptible to the consequences of hypertension than more future-oriented respondents. Among African Americans, present-time orientation may contribute to lowered susceptibility regarding hypertension. Hypertension is the leading risk factor for cardiovascular disease. The consequence of this thinking is that if a person believes that he or she is not susceptible to the consequences of hypertension (i.e., stroke, cardiovascular impairment), he or she may engage in less effective preventive hypertension management.

Theory of Planned Behavior

The theory of planned behavior was developed by Fishbein and Ajzen (1975) to study predictive behaviors across several domains, including physical health (Fisher, Fisher, & Rye, 1995). According to the theory, one's intentions to perform a certain behavior are the best predictor of that behavior. Behavioral intentions are determined by attitudes toward the behavior and beliefs about subjective norms (e.g., expectations and values of significant others). Attitudes toward performing a certain behavior are a function of the individual's beliefs about the consequences of performing the behavior, multiplied by his or her evaluations of these consequences. An individual's subjective norm is a function of his or her perception of social support from important others for performance of a preventive behavior multiplied by his or her motivation to do what he or she believes the significant other wants. The model is depicted on the next page.

An example will illustrate how beliefs, salient in the theory of planned behavior, affect subsequent behavior. One's intention to engage in HIV/AIDS preventive behavior, such as condom use, is determined by one's intention to wear a condom during a specific sexual encounter. Intentions are shaped by attitudes toward condom use and whether or not significant others also have favorable attitudes toward condom use. Attitudes are influenced by positive or negative beliefs about the effectiveness of condoms. If one believes that condoms are effective, resulting condom use is likely to occur.

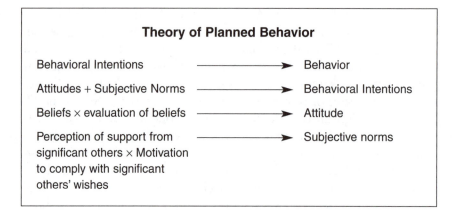

The theory of planned behavior has been used to explain other health behaviors among African Americans, including violence (Evans & Taylor, 1995), HIV/AIDS prevention behaviors (Jemmott & Jemmott, 1991), and cigarette smoking (Hanson, 1997). Jemmott and Jemmott (1991) found that, consistent with the theory of planned behavior, African American participants who had more favorable attitudes toward condoms and who perceived subjective norms as being supportive of condom use reported stronger intentions to use condoms in the following 3 months.

Self-Efficacy Theory

Self-efficacy theory is concerned with whether or not people can exert control over their motivation, behavior, and social environment (Bandura, 1977). Self-efficacy theory, like the theory of planned behavior, was not developed exclusively as a theory of health behavior but has been used extensively to understand and predict health behaviors. The theory predicts that one's beliefs about one's capability to perform a desired task will predict one's success at completing that task. Self-efficacy beliefs are usually specific; that is, one has efficacy with regard to a specific task or effort (e.g., Jean has high self-efficacy regarding her academic performance). Self-efficacy affects behavior by increasing the goals one sets. Persons with high self-efficacy will set higher goals and show persistence when goals are not met. High self-efficacy influences the strategies one uses to achieve goals and favorably influences the effectiveness of problem solving. Persons with low self-efficacy beliefs doubt their abilities and may be inefficient and ineffective problem solvers. Self-efficacy influences affect and emotional responses. Low self-efficacy beliefs lead to anxiety and less successful coping efforts. High self-efficacy beliefs are developed through knowledge, skills, practice, and the support of significant others (Bandura, 1977; Maddux & Lewis, 1995). Competency in desired behavior contributes to strong self-efficacy beliefs. A model of self-efficacy theory is depicted on the next page.

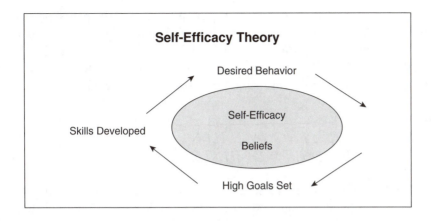

The three models of health behavior discussed have several similarities: (a) They all make the assumption that health is a valued priority of individuals; (b) they assume that individuals have the potential to engage in actions on their own behalf; (c) they are cognitively based, with an emphasis on beliefs; and (d) they all have a vast amount of health literature devoted to them. In general, the models are useful for predicting health-related behavioral changes (Cochran & Mays, 1993; Fisher et al., 1995). Health promotion behaviors such as exercise and diet have been predicted by these health models (Maddux & Lewis, 1995). Health care utilization and compliance behaviors, such as adherence to medication and having regular checkups, have also been predicted by these models (Fischera & Frank, 1994; Oldridge & Streiner, 1990). Finally, these models have been useful for explaining illness-related behaviors such as coping with chronic illness and disabilities (Belgrave, 1998). The health belief model has been used to account for drug prevention (Hahn & Rado, 1996) and the prevention of sexually transmitted disease (Simon & Das, 1984) among African Americans.

On the other hand, the usefulness of the health belief model, the theory of planned behavior, and self-efficacy theory for understanding health outcomes among African Americans has been questioned by some scholars (Belgrave, 1998; Cochran & Mays, 1993; Marin et al., 1995). In a critique of the usefulness of these models for understanding HIV/AIDS prevention behavior among African Americans, Cochran and Mays (1993) note that the models rely on the assumption that behavior is individualistic and rational. However, among African Americans, behavior may be engaged in because of social, family, and community obligations. The second limitation noted by these authors is the minimization of the importance of economic and ethnic discriminatory factors in health behaviors. For example, access to regular physical examinations may not be possible for people without adequate health insurance even if so desired.

Thus, these three models may not be as useful for explaining the health behaviors of African Americans as they are for Whites. Steers, Elliot, Nemiro, Ditman, and Oskamp (1996) found that the health belief model predicted safer sex behaviors for European American participants more so than for African American, Hispanic American, and Asian American participants. Others have found that the variables in the health belief model were not significantly associated with preventive health practices such as getting mammograms (Duke, Gordan-Sosby, Reynolds, & Gram, 1994).

WESTERN VERSUS NON-WESTERN CONCEPTUALIZATION OF ILLNESS

Landrine and Klonoff (1992) analyze how culture influences health and illness beliefs of ethnic and cultural groups from Western and non-Western cultures. According to Landrine and Klonoff, European Americans espouse a Western cultural view of illness. This view treats illness as person centered and as an interpersonal condition caused by microlevel, natural, and etiological agents such as genes, viruses, bacteria, and stress. Illness or disease is seen as discrete, episodic, or both. The implication of holding these beliefs is that treatment will be time limited, specific, and not holistically integrated into all aspects of the treated person's life. This view also assumes that only experts are trained in the diagnosis and treatment of disease.

In contrast to the person-centered approach of Western culture regarding illness and disability, Landrine and Klonoff (1992) note that many non-Western groups, including some ethnic minority groups in the United States, view illness as a long-term, fluid, and continuous manifestation of long-term and dynamic relationships within the family, the community, or nature. The beliefs of these individuals include macrolevel, interpersonal, and supernatural causes as explanations for illness or disease.

According to Landrine and Klonoff (1992), cultures that support the non-Western worldview of health and illness provide several alternative explanations for the causes of illness. These explanations assume that illnesses are caused by (a) violations of interpersonal norms, (b) deviations from social roles and norms, (c) certain emotions such as jealousy and envy, (d) violations of religious and moral norms, and (e) certain agents found in nature such as weather conditions and hot or cold foods.

Some ethnic minority and cultural groups in the United States, including African Americans, may also hold supernatural beliefs about the causes of illness. For example, within the African American community, there were healers such as "root" doctors who were used to cure illness and disease. Root doctors used roots and herbs in the treatment of physical, mental, and social conditions. When a hex or spell was cast, it could only be broken by a root doctor. Earlier in the 20th century, the root doctors held positions of high status and prestige in some regions of the United States (most often the South). While root doctors are no longer prevalent within the African American community, there are some anecdotal accounts that they still exist, especially in certain areas of the South. It is interesting that today people from all ethnic groups are using herbs and roots to maintain health and treat disease.

CULTURAL MODELS OF HEALTH AND ILLNESS

A culturally congruent model of health recognizes core values and ways of being. The significance of spirituality in the lives of African Americans is acknowledged in a culturally congruent model. African Americans are more likely than Whites to use spirituality in health promotion efforts and to provide a framework for coping with stressful circumstances (Belgrave, 1998; Potts, 1996; Swinney, 2002; Taylor, Chatters, Jayakody, & Levin, 1996). Consequently, spirituality should be integrated into treatment practices and health promotion efforts.

African American churches contribute to positive health outcomes within the African American community. Black churches provide the mechanism for health screenings (e.g., for high blood pressure or sickle cell disease) and prevention activities (e.g., exercise classes). African American churches have also been used as recruitment sites for health promotion activities (Weinrich et al., 1998).

The role of the family—including the extended family—must also be considered in understanding health and illness outcomes among African Americans. The Black extended family has been considered a source of emotional, material, and social support for African Americans with medical and health care needs (Belgrave, 1998). Compared with Whites, African Americans are more likely to care for an elderly or infirm family member in the home (Belgrave, 1998).

The extended family can be an asset for a person with a disability who may need support to carry out routine and daily activities. Some individuals with disabilities may be isolated and have limited participation in everyday activities outside the home. Within African American extended families, there may be less isolation because of ties to persons within and outside of the immediate family.

Belgrave, Davis, and Vajda (1994) studied the presence of the extended family among African Americans with disabilities. Belgrave et al. found that African Americans listed more kin than White Americans although there was no difference between the two groups in the number of immediate family members listed. The findings from this study suggest that the networks of African Americans with disabilities are more likely to include more significant others outside of the immediate family.

The extended family may provide emotional support and reassurance, as well as material support (e.g., help with transportation, babysitting, etc.). Extended family also provides an additional buffer for dealing with stress or problems within the household. The extended family is likely to live in the community and be in frequent contact with the family.

RACISM AND PHYSICAL HEALTH

Racism affects the health status of African Americans in several ways (Clayton & Byrd, 2001; Jackson et al., 1996). First, racial discrimination can negatively impact the quality and quantity of medical care. Second, racism can create differences in life opportunities and living conditions across a range of socioeconomic conditions, such as housing quality, employment, and education. Third, the experience of specific racial incidents may adversely affect health by causing psychological distress and other changes in physiological processes (this explanation is discussed more thoroughly in the section on hypertension). Fourth, some of the negative coping strategies used by members of oppressed groups may also impair physical and mental functioning (see Chapter 13 on drug use).

Selected Health and Illness Conditions Among African Americans

In this section, we review four health conditions common among African Americans. These conditions were selected because their prevalence is substantially higher among African Americans than among other ethnic groups.

HYPERTENSION

Hypertension is defined by either having elevated blood pressure (systolic pressure of at least 140 mmHg or diastolic pressure of at least 90 mmHg) or taking antihypertensive medication. Hypertension is a risk factor for heart disease and stroke, the first and third leading causes of death in this country (National Center for Health Statistics, 1998).

Hypertension is substantially higher among African Americans than among other ethnic groups. In 2001, for every 100,000 people in the population, hypertension was the cause for 836.5 deaths of Whites and 1,101.2 deaths of African Americans. This disease claims 1.3 times more African Americans than Whites. Thirty-three percent more African Americans than Whites have a risk of death from hypertension. About 35% of African Americans within the 20- to 74-year-old range have hypertension, compared with 24% of White males and 19% of White females. Hypertension kills 15 times as many African American males as White males in the 15- to 40-year-old age-group and 7 times as many African American females as White females in any age-group (Hopp & Herring, 1999).

Income is a factor in hypertension prevalence and control among African Americans. The prevalence of hypertension is higher among African Americans who are poor because it is less likely to be controlled.

The etiology of hypertension is complex. Genetic and physiological differences may account for some of the ethnic differences in hypertension prevalence. Environmental and social factors also account for some of the differential. Research has suggested that blood pressure within racial groups varies by geographical or social context. According to Williams (1992), blood pressure levels of West Africans are generally lower than those of Blacks in the United States and the Caribbean. Blood pressure increases when Blacks move from original communities to large urban communities (Hopp & Herring, 1999).

Furthermore, research has shown that African Americans who are darker in skin color have higher levels of blood pressure than those who have lighter skin color. The effects of skin color on elevated blood pressure seem to be mediated by socioeconomic status. One study found an association between skin color and blood pressure only in African Americans who were of low socioeconomic status (Klag, Whelton, Coresh, Grim, & Kuller, 1991). This may be due to the lesser ability of darker skinned Blacks to deal with the psychosocial stress associated with darker skin color. Ernst, Jackson, Robertson, Nevels, and Watts (1997) found a small positive relationship between darker skin tone and systolic blood pressure. However, because the males in this study were significantly darker than the females, this difference could be due to gender. The findings of the relationship between skin color and hypertension show an interaction between socio-environmental factors such as socioeconomic status and a susceptible gene that has a higher prevalence in persons with darker skin color.

Dietary habits of African Americans also may contribute to higher rates of hypertension. Pork, fried foods, and foods high in saturated fat, total fat, and sodium content may contribute to increased prevalence. Also, obesity, which is higher among African Americans, is a contributor to hypertension (Kumanyika, 1997b).

Research has shown a link between John Henryism and hypertension (James, 1994). John Henryism is a condition characterized by prolonged, high-effort active coping in the face of difficult environmental stressors. This association occurs among lower- as well as higher-income African American males (Fernander, Duran, Saab, & Schneiderman, 2004). Dressler, Bindon, and Neggers (1998) found that for men, as the degree of John Henryism increased, so did blood pressure and the risk of hypertension. Among women, increased John Henryism correlated with decreases in blood pressure and the risk of hypertension. Increased anger and hostility are also associated with increased blood pressure and risk for hypertension (Johnson & Gant, 1996).

Increased hypertension among African Americans is attributed in part to exposure to more chronic social stressors (e.g., racism, unemployment, economic problems; Anderson, McNeilly, & Myers, 1993; Steffen, McNeilly, Anderson, & Sherwood, 2003). In a study of African American men and women, greater perceived racism was related to higher ambulatory blood pressure. In one study, Krieger (1990) interviewed Black and White women about unfair race and gender treatment. Respondents were interviewed by phone in Alameda County, California. Black women who reported they usually accepted and kept quiet about unfair treatment were over four times more likely to report hypertension than women who said they took action and talked to others. There was no association between unfair treatment and hypertension among White women. Thus, it appears that differences in blood pressure between Blacks and Whites can be due, in part, to experiences of racial discrimination and responses to unfair treatment.

According to Kumanyika (1997a), the potential for hypertension control may be greater for African Americans than for Whites. Sodium reduction shows greater benefits in blood pressure reduction among African Americans than among Whites. Also, a high proportion of African Americans are overweight (32% of men and 49% of women). Changing these health habits could result in substantially reducing hypertension.

SICKLE CELL DISEASE

Sickle cell disease is a group of genetic blood disorders that affect 1 out of every 400 to 500 African Americans (Desforges, Milner, Wethers, & Whitten, 1978). The sickle cell gene is more common among those whose ancestry can be traced to a geographical region where malaria was a significant threat. The sickle cell gene provided protection against malaria for people of African and Mediterranean descent. The symptoms of sickle cell disease are variable and can range from mild to severe. One of the complications of sickle cell disease is vasco-occlusion. This is a process whereby blood flow is affected due to the involved red blood cells that are sticky and rigid and flow poorly throughout the body. These vasco-occlusions are painful and can result in destructive changes in the body's organs, involving the eyes (blindness), brain (stroke), heart (failure), lungs (scarring), liver/spleen (failure), kidneys (loss of function), or sex organs (impotence; Holbrook & Phillips, 1994).

New medication and treatment regimens have made the complications of sickle cell disease less severe today than in the past. Nevertheless, individuals with sickle cell disease will have to cope with many health challenges throughout their lives. Since pain is a most common symptom, learning to cope with pain is important.

In terms of psychological well-being, people with sickle cell disease have a higher incidence of social and psychological problems (including anxiety and depression) than people without sickle cell disease (Burlew, Telfair,

Colangelo, & Wright, 2000; Hasan, Hashmi, Alhassen, Lawson, & Castro, 2003; Molock & Belgrave, 1994). These increased problems are attributed to chronic pain and increased anxiety that may be associated with concerns about body deterioration or mortality (Barrett et al., 1988). Among children, the disease may disrupt patterns of normal functioning such as going to school, developing independence from adults, playing with peers, dating (among adolescents), and so forth.

There has been stigma attached to having sickle cell disease in part because it is a disease that primarily affects African Americans in this country. People with sickle cell disease have been concerned that the diagnosis will lead to more stereotyping and discrimination in the work environment. For example, a famous singer, Tionne (T-Boz) Watkins, did not initially disclose that she had sickle cell disease, until she became ill on tour. She later became a spokesperson for persons with sickle cell disease.

It is possible for people with sickle cell disease to have a good quality of life. Management of the psychological as well as the medical aspects of the disease is important. Thompson and colleagues (1996) found that good psychological adjustment among persons with sickle cell disease was enhanced by lower levels of perceived daily stress, less negative thinking, high levels of family support, and low levels of conflict and control.

LUPUS

Systemic lupus erythematosus (Lupus) is a chronic inflammatory disease that strikes an individual's immune system. The disease produces large quantities of antibodies that attack healthy tissue in the skin, joints, kidneys, lungs, heart, nervous system, blood, and other organs. The symptoms are many and varied; the fact that the illness mimics other diseases makes it difficult to diagnose, and sometimes Lupus is overlooked as a diagnosis (Lupus Foundation of America, 2001).

Common symptoms of lupus include painful swollen joints, extreme fatigue, skin rashes, sun or light sensitivity, hair loss, anemia, butterfly rash, kidney problems, and frequent fevers. Research suggests there is a genetic predisposition for Lupus (Tsao, 1998).

Lupus is much more prevalent among women than men and often starts between the ages of 15 and 44. With as many as 1 in 250 African American women acquiring the disease, lupus is three times more common in African American women than in White women; the reason for this is unknown. Also, symptoms and complications of the disease appear to be more severe among African Americans than among Whites (Alarcon et al., 1998).

Psychological and social consequences of lupus include loss of physical and social function, fear of death, fear of increasing disability, and depression (McCracken, Semenchuk, & Goetsch, 1995). Adaptive coping strategies can help individuals with lupus to have positive social and psychological outcomes. Individuals who use passive coping strategies such as avoidance and self-blaming demonstrate poorer psychological adjustment and functional status. On the other hand, active coping strategies such as making a plan of action are associated with better adjustment and ability to perform activities of daily living (McCracken et al., 1995).

DIABETES

Diabetes mellitus is a group of diseases characterized by high levels of blood glucose. It results from defects in insulin secretions, action, or both (Diabetes Prevention Program Research Group, 2002). Approximately 90% to 95% of African Americans with diabetes have type 2 (rather than type 1) diabetes. Type 2 diabetes occurs later in life and is caused by the body's resistance to the action of insulin and to impaired insulin secretions. It can be treated with diet, exercise, pills, or injections. A much smaller percentage of African Americans have type 1 diabetes, which usually develops before age 20. It is always treated with insulin.

African Americans are twice as likely as Whites to have diabetes. About one third of the U.S. population with diabetes is African American, and approximately 13% of all African Americans have diabetes. Diabetes is much more likely to occur among older than younger African Americans (Harris et al., 1998). Among African Americans younger than 20 years old, 1% have diabetes compared with 32% of African Americans in the 65 to 74 year age range.

Several factors contribute to the higher incidence of diabetes among African Americans. Genetics may play a role. For example, some researchers speculate that for type 2 diabetes, there is a gene that came from Africa. Years ago this gene was functional and enabled Africans, during feast and famine cycles, to conserve food energy more efficiently when food was scarce. The gene that developed to help survival in Africa may instead make a person more susceptible for developing type 2 diabetes now (Harris et al., 1998).

A second risk factor for diabetes is prediabetes, also known as impaired glucose tolerance. This occurs in people whose blood glucose levels are higher than normal but not high enough for them to be diagnosed with diabetes (Harris et al., 1998).

Being overweight is a third risk factor for diabetes (Crespo, Keteyian, Heath, & Sempos, 1996; Troiano, Flegal, Kuczmarski, Campbell, & Johnson, 1995). In addition to being overweight, the location in which the excess weight is carried contributes to the risk. African Americans are more likely to have upper-body fat. Related to this factor is another: physical activity. Researchers speculate that lower levels of physical activity may be one of the major contributors to increased diabetes among African Americans.

African Americans with diabetes experience more complications such as kidney failure, eye disease, and amputations than do Whites with diabetes. They also have greater disability, functional limitations, and deaths due to diabetes than do Whites (National Diabetes Information Clearinghouse, 2002).

Individuals can lower their risk for diabetes, however. The Diabetes Prevention Program Research Group conducted a study that looked at how type 2 diabetes could be prevented or delayed among people with impaired glucose tolerance, a risk factor for diabetes (National Diabetes Information Clearinghouse, 2002). The findings of this study show that people at high risk for type 2 diabetes can lower their chances of developing diabetes with lifestyle modifications such as diet and exercise.

Methodological Issues in Studying Health and Illness Among African Americans

When conducting health and medical research among African Americans, researchers must address several methodological issues. These include (a) researchers' lack of access to participants and participants' mistrust of research intent, (b) inadequate data collection protocols and measures, and (c) the cultural context of participants.

LACK OF ACCESS AND MISTRUST

One often-cited problem in conducting research on African American samples is gaining access to communities and participants within these communities. Some African Americans may be distrustful of health research and programs, especially those that do not originate from within the African American community. African Americans have been used in programs of research to gain insight into a medical problem or health issue without the knowledge gained coming back to the African American community. This was seen in the Tuskegee study discussed previously.

When African Americans are approached about participation, they may meet such requests with guarded suspicion. The researcher who is not a member of the community may not be perceived as credible or sincere. To gain support for conducting research and planning appropriate programs, it is necessary to forge positive alliances with both the formal and informal leadership of the community. These may include religious and civic leaders, local citizen groups, sororities, fraternities, and historically Black colleges and universities.

INADEQUATE DATA COLLECTION
PROTOCOL AND MEASURES

A second methodological consideration is that measures and data collection protocols that have been developed for White participants may not be appropriate for African Americans. African American families may not have the resources to come to the researcher's office to complete a questionnaire or to have a medical assessment done. In such cases, coordination of time and money to engage participants is necessary. In our research, we have found it necessary to go to the participant's home to collect data. In addition, some research participants may have responsibilities such as in-home child care and may lack transportation to research facilities.

When surveys and questionnaires are collected in the participant's home, researchers need to be aware that this setting may affect respondents' answers. In a participant's home, in contrast to a research office, there are likely to be more distractions, and all members of the household will feel the researcher's presence. Under these circumstances, the researcher has to be sensitive to how her presence is disruptive to the functioning of the household. Other places to collect data include public places such as libraries, fast-food restaurants, and clinics. The main point is that the researcher must be flexible when collecting data and conducting assessments.

Another problem in conducting health and medical research is that often health and medical status measures and instruments have not been developed with consideration given to the health problems and diseases that affect African Americans. Consider research on health and psychological outcomes among persons with sickle cell disease. The health status measures that have been developed for other types of chronic illnesses may not be appropriate for sickle cell disease. For example, pain and accompanying physical and psychological symptoms from a sickle cell crisis may differ from the pain and/or discomfort from other types of medical conditions (e.g., asthma).

CULTURAL CONTEXT OF PARTICIPANTS

The cultural context in which individuals experience a chronic illness must also be considered. Researchers should be aware of other social and economic issues that the individual has to deal with in addition to the disease. Treatment recommendations are not likely to be taken seriously if the clients or research participants are concerned with basic shelter, food, and safety. In addition, concerns with diseases and chronic illnesses that some African Americans perceive as stigmatizing must be considered, regardless of whether or not others actually stigmatize individuals with these conditions.

Summary

The proverb at the beginning of this chapter, "He who conceals his illness cannot expect to be cured," conveys the importance of acknowledging one's health condition and engaging in corrective actions and behavior. As we have noted throughout this chapter, many of these behaviors are influenced by culture.

There are disparities between African Americans and Whites in health, medical, and rehabilitation utilization patterns. Several factors contribute to these disparities, including access factors, attitudinal barriers, cultural differences, and various forms of racism. Strategies for improving utilization patterns and adherence can be implemented at the individual, family, community, and institutional levels. Increased empowerment of African Americans for assuming responsibilities for health and related outcomes is an important first step. Models of health, particularly the health belief model, the theory of planned behavior, and self-efficacy theory, have been used to understand and predict health-related outcomes, but they have limited use for predicting health outcomes among African Americans. Theories that consider culture, race, ethnicity, and class could be used to augment these models.

Hypertension, sickle cell disease, lupus, and diabetes are found among African Americans at rates much higher than those of other ethnic groups. Although the symptoms and consequences of these diseases can lead to serious health problems, these diseases can also be managed with appropriate medical and psychological treatment delivered in a culturally appropriate manner.

There are several methodological problems to consider when conducting health-related research and interventions with African Americans. These include (a) lack of access and mistrust, (b) inadequacy of data collection and measures, and (c) cultural context of participants.

12   Psychosocial Adaptation and Mental Health

The wind does not break a tree that bends.

—Sukuma proverb

Pretending There's No Racism Hurts Kids

Dec. 7, 2004

By Alison McCook

NEW YORK (Reuters Health)—African-American preschoolers whose parents say they don't believe racism is a problem are more likely to be depressed or anxious, a new study indicates.

"Racism is a reality," lead author Dr. Margaret O'Brien Caughy said. "It does have impact on very young children. And we have to acknowledge that," she noted.

Caughy said that there are many reasons why young children may become anxious if their parents deny the existence of racism. For one thing, parents who experience racism but don't acknowledge it may be anxious or depressed themselves, and pass that onto their children, she noted.

Otherwise, young children may witness signs of racism around them, and become upset when their parents' opinions don't match their experience.

"If (children) see in their day-to-day lives that racism is real, but their parents don't acknowledge it, could that create anxiety?" Caughy asked.

Traditionally, people who report they have experienced racism are more likely to have problems with their physical or mental health. In order to investigate whether denying instances of discrimination hurts health even more, Caughy and her team interviewed 200 African-American families with children aged 3 or 4.

Caughy, who is based at the University of Texas Health Sciences Center in Dallas, along with her colleagues, asked parents how often they experienced racism and how they coped with it, then measured children's behavior.

Approximately 7 percent of parents denied that racism was a problem for their friends and family, the authors report in the *American Journal of Public Health*.

In an interview with Reuters Health, Caughy explained that parents who said they didn't think racism was a problem for African-Americans in general were more likely to have young children with problems such as anxiety or depression.

She noted that parents who denied that they had experienced racism personally were no more likely to have children with these problems, and denying racism in general did not increase kids' risk of so-called "externalizing" behavior problems, such as aggression or acting out.

Although the team did not measure whether or not people had actually experienced racism, research suggests that 90 percent of African-Americans who say they are not discriminated against indeed are, according to objective measurements.

Parents who responded to racism by confronting the people involved or taking some kind of action were less likely to report that their children had behavior problems.

The findings suggest that parents should try to talk to children about racism, on a level they can understand, Caughy said. "Acknowledging it, that it's real . . . and then trying to help children develop realistic coping skills" appears to do the most good, she noted.

Introduction and Definitions

When we are able to work, play, love, and handle the challenges that life throws our way, we enjoy a sense of well-being, contentment, competence, peace, and perhaps even happiness. Although most of us experience times when we feel down, overwhelmed, upset, or disappointed, the extent to which difficult emotions or behaviors interfere with our ability to cope and function may reflect difficulties and problems in adaptation and mental health. In this chapter, we consider issues of well-being and health in the psychosocial domain for African Americans. As illustrated in the news release above, there may be important aspects of the experience of African Americans that may affect, support, or interfere with well-being, coping, and adaptation.

In this chapter, we examine a range of issues to support our understanding of the psychosocial adaptation of African Americans. This includes an overview of definitions and conceptual perspectives on adaptation, as well as conceptual and theoretical models of adjustment and maladaptation. We examine methodological issues relevant to adjustment, including assessment, and we review the research on the adaptation of African Americans. We also consider ways in which African Americans respond to problems in adaptation, including their use of mental health services and the ways in which these services can be provided most effectively. Finally, we consider theoretical applications and empirical lessons. The chapter ends with a summary.

DEFINITIONS AND PERSPECTIVES

Individuals and cultures make attempts to understand and sometimes change the behavior, emotions, or thinking of members of their group that most group members consider strange, troubling, or abnormal. These behaviors and experiences become troublesome when they cause some significant level of distress either to the individual or to others in the surrounding social environment. According to the World Health Organization (WHO),[1] 5 of the top 10 causes of disability internationally are mental and neurological disorders. Mental and neurological problems result in increasing levels of economic and social burden to individuals, families, communities, and nations.

In the psychological traditions of Western Europe, psychological maladjustment has been viewed from multiple theoretical frameworks. In the Western tradition, there are developmental models that emphasize deviations from a "normal" sequence of maturation or skill development. These perspectives consider maladaptation as a lag in or arrest from acquiring the abilities or skills that an individual is expected to achieve during a specific developmental period. For example, Freud viewed psychological dysfunction as an arrested development in an individual's expected progression through normal stages of psychosexual development. These problems in development most often result in the use of maladaptive strategies (e.g., defense mechanisms) in response to the distress or anxiety generated because of competing internal and external presses.

Other views of maladaptive psychological functioning include behavioral perspectives from the early work of Skinner, Pavlov, and Watson. Behavioral perspectives define psychological dysfunction as the set of undesirable (to the individual in his or her social context) behaviors. Dysfunction is based on the learning and maintenance of maladaptive behavioral responses through reinforcement, association (e.g., classical conditioning), or modeling. Behavioral perspectives often compare individuals' behaviors to age norms or averages. For example, the Child Behavior Checklist (Achenbach & Edelbrock, 1984) is an instrument used to examine behavioral problems in children and adolescents and is based on comparing reports made by parents, teachers, or children/adolescents of how frequently a young person engages in a specific behavior (e.g., lying) to how often other children of that individual's similar age and gender engage in that behavior.

Those who hold the humanistic perspective (e.g., Rogers, Maslow) view maladaptation as rising from the conflicts individuals experience in trying to meet their needs and the conflicts they might experience between their view of themselves (i.e., their actual or "real" self) and the person that they believe they should be (i.e., their "ideal" self). In contrast, family system theories view individuals as part of a system (i.e., the family) and see psychological problems in an individual as stemming from ineffective strategies and problems in the ways that the family functions and interacts.

Currently in the United States, the primary classification system used by professionals to understand psychological maladaption is the *Diagnostic and Statistical Manual of Mental Disorders, Fourth Edition–Text Revision (DSM-IV-TR)* of the American Psychiatric Association (APA; 2000). This system, grounded in the medical model, is based on illness concepts and defines psychological dysfunctions as deviations from a state of health.

Conceptualization of Psychological Dysfunction Among African Americans

In conceptualizing psychological dysfunction among African Americans, several authors have used European models as a point of departure. Building somewhat on the psychodynamic tradition, Welsing (1991) emphasizes the role and importance of symbolism. For example, Welsing suggests that the shape, color, and size of balls used in American sports, as well as weapons (e.g., guns and missiles) and historical monuments, reflect dynamic and symbolic issues that have deeper racial and sexual implications. (For a broader discussion of Black-White issues incorporating a psychodynamic perspective, also see Fanon's [1967] *Black Skin, White Masks*).

In contrast to European perspectives, other theoreticians have articulated Africentric perspectives on adaptation. For example, Azibo (1989) writes,

> Mental health is the achievement in the psychological and behavioral spheres of life of a functioning that (a) is in harmony with and (b) embraces the natural order . . . [and is] that psychological and behavioral functioning that is in accord with the basic nature of the original human nature and its attendant cosmology and survival thrust. (pp. 176–177)

Rather than a focus emphasizing mental "illness" (from a health or medical model perspective), the focus from an Africentric perspective is on mental "order" and "disorder." Azibo criticizes the Eurocentric perspective for its lack of a conceptually and theoretically grounded articulation of the concepts of mental health. Grounded in the African cosmological principle of *Anokwalei Enyo* ("two relative truths"; Wobogo, as cited in Azibo, 1989),

Azibo writes that mental order and disorder must be seen in relation to one another. Azibo further emphasizes the importance of the self and survival; one's sense of communal self, and the acknowledgment of the role of cultural values is important in understanding mental health and personal adjustment. Mental order is considered "correct psychological and behavioral functioning" (Azibo, 1989, p. 179) that is congruent with the natural order, universal forces, and God.

Based on results from her qualitative study of 117 college-age, adult, and older adult African Americans, Edwards (1999) provides a hierarchy of dimensions that define the "essential characteristics of a psychologically healthy African American/Black person" (p. 306). Starting with the most important dimension of African American psychological health are the following:

1. Ideological/Belief references: spiritual guidance, needing a belief in God, treating fellow man correctly, being in touch with Supreme Being, being what and who you are and getting blessings from God, putting Christ Jesus at the head of the house, strong cultural identity, being Black and proud, being pragmatic, common sense, and realizing that not all days will be happy

2. Moral Worth: self-respect, self-love, good esteem, strong self-worth, satisfied with God-created self, truth, honesty, responsible to love, being happy with what you do, being true to self and others, respect for others, compassion, empathy, understanding, caring, God, Godliness

3. Interpersonal Style: Communicating to strengthen relationships, to express yourself and your true feelings and a message, assertive, respect for others, caring, loving, secure relationships, understanding significant others, having compassion, being friendly

4. Competence: intelligent, able, mentally strong, adaptable, resilient, survival skills, educated, reading a lot, know limits

5. Determination: determined, will-power, control over one's life, goal-oriented, working toward objectives and being true to objectives

6. Unity: inner peace and beauty, know yourself, understand yourself, strive for fullest potential

7. Health/Physical: good health, health and diet, appearance, beauty of self (especially with darker skinned women), cleanliness, and personal hygiene (pp. 292–293)

This list is congruent with many of the core Africentric values of spirituality, communalism, a relational orientation, and interdependence. (See Chapter 2 for a more detailed discussion of these core values.)

Theoretical and Conceptual
Models of Mental Health

Several schools of thought have been utilized within American psychology to understand and intervene with behavior that is viewed as maladaptive. More recently, more integrative models of psychology have evolved which underline the interaction of human systems in understanding adaptation and maladaptation.

BIOPSYCHOSOCIAL PERSPECTIVE ON ADAPTATION

Biopsychosocial perspectives emphasize the interaction of biological, psychological, and social systems in our understanding of an individual's behavioral, emotional, and cognitive functioning. A behavioral problem (i.e., a psychological symptom) may be rooted in a genetic vulnerability (i.e., a biological factor), which may or may not be exacerbated by an environmental condition (e.g., higher levels of stress experiences because of social stratification and limited access to resources).

An example of this work can be found in the literature on African Americans and stress and coping. Lazarus and Folkman (1984) define stress as the experience of threat, loss, or challenge by individuals when they perceive that they do not have the personal resources to respond to the demands they are facing. Coping is defined as the emotional, behavioral, and cognitive strategies and responses used by a person in response to these demands. One's experience of stress is related to both one's cognitive perception of an event or circumstance as causing threat, loss, or challenge (i.e., primary appraisal) and one's sense of whether one has enough resources with which to respond to the demand (secondary appraisal). Research using the stress and coping model has found that as a group, African Americans experience higher levels of stress than European Americans (e.g., Askenasy, Dohrenwend, & Dohrenwend, 1977), and that both race and socioeconomic status (SES) contribute to stress experiences. In addition, race and SES may interact such that Blacks at lower levels of SES are at higher risk of negative stress-related outcomes (Ulbrich, Warheit, & Zimmerman, 1989).

In addition, Blacks may have high levels of stressful life experiences linked directly to individual and specific experiences of overt racism. Landrine and Klonoff (1996b) developed the Schedule of Racist Events to measure an individual's exposure to such experiences. This 18-item inventory assesses how often respondents have experienced racist events (e.g., "How many times have you been treated unfairly by people in service jobs [store clerks, waiters, bartenders, bank tellers, and others] because you are Black?") over the past year and in their lifetime. The authors found that

African American adults who reported greater exposure to racist events were more likely to report higher levels of smoking, health problems, and stress-related symptoms (e.g., depression, anxiety, and interpersonal sensitivity). Research has also suggested that African Americans who minimize or ignore experiences with racism may be at higher risk of cardio-vascular disease (e.g., Johnson & Greene, 1991; Krieger, 1990).

In addition to overt experiences of racism, African Americans may also experience what is referred to as "mundane extreme stress" (Peters & Massey, 1983), that is, stress which is attributed to the chronic and often subtle daily experiences of bias, discrimination, and racism.

In conceptualizing work with diverse ethnic groups including African Americans, Slavin, Rainer, McCreary, and Gowda (1991) have proposed an adaptation of Lazarus and Folkman's model that considers the explicit role of culture in the experience of stress. These authors suggest that culture may be important in shaping the experience of stress at each step of the stress and coping process. This may involve cultural variations in the ways that events are perceived. For example, someone who is African American may believe an event is occurring because of his or her race and ethnicity. Culture may also shape the types of coping resources to which an individual has access or which an individual decides to use. For example, African Americans may be more likely than members of other cultural groups to use fictive kin as coping resources (Stack, 1974). Culture may also shape the specific types of outcomes that are linked to stress exposure. For example, Blacks are overrepresented among individuals suffering from a range of stress-related diseases (e.g., heart disease, stroke; Flack et al., 1995). (For a review of stress and coping work that focuses on issues of prejudice, racism, and culture, see Allison, 1998.)

AFRICENTRIC PERSPECTIVES ON ADAPTATION

In addition to the Africentric perspective presented earlier in Azibo's definition of mental order and disorder, several Africentric theorists have provided conceptualizations of psychological adaptation and maladaptation. For example, Myers (1991, 1992) writes that an African worldview is an optimal worldview that not only promotes an individual's well-being but also provides a scientific and therapeutic perspective on psychological adjustment that supports optimal human functioning at both individual and societal levels. (See Chapter 2 for additional information on the optimal worldview.)

Azibo's Model of Mental Health and Disorder

Azibo's (1989) model of mental health and disorder takes "*the Black perspective* (cultural, historical, and conceptual analysis that employs and affirms principles deriving from the African social reality) *as the conceptual base for addressing the psychology of African people* [italics per original]" (p. 175) and involves the assumption that "personality has a biogenetic basis" (p. 175) and that there is a natural order to all things. Azibo operates from a "meta-personality" perspective that articulates three levels or components of a racially (i.e., genetically) based human personality. The "inner core" includes physical or biological factors such as spirituality, melanin, and rhythm. The "outer core" consists of cognitive components such as attitudes, values, and beliefs, as well as the behavioral manifestations of these components in action. Azibo also identified a third core of "nonracial" aspects of personality. These are peripheral individual differences such as shyness and assertiveness.

Azibo (1989) provides a conceptual model of maladaptation for African Americans that includes "psychological misorientation," a basic Black personality disorder that results from an individual operating without an African belief system. When this disorder is present, Azibo indicates there is incongruence between a person's biologic-genetic base and that person's behavior and cognition. Another important concept in Azibo's model is *mentacide*, the process by which individuals lose their psychological Blackness.

Mentacide has been defined as the intentional destruction of an ethnic group's collective mind or the oppressive imposition of another culture as a means of dominating the oppressed group. Mentacide includes forms that affect peripheral aspects of the self (i.e., major depression, generalized anxiety, or eating disorders) or that are alienating in nature (i.e., that undermine an individual's psychological sense of Blackness).

According to Azibo, misorientation is a precursor to another Black personality disorder, materialism depression. Materialism depression is grounded in a sense of relative deprivation and need for possessions to support one's sense of self. Azibo notes that misorientation and mentacide may play a role in a range of personal identity conflicts (e.g., individualism and anxiety over one's collective identity); reactionary disorders (e.g., psychological brainwashing, burnout, and oppression violence reactions), as described by Fanon (1963); self-destructive disorders (e.g., suicide, prostitution, drug and alcohol abuse, Black-on-Black crime), described by Akbar (1981); and theological (i.e., religious) misorientation. It is important to note that mentacide may occur without misorientation. For example, persons may suffer problems in psychological adaptation from the process of mentacide (e.g., developing a generalized anxiety disorder associated with life stress) without their being misoriented (i.e., the individual would still have a "correct" Black cognitive orientation).

Extending this work, Abdullah (1998) discusses disorders such as "mammy-ism" as a subcategory of psychological misorientation. Mammy-ism involves the dysfunctional assumption of caretaking behaviors and roles by Black women to the detriment of themselves and their own families and social networks.

Akbar's Perspectives on Mental Disorder

Akbar (1981) has articulated a nosology of mental disorders based on the premise that a pathological society (i.e., a social system that incorporates racism, oppression, and unnaturalness) leads to four types of disorders: self-destructive (described earlier), alien-self, anti-self, and organic. Within the alien-self disorder, individuals behave in ways that do not support their survival. Akbar indicates that individuals may manifest this disorder through neurotic anxiety and identity disturbances such as low self-esteem. A person with an anti-self disorder identifies with and has internalized the majority culture's negative stereotypes and pejorative attitudes regarding Blacks. Anti-self individuals express overt and covert hostility toward their own group. Akbar argues that organic disorders (e.g., hypertension, schizophrenia) may also be related to pathological social processes and linked to anti- and alien-self disturbances.

Recent research supports the idea that cultural factors are relevant to adjustment. For example, Yasui, Dorham, and Dishion (2004) found that ethnic identity is important to the adjustment of African American adolescents.

Approaches to Studying the Mental Health of African Americans

There are several approaches to studying the mental health of African Americans. Three include service utilization data, epidemiological studies, and the national survey of Black Americans.

SERVICE UTILIZATION DATA

Before the 1980s, service utilization data was used as an indicator of psychopathology. These data suggested that African Americans were more likely to have higher rates of mental health service use than other ethnic groups, especially when considering inpatient and residential care (Cheung, 1991). However, service utilization data, especially service use data that exclude clients seen in private settings, offer very limited information about differences in actual rates of psychopathology between cultural groups. This is due to a number of reasons. Various cultural groups may have different values about seeking services for mental health problems or may see these difficulties as medical, spiritual, or family problems as opposed to mental health problems. Some cultural groups may distrust available service centers or service providers, may not know of available services, or may find them unfamiliar, unwelcoming, or not congruent with their cultural beliefs and practices. These factors may contribute to African

Americans not coming in for mental health services when problems are less severe, resulting in delayed access to intervention and greater utilization of emergency and inpatient services. Who ends up using mental health services depends on a number of different factors, of which type and level of psychopathology are only two.

EPIDEMIOLOGICAL STUDIES

Epidemiological studies are a better means of understanding rates of psychopathology in a group and variations between groups than are service utilization studies. *Epidemiology* is the study of the rates of the incidence and prevalence of a health or mental health condition in a population (i.e., an entire group of people, e.g., Americans) or a representative sample of those people. The *incidence* of a disorder is the number of new cases that occur within a particular time period (e.g., within a year), whereas *prevalence* involves the total number of people within a population or a representative sample of a population that have a specific disorder at a particular point or period in time (e.g., over a lifetime). To better understand the incidence and prevalence of mental disorders within the United States, a number of epidemiological studies have been conducted. These can assist us in understanding similarities and differences between ethnic and racial groups in types and rates of psychopathology.

The National Institutes of Mental Health (NIMH) Epidemiological Catchment Area (ECA) study (Robins & Reiger, 1991) is one epidemiological study. Five research teams conducted household surveys in Baltimore, Maryland; Durham, North Carolina; Los Angeles, California; New Haven, Connecticut; and St. Louis, Missouri, using the NIMH Diagnostic Interview Schedule (DIS). This is a structured interview that allows researchers to make a diagnosis based on *DSM-III* criteria. Results from this study indicated few differences in the lifetime prevalence of mental disorders across race and ethnicity. African Americans had a significantly higher lifetime risk for phobia and lower risk of depression (Robins et al., 1984) and cognitive disorders among those 45 and over, and slightly higher rates of somatization as compared with Whites.

A second epidemiological study, the National Comorbidity Survey, likewise found few differences, but noted slightly lower rates of substance abuse and affective disorders, as well as lower levels of comorbidity and overall levels of lifetime prevalence of mental illness among African Americans as compared with Whites (Kessler et al., 1994).

NATIONAL SURVEY OF BLACK AMERICANS

Another study that has provided important information on the mental health of African Americans is the National Survey of Black Americans

(NSBA). The original sample included 2,107 Black Americans 18 years of age or older. The study used a national probability sample, selecting participants so that they are representative of the range of African Americans in the United States. Wave I of data was collected in 1979–1980. Three subsequent waves of data were collected (Wave II, a 1987–1988 telephone survey follow-up of 951 adults; Wave III, a 1988–1989 telephone survey follow-up of 793 adults; and Wave IV, a 1992 telephone survey follow-up of 659 adults interviewed in the 1987–1988 and the 1988–1989 surveys). In contrast to many research questions that focus on making between-group comparisons, in most cases examining differences between African Americans and European Americans, the NSBA provides an important opportunity to examine the variability (i.e., within-group differences) of mental health issues among African Americans. Research based on this data set has indicated that prayer is an important coping strategy for African Americans, especially among those with lower incomes, females, and older adults (over age 55; Neighbors, Jackson, Bowman, & Gurin, 1983). Across time (from 1979 through 1992), responses from African American study participants demonstrate a significant decrease in self-reports of happiness and an increase in environmental and serious personal problems but overall, an increase in reports of life satisfaction (Neighbors & Jackson, 1996). (For a full report of findings from the NSBA, see Neighbors & Jackson, 1996.)

OTHER APPROACHES TO STUDYING MENTAL HEALTH

There are other alternative indices that provide some insight into the psychosocial functioning and adaptation of cultural groups. For example, researchers have examined rates of suicide across different ethnic groups. White males account for a considerable majority of completed suicide among American ethno-gender groups (i.e., groups defined by both ethnicity and gender). Also some Native American and Asian American groups are disproportionately represented among individuals who commit suicide. It is notable, however, that between 1980 and 1992, African American males had the largest increase in rates of suicide. Within the 15- to 19-year-old age group, from 1980 to 1996 the rate of suicide for African American males increased 105% (Centers for Disease Control and Prevention [CDC], 1998). These data may not reflect the actual number of deaths by suicide among African American males because the data do not take into account phenomena such as "suicide by police," high rates of homicide, and other related forms of self-endangerment.

MENTAL HEALTH AND SOCIAL STATUS: THE CONFOUNDING OF RACE AND SOCIOECONOMIC STATUS

One important issue in trying to understand data on the mental health status of African Americans is the confounding of SES and ethnic group membership within the United States. For example, census data clearly indicate that African Americans have overall lower levels of income and educational attainment than do Whites and are more likely to live below the poverty level. Research also indicates that SES is related to mental health. Individuals with lower levels of resources are more likely to have a psychiatric diagnosis. Two models have been proposed to explain the link between SES and psychopathology. The social causation hypothesis suggests that the greater experience of stress and more limited access to resources and supports lead to problems in adaptive functioning. In contrast, the social selection hypothesis suggests that vulnerabilities, potentially biological in nature, lead to problems in adaptation, which in turn lead to individuals entering (or being "selected" into) a lower socioeconomic level. There is reasonable support for the social causation hypothesis, and data suggest that social selection also may occur, but not such that individuals drift downward within their lifetime or cohort, but that they may fail to progress economically or replicate their parents' SES level (Hudson, 1988). Related research by Kessler and Neighbors (1986) found that ethnicity and SES interact such that members of ethnic minority groups low in SES are at higher risk of mental disorder.

Issues in Mental Health Services Utilization

Although service use data may not be very useful in understanding differences between ethnic groups in adaptive functioning, these data can help us understand how people respond to mental health issues, how different types of services are used by various cultural group members, and to which services different groups have access.

DROPOUT, RETENTION, AND UTILIZATION

Early data on dropout and retention in psychotherapy indicated that African Americans (and members of other ethnic minority groups) were more likely to drop out or "prematurely" terminate therapy than White clients (Wierzbicki & Pekarik, 1993). Terrell and Terrell (1984) found that Blacks high in cultural mistrust who were seen by White therapists for their initial visits to a community mental health center were less likely to return than Blacks high in mistrust seen by Black therapists. Black clients with severe disturbance who are also high in cultural mistrust prefer Black clinicians, although they also believe that White clinicians are better trained (Whaley, 2001). In addition, cultural mistrust is linked to greater wariness about help seeking in general (Nickerson, Helms, & Terrell, 1994).

More recent work on cultural differences in service utilization documents fewer ethnic differences in dropout rates, but has noted important variations in service utilization by context (Snowden & Hu, 1997). For example, O'Sullivan, Peterson, Cox, and Kirkeby (1989) conducted a 10-year follow-up of Sue's (1977) early and mid-1970s examination of service delivery to ethnic minority groups and provide an examination of historical changes in service use. These data indicate that by the early to mid-1980's, Blacks (and Native Americans) continued to be overrepresented in community mental health center client populations, but that failure-to-return rates for African Americans, which had been 52% in 1971–1972, decreased to 22% in 1983, not significantly different from Whites (18% in 1983, down from 30% in 1971–1972). More recently, Takeuchi, Sue, and Yeh (1998) used data from the Los Angeles County Department of Mental Health to examine treatment outcomes (i.e., continuation, total number of sessions, and Global Assessment of Functioning scores [GAF]) comparing "ethnic specific" programs (i.e., mental health sites in which more than 50% of clients were from a specific ethnic group) and mainstream programs (i.e., sites in which more than 50% of clients were White). In culturally specific sites, African American clients were more likely to have an African American therapist (70%) than in a mainstreamed site (17%). African American clients in culturally specific programs, even after controlling for client-therapist match, were more likely to return for a second session (77% vs. 60% in mainstream programs), and were more likely to stay in therapy for more sessions. At intake, African American clients were more likely to show lower GAF scores, but there were no significant differences at discharge for African Americans or any of the other ethnic groups examined (i.e., Asian Americans and Mexican Americans).

Data from the NIMH ECA study (Robins & Regier, 1991) indicate that individuals who have a recent psychiatric disorder are between the ages of 25 and 44, female, White, of higher educational attainment, and single. They have a greater likelihood of using any type (either public or private) of mental health services (Swartz et al., 1998). Likelihood of treatment in a public setting is higher for males, African Americans and individuals with lower educational attainment and income. It is also notable that use of public services is significantly lower for the elderly.

Data on service experiences of children and adolescents suggests that there may be some important racial differences. Kodjo and Auinger (2004) found that among adolescents scoring relatively high in distress in the National Longitudinal Study of Adolescent Health, African American youth were less likely to receive counseling than their Hispanic or White peers, even when family income was controlled. Using data from the Integrated Database on Children and Family Services in the state of Illinois, Pavkov, George, and Czapkowicz (1997) found that African American youth had longer psychiatric hospital stays than youth from other ethnic groups; however, once other factors were considered (e.g., age, gender, dangerousness, diagnostic category, ethnicity), being an African American youth with a psychotic disorder increased likelihood of discharge (i.e., shorter stays). African American youth are also more likely to receive shorter outpatient treatment than White youth (Cuffe, Waller, Cuccaro, Pumariega, & Garrison, 1995).

INSURANCE

Another important consideration relating to the use of and access to mental health services is the ability to pay for services and having insurance. Recent attention has turned to the increasing role of managed care in the provision of mental health services for different racial and ethnic group members. Dana (1998) suggests that mental health services offered by managed care systems emphasize cost-effectiveness and assume that treatment effectiveness is similar across all cultural groups. However, because the research on which managed care treatment guidelines are based has largely not addressed multicultural issues in equal treatment outcomes, members of multicultural populations may receive inappropriate or inadequate care.

Similarly, Snowden (1998) indicates that managed care may create incentives that discourage African Americans from using services. Snowden cites data from the National Medical Expenditure Survey (Frieman, Cunningham, & Cornelius, 1994) that indicated that average mental health service costs for Whites were $975.00 in 1987, compared with $1,445.00 per African American service user. This discrepancy is due to the greater likelihood of inpatient care for African Americans. The increasing use of managed health care services in the public sector, and steps to include mental heath services within this service delivery model, make these concerns increasingly important.

INVOLUNTARY COMMITMENT

In considering treatment and intervention for mental health services, it is also notable that research has found Blacks to be overrepresented among individuals involuntarily committed to public mental hospitals in the United States (Lindsey & Paul, 1989). Based on principles of dangerousness (because of the risk of injury to self or others) or grave disability (i.e., inability to function in independent self-care) because of mental illness, the majority of states allow individuals to be legally hospitalized without their voluntary consent. Although rates of involuntary commitment have declined since the 1960s because of legal protections for individuals and patient rights and increased utilization of psychotropic medications, Blacks were at greater risk of involuntary commitment. Early arguments linked higher rates of involuntary commitment for Blacks with several factors, including greater genetic propensity to mental illness, greater vulnerability because of lower SES, more limited access to alternative intervention service treatment, and coming to a more deteriorated stage of illness.

MENTAL HEALTH AND OTHER SOCIAL SYSTEMS

In understanding race and culture in interventions for African Americans, it is important to examine the ways in which other social structures may be related to mental health interventions for African Americans. Two system interfaces may be particularly important to consider: schools and criminal justice. Work in the area of criminal justice raises important concerns regarding the differential treatment of youth and adults based on ethnicity and mental health status. For example, work by Cohen et al. (1990) found that in a disposition program, the only difference between youth referred for psychotherapeutic treatment as opposed to detention was race.

Mental health issues are also relevant in education settings. For example, African American youth are more likely than Whites to be identified for special educational placement both because of cognitive functioning and because of emotional or behavioral functioning. School systems, parents, advocates, legislators, and educational and psychological researchers have struggled with the distinctions between youth who demonstrate "social maladjustment" as opposed to "emotional disturbance," because Public Law 94-142 (the Education for All Handicapped Children Act of 1975) and the recent amendments to the Individuals with Disabilities Education Act in 1997 require that all children have access to a "free and appropriate" education in the least restrictive environment. Student safety and school system financial concerns have been important and difficult factors linked to decisions in providing services for socially maladjusted youth who do not have the same legal protections (e.g., from school expulsion) as do emotionally disturbed youth.

AFRICAN THERAPEUTIC PRACTICES

In contrast to American service delivery models, Maiello (1999), a White, Western psychotherapist, describes the work of a South African healer, a *sangoma*. This description involves the successful traditional healing of a young man who had experienced confusion, hallucination, stereotypic movement, and loss of reality contact. The sangoma's treatment involved the young man coming to live with the healer, "day and night." For two and a half weeks, the sangoma observed, to understand "what was 'not right' with him." The sangoma then prepared an appropriate *muthi* (medicine) for the patient to drink. Another muthi was applied to the patient's legs "to prevent the patient from running away from the therapy," and a third muthi was placed in the patient's nose and ears during sleep to stop the patient from hearing "his own stuff" and to bring him back to hearing and listening to his fellow human beings.

> One day . . . he gets up and recognizes you." This is the beginning of the last phase of treatment, which is given during daytime. From the moment when the patient can hear and recognize another person again, he must go back to work. The therapy becomes verbal, but the words remain closely related to concrete external reality . . . [the sangoma] worked with him, day by day, until he was "right" again, that is, until objects and names, words and actions matched as they had done before the illness. (pp. 221–222)

Work by scholars focusing on African perspectives on mental health and adaptation underline the role of culture and the importance of indigenous healers in psychotherapeutic interventions. Tsa-Tsala (1997) suggests that conceptions of health and disease from an African perspective reflect a holistic perspective, encompassing an understanding of a world where wellness is a matter of harmony. In contrast, disharmony has ancestral, intergenerational, and spiritual genesis and social and communal implications. Recent work has noted the complementarity and similarity between professional and traditional healing practices, and these examinations stress the importance of including traditional and religious healing practices, often that may involve herbal remedies (Madu, Baguma, & Pritz, 2000).

Improving Mental Health Services

Several psychotherapists have conceptualized models for organizing, understanding, and improving mental health services provided to African Americans. Early work in this area by Grier and Cobbs (1968) and Kardiner and Ovesey (1951) emphasized the negative impact of racism on the adaptation and functioning of African Americans. Advocates have called for improved mental health services for African Americans and members of other American ethnic groups because of the perceived "cultural encapsulation" of available mental health services. Cultural encapsulation involves the chauvinistic and inflexible use of a worldview or set of cultural values incongruent with the client group being served. These incompatible values are used to interpret behavior and enact treatment without the awareness, appreciation, or skills sets in the therapist to consider the role that culture may play in the therapeutic process. These perspectives are based on etic (i.e., universal) assumptions that everyone is similar in their display of behaviors related to psychosocial functioning and that therapeutic change processes are identical and equally effective across different cultural groups.

ACCULTURATION MODEL
AND MENTAL HEALTH TREATMENT

In contrast, other authors have considered models to describe and understand the role that culture may play in the therapeutic process. For example, Berry and colleagues (Berry, 1980; Berry & Kim, 1988) suggest that a client's level of acculturation can play an important role in his or her experience of mental health services. Berry argues that acculturation can be viewed as a series of stages with multiple outcomes. The first phase is that of precontact, when each culture is independent and has its own unique characteristics. In the contact phase, different cultural groups begin to interact with one another. This is followed by a conflict stage, during which pressure is exerted on the minority group to accommodate to the majority group behaviors and values. In the crisis phase, this conflict comes to a head. The final phase, adaptation, involves the two groups stabilizing their interactions (or lack thereof) into one of several modes of acculturation.

These resolutions may involve assimilation, a status where one group gives up its cultural practices and assumes the cultural practices of the majority group, or integration, where the minority group retains its own cultural practices but also participates in the cultural practices and social world of the majority group. Other modes of acculturation include separation, a status where groups choose not to interact with one another, and segregation, a status where the minority group is forcibly separated from social interaction with the majority group. There may also be accommodation, such that there are changes in the cultural practice of the majority group to include some of the practices of the minority group. When this occurs and there is some sense of merging and balance in the integration of the cultures, this is considered a fusion of the cultures. Finally, in a status of marginalization, an individual or group does not engage in the cultural practice of either the majority or minority group and is effectively excluded from their social worlds. Berry suggests that these stages of intercultural contact and modes of acculturation have an important impact on cultural group functioning and use of services and are reflected in assumptions of both the client and the therapist. A therapist can use the acculturation framework to better understand how an individual has organized the role of ethnicity in his or her life, how acculturation may have played a role in the individual's dysfunction, and how acculturation can play a role in interventions to improve functioning.

ETHNIC VALIDITY MODEL AND MENTAL HEALTH TREATMENT

The ethnic validity model of Tyler, Brome, and Williams (1991) has been used to understand therapeutic encounters. This model suggests that therapeutic encounters can involve the interaction between culture defining group and non-culture defining group members. Different types of pairings (e.g., a culture defining group therapist with a non-culture defining group client, or a non-culture defining group therapist with a non-culture defining group client) have the potential to result in different types of gains, losses, advantages, and disadvantages. For example, when a Black therapist works with a Black client (i.e., a non-culture defining group therapist with a non-culture defining group client), there may be the assumption that both individuals operate from the same cultural framework or worldview; however, this may not be true. Consider the pairing of a therapist working from an Africentric perspective with a client who views his or her ethnic group membership negatively or sees this group membership as unimportant. Tyler et al. (1991) suggest that this type of pairing illustrates that race (i.e., the physical characteristics associated with racial group membership) may tell us very little about more proximal factors (e.g., similarity in values or respect of differences in cultural values) that may be more important in effective therapy. Use of this model can assist therapists in avoiding assumptions about clients.

Related work by Helms and colleagues further suggests that client racial attitudes are related to preference for race of therapist (Parham & Helms, 1981) and emotional reactions to therapeutic experiences (Richardson & Helms, 1994).

PROFESSIONAL IMPLICATIONS AND APPLICATIONS

Several professional groups have called for improved service delivery to African Americans and other ethnic minority populations. Within the APA, there are several groups and programs that support these efforts. The Office of Ethnic Minority Affairs of the APA exists to promote an understanding of the influence of culture and ethnicity on behavior and encourage increased public knowledge of the special psychological resources and mental health needs of communities of color. The Society for the Psychological Study of Ethnic Minority Issues, Division 45, is the professional group within the APA whose members' work focuses on ethnic minority issues and concerns. The Association of Black Psychologists (ABPsi) has within its mission the improvement of mental health of all people of African descent.

Several programs have worked to increase the number of ethnic group psychotherapists, including African Americans. Within the Association of Black Psychologists, the Student Circle (originally the Student Division) was organized in 1993 to respond to student members' needs within ABPsi. The goals and activities of the Student Circle include work to "aid students in the process of entering and succeeding in graduate school; and to promote psychology as a major and as a profession among both graduate and undergraduate students." Programs and resources to increase the numbers of psychologists of color include NIMH's NIMH-COR (Career Opportunities in Research Education and Training), as well as NIMH's programs to strengthen the infrastructure of undergraduate programs at historically Black colleges. The American Psychological Association has also worked to increase the number of ethnic group psychologists to increase access to professionals that provide services to ethnic group members. APA also promotes the development of a knowledge base that supports better understanding of psychological issues relevant to persons of color through funding of the APA Minority Fellowship program.[2] This program was initially led by Dr. Dalmas Taylor and subsequently by Dr. James M. Jones.

Training in Cultural Sensitivity

In 1993, the APA published Guidelines for the Provision of Services to Cultural and Linguistic Minority Groups. These guidelines argue that psychological service providers need

• A sociocultural framework to consider diversity of values, interactional styles, and cultural expectations in a systematic fashion

• Knowledge of and skills for conducting multicultural assessments and interventions, including the ability to recognize cultural diversity

• An understanding of the role that culture and ethnicity-race play in the sociopsychological and economic development of ethnic and culturally diverse populations

• An understanding of the socioeconomic and political factors that significantly impact the psychological, political, and economic development of ethnically and culturally diverse groups

• Skills to help clients understand/maintain/resolve their own sociocultural identification

• An understanding of the interaction of culture, gender, and sexual orientation on behavior and needs

A body of literature indicates that culturally compatible interventions may affect the service experience of clients (e.g., Flaskerud, 1986).

Comparing use of services and dropout rate during the 6 months before and the 6 months after an intensive 8-day cross-cultural training program, Lefley and Bestman (1991) report a significant increase in service use and a decrease in dropout rates.

Using several different training models, D'Andrea, Daniels, and Heck (1991) have shown significant increases in scores on all three subscales of the Multicultural Awareness, Knowledge, and Skills Survey for participants in their multicultural training course. Other measures developed to assess therapist or counselor cultural competence include the Cross-Cultural Counseling Inventory–Revised (LaFramboise, Coleman, & Hernandez, 1991); the Multicultural Counseling Awareness Scale (Ponterotto, Sanchez, & Magids, 1991); and the Multicultural Counseling Inventory (Sodowsky, Taffe, Gutkin, & Wise, 1994).

Yutrzenka (1995) and Allison, Crawford, Echemendia, and Robinson (1994) argue that growing evidence links the provision of training and the acquisition of cultural competence in providing mental health services. For example, Wade and Bernstein (1991) found that Black female clients perceived experienced therapists who had received culture sensitivity training to be more credible, rated the therapeutic experience as more positive, and returned for more follow-up sessions than did clients whose therapists did not receive such training. Clients were also more likely to return to see Black counselors than White counselors.

RACE AND CULTURE IN PSYCHOTHERAPY

Once African Americans have decided to pursue mental health treatment, there are a number of treatment options and a number of factors involving race, culture, and ethnicity that may play a role in their experience of psychotherapy.

Williams (1996) discusses from a psychoanalytic perspective the role that skin color may play in therapeutic exchanges. Williams notes that the historical significance of skin color and hair texture in the United States and cultural ideals of beauty may have important implications for parenting, child socialization regarding race, family dynamics, and the internalization of social constructions of race. (See Chapter 6 for further discussion of the topic of skin color.) This argument builds on work by Neal and Wilson (1989) on the importance of social constructions of skin color within and between races, particularly for African American women. Issues of self-hatred and family processes involving greater protectiveness or rejection based on skin color may play a role within therapeutic encounters in transference relations in both intra-ethnic and interethnic relationships. These issues may also be reflected in projections of the client, or in countertransference experiences of the therapist.

A. C. Jones (1991) proposes four interacting sets of factors that may influence the presenting problems of African Americans and the conduct of psychotherapists in addressing these problems

1. "Reactions to racial oppression," involving an individual's development of coping strategies to respond to experiences of prejudice and discrimination

2. "Influence of the majority culture," including the potential internalization of cultural stereotypes regarding Blacks by both clients and therapists

3. "Influence of traditional African culture," such as a communal orientation, the use of spirituality as a coping resource, and sensitivity to and use of affect

4. "Individual family experiences and endowments" (e.g., experiences of trauma, family interaction patterns, individuals' abilities and disabilities) that may or may not be related to one's ethnic group membership (p. 585)

Boyd-Franklin's work with African American clients is based on a multisystemic model of psychotherapy. Boyd-Franklin (1989) proposes that therapeutic work with African Americans should focus on the family and that therapy with African American families involves work across multiple systems including the individual, the "real" (i.e., the functional as opposed to nuclear or biological) family and household, the extended and non-blood family, and church, community, and social service organizations. Boyd-Franklin suggests that the treatment process is circular, involving (a) joining and engaging the family, (b) initial assessment of the family, (c) problem solving, (d) family prescriptions and assignments, (e) information gathering through completing a family genogram (i.e., a family tree), and (f) work to "restructure" the family.

Resources have been developed to assist and support those providing culturally appropriate psychological services to African American clients. These would include books, such as *The First Session With African Americans: A Step by Step Guide* by Janet Sanchez-Hughley (2000), *Issues in Counseling African American Clients* by Thomas Parham (1992b), and professional training videotapes on psychotherapy with African Americans. Therapeutic perspectives focusing on African Americans have also incorporated issues of spirituality into psychotherapy (e.g., Dunn & Dawes, 1999). Readers might also be interested in bell hooks's (1993) book, *Sisters of the Yam,* a critical analysis and reflection on issues of healing and wellness for Black women grounded in the author's experience in a support group for Black women.

Not all therapeutic interventions are traditional psychotherapy encounters. Gregory and Phillips (1997) describe *NTU* (a Bantu word that means "essence") therapy, an Africentric approach to therapy that integrates concepts of harmony, balance, interconnectedness, and authenticity. The approach can consider a range of treatment and prevention services including in-home family therapy, case management, crisis intervention, parenting skills, and other cultural programming including a rites of passage program. DeCarlo and Hockman (2003) have recently reported the effective use of RAP therapy in promoting the development of prosocial skills.

Methodological Issues

As suggested throughout this chapter, there are several methodological issues that are central to examining mental health issues among African Americans. We have discussed rates and types of psychopathology among African Americans and approaches to treating African American clients. An additional issue is what assessment measures and strategies are most appropriate for use with Blacks. We discuss assessment issues next.

ASSESSMENT

Assessment is the process that mental health professionals use to understand what type of problem(s) an individual is experiencing. Assessments may involve unstructured or structured interviewing of the identified client or other important people (e.g., parents, spouse, teacher) to better understand the presenting problem. The client or other informants may also be asked to complete questionnaires, checklists, or other measures that assist the mental health professional in making a diagnosis that classifies the individual according to a set of established criteria or symptoms associated with a specific type of problem. As noted earlier in this chapter, the *DSM-IV-TR* (APA, 2000) is the diagnostic framework most frequently used by American psychologists, hospitals, and insurance providers.

Butcher, Nezami, and Exner (1998) identify a number of challenges in psychological assessment across different cultural groups, including language limitations, exposure to and experience with assessment processes, and variations in the manifestation of the same disorder. The definition of what is considered "normal" varies from culture to culture, and individuals undergoing an assessment may be influenced by cultural differences in motivation and differences in expectations for how they should interact with other people. Psychologists must consider whether a specific assessment task is culturally appropriate and whether it has the same psychological meaning (or equivalence) across different cultural groups.

Assessment With Adults:
The Minnesota Multiphasic Personality Inventory

The Minnesota Multiphasic Personality Inventory (MMPI; Hathaway & McKinley, 1940) was created as an adult assessment tool for use by mental health professionals and researchers. The MMPI-2 (Butcher, Dahlstrom, Graham, Tellegen, & Kaemmer, 1989) is a revision of the original measure and is the current version in use. The MMPI-2 contains 567 true-false items and takes approximately 60 to 90 minutes to complete. There are a variety of scoring options, but the 10 clinical scales—Hypochondriasis [Hs], Depression [D], Conversion Hysteria [Hy], Psychopathic Deviate [Pd], Masculinity-Femininity [Mf], Paranoia [Pa], Psychasthenia [Pt], Schizophrenia [Sc], Hypomania [Ma], and Social Introversion [Si]—and validity scales (e.g., F, L Lie, and K Correction) are the options used most frequently by clinicians and researchers.

In part because the standardization samples for the original MMPI contained no African Americans, there were concerns that the measure might be biased for use with African Americans. Despite inclusion of African Americans in the standardization sample of the MMPI-2, concerns of bias remain (e.g., Dana & Whatley, 1991). Numerous studies were conducted on the MMPI and questions were raised as to whether there were differences in psychopathology between African Americans and Whites. Reviews of this work, with a range of study samples (e.g., normal, substance abuse, psychiatric), have found no consistent pattern of racial differences (e.g., Greene, 1987), and studies controlling for other demographic factors (e.g., sex, age, SES, education, urban vs. rural residence, marital status, hospital status, and timing of testing) report few differences in MMPI scores due to ethnicity (Bertelson, Marks, & May, 1982).

In a recent review of 25 studies that used both the MMPI and MMPI-2, Hall, Bansal, and Lopez (1999) report differences between the scores of African American and European American males on Scales L, F, Sc, and Ma and between African American and White females on Scales Mf and Ma. The differences, however, were small and have little clinical significance.

Other Problems in Assessments With Adults

Even when clinical assessment tools are valid and reliable in research settings, we cannot be sure that they are reliable and valid in actual clinical practice. For example, Garb's (1997) review of studies on bias in clinical judgment (e.g., in diagnosis, ratings of adjustment, and descriptions of personality and symptoms that occur in actual community-based clinical practice) reports that African Americans are more likely to be diagnosed as having schizophrenia and less likely to be diagnosed as having a psychotic affective disorder than are Whites. The comparison of epidemiological data and clinical data from mental health service settings similarly suggests a discrepancy, such that African Americans are more likely to be overdiagnosed with schizophrenia and underdiagnosed with depression (Adebimpe & Cohen, 1989; Neighbors, Jackson, Campbell, & Williams, 1989). The overdiagnosis of schizophrenia may be related to African Americans' possible greater likelihood of presenting in clinical settings with Schneiderian first-rank symptoms (i.e., auditory hallucinations, delusions, and loss of agency; Carter & Neufeld, 1998). Whaley's (1998) work also suggests that issues of mistrust may play a role in the overdiagnosis of schizophrenia and underdiagnosis of depression among African Americans. Whaley argues that the concept of "paranoia" represents a dimension ranging from low or relatively minor levels of mistrust to extreme paranoia including severe delusions and hallucinations. He presents data suggesting that Blacks demonstrate higher levels of general distrust than Whites and that when SES is controlled, this ethnic difference is no longer significant. Whaley also notes a stronger association between mistrust and depression among African Americans than among Whites. This difference in levels of association raises questions as to whether assessment strategies[3] may confuse mistrust and paranoia and contribute to problems in accurately diagnosing both depression and schizophrenia among African Americans. The issue of mistrust may also be reflected in nondisclosure by African American clients, which is sometimes interpreted as resistance. Related to this, Ridley (1984) suggests that some tendencies by Blacks to initially mistrust a therapist may be healthy or adaptive.

Assessment of Hyperactivity Among African American Children

There has been considerable interest in the assessment and diagnosis of attention deficit hyperactivity disorder (ADHD) among African American children. In their review, Gingerich, Turnock, Litfin, and Rosen (1998) suggest that although the disorder is believed to be biological in nature, cultural factors also may play an important role in the manifestation of the disorder and its diagnosis. Findings from comparative studies conducted in the 1970s show African American children are rated higher than White children on symptoms of ADHD on parent and teacher rating scales (e.g., Anderson, Williamson, & Lundy, 1977; Blunden, Spring, & Greenberg, 1974; Goyette, Conners, & Ulrich, 1978).

More recently, in a sample of rural children (aged 10 to 16) from North Carolina, Epstein, March, Conners, and Jackson (1998) found that teachers tended to rate African American boys higher in conduct problems and hyperactivity and lower in anxious/passive symptoms than White boys. African American girls were rated as higher on conduct problems and anxious/passive symptoms than White girls. It is still important to note, however, that these differences are based on teacher ratings and not on observations of children's actual behaviors. No information about children's socioeconomic resources or teacher ethnicity is available from this study; therefore, it is not possible to ascertain the extent to which differences were real (i.e., actual differences in children's behaviors) or perceived (e.g., potential variations in rater's perceptions or related biases in rating).

McDermott and Spencer (1997) present data on a nationally representative sample of 1,400 children and adolescents ranging in age from 5 to 17. Rates of psychopathology were examined across racial and social class groups. Again, based on teacher observations, African Americans (as compared with Whites) showed higher rates of impulsive aggression (e.g., hitting without provocation) and opposition (e.g., purposively not following directions, defying authority) and lower levels of "diffident" problems (i.e., timidity and fearfulness), but similar rates of solitary aggression (e.g., engaging alone in destruction of property), attention-hyperactivity, and avoidance. Overall, rates of psychopathology did not differ by social class. Barbarin and Soler (1993) argue that due to living in conditions of chronic unpredictable stress, African American boys are more likely to exhibit behaviors of poor concentration, impulsivity, and distractibility. Boykin's (1978) work has also raised the question that symptoms of hyperactivity among African American children are sometimes confused with "verve," a cultural preference for high levels of stimulation and activity in the environment.

Assessment From an Africentric Perspective

When considering assessment from an Africentric perspective, clinicians and therapists have several scales to choose from that can assist them in understanding a client's "correct orientation," including Baldwin's African Self-Consciousness (ASC) scale (Baldwin, 1984; Baldwin & Bell, 1985). ASC "is a theoretical construct that attempts to explain the psychological functioning and behavior of persons of African descent from their own cultural perspective" (Baldwin, Duncan, & Bell, 1992, p. 284). Baldwin (1981, 1984) proposes a model of Black personality consisting of two core components: the African self-extension orientation (ASEO) and African Self–Consciousness (ASC). ASEO is based in spirituality and allows for self-extension; that is, the self, consciously and unconsciously, is defined in group or "corporate" terms (in contrast to the Eurocentric conceptualization of the self emphasizing individual identity). The African self-consciousness scale that uses these constructs is described in further detail in Chapter 2. Another index that assesses Black consciousness is Williams's Black Personality Questionnaire (Wright & Isenstein, 1975).

Summary

In this chapter, we presented an overview of issues supporting our understanding of the psychosocial adjustment of African Americans. Our understanding of adaptation has been based on multiple theoretical perspectives including Africentric models. We presented an overview of mainstream (e.g., MMPI) and African-centered (e.g., ASC scale) measures of well-being and maladaptation. We also considered the difficulty in using service data to make estimates of psychopathology rates among African Americans, and we presented overviews of research databases for studying psychopathology among African Americans. Data indicate few significant differences in rates of mental illness between African American and White adults; however, there are notable differences in mental health service utilization by Blacks and members of other ethnic groups.

Mental health professionals have called for improved access to culturally appropriate services for African Americans, and research has suggested that training can be important in improving the service experience of African Americans. There are increasingly more and more resources to support effective psychotherapy with specific subgroups of African Americans.

In closing this chapter, we feel it is important to acknowledge that there is a massive literature encompassing a broad range of issues related to psychological adaptation of African Americans. This chapter has presented only a select overview of issues representing both classic questions and new directions. For additional information, readers might consult Chapter 3: "Mental Health Care for African Americans" in the supplement to the Surgeon General's 2001 report, *Mental Health: Culture, Race and Ethnicity*.[4]

The Sukuma proverb "The wind does not break a tree that bends" suggests that individuals' ability to cope with the challenges they face supports their adaptation and adjustment. Having the capacity to bend, to be flexible, but to remain firmly rooted, reflects a sense of maintaining the connection to one's footing, but being able to handle and effectively respond to life's stresses.

Notes

1. WHO is an international organization founded by the United Nations in 1946 to promote "the attainment by all peoples of the highest possible level of health." For more information on WHO, visit their Web site at http://www.who.int/home_page

2. Individuals who are interested in careers in clinical or counseling psychology might consider contacting http://www.apa.org/students/student1.html for general information on undergraduate and graduate training. Information on the APA Minority Fellowship Program can be accessed at http://www.apa.org/mfp/rprogram.html. It is also important to note that individuals interested in careers relevant to mental health research and services have a range of professional options in other disciplines including clinical social work, psychiatry, psychiatric nursing, and rehabilitation counseling.

3. This may be particularly problematic when assessments involve dichotomous questions (e.g., yes-no questions) that do not consider the potential variability on the dimension of mistrust.

4. See http://www.surgeongeneral.gov/library/mentalhealth/home.html

Drug Use and Abuse

13

When the cock is drunk, he forgets about the hawk.

—Tshi proverb

*Maryland's prison budget is approaching $1 billion. Meanwhile, more than 200,000 Marylanders needed, but were unable to get, treatment last year.

*Seventy-three percent of Marylanders polled believe that treatment is a better way to stop drug use than prison is.

Every dollar spent on drug rehabilitation yields between $7 and $8 in cost benefits, primarily because of decreased crime and increased productivity. Community-based treatment also has been found to be better at reducing drug use and crime rates than treatment administered inside prisons.

When the governor signs this legislation, Maryland will join Texas, Arizona, California, Kansas, Colorado and Washington in diverting drug offenders from prison into treatment. In Texas, the Republican chairman of the Corrections Committee similarly teamed up with the Democrat who chairs the Legislative Black Caucus to pass a law that each year diverts 2,500 people from Texas's prisons into treatment. Arizona's diversion legislation was enacted through a ballot initiative led by the late conservative icon Barry Goldwater and passed with overwhelming bipartisan support.

Introduction, Definitions, and Historical Perspectives

The news story tells how one state is attempting to deal with the devastating problem of drugs. Treatment rather than incarceration will address the fact that the majority of those incarcerated are imprisoned for drug use. Those incarcerated are more likely to be African Americans.

Involvement with drugs and alcohol is a major problem within many African American communities, particularly urban, low-resource communities. Although African Americans consume fewer drugs than White Americans, they are more likely to suffer negative social and health consequences from their use. In a 1998 Annual Report on the State of Black America, the Urban League wrote that substance abuse was the single major social, economic, and public health problem in the African American community (Dei, 2002). For example, drug possession, sales, and use account for a large percentage of incarceration among African Americans. The increase in the number of African American males sent to prison over the past two decades is directly linked to the increase in the number of persons incarcerated for drug-related offenses (Nunn, 2002). Despite the fact that African Americans represent 12% of the population in the United States, they accounted for 32.5% of state and local arrests for drug abuse violations in 2002, compared with Caucasians, who accounted for 66.2% of arrests (U.S. Sentencing Commission, 2002). Of the drug offenders convicted in State courts during 2000, 53% were Black and 46% were White (Bureau of Justice Statistics, 2000).

In inner cities, home to many African Americans, drug trafficking and use cause high levels of crime, violence, and other social problems. As noted in Chapter 11, legal drugs such as alcohol and cigarettes contribute to increased morbidity, disability, and mortality among African Americans.

We begin this chapter with definitions and then give a historical overview of drug use in Africa, drug use among enslaved Africans, and current drug use among African Americans. Next we discuss the etiology and consequences of drug use for African Americans, covering the topics of drug initiation, drug use theories, and the role of cultural factors in drug use. We then examine institutional and societal influences, including the role of poverty, the media, and differences in drug-related incarceration rates for African Americans and members of other racial-ethnic groups. We follow this with an examination of several prevention and treatment models and programs used to address problems associated with drug use. Next, we provide an overview of methodological issues that are relevant to research on drug use and abuse among African Americans. Finally, we provide a chapter summary.

DEFINITIONS

Drugs are substances intended for use in the diagnosis, cure, mitigation, treatment, or prevention of disease. Drugs are also illicit substances that cause addiction, habituation, or a marked change in consciousness (*Merriam-Webster*, 2002). An illicit drug is a drug that is illegal, such as marijuana, cocaine, or heroin. Drug abuse is the use of any chemical substance (especially controlled substances such as psychoactive drugs, narcotics, hormones, prescription medication, or over-the-counter medicines) in a way that society deems harmful to the user or others.

HISTORICAL PATTERNS OF DRUG USE

Drug Use in Africa

Historical perspectives provide insight into current patterns of alcohol use among African Americans by examining drinking patterns of indigenous Africans. In their book, *Doing Drugs: Patterns of African American Addiction*, James and Johnson (1996) write that enslaved Africans arriving in America came from tribes that used fermented maize (corn) or millet as a food and a trade product, in social interactions, and as a sacred drink. Beer was used as an offering to gods and as a reward to those who had worked the land (Gordon, 2003). From the 16th to the 18th centuries, West and East Central Africans brewed beer and wine, and Southern Africans engaged in some use of cannabis (marijuana; Ambler, 2003). Among tribal Africans, alcohol was drunk in a group context—in religious and sacred events—rather than individually. For example, when the Asante celebrated the harvest festival, *odwira*, it was commonplace to have liquor as an integral part of the festivities: "The . . . King ordered a large quantity of rum to be poured into brass pans in various parts of the town: the crowd pressing around. . . . All wore their handsomest cloths, which they trailed after them in a length, in a drunken emulation of extravagance" (Ambler, 2003). Although alcohol was consumed at these special occasions, drugs were not seen in West African society.

Role of Drugs in the Slave Trade

By the 1700s, alcohol had acquired an economic function and was used as currency in slave trading. It is estimated that alcohol purchased from 5% to 10% of all slaves in West Africa (Ambler, 2003). The connection between alcohol and the slave trade was circular, and it involved New England, Africa, and the West Indies (James & Johnson, 1996). Sugar and molasses from the British and Spanish West Indies were shipped to New England, where they were distilled into rum. The rum was then sent to Africa where it was exchanged for slaves. These slaves were shipped to the West Indies to work in the fields.

Drug Use During Slavery

The social drinking patterns of African Americans living in slavery included weekend and holiday use and drinking at celebrations. This drinking pattern was shaped, in part, because of the dawn-to-dusk work demands on slaves. Slave masters permitted and encouraged the use of alcohol as a reward during harvest times (Suggs & Lewis, 2003).

Drug Use Following the Civil War

Immediately after the Civil War, many Blacks became more involved in the Protestant Church. Church doctrine forbade alcohol consumption, and this prohibition restricted drug use. Black churches of all denominations grew dramatically after the Emancipation Proclamation, and they promoted abstinence and moderation in drinking. However, following the Civil War, many African Americans migrated north, frequently to urban areas, in search of employment. Greater exposure to urban life contributed to heavier drinking patterns and addiction among African Americans. Rather than restricting alcohol use to celebratory occasions, many African Americans began to use alcohol to cope with problems of daily living brought on by poverty and racism. Around this time, opium use also increased in the United States. Chinese workers, brought to the western United States to build railroads, are largely credited with introducing opium into the United States (James & Johnson, 1996).

Drug Use From 1900 to 1930

Illegal drug use in the early 1900s was mostly limited to ex-convicts and criminals. However, by the 1930s, African Americans were disproportionately represented in the known addict populations of major urban areas. There was an expansion of clubs and bars in African American cities and communities during the 1930s; with this expansion came increased opportunity for alcohol and other drug use (James & Johnson, 1996).

Drug Use in the 1940s and 1950s

During the late 1940s and 1950s, heroin use increased in urban African American communities. Marijuana, which had previously been used only by specific subgroups of African Americans, such as prisoners, was also beginning to be used by more diverse groups of African Americans. However, the overall impact of heroin addiction, which was concentrated in urban areas, was relatively small compared with the broader impact of alcohol on both rural and urban Black communities (James & Johnson, 1996). During this period, African American communities tolerated high levels of alcohol use because of the oppressive circumstances and high levels of stress under which many African Americans lived. Options for those who wanted alcoholism treatment were very limited in the 1950s and 1960s. Hospital treatment programs were designed for middle-class Americans, and self-help programs such as Alcoholics Anonymous were not available in African American communities. Many African Americans who were addicted to alcohol could not get treatment.

During the 1950s and 1960s, organized drug syndicates gained control of drug production and distribution. With limited employment options available to them, many younger African Americans in urban communities became involved with drug preparation, packaging, and sales. This involvement of some younger African Americans in the drug trade continues today, as does control by organized drug syndicates.

Drug Use From the 1970s to the Present

The 1970s, 1980s, and 1990s saw the rise of cocaine, which led to the appearance of crack cocaine. Perhaps more than any other drug, crack cocaine has had a devastating impact on African American families and communities. Although cocaine has been used since 1890 in medicines and drinks, it was not introduced to the African American community until the 1980s. Its introduction had a detrimental effect on the people of the community: As addiction emerged, the social problems of crime, family disruptions, and disease drastically increased. Another distressing effect of cocaine was the staggering number of African American men who

Table 13.1 Prevalence of Selected Substance Use in the Past Month by Age and
Ethnicity

	Ages 12–17		Ages 18–25		Ages 26 & Over	
	Black (Non-Hispanic)	White (Non-Hispanic)	Black (Non-Hispanic)	White (Non-Hispanic)	Black (Non-Hispanic)	White (Non-Hispanic)
Cigarettes	6.6	15.6	27.7	47.7	28.3	25.2
Alcohol	10.9	20.1	48.3	66.8	43.6	57.5
Heavy Alcohol*	0.6	3.2	5.9	19	4.8	6.3
Illicit Drugs**	10	12.6	18.21	22.9	7.8	5.9

Source: Substance Abuse and Mental Health Services Administration, Office of Applied Studies,
National Survey on Drug Use and Health (2002).

*Five or more drinks on the same occasion at least once in the past month.

**Illicit drugs include marijuana/hashish, cocaine (including crack), heroin, hallucinogens,
inhalants, or any prescription-type psychotherapeutic drug used nonmedically.

were prosecuted for its distribution. The Anti-Drug Abuse Act of 1986
created a disparity in sentencing those arrested for crack versus those
arrested for powder cocaine. This has been particularly debilitating for the
African American community, where crack cocaine is the drug most likely
to be used.

Current Drug Use Among African Americans

The National Survey on Drug Use and Health provides data on patterns
of drug use among different age, gender, and ethnic groups (Substance
Abuse and Mental Health Services Administration [SAMHSA], 2002). The
National Survey is a national sample of the civilian noninstitutionalized
population age 12 and older. Table 13.1 provides the percentage of drugs
consumed by African Americans and Whites by age-group over a 30-day
period just prior to the 2002 survey. Across most drug and age categories,
a smaller percentage of African Americans than Whites reported consum-
ing drugs. This gap is most notable in the age-groups 12 to 17 and 18 to 25
years old. More Whites than African Americans reported smoking cigarettes and drinking alcohol. The gap between African Americans and
Whites in drug consumption decreases in the 25 and older group.

Although overall drug use is less common among African Americans
than among Whites, it is important to note that there are disproportionately higher rates of drug-related problems among African American
youth relative to White youth. Black and Hispanic youth show higher
prevalence for alcohol-related social problems than do Whites, despite

higher drinking rates among Whites (Barnes & Welte, 1986). This may be due to fewer resources available to assist African Americans with drug-related problems. The consequences of smoking are also worse for African Americans than for Whites. For African American men and women, lung cancer is the second most common cancer, and it kills more African Americans than any other cancer (CancerCare, 2004). African American men are at least 40% more likely to develop lung cancer than are White men. Whereas 107 out of every 100,000 African American males succumb to lung cancer, only 78 out of 100,000 White men die from lung cancer (CancerCare, 2004). These high rates of mortality are linked to socioeconomic factors, such as limited access to health care (American Cancer Society, 2004).

ALCOHOL

Although alcohol is a legal drug for those of drinking age, alcohol consumption and abuse is a major cause of morbidity, mortality, disability, and property destruction in this country. Table 13.1 shows the percentages of 30-day alcohol use by age and ethnic group. Among youth aged 12 to 17 in 2002, African Americans (10.9%) and Asians (7.4%) were least likely to report past month alcohol use. The percentage of persons who reported alcohol consumption is lower for African Americans than for Whites in each age-group.

The discrepancy in alcohol use is especially large between African American and White adolescent females. The prevalence of heavy drinking patterns among White adolescent females is about twice that for African American adolescent females. For example, 10.8% of African American females aged 12 to 17 years old reported being current drinkers compared with 20.4% of White adolescent females. Heavy alcohol usage was reported by 2.5% of White adolescent females compared with 0.4% of African American female adolescents (SAMHSA, 2002).

CIGARETTES

Tobacco use is a leading contributor to disability, illness, and death in the United States. Table 13.1 shows the rate of smoking for African Americans and Whites across three age-groups in 2002. As shown in Table 13.1, cigarette smoking was substantially less common among African Americans than among Whites aged 12 to 17 and 18 to 25 years old. However, cigarette smoking among Whites decreases after age 25. For example, among those 26 and older, slightly more African Americans than Whites reported smoking. Smoking among African Americans increases at all age levels.

COCAINE

Cocaine is an illicit drug whose use has been associated with many severe consequences. Use of cocaine, especially crack cocaine, has been incredibly destructive especially within African American communities. Health, social services, medical, and judicial systems are burdened with the consequences of cocaine use. The distribution of crack cocaine within many low-income African American communities accounts in large part for elevated criminal activity, high incarceration rates, and other social problems. The most common drug for which African Americans are charged with drug-related crime offenses is crack cocaine (U.S. Sentencing Commission, 2002).

Cocaine is highly addictive and is characterized by a high frequency of relapse following treatment (James & Johnson, 1996). The nature of cocaine addiction makes it very difficult to treat.

One indicator of a community's cocaine problems is the number of emergency room episodes arising out of cocaine use. Table 13.2 shows emergency room episodes according to ethnicity and gender. The prevalence of emergency room episodes are substantially higher for African Americans than for Whites. As seen in Table 13.2, about the same number of African American men as White men were treated in emergency rooms for cocaine-related episodes in 2002. Similar trends exist for females, with about the same number of African American females and White females treated for cocaine-related emergency episodes despite the fact that African Americans comprise 12% of the population. Several explanations exist for this disparity. African Americans are more likely to use the cheaper but more potent form of cocaine (crack), which may be more dangerous. African Americans may have less access to cocaine and crack that is pure. In addition, African Americans who are addicted may have less access to treatment than Whites.

ILLICIT DRUGS

An estimated 19.5 million Americans consumed illicit drugs in 2002 (SAMHSA, 2002). The rate of illicit drug use for African Americans of all age groups was 9.7%, which was slightly higher than for Whites at 8.5%. Among White youth aged 12 to 17 years old, boys and girls were about equally likely to be illicit drug users (12% of females, 13.1% of males). However, the rate of drug use was higher among Black males (11%) than among Black females (8.9%).

Causes and Consequences of Drug Use

The etiology of drug use focuses on why people start using drugs. Experimentation with drug use most often begins during adolescence.

Table 13.2   Cocaine-Related Emergency Episodes

Black Males (Non-Hispanic)	White Males (Non-Hispanic)	Black Females (Non-Hispanic)	White Females (Non-Hispanic)
52,463	49,305	27,089	29,736

Source: Substance Abuse and Mental Health Services Administration, Office of Applied Studies, Drug Abuse Warning Network, 2002.

We now focus on the etiology of drug use among youth as opposed to drug use among adults. Factors that contribute to initial drug use are different from factors that contribute to continuing drug use and addiction. Once use turns to abuse and addiction, psychological and physiological mechanisms strongly support continued use. Consequently, we devote more attention to understanding initial drug use.

DRUG USE INITIATION

Drug use is often initiated in early adolescence. During adolescence, one explores new activities, and drug experimentation may be one such activity. Initiation often begins with cigarettes and liquor, which are considered "gateway" drugs to other drugs such as marijuana (Schilling & McAlister, 1990). Drug initiation starts around the age of 11 to 12 for youth of all ethnic groups. Fifty percent of African American youth report that they have tried alcohol before the age of 12 (Forney, Forney, & Ripley, 1991; Vega, Gil, & Zimmerman, 1993). However, the period of greatest risk for initiation to cigarettes, alcohol, and marijuana is between the ages of 16 and 18 (Beman, 1995). Youth who do not use these substances during the adolescent period are less likely to use drugs as adults.

CO-OCCURRING BEHAVIORS

Drug use among adolescents is often associated with other problem behaviors, such as low academic achievement, delinquency, and early, risky sexual activity. According to problem behavior theory, drug use is part of a syndrome of other problems including juvenile delinquency, low interest in school, and aggressive and violent behavior (Jessor & Jessor, 1977).

There is a strong association between youth delinquency and violence and drug use. There may be common etiological factors for all of those problem behaviors (Botvin & Scheier, 1997). Research on drug abuse and violence suggests that drug use does not precede or follow violence but tends to co-occur at similar levels of frequency and severity. The underlying cause of violence may be the same as the underlying cause of drug use.

CONSEQUENCES

Early use of drugs has been associated with serious consequences of drug use and problems in later life. Youth who begin using drugs early are at increased risk for drug abuse in later adolescence and adulthood. As noted earlier, adolescent drug use has been linked to higher risk of other negative behaviors such as school failure, poor school performance, and delinquency (Brook, Whiteman, Balka, Win, & Gursen, 1997). Other serious consequences of drug use are accidental overdose, motor vehicle accidents, injury, disability, and morbidity. In addition, illicit drug use has pervasive negative effects at individual, family, community, and societal levels.

RISK AND PROTECTIVE FACTORS

There are both risk and protective factors for drug use. Risk factors are those characteristics or circumstances that predispose youth to begin using drugs. These could include individual attributes, situational conditions, or environmental contexts. Research shows that not one but several risk factors contribute to drug use among youth. In general, the greater the number of risk factors, the greater the probability of drug use (Hawkins, Catalano, & Miller, 1992). Risk factors can be categorized under the individual, family, peer, school, and community domains.

More recently, research has examined protective factors against substance abuse. These factors are hypothesized to buffer individuals against stressors that might occur in the midst of risk factors such as neighborhood and family disorganization (Grover, 1998). Protective factors may interact with risk factors and prevent, moderate, or lessen the effects of risk factors. Protective factors can prevent drug use by providing the youth with a strong sense of self-competence that results in drug refusal efficacy.

Protective factors can be categorized in the same domains as risk factors and include the individual, family, peer, school, and community. The following protective factors have been found to be associated with less drug use and antidrug attitudes: (a) having a range of adaptive social coping skills; (b) self-efficacy and the ability to adapt to changing circumstances; (c) positive social interaction; (d) family cohesion, attachment, and bonding; (e) parental supervision; (f) school and community norms and standards against substance use; and (g) school achievement and commitment. The concept of resilience has also been used to explain why some youth with multiple risk factors do not use drugs. Masten and Coatsworth (1998) defined resilience as "manifested competence in the context of significant challenges to adaptation or development" (p. 206).

In general, risk and protective factors for drug use among all youth are useful for understanding drug use among African Americans, with exceptions that will be noted.

Individual Factors

Individual factors are those that characterize individual level susceptibility to drug use. These include dispositional and psychological factors,
demographic factors, and biological factors.

Several dispositional factors are associated with drug use. These include
sensation seeking and rebelliousness (Stanton, Li, Cottrell, & Kaljee, 2001),
lower achievement needs (McCluskey, Krohn, Lizotte, & Rodriguez, 2002),
and low self-worth (Adger, 1991). Aggression, rebelliousness, alienation,
and delinquency (Botvin & Scheier, 1997) are also associated with drug use.

Individual-level protective factors against drug use include social skills,
problem-solving skills, social responsiveness, cooperativeness, emotional
stability, and a positive self-concept (Grover, 1998).

Genetic or biological factors may also play a role in drug use. Studies
of twins show that there may be a genetic predisposition for drug abuse.
For example, researchers have found that adopted offspring of alcoholic
parents show more alcoholism than those whose biological parents are
nonalcoholic (Center for Substance Abuse Prevention [CSAP], 1993).

Regarding smoking, studies suggest that African Americans absorb more
nicotine from smoking than do White or Hispanic smokers. The results of a
study conducted by the Centers for Disease Control showed that African
American participants had cotinine levels that were significantly higher than
White and Mexican American participants (Carabello et al., 1998). Cotinine
is nicotine that has been metabolized by the body and is a marker for nicotine levels. In a related study conducted at the University of California, San
Francisco, the authors found that nicotine intake per cigarette was 30%
greater in Blacks than in Whites and that Blacks retained cotinine in their
bodies longer than Whites. The higher levels of cotinine could account, in
part, for why African Americans have a higher incidence of smoking-related
diseases and have a more difficult time quitting than their White and Hispanic
counterparts. The researchers speculate that if higher cotinine levels are
linked to higher absorption of other health-compromising ingredients in
cigarette smoke, it may help explain the higher rates of lung cancer deaths
among Black smokers than among White smokers (Langreth, 1998;
Schwartz, 1998).

Family Factors

Parental and family variables affect youth drug use. Family conflict,
poor communication, and negative interactions with parents have been
associated with adolescent drug use (Bray, Adams, Greg, & Baer, 2001;
Brook et al., 1997). Positive family interactions, communication, and support have been associated with reductions in drug use (Grover, 1998).

Parental monitoring and supervision of adolescents' behavior have been
linked to lower levels of substance use (Miller & Volk, 2002). Monitoring by

adults is especially beneficial during middle school, when children may be most susceptible to peer influence (Dei, 2002). A qualitative study of five Black adolescents from the inner city suggested that although schools, media, and peers are contributors to drug use, adult household members and neighbors are the essential contributors (Dei, 2002).

Family structure has also been associated with adolescent drug use (Miller & Volk, 2002). Among the general population, youth in single-parent homes are somewhat more likely to use drugs than youth who reside with both parents. African American youth are more likely than White youth to reside with one biological parent. Only about one third of Black youth compared with two thirds of White youth currently live with both biological parents (Johnson, Hoffmann, Su, & Gerstein, 1997). The assumption is that two parents can provide more supervision and serve as a buffer for problems and stressors youth may face. However, family structure differs between African American and White families, and some research suggests that drug use among African American youth is not greater in one- versus two-parent households (Amey & Albrecht, 1998).

Recognizing the importance of supportive adults, federal agencies, such as the CSAP, have funded many prevention programs that pair youth with role models, mentors, and supportive adults. Supportive adults are provided to youth who may be at high risk for substance use and problem behaviors because of contextual factors. It is hypothesized that supportive adults can help youth meet many of their needs for affiliation, esteem, and achievement, and can provide a buffer against stressors that may occur as a result of living under challenging socioenvironmental conditions (CSAP, 2001).

Parental drug use has also been identified as a contributor to child drug use. Kandel, Kessler, and Margulies (1978) found that 82% of parents who drank had adolescents who also drank, and 72% of parents who abstained had adolescent children who also abstained. Higher rates of drug use among children of parents who use drugs can be due to several factors: parents acting as a model for drug use behavior, greater access to drugs, lack of parental monitoring of drug-using peers, and excessive parental drug use. All are causes of family dysfunction and dysfunctional behavior that can lead to drug use and abuse.

Peer Factors

Peer influence is a strong predictor of drug use during adolescence (Farrell & White, 1998; Hawkins, Catalano, & Miller, 1992). Youth who have peers who use drugs are more likely to use drugs than those whose peers do not use drugs. Peer cluster theory assumes that peers influence drug use both directly and indirectly (Oetting & Beauvais, 1986). Youth try their first drugs with peers, and peers provide drugs, model drug-using behaviors, and influence attitudes toward drugs. Both peer pressure and peer drug use were related to the frequency of drug use as reported by

African American 10th graders attending urban high schools (Farrell & White, 1998).

Given the strong influence of peers, many drug prevention programs have been designed to increase skills to resist peer pressure for drug use. These programs teach children to identify negative drug influences, to develop the skills needed to resist peer persuasion, and to cope with peers who may be critical of the non-drug using youth (Botvin & Kantor, 2000).

School Factors

In general, school problems are markers for a number of risk factors, including drug use. Lack of attachment with, commitment to, and interest in school have been associated with drug use among youth (McCluskey et al., 2002). School-related problems, such as school failure, truancy, and special placements, are higher among drug users (McCluskey et al., 2002). High academic performance and interest is a protective factor against drug use.

Poor school management characterized by disorganization and poor school morale has also been linked to increased drug use (Brook, Nomura, & Cohen, 1989). School policy also contributes to drug use. Schools that have lax drug policies tend to have higher levels of drug use among students than those schools where there are strictly enforced policies against drug use (Beman, 1995).

Community Factors

There are several community level influences on drug use for youth. Access and availability of drugs are predictors of drug use. Youth who live in communities where drugs are more easily accessible use more drugs than those who do not have such access. For example, liquor stores are more common in low-income communities than in middle-income communities. These liquor stores are often small convenience stores where community residents go to purchase food and other household items because of the absence of large supermarket chains in their neighborhoods. These liquor stores make alcohol much more accessible than it is in middle-income neighborhoods.

Drug use is also prevalent in communities that have high levels of social disorganization and stress. Communities with densely packed low-income housing developments, high crime rates, youth gangs, low surveillance of youth, and adult illicit behavior show higher rates of youth drug use. Residential mobility is also associated with higher rates of drug use (Hawkins et al., 1992). Like their adult counterparts, youth may turn to drugs to deal with the stress of their environment.

Economic and employment opportunities within a community play a role in drug use and associated negative behaviors. The availability of jobs, recreational activities, and community resources are dependent on the economy of a community. Distressed communities provide few alternative activities in which youth can engage. These communities provide little employment and few legitimate opportunities for youth to earn money. Among some youth, drug use and drug selling are distinct and separate activities and drug selling may not be seen as a negative activity. Feigelman, Stanton, and Ricardo (1993) conducted focus group discussions with youth who resided in inner-city communities regarding their perception of drug selling and drug use. Participants were 10 to 14 years of age. Most of the youth felt that dealing drugs was not as problematic as using drugs. Youth interviewed identified many rewards of selling drugs. These included material items and wealth, attention received from being a drug dealer, and affiliation with something special.

CULTURAL FACTORS

Recently, there has been research on the positive role of cultural variables in preventing drug use and abuse among African American youth. The findings from this research assume that spirituality, a positive ethnic identity, and strong cultural values serve as protective factors for African American youth (Belgrave, Townsend, Cherry, & Cunningham, 1997; Chipungu et al., 2000). There has been a call for the development of culturally specific drug prevention and intervention programs (Botvin, Dusenburg, Baker, James-Ortiz, & Botvin, 1992; CSAP, 1992; Nobles & Goddard, 1993; Rebach, 1992; Rowe & Gills, 1993). The assumption is that drug prevention information presented in culturally meaningful and relevant formats can be effective in inoculating youth from those personal attributes and ecological factors that are associated with initiation of drug use. Culturally specific values and beliefs about self and about how to relate to others—especially to one's community—can be protective for African American youth. African American youth who have internalized spirituality, Africentric values, and a positive racial identity are better able to resist and/or delay drug initiation (Belgrave et al., 1997; Belgrave, Brome, & Hampton, 2000).

Spirituality

One dimension of an Africentric worldview, spirituality (and religiosity), is linked to attitudes toward drug use. In a study of over 1,000 students from two historically black colleges and universities, Bowen-Reid and Rhodes (2003) found that students who use marijuana are less spiritual than those who either stopped using or who have never used marijuana. Belgrave et al. (1997) found that African American youth who attend church and who discuss religious and spiritual topics within the home are less likely to use drugs (cigarettes, beer, wine, etc.) than those with fewer religious practices. Belgrave and colleagues note that the religiosity of youth in their relatively young (i.e., ages 9 and 10) probably reflects the religiosity of parents and other adults in the home. In households where experiences are organized around spiritual and religious activities, there may be fewer opportunities for youth to experiment with drugs. In addition, in households where parents and other adults do not use drugs, there is less access to drugs.

Ethnic Identity

Ethnic identity has been defined as feelings of belongingness, attachment, and behavioral dispositions toward one's own ethnic group (Phinney, 1992). Several studies have shown a relationship between ethnic identity and reduced problem behaviors among youth. Ethnic identity is associated with increased academic achievement (Wong, Eccles, & Sameroff, 2003), better coping (Greig, 2003), and lower sexual risk (Beadnell et al., 2003) among African American youth. Adolescents with strong ethnic identity are less likely to use drugs (Belgrave et al., 2000; Marsiglia, Kulis, & Hecht, 2001).

Africentric Values

Ethnic identity has to do with one's affiliation toward one's ethnic and cultural group. Africentric values, on the other hand, have to do with the beliefs, values, and cultural dispositions of people of African descent. Like ethnic identity, Africentric values have been associated with prosocial behavior and good coping strategies (Thompson & Chambers, 2000). Belgrave and colleagues (1997) investigated the influence of Africentric values on drug knowledge, attitudes, and use. Participants were 189 fourth and fifth graders attending public schools in two urban cities on the East Coast. Their findings indicated that Africentric beliefs about collective work and responsibility were associated with negative drug attitudes and less drug use. Also, participants with stronger Africentric values were more likely to perceive drugs as harmful. It is likely that students at this age have beliefs and values similar to their parents. Parents with strong Africentric beliefs and values may find drug use incongruent with a culturally grounded lifestyle. These beliefs may be transferred to children.

In another study, Belgrave and colleagues (2000) examined the relative contribution of culturally specific variables to drug use. The authors investigated the incremental contribution of culturally specific factors in predicting drug outcomes, when other variables that have traditionally been identified as correlates and/or predictors of drug use among adolescents were controlled for. These other variables included individual variables (e.g., self-esteem), family variables (e.g., family cohesion), and peer variables (e.g., peer drug attitudes). The results of this study indicated that cultural variables, such as Africentric values, along with racial identity, contributed significantly to understanding drug knowledge, drug use, and drug attitudes among African American youth. Cultural variables were as strongly associated with drug variables as more traditional variables.

There are several reasons why Africentric values may be related to drug attitudes and use. Africentric values may, in general, promote positive behaviors and a healthy drug-free lifestyle. Families who adhere to strong Africentric values may be less affected by stressors and may be more protected under adverse or stressful conditions that could lead to drug use. In essence, drug use is probably antithetical to Africentric values and beliefs.

Acculturation

Acculturation is the extent to which ethnic and cultural minorities participate in the cultural traditions, values, beliefs, and practices of their own culture versus those of the dominant "White" society, in the United States (Landrine & Klonoff, 1996a). African Americans as an ethnic group can function on a continuum from traditional to acculturated. People with traditional beliefs (similar to Africentric beliefs) remain immersed in the beliefs, practices, and values of their own culture. Thus, those who are acculturated are immersed in the values, beliefs, and behaviors of the dominant society. There has been limited research on acculturation and drug use. In one study on cigarette smoking and acculturation, Landrine and Klonoff (1996a) found that African American smokers tend to be more traditional (i.e., less acculturated) than African American nonsmokers. In a study of 128 African American adults, the authors found that smokers have greater distrust of Whites, hold more traditional health beliefs, believe in more superstitions, and are more likely to eat traditional foods than are nonsmokers. The authors offered several explanations for why smoking may be associated with less acculturation. Traditional African Americans may distrust Whites to such an extent that they distrust information about smoking. Highly traditional African Americans may be members of the culture who retain the unhealthy lifestyle (i.e., unhealthy diet and too little exercise) that is no longer adhered to in the larger, European American culture. African American smokers may believe that they are not vulnerable to the negative consequences of smoking, because they engage in traditional health practices. And African Americans with traditional beliefs may experience greater emotional distress than more acculturated African Americans and may be treated more harshly by Whites. This could lead to higher levels of stress, depression, and anxiety that could then lead to greater rates of smoking. This last hypothesis is consistent with the results of a study by Gottlieb and Green (1987). These authors found a link between high stress and high rates of smoking among African American adults.

Culturally Specific Drug Prevention Programs

There are several types of culturally specific prevention programs. Culturally focused prevention programs funded by the Center for Substance Abuse Prevention can be categorized into three broad categories (Chipungu et al., 2000). The first program type addresses the potential of cultural tradition, values, and spirituality as protective factors. These factors are incorporated in prevention programs. The second program type explores African American and African history and the contributions of Blacks as sources of identity and positive affirmation. This type of program might also include trips to Black museums or exhibits. The third program type focuses on contemporary cultural experiences among African Americans and addresses a range of topics related to external risk. This program may, for example, address racism and discrimination as factors in drug use and incarceration. Most culturally focused prevention programs include a combination of these three program types.

INSTITUTIONAL AND SOCIETAL FACTORS

In addition to cultural and identity factors that operate on an individual level, there are several institutional and societal influences on drug use among African Americans. The majority of African Americans (55%) live in families classified as poor or near poor (Centers for Disease Control and Prevention, 2002c). Poverty is almost always associated with living in neighborhoods with low economic viability and other social problems. We now review how poverty contributes to drug use. The media also affect how drugs are perceived. In general, the media represent's African Americans more negatively than Whites in scenes depicting drug use. Finally, we review cocaine as an example of how institutional discrimination affects sentencing differentials between African Americans and Whites.

Poverty

Poverty is a risk factor for drug use. Data from the National Household Survey revealed that drug use is associated with poverty (Kaestner, 1998). Whitehead, Peterson, and Kaljee (1994) conducted interviews with 600 African American residents of inner-city neighborhoods. They note that among African American males who have been denied mainstream employment opportunities, engaging in nonmainstream activities such as drug trafficking may be perceived as an opportunity for economic freedom and as a power base.

Media

Children and adolescents are the major consumers of television and movies, and the media have considerable potential to encourage drug use in portrayals that legitimize, normalize, trivialize, or glorify substances. Roberts, Henriksen, and Christenson (1999) conducted a comprehensive study of depictions of substance use in popular movies and music. The authors examined the 200 most popular movie rentals and 1,000 of the most popular songs from 1996 and 1997. Substances that were analyzed included illicit drugs, alcohol, tobacco, and over-the-counter and prescription medicines. The researchers examined what drugs were used, by whom, how often, and under what circumstances. The authors found that 98% of movies depicted illicit drugs, alcohol, tobacco, or over-the-counter medicines. Alcohol and tobacco appeared in more than 90% of the movies, and illicit drugs appeared in 22%. Twenty-six percent of the movies that showed illicit drugs contained explicit, graphic portrayals of their preparation and/or use. Forty-nine percent showed short-term consequences of substance use, and about 12% showed long-term consequences. Five percent of the major characters used illicit drugs, 25% smoked tobacco, and 65% drank alcohol.

In terms of the characters in the movies, the authors noted that more White than African American characters used illicit drugs. However, although African Americans represented a small portion of all major characters, their proportional illicit drug use was higher (10%) than that of White characters (5%).

The analysis of music content revealed differences in whether or not drugs were mentioned in rap and non-rap music categories. Drug references were most common in rap music; illicit drugs were mentioned in 63% of rap songs. Illicit drugs were mentioned in 10% of the lyrics of the other song categories. Alcohol was mentioned in about half of the rap lyrics and in about 13% of the other categories. Marijuana was the most frequently mentioned illicit drug.

Incarceration and Drugs

African Americans have much higher rates than other ethnic groups of being investigated and charged with drug use, possession, and sale of illegal drugs. African Americans have been disproportionately affected by former U.S. President Ronald Reagan's war on drugs, which began in 1982. According to Nunn (2002), drugs are one of the primary reasons why the percentages of Blacks in prison have increased dramatically over the past two decades. Since the war on drugs was declared, prison populations have tripled, especially in federal institutions. The federal prison population was only 24,000 in 1980 but exceeded 145,000 by 2000. Fifty-seven percent were incarcerated for drug offenses.

In some cities, such as Baltimore, African Americans account for 86% of those arrested for drug offenses. The higher arrest rates for African Americans cannot be accounted for by greater illicit drug use, in that most drug arrests are made for the crime of possession. Yet most drug users are White. This can be partly attributed to where arrests are made. Police are more likely to concentrate their arrests in socially disorganized neighborhoods where drug dealing is at the street level.

Differences in mandatory minimum sentences for crack and powdered cocaine illustrate the role of race in convictions and lengths of sentencing. Crack is a form of cocaine whose market is concentrated in urban communities that are largely Black and Hispanic (Banks, 1997). These communities have elevated levels of poverty, unemployment, and other indicators of community distress. The Omnibus Bill, implemented in 1987, imposes mandatory minimum sentences of 5 years for first offenders convicted of trafficking 5 or more grams of crack cocaine. An equivalent sentence for powdered cocaine would require trafficking 500 grams. Conviction for possession of 5 grams of crack carries a minimum penalty of 5 years for a first offense. In contrast, conviction for possessing powdered cocaine is a misdemeanor with a maximum penalty of one year's imprisonment. The Omnibus Drug Bill was upheld in 1995, despite efforts to address and overturn the 100-to-1 quantity ratio between sentences for trafficking in crack and powdered cocaine and the penalties for simple possession of crack (Banks, 1997).

These sentencing differentials have had a large effect on African Americans' convictions in federal courts (Banks, 1997; Nunn, 2002). For example, in 1993 the racial distribution of all convictions for drug trafficking in the federal courts was fairly even (Whites, 30.8%; Blacks, 33.9%; Hispanics, 33.8%). However, persons convicted of crack offenses have been overwhelmingly Black (88.3%) as opposed to White (4.1%) or Hispanic (7.1%). Because most drug cases are tried at the state and local levels, mandatory minimum sentences also result in an overwhelming majority of those convicted at the state and local level for crack cocaine offenses to be African American.

Approaches to Drug Use Prevention

The best way of dealing with substance and drug use is to prevent it from occurring. Several types of prevention programs have been successfully used to prevent alcohol, tobacco, and other drug use among African Americans. Some of these programs are universal, meaning that they are applicable to all ethnic and cultural groups. Others are more culturally specific, meaning that they are designed specifically for African Americans.

We first discuss universal approaches to substance abuse prevention, and then we offer an overview of culturally specific approaches.

Several approaches have been used for preventing and reducing substance use and abuse among youth (CSAP, 1996). *Knowledge-based programs* are designed to provide information about drugs and the negative consequences of drugs. Evaluations of knowledge-based programs have indicated that when used alone, these programs have not been effective in changing drug behaviors. *Personal, interpersonal, and enhancement programs* promote feelings of self-worth and competence that make the individual less likely to engage in drug use. *Life skills and social skills programs* teach youth skills for refusing drugs, make youth aware of the social context of drug use, and provide youth with skills for coping with anxiety and/or social and interpersonal relationships that may lead to drug use. *Family-based programs* improve parenting skills and family cohesiveness, and foster competence and connections among children to deter drug use. *Community-based programs* target aspects of the community that affect drug accessibility and attitudes. Actions can include removal of liquor stores, policing of drug trade, and advertising. *Alternative programs* provide youth with constructive and healthy activities that offset the attractiveness of drugs. These may include community service programs for youth, athletic and recreational programs, and tutoring and educational enhancement programs (CSAP, 1996). *Cultural enhancement programs* focus on the infusion of cultural values, attitudes, and behaviors that are protective against drug use. Most programs use a combination of these strategies and approaches for drug prevention.

LIFE SKILLS TRAINING PROGRAM

One prevention approach with demonstrated effectiveness is the Life Skills Training Program. This approach involves teaching youth skills for resisting social and peer influences. The life skills training approach has shown successful outcomes among many youth populations including African Americans (Botvin & Kantor, 2000). Life skills training is designed to help youth gain skills necessary to resist peer pressures to smoke, drink, and use drugs; to help participants to develop greater self-competence; to effectively cope with social anxiety; and to increase knowledge of the consequences associated with substance use (Botvin & Kantor, 2000).

The Life Skills Training Program has shown effectiveness in reducing tobacco, alcohol, and marijuana use (Botvin & Kantor, 2000). The program has been effective with Hispanic and African American youth. The Life Skills Training Program is mostly implemented in school settings, but it can also be implemented in other settings, such as recreational centers, churches, and community centers.

CULTURALLY FOCUSED APPROACHES TO DRUG PREVENTION AND TREATMENT

Considering how important cultural beliefs and behaviors are in drug prevention and intervention, programs that consider culture in such efforts should be beneficial (Castro & Alarcon, 2002). There has been some recent work in which culturally congruent drug programs have been developed, implemented, and evaluated. We will describe two programs with strong cultural foci: a drug prevention program for African American youth and a drug treatment program for African American women. Common to both programs is the use of culture both in content (i.e., topics, lessons, curriculums) and in process (i.e., method by which the program is implemented).

A Culturally Appropriate Drug Prevention Program

Belgrave and colleagues (2004) provided a culturally enhanced drug prevention intervention to African American girls aged 10 to 14, called Sisters of Nia. The intervention was a combination of cultural and life skills training curricula (described previously). The cultural curriculum consisted of sessions that focused on the culture of being female and of African descent. Each session began with a unity circle following by small group discussion and activities. These small groups, called *jamaas* (Swahili for "family"), were led by *mzees* (Swahili for "female elder"). The principles of Nguza Saba (seven principles of Kwanzaa) and an African proverb were used to introduce and guide the discussion for the topic of the week. Some of the topics were relationships, Africa and African culture, appearances, leadership among African American women, life course expectations, and goals. Drug prevention topics were included as part of the life skills training curriculum. At the end of each session, the groups came together again in a closing unity circle. An important component of the cultural curriculum was to foster positive relationships among participants and program staff. Therefore, activities were structured to be interdependent with a focus on the group rather than the individual participant.

Participants met once a week for 17 weeks for 1.5 hours. Data on drug refusal efficacy were collected at the beginning and the end of the program from girls in intervention and comparison groups. Participants in the drug prevention program reported greater alcohol and drug refusal efficacy and resistance than participants in the comparison group at post–test.

An Africentric Approach to Substance Abuse Treatment

An example of a culturally congruent drug treatment program for African American women is one implemented by Jackson, Stephens, and Smith (1997). This program, called the *Iwo San* (Swahili for "House of Healing"; Jackson et al., 1997), was a residential treatment program for drug and alcohol abusing African American women and their dependent children. The program was based on the assumption that addiction arises as a coping mechanism for escaping stressors and the problems of daily life.

Iwo San incorporated a rites-of-passage component engendering the Africentric perspective. The rites of passage fostered a sense of responsibility for self, family, and community. Spirituality played a key role in this program and spirituality was interwoven throughout the treatment in Iwo San. A council of elders was one component of the rites program. Elders were selected by age, recognition, and standing in the community and consisted of representatives from all program components (staff, residents, community residents, etc.). The Council of Elders expressed wisdom, offered guidance and leadership, and facilitated moral and spiritual development.

The Iwo San program also emphasized respect for tradition. Respect for tradition was accomplished by ceremonies to celebrate rites of passage and holidays such as Kwanzaa and by the preparation of traditional African foods. All clients and their children were taught African and African American history. Another feature of the program was to promote harmony within the spiritual, mental, and physical self. Accordingly, each client was taught meditation in order to facilitate self-understanding. The program also focused on the "we," and the entire community shared responsibilities—from chores to problems.

In terms of treatment length, most drug treatment programs establish set days for participation. However, it is incompatible with an Africentric perspective to establish a set number of days for a client to complete treatment. In Africentric tradition, the will of the people, not the clock, defines time. Because the client's treatment progress was individual, so was her period of participation.

Although the research on cultural approaches to prevention and treatment is limited, the few studies that have been conducted are promising. They suggest that culturally based approaches used in conjunction with other prevention and treatment methods will support reduction of drug use among African Americans.

Methodological Issues

There are two methodological issues to consider when conducting research on drugs and African Americans. They are the validity of self-reports of drug use and the identification of appropriate constructs and measures in drug research.

SELF-REPORT OF DRUG USE

When respondents are asked to report any illicit or stigmatizing behavior, there is always a concern as to whether the respondent will answer questions in a truthful way. People may lie for fear of stigmatization and/or punishment. They may not want the interviewer to know that they are engaging in negative behaviors. Moreover, illicit drugs are illegal, and identification of use may hold punitive (i.e., expulsion from school) or criminal consequences. This may be a concern if an interviewer represents an organization or agency that the individual distrusts or does not know. In order to get valid results, respondents must feel that the information they share is confidential and will not be used against them. The development of a trusting and honest relationship between the interviewer and the respondent is essential if this is to occur.

IDENTIFYING CORRELATES OF DRUG USE FOR AFRICAN AMERICANS

Identifying the appropriate constructs and measures to understand predictors or contributors of drug use are also prime methodological concerns. Most researchers have assumed that the same factors that are correlated with drug use among the general population hold true for African Americans. However, this is not always the case. For example, several studies reviewed earlier in this chapter showed that strong cultural beliefs and values were associated with less drug use and more negative drug attitudes among African Americans (Belgrave et al., 1997; Belgrave et al., 2000; Cherry et al., 1998). Other studies have shown an association between drug use and religiosity and spirituality for African Americans (Belgrave et al., 1997; Wallace, Brown, Bachman, & Laveist, 2003). The relationship between drug use and spirituality may not be as strong for Whites. In analysis of data on African American and White adults, Belgrave, 2005 found that spirituality was associated with less drug use for African Americans than it was for Whites.

Finally, some research suggests that family factors may play a differential role in drug use among White and African American youth. Research on White youth has suggested that those who reside within single-parent households are more likely to use drugs than those who reside in two-parent households (Miller & Volk, 2002). However, Belgrave et al. (1997) found no correlation between family structure and drug attitudes or use for African American adolescents. That is, youth who lived with one parent were not any more likely to use drugs than those who lived with two parents.

Summary

The proverb at the beginning of the chapter states, "When the cock is drunk, he forgets about the hawk." Similarly, alcohol and other drugs have had devastating consequences for African Americans. In this chapter we have explored some of the reasons for drug abuse and what can be done about the problem.

Africans drank alcohol during celebrations and special events, and alcohol was also used as currency in the slave trade. The use of alcohol and other drugs continued among enslaved Africans in the New World. Following the Civil War, increased use of drugs occurred as African Americans began migrating north and to urban areas.

Surveys of the prevalence of drug use among youth show that African Americans use less alcohol, cigarettes, and other drugs than White youth. However, patterns of use change with age, and African Americans are more likely to increase their drug use as they get older.

Drug initiation begins during early adolescence and tends to co-occur with other social problems. There are several risk and protective factors for drug use. These include risk and protective factors at the individual, family, peer, school, and community levels.

Institutional and societal influences on drug use include poverty and stereotypical media portrayals of African Americans. Drug incarceration policies result in higher rates of incarceration for African Americans than other ethnic groups because of differentials in crack and cocaine sentencing. Cultural beliefs and values may reduce risk for drug use. Strong spirituality, ethnic identity, and Africentric values have been found to correlate with less drug use and more negative drug attitudes. Programs that infuse cultural values, beliefs, and ethnic consciousness enhance these protective factors against drug use.

There are several approaches to preventing drug use. These include life skill training approaches and cultural approaches or a combination of these.

Aggression, Violence, and Crime 14

> *To fight once shows bravery, but to fight all the time is stupid.*
>
> —Oromo proverb

In Search of Fairness
Monday, January 3, 2005
North Jersey Media Group, Inc.
Editorial by the record

New Jersey has more than 23,000 people in state prison. And for each one, it spends on average a staggering $28,000 per year. That's enough to pay for a year in college, or for a lengthy period of drug treatment—which many of the folks behind bars in New Jersey could use. To be sure, cost shouldn't be the only thing the criminal justice system takes into account in deciding who gets locked up and for how long. The need for justice, fairness and the protection of society from dangerous criminals all must be of primary consideration. But the price of imprisoning people can serve as an impetus in examining sentencing rules and procedures. Are they fair? Do they benefit society?

New Jersey has begun such an examination through its creation in 2004 of the Commission to Review Criminal Sentencing. The panel has a broad mission to review all aspects of sentencing. But one area it will focus on is laws passed in 1979 setting mandatory minimum sentences for drug offenses and other crimes. Mandatory minimum sentences are one reason why the nation's prison population has swelled even as crime has plummeted. That's because these laws tie the hands of judges, forcing them in many cases to hand down lengthy prison sentences even to first-time, non-violence drug offenders. One particularly unjust law in New Jersey mandates a 10-year sentence for anyone caught selling drugs within 1,000 feet of a school.

The intent of the law was to keep drug dealers away from schoolchildren. But its effect is that drug dealers in densely packed cities, where just about every place is close to a school, are subject to harsher punishments than their counterparts in small towns. The sentencing commission, to its credit, has made review of this law a priority.

Mandatory minimums became popular in the 1970s when the United States declared war on drugs. But their highly punitive approach clearly hasn't solved the drug problem. The laws have also become hard to defend in the face of declining crime rates.

In 2003, rates of violent and property crime reached the lowest level since the government began surveying crime victims 30 years ago. That downward trend continued in the first half of last year.

New Jersey has seen a similar drop in crime. And the good news is that state's prison population has fallen in recent years. Still, in 2003 the number of state inmates was 375 percent higher than in 1980. So, whom are these people packing our prisons? Thirty-five percent were convicted of drug offenses. Only 40 percent are in for violent crimes. But here's the most disturbing statistic: 63 percent of New Jersey's inmates are black, even though African-Americans make up only 14 percent of the state's population. New Jersey has the biggest racial disparity in imprisonment in the nation.

That shameful standing alone calls into question the fairness of state sentencing laws. Change can't come soon enough.

Introduction and Definitions

This news story points out the harsh reality of crime for African Americans. African Americans are more likely to be incarcerated than any other racial group in the United States. Biased institutional laws, disadvantaged communities, and racial inequalities account for the high incidence of incarceration. In this chapter, we review data on arrests and incarceration of African Americans and provide some historical and contemporary explanations.

Aggression and violence are part of the fabric of life in the United States. Aggression and violence are expressed by individuals (e.g., the 1999 killings at Columbine high school in Colorado), within a community or collective group (e.g., high levels of crime in some neighborhoods), and at a societal level (e.g., war). Aggressive and violent acts are sanctioned (e.g. executions of death row inmates) and enjoyed as a source of entertainment (e.g., boxing, football). Movies and television, major sources of entertainment and information, depict aggression and violence constantly. The quality of life and well-being of African Americans are very much influenced by aggression and violence in this country.

This chapter examines the topics of aggression, violence, and crime from the perspective of African Americans. We first define related terms and then we provide the historical context of aggression and violence against enslaved Africans and African Americans during their early years in the United States.

In trying to understand the origin of violence, we examine the theoretical debate over whether or not aggression is inborn or learned. We also explore three major theoretical perspectives on crime and violence: social learning theory, social organization theory, and cultural theory.

Because African Americans are more likely than White Americans to face the consequences of aggression, violence, and crime, we give an overview of the statistics on crime and incarceration among African Americans. We also discuss community violence and co-victimization, violence against women, and prevention and reduction of aggression, violence, and crime. Methodological issues related to research on violence, crime, among African Americans are reviewed, and finally, a chapter summary is given.

DEFINITIONS

Aggression is an intentional behavior aimed at causing physical or emotional pain. Aggression can be instrumental or hostile (Berkowitz, 1993). Instrumental aggression is intentional behavior to hurt someone as a means to an end, as for example, between boxers in a boxing match. Hostile aggression is a type of aggression that comes from feelings of anger and is aimed at inflicting pain, such as when a person initiates a fight because he or she has been insulted. Aggression can be physical or verbal, and direct or indirect. Examples of physical aggression are hitting, using weapons, and kicking. Examples of nonverbal aggression are gossiping about others, isolating others, and insulting others.

Violence is an extreme form of aggression. "Violence is the exertion of physical force in order to injure or abuse another" (*Merriam-Webster Online Dictionary*, 2004). Violence and aggression can also lead to criminal acts. "A crime is an act or the commission of an act that is forbidden or the omission of a duty that is commanded by a public law and that makes the offender liable to punishment by that law" (*Merriam-Webster Online Dictionary*, 2004).

Violence Against Africans From the Middle Passage to the 20th Century

In the popular media and academic literature, much attention has been directed at aggressive and violent behavior, especially within inner-city and urban communities whose residents are primarily African Americans and other ethnic minorities. High levels of violence and crime have especially been noted among African American males. However, violent behavior among African Americans is a fairly recent phenomenon. A discussion of violence and aggression among contemporary African American males must include a consideration of the historical context of violence against Africans and African Americans.

VIOLENCE DURING THE MIDDLE PASSAGE

King (1997) provides a thoughtful discussion of the historical context of violence against Africans and African Americans in an article titled "Understanding Violence Among Young African American Males: An Afrocentric Perspective." He begins by discussing violence by Europeans against Africans and then enslaved Africans in the United States. According to King, present-day violent behaviors among young African American males were almost nonexistent in Africa prior to the slave trade. Given this historical framework, how can we account for the violence that appears to be a part of the contemporary African American male experience?

According to King (1997), the enslavement of African people was the single most violent and brutal act committed against any group of people in the history of the world. The roots of violence began with the brutal and inhumane enslavement of millions of Africans on land stolen from Native Americans. The 365 years of enslavement was a violent period. There were more than 40 million (some estimates are as high as 150 million) African people throughout the Americas. Mortality among Africans was very high. One out of every three Africans captured during slave raids died before reaching the coast where they were shipped out; another third died at sea prior to reaching their final destination.

VIOLENCE DURING AND AFTER SLAVERY

Following the middle passage, violence continued under American slavery. Africans were considered property and were forced to work under strenuous conditions for more than 220 years (King, 1997). Male Africans (compared with female Africans) were treated more violently and received all types of physical punishment including lynching, beatings, body mutilations, and castration. Violence in the form of rape was directed against African women.

After slavery ended, violence against African Americans, especially males, continued. During the late 19th and early 20th centuries, thousands of African American males were incarcerated, injured, and murdered. Between 1885 and 1921, 4,096 lynchings were recorded in the United States, an average of 113 per year (Fishel & Quarles, as cited in King, 1997). The number of actual lynchings was most likely higher than 4,096, as many were not recorded. Many of the victims of lynchings were accused but rarely confirmed of raping a White female. Burning by mobs was another form of violence. Lynchings were well publicized in newspapers and were cause for celebrations among members of the White community, especially in the southern states. White race riots between the years 1865 and 1940 led to the deaths of over 500 African Americans (Staples, as cited in King, 1982). There was little interference or punishment of the rioting offenders from local law officials.

Police brutality did not begin with the publicized Rodney King incident of 1992. Between 1920 and 1932, out of 479 Blacks killed by White persons in the South, 54% were killed by White police officers. Seventy-five percent of the civilians killed by police in seven cities between 1973 and 1974 were Black males (Staples, as cited in King, 1997). According to King (1997), the institutional and legal violence against African Americans has led to an undervaluing of their lives. How does this historical context relate to the violence seen among African American males currently taking place in African American communities, especially inner-city communities? The systemwide expression of violence directed at African Americans has affected African American males' perceptions of opportunities and life course expectations. African Americans observe that adult males in their community have high rates of underemployment, unemployment, poverty, and poor health. High rates of mortality and incarceration leave adolescent males without exposure to adult males who can serve as positive mentors to show them how to be a man and how to succeed in this society. Males who are considered successful often obtain funds illegally through drug sales and other illegal activities. Role models for legitimate routes to success are often lacking. The availability of drugs is a major contributor to violence in urban African American communities. Involvement in the drug culture results in violence, turf wars, and illegal activities.

Furthermore, the glorification of materialistic acquisition and wealth by the media also plays a role in violence within African American communities. According to King (1997),

> The conspicuous consumption, irresponsible sexual behaviors, and gratuitous violence depicted in the media undermine the development of a culturally and socially appropriate value system in millions of African American boys, adolescents, and young adults. These conditions lead to feelings of frustration and emotional pain that destroys the moral character and conscience of many young men and boys. (p. 89)

In overview, a history of violence and oppression against African Americans in the U.S. has contributed to feelings of hopelessness and lower life course expectations, which in turn have led to aggression and violence among African American males.

Theories of Aggression and Violence

Is aggression learned or inborn? The answer to this question has long been debated. Some researchers point out that the universality of aggression among vertebrates suggests that aggression has been maintained over the years because it has some survival value. However, cultures differ greatly in their degree of aggressiveness. In the history of Europe, there has been one major war after another. In contrast, cultural groups such as the Pygmies of Central Africa and the Arepesh of New Guinea have extremely rare acts of aggression (Baron & Richardson, 1994).

Aggression and violence have been viewed from several theoretical perspectives. The innate perspective is that aggression is instinctual and that humans are biologically programmed to be aggressive for survival purposes. Another theoretical perspective is that aggression occurs under conditions of frustration. Aggression is used to reduce this frustration. A frustration reduction drive theory would account for the riots of the 1960s that took place in several cities following the assassination of Dr. Martin Luther King Jr. African Americans frustrated by civil rights injustices and other violations of human rights dealt with this frustration through rioting. Three major theories of aggression and violence are reviewed next.

SOCIAL LEARNING THEORY

Social learning theory assumes that we learn aggressive behavior by observing others and imitating them. One of the earliest studies that demonstrated the modeling of aggressive behavior showed children observing an adult kicking a plastic air-filled "Bobo" doll. The doll was the type of doll that when kicked would bounce back up. Then the doll would be kicked again (Bandura, Ross, & Ross, 1963). Following this observation, children were allowed to play with the doll. The children imitated the adult they had seen and treated the doll in the same aggressive way. This study was a forerunner to many subsequent studies on media violence.

Media violence (i.e., violence that occurs after exposure to violence seen or heard in the media) has been cited as a major contributor to aggression and violence. Fifty-eight percent of all TV programs contain violence and of these, 78% do not contain remorse, criticism, or penalty for that violence (Seppa, 1997). The average 12-year-old has seen more than 100,000 acts of violence on television (Signorielli, Gerbner, & Morgan, 1995). Long-term studies have shown that the more violence children watch on television, the more violent they are as teenagers and young adults; this effect seems to be strongest for children who are already somewhat prone to violence. African American children, especially low-income African American children, have increased exposure to media violence and spend more time watching television than do White children (Ford, McDonald, Owens, & Robinson, 2002). Media violence can affect adults as well as children.

A series of studies have shown that exposure to violent weapons increases aggressive acts especially under conditions of provocation and frustration. Exposure to violent stimuli such as guns may prime a person for aggression and violence. Berkowitz (1993) showed that exposure to a gun leads to increased aggression under conditions of provocation and frustration. In Berkowitz's study, a "subject" who had been frustrated was more likely to react aggressively to a "confederate" when a gun was left lying on the table than when it was not. This study has been cited often as a reason to discourage easy access to guns and other lethal weapons.

In another study, teenagers from the United States and 10 other countries were asked to read stories involving conflict among people and to guess the outcome of the conflict (Archer & McDaniel, 1995). American teenagers were more likely to anticipate a violent resolution to the conflict than were teenagers from other countries. The U.S. teenagers were also more likely to suggest more lethal ways (such as using guns) to resolving the conflict.

In summary, the social learning perspective can be used to account for violence seen in some African American communities. First of all, there is the modeling of adult violence by older teens in these communities. Teens in turn model aggression and violence to younger children. The availability of and display of weapons, as well as the increased exposure to violence through the media, are additional factors that promote violence in these communities.

SOCIAL ORGANIZATIONAL THEORY

Social organization refers to the extent to which residents of a neighborhood are able to achieve and maintain effective social control and realize collective goals. Socially disorganized neighborhoods are characterized by dysfunctional households; ethnic, racial, and class segregation; hostile behavior; and norms tolerant of crime. These neighborhoods are further characterized by unemployment, poverty, and residential mobility (Bennett & Fraser, 2000). The social organizational perspective assumes that violence is the result of structural disadvantages that deny African Americans in general, and African American males in particular, access to economic opportunities and social mobility (Gibbs, 1988).

Social organizational theory assumes that violence may be embedded in structural disadvantage in communities. These disadvantages are more likely to exist among African Americans than among Whites. The social organizational perspective considers the effects of racism and poverty and social policies that increase risk factors, especially among young men in high-risk neighborhoods.

Social organizational theory also takes into account the relationship between oppositional and destructive behaviors and violence (Bennett & Fraser, 2000). Within many low-income communities, destructive behaviors are tolerated. These behaviors range from littering to destroying property to stealing. Drug addiction and trafficking, along with other criminal activities, are further evidence of social disintegration. These acts contribute to the fear and isolation of residents.

Incarceration and Police Presence

High rates of incarceration in low-income, urban neighborhoods may contribute to social disorganization by creating a heavy reliance on law enforcement to correct deviant and criminal behavior (Bennett & Fraser, 2000). Monitoring by law enforcement replaces community-generated norms that may informally control and correct deviant behavior. High levels of incarceration may undermine informal social, political, and economic systems in a neighborhood. In addition, the presence of law enforcement may reduce neighborhood cohesion. Neighborhood cohesion also may be reduced when law enforcement focuses on arrest and incarceration and not on preventive measures such as would be found in community policing.

Family Disruption and Violence

Poverty, unemployment, and other social disadvantages directly and indirectly contribute to violence through family disruption. People in poverty view their future as uncertain and may be less willing to assume family and marriage responsibilities. One perspective considers that single-parenthood, specifically the absence of fathers in the household, is a primary contributor to violence. Researchers have noted an association between increasing rates of father-absent homes and violence among young African American males (Bennett & Fraser, 2000). To account for the father-absent hypothesis, some violence prevention programs have included mentoring by adult males.

The father-absent hypothesis has been criticized for not adequately accounting for the complexity of African American families. Father absence can be offset by the presence of other male family members, including extended family members and friends. Furthermore, some studies have found no association between father absence and delinquent behavior (Salts, Lindholm, Goddard, & Duncan, 1995). What seems to be more important than whether or not the father is present in the household is caregiver-child communication, discipline, and supervision.

Residential Segregation

Racial residential segregation has also been suggested as an explanation for higher rates of violence among African Americans (Peterson, Krivo, & Velez, 2001). Racial segregation is associated with racial inequality, and such inequality in turn is associated with increased violence. Under conditions of racial inequality, deviant and criminal behavior is seen as a response to frustration due to the lack of economic success and socioeconomic resources. Moreover, the expression of such frustration is likely to be enhanced when the inequalities are based on race.

Because the residents of segregated neighborhoods tend to have low socioeconomic power, racially segregated minorities are not able to organize collective protests (e.g., strikes, boycotts, and voting) for inequities. Instead, protest may be expressed in other forms such as aggressive behavior and criminal activity.

What role does segregation play in promoting violence? Black-White residential segregation is a defining feature of racial inequality. In many places, Blacks have virtually no contact with Whites in their own or neighboring communities. High levels of segregation are associated with several problems including poverty, physical deterioration of housing and business units, poorer schools, and high levels of crime (Peterson et al., 2001). To Blacks, residential racial segregation symbolizes barriers to upward mobility and life opportunities. Limited opportunities for achievement can lead to frustration, resentment, hopelessness, and alienation, which in turn can lead to violence.

The social isolation people feel as a result of living in segregated neighborhoods also contributes to violence. Segregation imposes a structural context in which disadvantage is concentrated in certain geographic areas of the city (Peterson et al., 2001). Rather than poverty and other social disadvantages being spread out over a larger geographical area, poverty is concentrated in the neighborhoods in which residents live. The concentration of poverty and disadvantage is the condition that leads to violence. Residents observe that violence is an acceptable response to conflict and stress. People witness violent acts, and young people begin to model this behavior. There are fewer informal networks among neighborhoods, families, businesses, and friends, and this makes it difficult for residents to identify strangers, monitor each other's property, and supervise peer groups and youth.

Peterson et al. (2001) argue that racially segregated neighborhoods may be a strong contributor to violence among African American youth because the conditions that encourage violence are particularly salient for persons who have not yet taken on adult roles and responsibilities. These consequences may be more drastic for youth in disadvantaged communities, where adult supervision by parents, neighbors, and other community members is less frequent. Community agencies that provide supervision to youth such as recreational facilities, gyms, libraries, and Churches may help to reduce crime and violence.

In summary, the social organizational theory of violence assumes that violence is a result of structural inequalities in one's neighborhood that prevent access to needed resources and positive role models.

CULTURAL THEORIES OF AGGRESSION AND VIOLENCE

Cultural theories of aggression and violence are another way to account for socialization of aggression and violence among people of African descent in this country. These theories also recognize the impact of the historical legacy of racism and oppression as a contributor to violence.

Cultural Racism

Cultural racism has been examined as a reason for violence among African Americans. Cultural racism is the systematic manner in which the White majority has established its primary cultural institutions (education, media, religion) to elevate and promote European physical characteristics, character, and achievement and to denigrate the physical characteristics, character, and achievement of non-White people (Oliver, 2001). An example of cultural racism is the absence of social science curricula that cover the contributions of Africans and African Americans to human civilization. Another example might be the mass media's portrayal of African Americans in a manner that promotes and justifies racial bias and stereotypes. For example, the majority of Black actors are employed in comedy roles (Schafer, 1993).

According to Oliver (2001), three factors have contributed to a cultural crisis among African Americans: (a) the loss of a history because of the structural and cultural practices in which African Americans have been disconnected from their history and traditional cultural practices, (b) the lack of appreciation of the cultural beliefs and practices unique to people of African descent, and (c) the lack of cultural confidence needed to effectively work toward accomplishing group goals.

Exposure to cultural racism contributes to the existence of violence, as it influences how African Americans define themselves, others, their community, and specific encounters (Oliver, 2001). Cultural racism has contributed to social disorganization among African Americans as it influences how African Americans see themselves. Racial stereotypes about violent, irresponsible Blacks are more likely to resonate with those African Americans who live in communities experiencing concentrated poverty. Those who are most at risk for participating in violent behavior have the tendency to accept as valid stereotypical negative images of African Americans.

The inability to achieve manhood through conventional means may lead some African American males to embrace exaggerated and stereotypical images of manhood. These alternative views of manhood are likely to increase one's risk of becoming involved in violence. For example, African American males who define manhood in terms of toughness, sexual conquest, and thrill seeking are most likely to spend more time hanging out in the street, using and selling drugs, and committing criminal acts as a way to maintain their lifestyles. These males are attracted to the street because they have been denied access to the conventional opportunity structure (Oliver, 2001).

Cultural and Ethnic Differences in Explanations of Violence

Factors that explain violence for African Americans may differ from those for Whites. Salts et al. (1995) tested a model of predictors of violent behavior for African American and White adolescents. Several variables were tested in the model, including school, family, and individual variables (i.e., self-esteem, drug uses, delinquent behavior, etc.). The findings showed that a higher percentage (58%) of the variance in violent behavior could be explained for Whites than for African Americans (39%). In other words, several factors could be identified to explain why Whites engaged in violence. Fewer factors could be identified for Blacks. The authors suggest that there may be other unidentified influences and conditions that explain the violent behavior of African Americans. These other factors may be community- and society-level factors discussed previously.

In another study, Caldwell, Kohn-Wood, Schmeelk-Cone, Chavous, and Zimmerman (2004) examined the effects of racial discrimination and racial identity attitudes on violent behavior. Participants were 325 African American young adults. They found that those who had experienced racial discrimination were more likely to engage in violent behavior. The authors speculate that violent behavior may represent an ineffective way of coping with life stressors. They further found that strong racial identity attitudes were a buffer between racial discrimination and violent behavior, especially for males. This means that for those African American males who reported strong ethnic identity, personal experiences of racial discrimination did not lead to much violence.

Crime and Punishment

Crime and incarceration are consequences of violence, and African Americans are more likely than Whites to be arrested, incarcerated, and put on probation and/or parole. In this section, we review statistics on arrest, incarceration, and probation and parole.

ARREST AND INCARCERATION

Although violence appears especially prevalent among African American males who live in inner cities, it is important to note that the vast majority of African American males are neither aggressive nor violent. African Americans are no more aggressive or violent than any other ethnic group. Yet, African Americans are much more likely than Whites to be arrested and convicted of crimes and to receive harsher sentencing.

Table 14.1   Percentage of Arrests by Offense and Race, United States, 2001*

Offense	White	Black
Total	69.5	28.1
Murder and nonnegligent manslaughter	48.4	48.7
Forcible rape	62.7	34.8
Robbery	44.5	53.8
Aggravated assault	64.0	33.7
Larceny–theft	66.1	31.2
Motor vehicle theft	57.5	39.8
Arson	76.9	20.7

Source: U.S. Department of Justice, Federal Bureau of Investigation (2002).

* Table does not include arrests of other ethnic groups.

Arrests by Offense

Table 14.1 shows arrest percentages by offense and race for the year 2001. Although only 12% of the total U.S. population, African Americans accounted for 28.1% of the total arrests in 2001. Arrests for murder and robbery are especially distorted. African Americans and Whites had a comparable percentage of arrests for murder in 2001, about 48%. African Americans also represented a large percentage of the arrests for robbery, 53.8%. For every arrest category, African Americans represented a substantially higher percentage than their representation in the population.

Incarceration Rates

Incarceration rates for African Americans are also substantially higher than for Whites and other ethnic groups. Table 14.2 shows the ethnicity of prisoners in state and federal prisons in the year 2002. In absolute numbers, 586,700 prisoners were African American males and 436,800 were White males. The table shows that African Americans made up 45.1% of the prison population and Whites made up 34.2% of the prison population in 2002. In the same year, the number of African American female prisoners was 36,000, which was close to the 35,400 for White females. Table 14.2 also shows that the percentages of prisoners for each ethnic group had not changed in the previous seven years.

Table 14.3 shows the numbers of prisoners under state or federal jurisdiction by ethnicity per 100,000 residents in the year 2002. Incarceration rates were alarmingly high for Black males in the 25- to 29-year-old group: approximately 10% (Harrison & Beck, 2003). This compares with 2.4% for Hispanic males and 1.2% for White males. Table 14.3 also shows incarceration

Table 14.2   Percentage of Prisoners Under State or Federal Jurisdiction, United States, 1995, 2002

	1995	2002
Total	100.0%	100.0%
White	33.5	34.2
Black	45.7	45.1
Hispanic	17.6	18.1
Other	3.2	2.6

Source: Harrison and Beck (2003, p. 9).

Note: Figures are for inmates with sentences of more than one year.

Table 14.3   Number of Prisoners Under State and Federal Jurisdiction per 100,000 Residents, by Gender, Race, Hispanic Origin, and Age, 2002

	Males				Females			
Age	Other[a]	White[b]	Black[b]	Hispanic	Other[a]	White[b]	Black[b]	Hispanic
Total	912	450	3,437	1,176	61	35	191	80
18–19	869	331	2,865	1,224	34	26	87	35
20–24	2,109	934	7,490	2,382	90	59	217	130
25–29	2,577	1,229	10,376	2,394	170	97	498	179
30–34	2,326	1,251	8,885	2,409	213	129	662	216
35–39	2,014	1,080	7,893	2,060	177	106	566	193
40–44	1,316	691	4,939	1,850	92	51	315	111
45–54	647	376	2,344	1,030	41	25	123	76
55 or older	141	96	479	272	5	4	17	8

Source: Harrison and Beck (2003, p. 9).

Note: Based on estimates of the U.S. resident population July 1, 2002.

a. Includes Native Indians, Alaska Natives, Asians, Native Hawaiians, and other Pacific Islanders.

b. Excludes Hispanics.

rates for other age-groups for males and females. African American females were five times more likely to be incarcerated than White females.

DEATH-ROW SENTENCING

Thirty-seven states and the federal prison system had a total of 3,557 prisoners under sentence of death at the end of 2002 (Bonczar & Snell, 2004). Three states reported 40% of the nation's death-row population: California (614), Texas (450), and Florida (366). During 2002, the total number of White inmates under sentence of death in the United States declined by 37; the number of Blacks increased by 16. Blacks composed 44% of all prisoners under sentence of death and Whites composed 54%. Of the Blacks who had a death sentence, 281 (9.8%) were executed during the period from 1977 to 2000. Of the Whites with a death sentence, 469 (13.9%) were executed. These data indicate that Blacks, relative to Whites, were disproportionately more likely to be on death row but slightly less likely to be executed if they were on death row.

TYPES OF OFFENSES AND SENTENCING

Drugs play a major role in sentencing for African Americans. Blacks are more likely to be sentenced for drug convictions than are Whites (Ditton & Wilson, 1999). In new court commitments to state prison in 1996, 36.8% of the Black convictions were for drug offenses (possession, trafficking), compared with 18.7% for Whites. Blacks and Whites had comparable rates of violent offenses (murder, rape, robbery, assault): 29% of Blacks and 28.7% of Whites were sentenced for violent offenses. Regarding property offenses, 24.9% of Blacks were sentenced for property offenses (e.g., burglary, larceny/theft, motor vehicle theft, fraud) and 38.1% of Whites were sentenced for property offenses.

Community Violence

Community violence exposure is defined as experiencing, seeing, or hearing about violence in one's home, school, or neighborhood. Co-victimization is the indirect experience of violence by directly observing the assault of another person (Shakoor & Chalmers, 1991).

Many inner-city communities have high levels of crime and violence. Community exposure to violence has been likened to living in a war zone. From 50% to 95% of children living in inner cities have been exposed to community violence. Several studies have examined prevalence of violence exposure, the effects of violence exposure, and factors that reduce some of the negative effects of violence exposure.

PREVALENCE OF EXPOSURE TO COMMUNITY VIOLENCE

African Americans living in inner cities experience a high degree of exposure to community violence. A study of 209 sixth graders in Philadelphia, of whom 95% were African American, indicated the following: 70% had witnessed a beating, 55% a stabbing, 47% a shooting, and 22% murder (Campbell & Schwartz, 1996). Similar findings have been found with older adolescents. One hundred seventy-eight African American inner-city youth from Detroit reported witnessing some form of community violence, and 85% had been victims of community violence (Myers & Thompson, 2000).

In an ethnographic study of third- and sixth-grade African American inner-city schoolchildren in Washington, D.C., Towns (1996) observed for 2 years the pervasive and recurring themes of community violence among children. In fact, the recurring themes of community violence forced her to change the original purpose of her study, which was to examine school interest and achievement among students. She writes,

> I discovered that school experience was not foremost on the children's minds: rather the violence they encountered in their community was these children's overriding concern. (pp. 377–378)
>
> On my first day at the school, an announcement boomed from the school's public [address] system warning everyone that an intruder was in the building and that all teachers should secure their doors until he was apprehended. Later that week, I returned from a lunch break to find police cars and fire trucks surrounding the building. (p. 376)

EFFECTS OF EXPOSURE TO COMMUNITY VIOLENCE

Exposure to violence results in both short- and long-term negative effects, including increased depression and anxiety, low self-esteem, posttraumatic stress disorder, fear, sleep disturbance, aggression and delinquent behavior, and poor academic performance (Kilpatrick et al., 2000). These symptoms can be categorized as externalizing and internalizing. Externalizing symptoms are aggressive acts directed at others, such as hitting other children, bullying, and engaging in disruptive behavior. Internalizing symptoms are directed at the self and include anxiety, depression, fear, and stress. In one study of female adolescents who witnessed violence, participants had problems with drinking, using drugs, carrying weapons to school, and trouble in school (Jenkins & Bell, 1994).

This is also the case with younger children. Youth who are exposed to community violence are more likely to be violent themselves. In a study of fourth-, fifth-, and sixth-grade students from inner-city schools, Hill and Madhere (1996) found that children who reported more co-victimization also had an increased need for retaliation and higher rates of confrontational behavior. These children also had higher levels of aggressiveness as rated by their peers.

Academic difficulties are another by-product of exposure to violence. Children who are exposed to violence concentrate less well and learn less. Low academic achievement and the inability to learn are risk factors for other problem behaviors, including drug use and delinquency.

YOUTH VIOLENCE

Youth are both perpetrators and victims of violence. Youth aged 12 to 19 are victimized at higher rates than are persons in any other age category (Peterson et al., 2001). This rate is at least twice that of any group 25 years and older. The availability of firearms is a major contributor to high rates of homicide among African American juveniles (Snyder, Sickmund, & Poe-Yamagata, 1996). The increase in juvenile homicide from the mid-1980s through the mid-1990s was firearm related. African Americans were more likely than Whites to be victims of firearm-related homicide. In the first half of the 1980s, firearms were involved in 46% of African American juvenile homicides. However, between 1990 and 1994, firearms were involved in 71% of African American juvenile homicides, compared with 54% of White juvenile homicides (Snyder et al., 1996).

WHAT PROTECTS CHILDREN AGAINST EXPOSURE TO COMMUNITY VIOLENCE?

Not every child from a socially disorganized neighborhood engages in violence; in fact, many do not. The concept of resilience explains this. Resiliency is defined as high functioning in the face of great risk or adversity (Rutter, 1990). In the absence of community-level risk factors, protective factors such as a supportive family and a resourceful neighborhood help the child to thrive. Attributes of the child, including self-esteem, self-efficacy, cultural identity, and social competence, also may buffer the individual from community-level risks for violence. One attribute of the child that seems to moderate the negative effect of violence exposure is emotional regulation. Children who are able to regulate their emotions and who have the ability to take a different perspective are less likely to be affected by community violence (Kliewer et al., 2004). This is because these youth are more likely to think through problems associated with violence instead of acting out aggressively.

Family relationships and cohesion is a second variable that helps children who live in violent communities. Children who feel valued, accepted, and loved are less likely to be negatively affected by community violence than those children in households without good relationships within the family. Also, parenting practices such as supervision, support, and engagement with youth affect how children react to violence exposure (Burton & Jarrett, 2000). Youth from more cohesive families have fewer aggression-related problems than youth from less cohesive families (Plybon & Kliewer, 2001). This support may also be found within the extended kin network. Low levels of family cohesion have been linked to increased symptoms of anxiety and depression among youth who have witnessed violence (Gorman-Smith & Tolan, 1998).

Also, the emotional or psychological state of the mother or primary caregiver influences how well the child responds to community violence. When the parent is calm and can problem solve in the face of danger, while at the same time not minimizing the seriousness of the situation, the child is better off. Kliewer et al. (2004) found that African American parents' emotional state had a protective effect on youth exposure to violence. A caregiver's ability to regulate his or her anger is helpful for youth exposed to violence.

At the neighborhood level, youth's perception of neighborhood cohesion affects perception of and reactions to community violence. When resources are available in a community, youth are less likely to experience the stress of community violence. These resources might include other adults to talk to, community centers, playgrounds, recreational facilities, and churches.

Violence Against Women

Despite the myth of the strong and resilient African American woman, she has been subject to violence both historically and contemporarily. In this section, we discuss rape and domestic violence from the perspective of African American girls and women. While rape and domestic violence are social problems that affect women in all ethnic groups, the nature and the extent of the violence may differ qualitatively for African American women than for women in other ethnic groups.

RAPE

Rape is the ultimate expression of aggression and violence. Although men are also victims of rape, we concentrate on females as rape victims because rape of females is more common than rape of males.

Rape of Enslaved Female Africans

Prior to setting foot on this continent, African women were raped and sexually exploited by Europeans who went to the coast of West Africa to select slaves for transport to the New World. Europeans who came to the West African coast had been at sea and away from home (and wives) for extended periods of time. In a visit to slave castles on the coast in Ghana and the open courtyards that surrounded these castles, the first author (Belgrave) was reminded of narratives that told of how female slaves were selected for sexual exploitation. The slave traders would require women to be brought unclothed into an open courtyard, where they could be viewed by the Captain in turn. Then one would be selected for sex with the slave trader. The selected women would be washed down (as their living quarters were filthy) prior to being taken to the trader.

Extreme sexual exploitation of African women continued throughout the period of slavery (Wyatt, 1992). The rape of enslaved African women not only was done for the pleasure of the slave owner but also for profitable reasons. Rape by slave owners increased slave populations and thus increased the slave owner's property. Justification for the sexual exploitation of enslaved Africans stemmed from 15th-century Christian missionary attitudes about the strong "sexual appetite" of Africans. Stereotypes about Black male sexual prowess and Black female promiscuity linger to this day. Until slavery was abolished, enslaved Africans had no legal recourse for rape. After slavery, the American legal system still treated the rape of African American and White women differently.

Wyatt (1992) conducted a study to investigate ways in which African American rape survivors differed from White rape survivors. She interviewed 55 persons who had indicated previous sexual victimization. She discovered that many rape victims were uncertain about whether to label their experiences as rape, especially if their assailant had been a friend or relative. Wyatt considered all incidents of involuntary sexual experience, whether perpetrated by friend, relative, or stranger, as rape. Wyatt found that African American women were less likely than White women to have disclosed incidents of sexual assault to others including the police and rape centers. African American women were also more likely than White women to report that where they lived placed them at risk for rape. African American women were more likely than White women to have repeated sexual assaults. And the African American women were more likely than the White women to have heard sexual and racial stereotypes regarding what kinds of women are likely to be raped. This last finding suggests that society conveys—more so to African Americans than to Whites—stereotypes about rape that ascribe some blame for the rape to the individual.

Wyatt (1992) provided several recommendations for rape prevention and also support of rape survivors. She recommended that rape prevention efforts focus on the effects of poverty on rape. Many girls and women live in environments that both place them at risk for being victimized and pose barriers to services after victimization. These barriers need to be addressed with groups at highest risk, specifically poor communities of ethnic minorities.

Part of the unwillingness of African American victims in Wyatt's study to disclose incidents of rape may be the perceived lack of community and societal support for their experiences. Inequity in the prosecution of rape African American rape victims supports this perception. Regardless of ethnicity, sexual assault has serious consequences for victims, including mental illness and increased drug abuse. Wyatt also recommended that continued efforts be made to educate law enforcement and those in the health and mental health professions about racial issues in the prevention, prosecution, and treatment of rape.

Acquaintance and Date Rape

Acquaintance rape occurs when sexual intercourse is forced or coerced, or the victim is manipulated into having the victim by someone with whom the victim is acquainted (Jenkins & Dambrot, 1987). Date rape occurs when this happens to who sexual intercourse is dating or who she has dated. Women who are raped by acquaintances are less likely to define and report this as rape than when they are victims of rape by a stranger. In nearly three out of four incidents, the victim knows or is acquainted with the assailant (Greenfield, 1997). Some argue that the increase in date rape is due to an increase in the availability of magazines, films, and videocassettes depicting explicit sexual behavior. Findings from studies suggest that exposure to violent pornography promotes greater acceptance of violence toward women (Dean & Malamuth, 1997).

Rape of an African American woman has historically been viewed as less serious than rape of a White woman. Foley, Evancic, Karnik, King, and Parks (1995) investigated the effects of the race of the assailant (Black or White), the race of the victim (Black and White), and gender of subjects (male and female) on subjects' perceptions of date rape. A sample of Whites and Blacks read a vignette of a date between two college students who had been dating. Foley et al. found that forced sexual encounter was perceived as less serious if the victim was a Black woman than when she was a White woman. If the victim was Black, participants were more likely to say that the forced encounter was an act of love than if she was a White woman. Also, females were more likely than males to define the forced sexual encounter as date rape and to think that the incident should be reported. Males were less likely than females to agree that the assailant should have stopped when asked to do so.

Based on their findings, Foley et al. (1995) suggest that Black women are more reluctant to report being sexually assaulted because they assume that their reports are not likely to be taken seriously.

DOMESTIC VIOLENCE

Domestic violence is defined as physical, emotional, or psychological violence occurring between sexual partners (Huang & Gunn, 2001). Twenty-eight percent of American couples experience at least one act of partner abuse during their marriage. Another 16% experience at least one act of violence a year, and 6% experience an act of severe violence in a given year.

In a study on the prevalence of violence in African American families, Gelles and Straus (1988) reported that African American husbands had higher rates of overall and severe violence toward their wives than did White husbands. The rate of wife abuse in African American families was 113 per 1,000 and 30 per 1,000 in White families. However, that study was published many years ago and more recent research is needed to see if the trend has continued.

Wyatt, Axelrod, Chin, Vargas Carmona, and Burns Loeb (2000) examined the prevalence of domestic violence and the risk factors for violence in a community sample of 128 African American women of mixed HIV seropositive status and mixed socioeconomic status ranging from low to middle class. Wyatt et al. found that violence was experienced by almost half of the women in this sample; 34% of the sample reported a moderate level of violence and 15% reported a severe level of violence. All of the respondents had experienced some nonphysical conflict from their partners such as sulking, quarreling, shouting, and insults. Furthermore, childhood abuse was related to partner violence. Women who had experienced abuse in childhood were more likely to report partner violence. Childhood abuse may be a factor in women entering into abusive relationships. Also, women who were HIV positive in this study were more likely to report abuse than women who were not. HIV positive women were also more likely to have experienced victimization in childhood.

Regarding risk factors for domestic abuse, Wyatt et al. (2000) found that childhood experiences of abuse increased the risk for partner violence in adulthood. Women who have been abused in the past seem to be more likely to enter into abusive relationships than those who have not experienced abuse in the past. Wyatt et al. also found that women with lower incomes and those with the highest income were most likely to report more frequent violence and nonphysical conflicts. It may be that women in both of these income categories are unable to support themselves and/or may be more dependent on their partners for economic survival.

Research suggests that Black women are more likely than White and Hispanic women to commit acts of severe violence against their husbands or boyfriends. The pattern of partner abuse among Black couples appears to be more reciprocal compared with its occurrence among White couples. For example, among Black married couples, wives were just about as likely to kill their husbands as husbands were to kill their wives; 47% of the victims of a Black spouse were husbands and 53% were wives (Dawson & Langan, 1994). Among White victims murdered by their spouses, wives were much less likely to be the killers: Whereas 38% of the White victims were husbands, 62% were wives.

Preventing Violence

Violence prevention programs typically target children and teens in order to reach youth prior to their engagement in violence. Because early adolescence (ages 11 to 13) is a critical period for instilling skills, beliefs, and values that support nonviolence, many prevention programs target this age-group.

There are many effective violence prevention programs. These programs are implemented within schools and communities and target individuals, families, schools, and communities.

VIOLENCE PREVENTION VIA SELF AND ETHNIC IDENTITY ENHANCEMENT

Improving self-worth and efficacy is one strategy for violence prevention. Efficacy and competency in decision making and conflict resolution skills can reduce conflict, anger, and violence. The ability to make good decisions promotes high self-esteem and worth. Issues related to self-worth may account for why some adolescents resort to violence. Accordingly, many violence prevention programs aim at improving self-worth via self-esteem and cultural identity enhancement.

A study by Okwumabua, Wong, Duryea, Okwumabua, and Howell (1999) used this approach. Their program was aimed at increasing self-esteem through social skills training and cultural awareness in order to prevent violence among African American youth. One hundred twenty-two African American male students, aged 8 to 14 and enrolled in public schools in West Tennessee, participated in the program. The program consisted of three components: (a) decision-making skills training, (b) conflict resolution training, and (c) cultural awareness. Participants met 48 weeks for 50 minutes per week. Students who participated in the program improved in self-concept and ethnic identity. Students in the 10- to 11-year-old group showed the most improvement relative to students in the younger (8 to 9) and older (12 to 14) age-groups.

SCHOOL-BASED PROGRAMS

Responding in Peaceful and Positive Ways (RIPP) is a school-based violence prevention program for students in middle and junior high schools (Farrell, Meyers, & White, 2001). The program can be delivered over 3 years and includes a classroom curriculum that focuses on problem solving and real-life applications. The RIPP program teaches concepts such as (a) the importance of significant friends or adult mentors, (b) the relationship between self-image and gang-related behaviors, and (c) the effects of environmental factors on personal health. Students learn about physical and mental development that occurs during adolescence, analyze the consequences of personal choices on health and well-being, learn that there are nonviolent options when conflicts arise, and learn how to be a positive family and community citizen.

The program has been evaluated. The findings showed that students in the RIPP program compared with students in a control group (a) had fewer disciplinary code violations for carrying weapons, (b) were less likely to have in-school suspensions, (c) had lower reported rates of fight-related injuries, (d) had more favorable attitudes toward nonviolence, and (e) were more likely to participate in their school's peer-mediation program (Farrell et al., 2001).

COMMUNITY POLICING

Community policing has been recognized as an effective way to combat criminal activity among adolescents and young adults. One such program was implemented in Boston neighborhoods with high crime rates (Bennett & Fraser, 2000). The program has four components: The Youth Violence Strike Force, Operation Nightlife, Operation Cease-Fire, and the Boston Gun Project. The program involved collaborative efforts between local and state law enforcement entities and other agencies. Law enforcement officials use criminal statutes and laws to remove violent offenders from the streets. Probation officers make nightly visits to the homes of youth who are under court supervision to ensure compliance with the terms of the probation, to reduce truancy, and increase parental involvement. Mediation specialists also known as "street-workers" visit "hot spots" in an effort to resolve conflict and link youth with community services. Overall, Boston's community prevention intervention is believed to be a significant contributor to the near 80% reduction in crime from 1990 to 1995 (Bennett & Fraser, 2000).

Midnight Basketball

Midnight basketball has been used as a violence and crime reduction strategy (Bennett & Fraser, 2000) since its beginnings in Glenarden, Maryland, in 1986. Its goal is to keep high-risk youth, mostly unemployed high school dropouts, off the street. Midnight basketball currently exists in hundreds of cities across the country. Games are scheduled between the hours of 12 midnight and 3 a.m. Midnight basketball programs generally provide more than late-night recreational activities. They also provide opportunities for participants to obtain high school diplomas or graduate equivalency degrees, parenting skills, and sometimes employment skills. Midnight basketball programs have been associated with reductions in crime (Bennett & Fraser, 2000).

Methodological Issues

Much of the media and statistics portray African Americans, especially young African American males, as violent. Disproportionately higher rates of incarceration among African Americans add credibility to this portrayal. Understanding the causes of aggression, violence, and crime among African Americans is incomplete without understanding the historical context of violence against Africans, enslaved Africans, and contemporary African Americans. Therefore, one methodological consideration is the way in which data and statistics are analyzed and reported. Analysis and presentation of data that highlight violence and the perpetuators of violence should also take into account the context of violence and aggression in the United States.

Another methodological issue that arises when discussing aggression and violence among young African Americans is what constitutes an aggressive and/or violent act. Within the context of some urban communities, to not aggress when one is aggressed against can be problematic. Learning how and when to respond or not respond in aggressive ways is essential to many African American males who reside in urban communities. This type of survival aggressiveness may be qualitatively different (and measured differently) from the type of retaliatory aggressive behavior seen in youth who have been bullied, such as those youth responsible for the Columbine killings.

In overview, a true understanding of aggression and violence within the African American community would be incomplete without understanding the historical context and the symbolic meaning of violence.

Summary

The proverb at the beginning of this chapter says, "To fight once shows bravery, but to fight all the time is stupid." In this chapter, we have shown the devastating consequences of aggression and violence that have been perpetrated both against and by African Americans. Three main theories that explain violence and aggression are social learning theory, social organizational theory, and cultural theory.

African Americans show higher rates of arrest and incarceration than any other ethnic group. Drug offenses play a large role in incarceration rates.

Youth who are exposed to community violence experience a multitude of problems from such exposure. The majority of children and teens who live in inner cities have been exposed to community violence.

Violence against women, including rape and domestic violence, has occurred throughout history. There are differences among African American and White women with regard to the perception and reporting of rape and domestic violence.

Programs to prevent violence have been implemented at the individual level, in schools, and in communities.

References

Abdullah, A. S. (1998). Mammy-ism: A diagnosis of psychological misorientation for women of African descent. *Journal of Black Psychology, 24*(2), 196–210.

Achenbach, T. M., & Edelbrock, C. S. (1984). Psychopathology of childhood. *Annual Review of Psychology, 35,* 227–256.

Adams, G. M. (2000). An ethnographic study of academic success in African-American doctoral recipients: The effects of persistence, psychological, and social psychological factors. *Dissertation Abstracts International, A (Humanities and Social Sciences), 60*(9-A), 3266, US: Univ. Microfilms International.

Adebimpe, V. R., & Cohen, E. (1989). Schizophrenia and affective disorder in black and white patients: A methodologic note. *Journal of the National Medical Association, 81*(7), 761–765.

Adger, H. (1991). Problems of alcohol and other drug use and abuse in adolescents. *Journal of Adolescent Health, 12,* 606–613.

Administration on Aging, U.S. Department of Health and Human Services. (2002). *A profile of older Americans: 2002.* Retrieved April 4, 2005, from http://www.aoa.gov/prof/Statistics/profile/8_pf.asp

Administration on Aging, U.S. Department of Health and Human Services. (2003). *A profile of older Americans: 2003.* Retrieved January 10, 2005, from http://www.aoa.gov/prof/Statistics/profile/2003/2003profile.pdf

Ainsworth, M. (1979). *Patterns of attachment: A psychological study of the strange situation.* Hillsdale, NJ: Erlbaum.

Akbar, N. (1981). Mental disorder among African-Americans. *Black Books Bulletin, 7*(2), 18–25.

Akbar, N. (1982). *From miseducation to education.* Jersey City, New Jersey: New Mind Productions.

Akbar, N. (1991a). The evolution of human psychology for African Americans. In R. Jones (Ed.), *Black psychology.* Berkeley, CA: Cobb & Henry.

Akbar, N. (1991b). Mental disorders among African Americans. In R. Jones (Ed.), *Black psychology.* Berkeley, CA: Cobb & Henry.

Akbar, N. (1996). African metapsychology of human personality. In D. A. Azibo (Ed.), *African psychology.* Trenton, NH: African World Press.

Akbar, N. (2004). The evolution of human psychology for African Americans. In R. Jones (Ed.), *Black psychology.* Hampton, VA: Cobb & Henry.

Alan Guttmacher Institute. (2004). *U.S. teenage pregnancy statistics: Overall trends, trends by race and ethnicity and state-by-state information.* Retrieved December 5, 2004, from http://www.guttmacher.org/pubs/covers/state_pregnancy_trends.html

Alarcon, G. S., Roseman, J., Bartolucci, A. A., Friedman, A. W., Moulds, J. M., Goel, N., et al. (1998). Systemic lupus erythematosus in three ethnic groups: II. Features predictive of disease activity early in its course. *Arthritis-Rheumatology, 41*(7), 1173–1180.

Alba, R. D., Logan, J., & Stults, B. J. (2000). How segregated are middle-class African Americans. *Social Problems, 47*, 543–558.

Albury, A. (1998). *Social orientation, learning condition and learning outcomes among low income black and white grade school children.* Unpublished doctoral dissertation, Howard University, Washington, DC.

Allen, B. A., & Boykin, A. W. (1991). The influence of contextual factors on Afro-American and Euro-American children's performance: Effects of movement opportunity and music. *International Journal of Psychology, 26*, 373–387.

Allen, B. A., & Butler, L. (1996). The effects of music and movement opportunity on the reasoning performance of African American and White school children: A preliminary study. *Journal of Black Psychology, 22*(3), 316–327.

Alliance for Health Reform. (2004). *Closing the Gap 2003: Racial and ethnic disparities in health care.* Retrieved October 15, 2004, from http://www.allhealth.org

Allison, K. W. (1998). Stress and oppressed social category membership. In J. K. Swim & C. Stangor (Eds.), *Prejudice: The target's perspective* (pp. 145–170). San Diego: Academic Press.

Allison, K. W., Crawford, I., Echemendia, R., & Robinson, L. (1994). Human diversity and professional competence: Training in clinical and counseling psychology revisited. *American Psychologist, 49*(9), 792–796.

Ambler, C. (2003). Alcohol and the slave trade in West Africa, 1400–1850. In W. Jankowiak & D. Bjradburd (Eds.), *Drugs, labor, and colonial expansion* (pp. 73–87). Tucson: University of Arizona Press.

American Cancer Society. (2004). Retrieved August 15, 2004, from http://www.cancer.org/docroot/home/index.asp

American Heritage Dictionary of the English Language (4th ed.). (2004). Retrieved June 1, 2004, from http://www.dictionary.com/

American Heritage Stedman's Medical Dictionary. (2002). Boston: Houghton Mifflin.

American Psychiatric Association. (1987). *Diagnostic and statistical manual of mental disorders* (3rd ed., text rev.)

American Psychiatric Association. (2000). *Diagnostic and statistical manual of mental disorders* (4th ed., text rev.). Washington, DC: Author.

American Psychological Association. (2004). *Office of Ethnic Minority Affairs.* Retrieved from http://www.apa.org/pi/oema/

American Psychological Association. (2005). *About the American Psychological Association.* Retrieved from http://www.apa.org/about/

American Psychological Association Research Office. (2000a). *Demographic shifts in psychology.* Retrieved from http://research.apa.org/gen1.html

American Psychological Association Research Office. (2000b). *2000 Graduate study in psychology.* Retrieved from http://research.apa.org/

Amey, C. H., & Albrecht, S. T. (1998). Race and ethnic differences in adolescent drug use: The impact of family structure and the quantity and quality of parental interaction. *Journal of Drug Issues, 28*(2), 283–298.

Anderson, E. (1994). The code of the streets. *Atlantic Monthly, 273*(5), 80–94.

Anderson, J. L., Crawford, C. B., Nadeau, J., & Lindberg, T. (1992). Was the Duchess of Windsor right? A cross-cultural review of the socioecology of ideals of female body shape. *Ethology and Sociobiology, 13,* 197–227.

Anderson, N. B., McNeilly, M., & Myers, H. F. (1993). A biopsychosoical model of race differences in vascular reactivity. In J. J. Blascovich & E. S. Katkin (Eds.), *Cardiovascular reactivity to psychological stress and disease* (pp. 83–108). Washington, DC: American Psychological Association.

Anderson, R. N., & Smith, B. L. (2003). Deaths: Leading causes for 2001. *National Vital Statistics Report, 52*(9), 1–86.

Anderson, R. P., Williamson, G. A., & Lundy, N. C. (1977). *Relationship between performance-based and observer-based measures of hyperactivity.* Paper presented at the meeting of the Southwestern Psychological Association, Fort Worth, TX.

Aneshensel, C. S., & Sucoff, C. A. (1996). The neighborhood context and adolescent mental health. *Journal of Health and Social Behavior, 37,* 293–310.

Ani, M. (1994). *Yurugu: An Afrocentric critique of European cultural thought and behavior.* Trenton, NJ: Africa World Press.

Annie E. Casey Foundation. (2003). *Kids count: African-American children pocket guide: State level measures of child well being from the 2000 census.* Washington, DC: Population Reference Bureau.

Anti-Drug Abuse Act. (1986). National Criminal Justice Reference Service, U.S. Department of Justice.

Archer, D., & McDaniel, P. (1995). Violence and gender: Differences and similarities across societies. In R. B. Ruback & N. A. Weiner (Eds.), *Interpersonal and violent behaviors: Social and cultural aspects* (pp. 63–88). New York: Springer.

Arias, E., Anderson, R. N., Kung, H., Murphy, S. L., & Kochanek, K. D. (2003). Deaths: Final data for 2001. *National Vital Statistics and Reports, 52*(3), 1–115.

Armstrong, T. D. (1999). The impact of spirituality on the coping process in families dealing with pediatric HIV or pediatric nephritic syndrome. *Dissertation Abstracts International: Section B: The Sciences & Engineering, 59*(12-B), Jun 1999, 6482. US: Univ. Microfilms International.

Aronson, E., Wilson, T. D., & Akert, R. M. (2002). *Social psychology* (4th ed.). Upper Saddle River, NJ: Prentice Hall.

Asante, M. K. (1991). *Kemet, Africentricity, and knowledge.* Trenton, NJ: Africa World Press.

Asante, M. K. (2003). *Afrocentricity: The theory of social change.* Chicago: African American Images.

Askenasy, A. R., Dohrenwend, B. P., & Dohrenwend, B. S. (1977). Some effects of social class and ethnic group membership on judgments of the magnitude of stressful life events: A research note. *Journal of Health & Social Behavior, 18*(4), 432–439.

Attaway, N., & Bry, B. H. (2004). Parenting style and black adolescents' academic achievement. *Journal of Black Psychology, 30*(2), 229–247.

Atwell, I., & Azibo, D. A. (1991). Diagnosing personality disorders in Africans using the Azibo Nosology: Two case studies. *Journal of Black Psychology, 17,* 1–22.

Azibo, D. (1983). Some psychological concomitants and consequences of the black personality: Mental health implications. *Journal of Non-White Concerns in Personnel and Guidance, 11,* 59–66.

Azibo, D. A. (1989). African-centered theses on mental health and a nosology of Black/ African personality disorder. *Journal of Black Psychology, 15*(2), 173–214.

Azibo, D. A. (1996). African psychology in historical perspective and related commentary. In D. A. Azibo (Ed.), *African psychology in historical perspective and related commentary.* Trenton, NJ: African World Press.

Baldwin, A. L., Baldwin, C., & Cole, R. E. (1990). Stress-resistant families and stress-resistant children. In J. Rolf, A. S. Masten, D. Cicchetti, K. H. Nuechterlein, & S. Weintraub (Eds.), *Risk and protective factors in the development of psychopathology* (pp. 257–280). New York: Cambridge University Press.

Baldwin, A. L., Baldwin, C. P., Kasser, T., Zax, M., Sameroff, A., & Seifer, R. (1993). Contextual risk and resiliency during late adolescence. *Development and Psychopathology, 5,* 741–761.

Baldwin, J. A. (1981). Notes on an Africentric theory of black personality. *The Western Journal of Black Studies, 5,* 172–179.

Baldwin, J. A. (1984). African self-consciousness and the mental health of African-Americans. *Journal of Black Studies, 15,* 177–194.

Baldwin, J. A. (1986). Black psychology: Issues and synthesis. *Journal of Black Studies, 16*(3), 235–249.

Baldwin, J. A. (1991). African (black) psychology: Issues and synthesis. In R. Jones (Ed.), *Black psychology* (pp. 125–135). Berkeley, CA: Cobb & Henry.

Baldwin, J. A., & Bell, Y. R. (1985). The African self-consciousness scale: An Africentric personality questionnaire. *The Western Journal of Black Studies, 9*(2), 61-68.

Baldwin, J. A., Brown, R., & Hopkins, R. (1991). The black self-hatred paradigm revisited: An Africentric analysis. In R. L. Jones (Ed.), *Black psychology* (3rd ed., pp. 141–165). Berkeley, CA: Cobb & Henry.

Baldwin, J. A., Brown, R., & Rackley, R. (1990). Some socio-behavioral correlates of African self-consciousness in African American college students. *The Journal of Black Psychology, 17*(1), 1–17.

Baldwin, J. A., Duncan, J. A., & Bell, Y. R. (1992). Assessment of African self-consciousness among black students from two college environments. In K. A. Burlew, W. C. Banks, H. P. McAdoo, & D. A. Azibo (Eds.), *African American psychology: Theory, research, and practice.* Newbury Park, CA: Sage.

Baldwin, J. R., Day, L. E., & Hecht, M. L. (2000). The structure(s) of racial attitudes among white college students. *International Journal of Intercultural Relations, 24,* 553–577.

Bandura, A. (1977). Self-efficacy: Toward a unifying theory of behavioral change. *Psychological Review, 84,* 191–215.

Bandura, A., Ross, D., & Ross, D. (1963). Imitation of film-mediated aggressive models. *Journal of Abnormal and Social Psychology, 66*(1), 3–11.

Banks, R. (1997). Race, representation, and the drug policy agenda. In C. Herring (Ed.), *African Americans and the public agenda.* Thousand Oaks, CA: Sage.

Banks, W. C., McQuater, G. V., Anthony, J. R., & Ward, W. E. (1992). Delayed gratification in blacks: A critical review. In A. K. Burlew, W. C. Banks, H. P. McAdoo, & D. A. Azibo (Eds.), *African American psychology: Theory, research, and practice.* Newbury Park, CA: Sage.

Barbarin, O. A., & Soler, R. E. (1993). Behavioral, emotional, and academic adjustment in a national probability sample of African American children: Effects of age, gender, and family structure. *Journal of Black Psychology, 19*(4), 423–446.

Barna Group. (2005). *African Americans.* Retrieved March 27, 2005, from http://www.barna.org/

Barnes, G. M., & Welte, J. W. (1986). Adolescent alcohol abuse: Subgroup differences and relationships to other problem behaviors. *Journal of Adolescent Research, 1,* 79–94.

Baron, R., Tom, D., & Cooper, H. (1985). Social class, race and teacher expectations. In J. B. Dusek (Ed.), *Teacher expectancies* (pp. 251–269). Hillsdale, NJ: Erlbaum.

Baron, R. A., & Richardson, D. R. (1994). *Human aggression* (2nd ed.). New York: Plenum Press.

Barrett, D. H., Wisotzek, I. E., Abel, G. G., Rouleau, J. L., Platt, A. F., Pollard, W. E., et al. (1988). Assessment of psychosocial functioning of patients with sickle cell disease. *Southern Medical Journal, 81,* 745–750.

Bauman, K. J., & Graf, N. L. (2003). *Educational attainment 2000, Census 2000 brief.* Retrieved April 5, 2005, from http://www.census.gov/prod/2003pubs/c2kbr-24.pdf

Baumeister, R. F. (Ed.). (1999). *The self in social psychology.* Philadelphia: Psychology Press.

Baumeister, R. F., & Muraven, M. (1996). Identity as adaptation to social, cultural, and historical context. *Journal of Adolescence, 19*(5), 405–416.

Beadnell, B., Stielstra, S., Baker, S., Morrison, D. M., Knox, K., Gutierrez, L., et al. (2003). Ethnic identity and sexual risk-taking among African-American women enrolled in an HIV/STD prevention intervention. *Psychology, Health & Medicine, 8*(2), 187–198.

Belgrave, F. Z. (1998). *Psychosocial aspects of chronic illness and disability among African Americans.* Westport, CT: Auburn House/Greenwood.

Belgrave, F. Z. (2002). Relational theory and cultural enhancement interventions for African American adolescent girls. *Public Health Reports, 117*(Suppl. 1), 76–81.

Belgrave, F. Z. (2005). *The development and validation of the Africentric worldview scale.* Manuscript under revision.

Belgrave, F. Z., Brome, D. R., & Hampton, C. (2000). The contribution of Africentric values and racial identity to the prediction of drug knowledge, attitudes, and use among African American youth. *Journal of Black Psychology, 26*(4), 386–401.

Belgrave, F. Z., Davis, A., & Vajda, J. (1994). An examination of social support source, type, and satisfaction among African Americans and White Americans with disabilities. *Journal of Social Behavior and Personality, 9*(5), 307–320.

Belgrave, F. Z., Reed, M. C., Plybon, L. E., Butler, D. S., Allison, K. W., & Davis, T. (2004). Sisters of Nia: A cultural program for African American girls. *Journal of Black Psychology, 30,* 329–343.

Belgrave, F. Z., Reed, M. C., Plybon, L. E., & Corneille, M. (2004). The impact of a culturally enhanced drug prevention program on drug and alcohol refusal efficacy among urban African American girls. *Journal of Drug Education, 34*(3), 267–279.

Belgrave, F. Z., Townsend, T. G., Cherry, V. R., & Cunningham, D. M. (1997). The influence of an Africentric worldview and demographic variables on drug knowledge, attitudes, and use among African American youth. *Journal of Community Psychology, 25*(5), 421–433.

Belgrave, F. Z., & Walker, S. (1991). Psychological predictors of adjustment to disability in African Americans. *Journal of Rehabilitation, 57*(1), 37–40.

Bell, J. (1995). Notions of love and romance among the Taita of Kenya. In W. Jankowiak (Ed.), *Romantic passion: A universal experience?* (pp. 152–165). New York: Columbia University Press.

Bell, Y. R. (1994). A culturally sensitive analysis of black learning style. *Journal of Black Psychology, 20*(1), 47–61.

Beman, D. S. (1995). Risk factors leading to adolescent substance abuse. *Adolescence, 30*(117), 201–208.

Bennett, M. D., & Fraser, M. W. (2000). Urban violence among African American males: Integrating family, neighborhood, and peer perspectives. *Journal of Sociology and Social Welfare, 27*(3), 93–116.

Berkowitz, L. (1993). *Aggression: Its causes, consequences, and control.* New York: McGraw-Hill.

Bernal, M. E., & Castro, F. G. (1994). Are clinical psychologists prepared for service and research with ethnic minorities? Report of a decade of progress. *Psychologist, 49*(9), 797–805.

Bernstein, A. B., Hing, E., Moss, A. J., Allen, K. F., Siller, A. B., & Tiggle, R. B. (2003). *Health care in America: Trends in utilization.* Hyattsville, MD: National Center for Health Statistics.

Berry, J. (1990). Psychology of acculturation. In J. Berman (Ed.), *Cross-cultural perspectives: Nebraska symposium on motivation* (pp. 201–234). Lincoln: University of Nebraska Press.

Berry, J. W. (1980). Acculturation as varieties of adaptation. In A. M. Padilla (Ed.), *Acculturation: Theory, model, and some new findings* (pp. 9–25). Boulder, CO: Westview Press.

Berry, J. W., & Kim, U. (1988). Acculturation and mental health. In P. R. Dasen, J. W. Berry, & N. Sarorius (Eds.), *Health and cross-cultural psychology: Toward applications* (pp. 207–236). Newbury Park, CA: Sage.

Berscheid, E. (1985). Interpersonal attraction. In G. Lindzey & E. Aronson (Eds.), *The handbook of social psychology* (3rd ed., Vol. 3, pp. 413–484). New York: McGraw-Hill.

Berscheid, E., Snyder, M., & Omoto, A. M. (1989). The relationship closeness inventory: Assessing the closeness of interpersonal relationships. *Journal of Personality and Social Psychology, 57*(5), 792–807.

Bertelson, A. D., Marks, P. A., & May, G. D. (1982). MMPI and race: A controlled study. *Journal of Consulting and Clinical Psychology, 50*(2), 316–318.

Billingsley, A. (1968). *Black families in white America.* Englewood, NJ: Prentice Hall.

Bird, G., & Melville, K. (1994). *Families and intimate relationships.* New York: McGraw-Hill.

Blumstein, P., & Schwartz, P. (1983). *American couples: Money, work, sex.* New York: William Morrow.

Blunden, D., Spring, C., & Greenberg, L. M. (1974). Validation of the Classroom Behavior Inventory. *Journal of Consulting and Clinical Psychology, 42*(1), 84–88.

Bonczar, T. P., & Snell, T. L. (2004). *Capital punishment, 2002* (BJS Report No. NCJ 201848). Washington, DC: U.S. Department of Justice, Bureau of Justice Statistics.

Bond, S., & Cash, T. (1992). Black beauty: Skin color and body image among African-American college women. *Journal of Applied Social Psychology, 22,* 874–888.

Borduin, C. M., Pruitt, J. A., & Henggeler, S. W. (1986). Family interactions in black, lower-class families with delinquent and nondelinquent adolescent boys. *Journal of Genetic Psychology, 147*(3), 333–342.

Botvin, G. J., Dusenberry, L., Baker, E., James-Ortiz, S., & Botvin, E. M. (1992). Smoking prevention among urban minority youth: Assessing the effects on outcome and mediating variables. *Health Psychology, 11,* 290–299.

Botvin, G. J., & Kantor, L. (2000). Preventing alcohol and tobacco use through life skills training. *Alcohol Research & Health, 24*(4), 250–257.

Botvin, G. J., & Scheier, L. M. (1997). Preventing drug abuse and violence. In D. K. Wilson & J. R. Rodriguez (Eds.), *Health-promoting and health-compromising behaviors among minority adolescents: Application and practice in health psychology.* Washington, DC: American Psychological Association.

Bowen-Reid, T. L., & Rhodes, W. A. (2003). Assessment of marijuana use and psychosocial behaviors at two historically black universities. *Journal of Black Psychology, 29,* 429–444.

Bowlby, J. (1982). Attachment and loss: Retrospect and prospect. *American Journal of Orthopsychiatry, 52*(4), 664–678.

Bowles, J., & Kingston, R. S. (1998). The impact of family function on health of African American elderly. *Journal of Comparative Family Studies, 29*(2), 337–347.

Bowman, P. J., & Forman, T. A. (1997). Instrumental and expressive family roles among African American fathers. In R. J. Taylor, J. S. Jackson, & L. M. Chatters (Eds.), *Family life in black America* (pp. 248–261). Thousand Oaks, CA: Sage.

Bowman, P. J., & Howard, C. (1985). Race-related socialization, motivation, and academic achievement: A study of black youths in three-generation families. *Journal of the American Academy of Child Psychiatry, 24*(2), 134–141.

Boyd, R. L. (1998). The storefront Church ministry in African American communities of the urban north during the great migration: The making of an ethnic niche. *The Social Science Journal, 35*(3), 319–332.

Boyd-Franklin, N. (1989). *Black families in therapy: A multisystems approach.* New York: Guilford Press.

Boyd-Franklin, N. (2003). *Black families in therapy: Understanding the African American experience* (2nd ed.). New York: Guilford Press.

Boyd-Franklin, N., & Lockwood, T. W. (1999). Spirituality and religion: Implications for psychotherapy with African American clients and families. In F. Walsh (Ed.), *Spiritual resources in family therapy* (pp. 90–103). New York: Guilford Press.

Boykin, A. W. (1978). Psychological/behavioral verve in academic/task performance: Pre-theoretical considerations. *Journal of Negro Education, 47*(4), 343–354.

Boykin, A. W. (1983). The academic performance of Afro-American children. In J. Spence (Ed.), *Achievement and achievement motives* (pp. 324–371). San Francisco: W. H. Freeman.

Boykin, A. W. (1994). The sociocultural context of schooling for African American children: A proactive deep structural analysis. In E. Hollins (Ed.), *Formulating a knowledge base for teaching culturally diverse learners* (pp. 233–245). Philadelphia: Association for Supervision and Curriculum Development.

Boykin, A. W., & Ellison, C. M. (1995). The multiple ecologies of black youth socialization: An Afrographic analysis. In R. L. Taylor (Ed.), *African American youth: Their social and economic status in the United States* (pp. 93–129). Westport, CT: Praeger.

Boykin, A. W., Jagers, R. J., Ellison, C., & Albury, A. (1997). Communalism: Conceptualization and measurement of an Afrocultural social ethos. *Journal of Black Studies, 27*(3), 409–418.

Boykin, A. W., & Toms, F. D. (1985). Black child socialization: A conceptual framework. In H. McAdoo & J. McAdoo (Eds.), *Black children* (pp. 33–51). Beverly Hills, CA: Sage.

Bradley, C. R. (1998). Child rearing in African American families: A study of the disciplinary practices of African American parents. *Journal of Multicultural Counseling and Development, 26,* 273–281.

Bramlett, M. D., & Mosher, W. D. (2002). Cohabitation, marriage, divorce, and remarriage in the United States. *Vital Health Statistics, 23*(22), 1–93.

Bray, J. H., Adams, G. J., Greg, G. J., & Baer, P. E. (2001). Developmental, family, and ethnic influences on adolescent alcohol usage: A growth curve approach. *Journal of Family Psychology, 15*(2), 301–314.

Brehm, S. S. (1992). *Intimate relationships* (2nd ed.). New York: McGraw-Hill.

Broman, C. (1988). Satisfaction among blacks: The significance of marriage and parenthood. *Journal of Marriage and the Family, 50*(1), 45–51.

Bronfenbrenner, U. (1977). Toward an experimental ecology of human development. *American Psychologist, 32*(7), 513–531.

Bronfenbrenner, U. (1979). *The ecology of human development.* Cambridge, MA: Harvard University Press.

Bronfenbrenner, U. (1986). Ecology of the family as a context for human development: Research perspectives. *Developmental Psychology, 22,* 723–742.

Brook, J. S., Balka, E. B., Brook, D. W., Win, P. T., & Gursen, M. D. (1998). Drug use among African Americans: Ethnic identity as a protective factor. *Psychological Reports, 83*(3, Pt. 2), 1427–1446.

Brook, J. S., Nomora, C., & Cohen, P. (1989). A network of influences on adolescent drug involvement: Neighborhood, school, peer, and family. *Genetic, Social, and General Psychology Monographs, 115*(1), 125–145.

Brook, J. S., Whiteman, M., Balka, E. B., Win, P. T., & Gursen, M. D. (1997). African American and Puerto Rican drug use: A longitudinal study. *Journal of the American Academy of Child & Adolescent Psychiatry, 36,* 1260–1268.

Brookins, C. C. (1994). The relationship between Afrocentric values and racial identity attitudes: Validation of the belief systems analysis scale on African American college students. *Journal of Black Psychology, 20*(2), 143–156.

Brookins, C. C. (1996). Promoting ethnic identity development in African American youth: The role of rites of passage. *The Journal of Black Psychology, 22*(3), 388–417.

Brookins, C. C. (1999). Afrikan and community psychology: Synthesizing liberation and social change. In R. L. Jones (Ed.), *Advances in African American psychology: Theory, paradigms, and research* (pp. 27–50). Hampton, VA: Cobb & Henry.

Brooks-Gunn, J., Duncan, G. J., Klebanov, P. K., & Sealand, N. (1993). Do neighborhoods influence child and adolescent development? *American Journal of Sociology, 99*(2), 353–395.

Brown, C. M., & Segal, R. (1998). Ethnic differences in temporal orientation and its implications for hypertension management. *Journal of Health and Social Behavior, 37*(4), 350–361.

Brown, J. C. (1993, February 1). Which black is beautiful? *Advertising Age, 64,* 19.

Bumpass, L. L., Martin, T. C., & Sweet, J. A. (1991). The impact of family background and early marital factors on marital disruption. *Journal of Family Issues, 12*(1), 22–42.

Bureau of Justice Statistics. (1997). *Corrections statistics.* Retrieved November 19, 2004, from http://www.ojp.usdoj.gov/bjs/

Bureau of Justice Statistics. (2000). *State court sentencing of convicted felons, 2000.* Washington, DC: U.S. Department of Justice.

Bureau of Justice Statistics. (2003). *Prisoners in 2002.* Washington, DC: U.S. Department of Justice.

Burgess, N. J. (1995). Looking back, looking forward: African American families in sociohistorical perspective. In R. B. Ingoldsby & S. Smith (Eds.), *Families in multicultural perspective* (pp. 321–334). New York: Guilford Press.

Burlew, A. K., & Smith, L. R. (1991). Measures of racial identity: An overview and a proposed framework. *Journal of Black Psychology, 17*(2), 53–71.

Burlew, K., Telfair, J., Colangelo, L., & Wright, E. C. (2000). Factors that influence adolescent adaptation to sickle cell disease. *Journal of Pediatric Psychology, 25*(5), 287–299.

Burton, L. M. (1992). Black grandparents rearing children of drug-addicted parents: Stressors, outcomes, and social service needs. *The Geronotologist, 32*(6), 744–751.

Burton, L. M., Allison, K. W., & Obeidallah, D. (1995). Social context and adolescence: Perspectives on development among inner-city African-American teens. In L. J. Crockett & A. C. Crouter (Eds.), *Pathways through adolescence: Individual development in relation to social contexts* (pp. 119–138). Hillsdale, NJ: Erlbaum.

Burton, L. M., & Dilworth-Anderson, P. (1991). The multigenerational family roles of aged black Americans. *Marriage and Family Review, 16,* 311–330.

Burton, L. M., & Jarrett, R. L. (2000). In the mix, yet on the margins: The place of families in urban neighborhood and child development research. *Journal of Marriage and the Family, 62*(4), 1114–1135.

Burton, L. M., Price-Spratlen, T., & Spencer, M. B. (1997). On ways of thinking about measuring neighborhoods: Implications for studying context and developmental outcomes for children. In J. Brooks-Gunn, G. Duncan, & J. L. Aber (Eds.), *Neighborhood poverty: Context and consequences for children* (Vol. 2, pp. 132–144). New York: Russell Sage.

Butcher, J. N., Dahlstrom, W. G., Graham, J. R., Tellegen, A., & Kaemmer, B. (1989). *Manual for the restandardized Minnesota Multiphasic Personality Inventory: MMPI-2.* Minneapolis: University of Minnesota Press.

Butcher, J. N., Nezami, E., & Exner, J. (1998). Psychological assessment of people in diverse cultures. In S. S. Kazarian & D. R. Evans (Eds.), *Cultural clinical psychology: Theory, research, and practice* (pp. 61–105). London: Oxford University Press.

Butler, J. (1992). Of kindred minds: The ties that bind. In M. A. Orlandi, R. Weston, & L. G. Epstein (Eds.), *Cultural competence for evaluators: A guide for alcohol and other drug abuse prevention practitioners working with ethnic/racial communities*. Rockville, MD: U.S. Department of Health and Human Services, Office for Substance Abuse Prevention.

Byrd, W. M., & Clayton, L. A. (2001). Race, medicine, and health care in the United States: A historical survey. *Journal of the National Medical Association, 93*(3), 11S–34S.

Caldwell, C. H., Kohn-Wood, L. P., Schmeelk-Cone, K. H., Chavous, T. M., & Zimmerman, M. A. (2004). Racial discrimination and racial identity as risk or protective factors for violent behaviors in African American young adults. *American Journal of Community Psychology, 33*(1–2), 91–106.

Calhoun-Brown, A. (1998). While marching to Zion: Other worldliness and racial empowerment in the black community. *Journal for the Scientific Study of Religion, 37*(3), 427–439.

Campbell, C., & Schwartz, D. F. (1996). Prevalence and impact of exposure to interpersonal violence among suburban and urban middle school students. *Pediatrics, 98*(3), 396–403.

CancerCare. (2004). Retrieved April 7, 2005, from http://www.cancercare.org/

Carabello, R. S., Giovino, G. A., Pechacek, T. F., Mowery, P. D., Richter, P. A., Strauss, W. J., et al. (1998). Racial and ethnic differences in serum cotinine levels of cigarette smokers. *The Journal of the American Medical Association, 280,* 135–142.

Carey, K. (2004). *A matter of degrees: Improving graduation rates in four-year colleges and universities* (Report by the Education Trust). Retrieved April 4, 2005, from http://www2.edtrust.org/NR/rdonlyres/11B4283F-104E-4511-B0CA-1D3023231157/0/highered.pdf

Carruthers, J. H. (1996). Science and oppression. In D. Azibo (Ed.), *African psychology in historical perspective and related commentary*. Trenton, NJ: Africa World Press.

Carter, J. R., & Neufeld, R. J. W. (1998). Cultural aspects of understanding people with schizophrenic disorders. In S. S. Kazarian & D. R. Evans (Eds.), *Cultural clinical psychology: Theory, research, and practice* (pp. 246–266). London: Oxford University Press.

Carter, R. T., & Helms, J. E. (1987). The relationship of black value-orientations to racial identity attitudes. *Measurement and Evaluation in Counseling and Development, 19*(4), 185–195.

Castro, F. G., & Alarcon, E. H. (2002). Integrating cultural variables into drug abuse prevention and treatment with racial/ethnic minorities. *Journal of Drug Issues, 32*(3), 783–811.

Center for Substance Abuse Prevention. (1992). *Drug attitude scale, COPA project*. Rockville, MD: Office of Scientific Analysis.

Center for Substance Abuse Prevention. (1993). *Prevention strategies based on individual risk factors for alcohol and other drug abuse*. Rockville, MD: Office of Scientific Analysis.

Center for Substance Abuse Prevention. (1996). *A review of alternative activities and alternatives programs in youth-oriented prevention*. Rockville, MD: Office of Scientific Analysis.

Center for Substance Abuse Prevention. (2001). *Mentoring and family strengthening programs*. Rockville, MD: Office of Scientific Analysis.

Centers for Disease Control and Prevention. (1997). Update: Blood lead levels—United States, 1991–1994. *Morbidity and Mortality Weekly Report, 46*(7), 141–146.

Centers for Disease Control and Prevention. (1998). Suicide among black youths—United States, 1980–1995. *Morbidity and Mortality Weekly Report, 47*(10), 193–206.

Centers for Disease Control and Prevention. (2002a). Cases of HIV infection and AIDS in the United States (*HIV/AIDS Surveillance Report 2002*, Vol. 14). Retrieved April 7, 2005, from http://www.cdc.gov/hiv/stats/hasr1402.htm

Centers for Disease Control and Prevention. (2002b). Infant mortality and low birth weight among black and white infants—United States, 1980–2000. *Morbidity and Mortality Weekly Report, 51*(27), 589–592.

Centers for Disease Control and Prevention. (2002c). Racial and ethnic disparities in infant mortality rates—60 Largest U.S. cities, 1995–1998. *Morbidity and Mortality Weekly Report, 51*(15), 329–332.

Chambers, J. W., Kambon, K., Birdsong, B. D., Brown, J., Dixon, P., & Robbins-Brinson, L. (1998). Africentric cultural identity and the stress experience of African American college students. *Journal of Black Psychology, 24*(3), 368–396.

Chase-Lansdale, L. P., & Gordon, R. A. (1996). Economic hardship and the development of five- and six-year-olds: Neighborhood and regional perspectives. *Child Development, 67*(6), 3338–3367.

Chase-Lansdale, P. L., Gordon, R. A., Brooks-Gunn, J., & Klebanov, P. K. (1997). Neighborhood and family influences on the intellectual and behavioral competence of preschool and early school-age children. In J. Brooks-Gunn, G. J. Duncan, & J. L. Aber (Eds.), *Neighborhood poverty: Context and consequences for children* (Vol. 1, pp. 79–118). New York: Russell Sage.

Chaskin, R. J. (1998). *Defining neighborhoods* (Growing Smart Working Paper). Retrieved March 17, 2005, from http://www.planning.org/casey/pdf/chaskin.pdf

Chaskin, R. J., & Richman, H. A. (1992). Concerns about school-linked services: Institution-based versus community-based models. *The Future of Children, 2*(1), 107–117.

Chatters, L. M., Taylor, R. J., & Jayakody, R. (1994). Fictive kinship relations in black extended families. *Journal of Comparative Family Studies, 25*(3), 297–312.

Chatters, L. M., Taylor, R. J., & Lincoln, K. D. (1999). African American religious participation: A multi-sample comparison. *Journal for the Scientific Study of Religion, 38*(1), 132–145.

Chavis, D. M., Hogge, J. H., McMillan, D. W., & Wandersman, A. (1986). Sense of community through Brunswik's lens: A first look. *Journal of Community Psychology, 14*(1), 24–40.

Cheatham, H. E., Slaney, R. B., & Coleman, N. C. (1990). Institutional effects on the psychosocial development of African-American college students. *Journal of Counseling Psychology, 37*(4), 453–458.

Cherry, V. R., Belgrave, F. Z., Jones, W., Kennon, D. K., Gray, F. S., & Phillips, F. (1998). NTU: An Africentric approach to substance abuse prevention among African American youth. *The Journal of Primary Prevention, 18*(3), 319–338.

Chestang, L. W. (1972). *Character development in a hostile environment* (Occasional Paper No. 3). Chicago: University of Chicago, School of Social Service Administration.

Cheung, F. K. (1991). The use of mental health services by ethnic minorities. In H. F. Myers & P. Wohlford (Eds.), *Ethnic minority perspectives on clinical training and services in psychology* (pp. 23–31). Washington, DC: American Psychological Association.

Children's Defense Fund. (2003). *Analysis: Number of black children in extreme poverty hits record high.* Retrieved December 20, 2004, from http://www.childrensdefense.org/pdf/extreme_poverty.pdf

Chipungu, S., Herman, J., Sambrano, S., Nistler, M., Sale, E., & Springer, J. F. (2000). Prevention programming for African American youth: A review of strategies in CSAP's national cross-site evaluation of high risk youth programs. *Journal of Black Psychology, 26*(4), 360–385.

Clance, P. R., & Imes, S. A. (1978). The imposter phenomenon in high achieving women: Dynamics and therapeutic intervention. *Psychotherapy: Theory, Research, & Practice, 15,* 241–247.

Clark, K. B., & Clark, M. K. (1939). The development of consciousness of self and the emergence of identification in Negro preschool children. *Journal of Social Psychology, 10,* 591–599.

Clark, K. B., & Clark, M. P. (1947). Racial identification and preferences in Negro children. In T. M. Newcomb & E. L. Hartley (Eds.), *Readings in social psychology* (pp. 169–178). New York: Holt.

Clark, M. S., & Mills, J. (1979). Interpersonal attraction in exchange and communal relationships. *Journal of Personality and Social Psychology, 37,* 12–24.

Clayton, L. A., & Byrd, W. M. (2001). Race: A major health status and outcome variable 1980–1999. *Journal of the National Medical Association, 93*(3), 35S–54S.

Clotfelter, C. T. (1976). School desegregation, "tipping," and private school enrollment. *Journal of Human Resources, 11*(1), 28–50.

Cochran, S. D., & Mays, V. M. (1993). Applying social psychological models to predicting HIV-related sexual risk behaviors among African Americans. *Journal of Black Psychology, 19*(2), 142–154.

Cohen, R., Parmelee, D. X., Irwin, L., Weisz, J. R., Howard, P., Purcell, P., et al. (1990). Characteristics of children and adolescents in a psychiatric hospital and a corrections facility. *Journal of the American Academy of Child and Adolescent Psychiatry, 29*(6), 909–913.

Coleman, J. S. (1988). Social capital in the creation of human capital. *The American Journal of Sociology, 94*(Suppl.), 95–121.

Coleman, K. (1998). *The effects of communal learning contexts on black and white children's problem solving ability.* Unpublished doctoral dissertation, Howard University, Washington, DC.

Colman, A. M. (1994). *Companion encyclopedia of psychology.* London: Routledge.

Coner-Edwards, A. F., & Edwards, H. E. (1988). The black middle class: Definition and demographics. In A. F. Coner-Edwards & J. Spurlock (Eds.), *Black families in crisis: The middle class* (pp. 1–13). New York: Brunner/Mazel.

Cook, D. (1993). Research in African-American churches: A mental health counseling imperative. *Journal of Mental Health Counseling, 15*(3), 320–333.

Cook, D. A., & Wiley, C. Y. (2000). Psychotherapy with members of African American churches and spiritual traditions. In R. P. Scott & A. E. Bergin (Eds.), *Handbook of psychotherapy and religious diversity* (pp. 369–396). Washington, DC: American Psychological Association.

Cook, J. M., Pearson, J. L., Thompson, R., Black, B. S., & Rabins, P. V. (2002). Suicidality in older African Americans: Findings from the EPOCH study. *American Journal of Geriatric Psychiatry, 10*(4), 437–446.

Coon, D. (1997). *Essentials of psychology.* Pacific Grove, CA: Brooks/Cole.

Copeland, N. L. (2000). Sociocultural perspectives on the stress process: The moderating effects of cultural coping resources. *Dissertation Abstracts International: Section B: The Sciences & Engineering, 61,* 1132. US: Univ. Microfilms International.

Cosby, C. & Poussaint, R. (2004). *A wealth of wisdom: Legendary African American elders speak.* New York: Atria Books.

Council on Independent Black Institutions. (1994). *CIBI's definition of Afrikan centered education: A position statement.* Retrieved March 20, 2005, from http://www.cibi.org/about.htm

Crane, J. (1991). The epidemic theory of ghettos and neighborhood effects on dropping out and teenage childbearing. *American Journal of Sociology, 96*(5), 1126–1159.

Crespo, C. J., Keteyian, S. J., Heath, G. W., & Sempos, C. T. (1996). Leisure-time physical activity among US adults. *Archives of Internal Medicine, 156,* 93–98.

Crocker, J., Luhtanen, R., Blaine, B., & Broadnax, S. (1994). Collective self-esteem and psychological well-being among White, Black, and Asian college students. *Personality and Social Psychology Bulletin, 20*(5), 503–513.

Crocker, J., & Major, B. (1989). Social stigma and self-esteem: The self-protective properties of stigma. *Psychological Review, 96*(4), 608–630.

Cross, W. E. (1978). The Thomas and Cross models of psychological nigrescence: A review. *Journal of Black Psychology, 5*(1), 13–31.

Cross, W. E., Jr. (1991). *Shades of black: Diversity in African-American identity.* Philadelphia: Temple University Press.

Cross, W. E., Parham, T. A., & Helms, J. E. (1998). Nigrescence revisited: Theory and research. In R. Jones (Ed.), *African American identity development* (pp. 3– 71). Hampton, VA: Cobb & Henry.

Cuffe, S. P., Waller, J. L., Cuccaro, M. L., Pumariega, A. J., & Garrison, C. Z. (1995). Race and gender differences in the treatment of psychiatric disorders in young adolescents. *Journal of the American Academy of Child and Adolescent Psychiatry, 34*(11), 1536–1543.

Cunningham, L. J., & Egan, K. J. (1996). *Christian spirituality: Themes from the tradition.* New York: Paulist Press.

Cunningham, M. (1986). Measuring the physical attractiveness: Quasi-experiments on the sociobiology of female facial beauty. *Journal of Personality and Social Psychology, 50,* 925–935.

Cunningham, M., & Meunier, L. N. (2004). The influence of peer experiences on bravado attitudes among African American males. In N. Way & J. Chu (Eds.), *Adolescent boys in context: Exploring diverse cultures of boyhood* (pp. 219–234). New York: New York University Press.

Cunningham, M. R., Barbee, A. P., & Pike, C. L. (1990). What do women want? Facialmetric assessment of multiple motives in the perception of male facial physical attractiveness. *Journal of Personality and Social Psychology, 68,* 261–279.

Cunningham, M. R., Roberts, A. R., Wu, C., Barbee, A. P., & Druen, P. B. (1995). "Their ideas of beauty are, on the whole, the same as ours": Consistency and variability in the cross-cultural perception of female physical attractiveness. *Journal of Personality and Social Psychology, 68,* 261–279.

Cunningham, M. R., Swanson, D. P., Spencer, M. B., & Dupree, D. (2003). The association of physical maturation with family hassles among African

American adolescent males. *Cultural Diversity and Ethnic Minority Psychology, 9*(3), 276–288.

Cunningham, R. T. (1997). *The effects of contextual differentiation and content imagery on the cognitive performance of African American and Euro-American low-income children: Movement/music explorations.* Unpublished doctoral dissertation, Howard University, Washington, DC.

Cunningham, R. T., & Boykin, A. W. (2004). Enhancing cognitive performance in African American children: Infusing Afro-cultural perspective and research. In R. Jones (Ed.), *Black psychology* (4th ed., pp. 487–507). Berkeley, CA: Cobb & Henry.

Damon, W., & Hart, D. (1982). The development of self-understanding from infancy through adolescence. *Child Development, 53,* 841–864.

Dana, R. H. (1998). Problems with managed mental health care for multicultural populations. *Psychological Reports, 83*(1), 283–294.

Dana, R. H., & Whatley, P. R. (1991). When does a difference make a difference? MMPI scores and African-Americans. *Journal of Clinical Psychology, 47*(3), 400–406.

D'Andrea, M., Daniels, J., & Heck, R. (1991). Evaluating the impact of multicultural counseling training. *Journal of Counseling & Development, 70*(1), 143–150.

Darling-Hammond, L. (1998). Unequal opportunity: Race and education. *Brookings Review, 16*(2), 28–33.

Dawson, J. M., & Langan, P. A. (1994). *Murder in families* (BJS Report No. NCJ 143498). Washington, DC: U.S. Department of Justice, Bureau of Justice Statistics.

Dean, K. E., & Malamuth, N. M. (1997). Characteristics of men who aggress sexually and of men who imagine aggressing: Risk and moderating variables. *Journal of Personality and Social Psychology, 72*(2), 449–455.

Deater-Deckard, K., Bates, J. E., Dodge, K. A., & Pettit, G. S. (1996). Physical discipline among African American and European American mothers: Links to children's externalizing behaviors. *Developmental Psychology, 32*(6), 1065–1072.

DeCarlo, A., & Hockman, E. (2003). RAP therapy: A group work intervention method for urban adolescents. *Social Work With Groups, 26*(3), 45–59.

Dei, K. A. (2002). *Ties that bind: Youth and drugs in a black community.* Prospect Heights, IL: Waveland Press.

Desforges, J., Milner, P., Wethers, D. L., & Whitten, C. F. (1978). *Sickle cell disease.* Los Angeles: National Association for Sickle Cell Disease.

Deutsch, M. (1985). *Distributive justice: A social psychological perspective.* New Haven, CT: Yale University Press.

Diabetes Prevention Program Research Group. (2002). The Diabetes Prevention Program (DPP): Description of lifestyle intervention. *Diabetes Care, 25*(12), 2165–2171.

Dillworth-Anderson, P., & Williams, S. W. (2004). Recruitment and retention strategies for longitudinal African American caregiving research: The family caregiving project. *Journal of Aging and Health, 16*(Suppl. 5), 137S–156S.

Ditton, P. M., & Wilson, D. J. (1999). *Truth in sentencing in state prisons* (BJS Report No. NCJ 170032). U.S. Department of Justice, Bureau of Justice Statistics.

Dixon, P., & Azibo, D. A. (1998). African self-consciousness, misorientation behavior, and a self-destructive disorder: African American male crack-cocaine users. *Journal of Black Psychology, 24*(2), 226–247.

Dolcini, M. M., Harper, G. W., Watson, S., Han, L., Ellen, J., & Catania, J. (2004). *The structure and quality of adolescent friendships in an urban African American neighborhood.* San Francisco: University of California, San Francisco, AIDS Research Institute.

Dornbusch, S. M., Ritter, P. L., & Steinberg, L. (1991). Community influences on the relation of family statuses to adolescent school performance: Differences between African Americans and non-Hispanic Whites. *American Journal of Education, 99*(4), 543–567.

Doss, R. C., & Gross, A. M. (1992). The effects of Black English on stereotyping in intraracial perceptions. *The Journal of Black Psychology, 18*(2), 47–58.

Dreger, R. M., & Miller, K. S. (1960). Comparative psychological studies of Negroes and Whites in the United States. *Psychological Bulletin, 57*, 361–402.

Dresseler, W., Bindon, J. R., & Neggers, Y. H. (1998). John Henryism, gender, and arterial blood pressure in an African American community. *Psychosomatic Medicine, 60*(5), 620–624.

DuBois, D., & Hirsch, B. (1990). School and neighborhood friendship patterns of Blacks and Whites in early adolescence. *Child Development, 61*(2), 524–536.

Du Bois, W. E. B. (1899). *The Philadelphia Negro.* Philadelphia: University of Pennsylvania.

Du Bois, W. E. B. (1903). The souls of black folks. Chicago: A.C. McClug.

Du Bois, W. E. B. (1908). *The Negro American family.* Atlanta, GA: Atlanta University Press.

Duke, S. S., Gordan-Sosby, K., Reynolds, K. D., & Gram, I. T. (1994). A study of breast cancer detection practices and beliefs in black women attending public health clinics. *Health Education Research, 9*(3), 331–342.

Duncan, G. J. (1994). Families and neighbors as sources of disadvantage in the schooling decisions of white and black adolescents. *American Journal of Education, 103*(1), 20–53.

Duncan, G. J., Brooks-Gunn, J. P., & Klebanov, P. K. (1994). Economic deprivation and early-childhood development. *Child Development, 65*, 296–318.

Dunn, A. B., & Dawes, S. J. (1999). Spirituality-focused genograms: Keys to uncovering spiritual resources in African American families. *Journal of Multicultural Counseling & Development, 27*(4), 240–254.

Durkheim, É. (1951). *Suicide: A study in sociology.* Translated from the French by John A. Spaulding and George Simpson. Edited by George Simpson. New York: Free Press, 1951. (Original work published 1897)

Eato, L. E., & Learner, M. M. (1981). Relations of physical and social environment perceptions to adolescent self esteem. *Journal of Genetic Psychology, 139*, 143–150.

Edwards, K. L. (1999). African American definitions of self and psychological health. In C. C. Yeakey & R. D. Henderson (Eds.), *Surmounting all odds: Education, opportunity, and society in the new millennium* (Vol. 1). Greenwich, CT: Information Age.

Ellison, C. G. (1991). Religious involvement and subjective well-being. *Journal of Health and Social Behavior, 32*, 80–99.

Emerson, M. O., Smith, C., & Sikkink, D. (1999). Equal in Christ, but not in the world: White conservative Protestants and explanations of black-white inequality. *GALE Group, 46*(3), 398–417.

Ensminger, M. E., Lamkin, R. P., & Jacobson, N. (1996). School leaving: A longi-
    tudinal perspective including neighborhood effects. *Child Development,
    67*(5), 2400–2416.

Ensminger, M. E., & Slusarcick, A. L. (1992). Paths to high school graduation or
    dropout: A longitudinal study of a first-grade cohort. *Sociology of Education,
    65*(2), 95–113.

Epstein, J. N., March, J. S., Conners, C. K., & Jackson, D. L. (1998). Racial differ-
    ences on the Conners Teacher Rating Scale. *Journal of Abnormal Child
    Psychology, 26*(2), 109–119.

Erikson, E. H. (1963). *Childhood and society* (2nd ed.). New York: Norton.

Erikson, E. H. (1968). *Identity: Youth and crisis.* New York: Norton.

Ernst, F. A., Jackson, I., Robertson, R. M., Nevels, H., & Watts, E. (1997). Skin tone,
    hostility, and blood pressure in young normotensive African Americans.
    Ethnicity and Disease, 7, 34–40.

Evans, B., & Lee, B. K. (1998). Culture and childhood disorders. In S. S. Kazarian
    & D. R. Evans (Eds.), *Cultural clinical psychology: Theory, research and prac-
    tice.* New York: Oxford University Press.

Evans, J. P., & Taylor, J. (1995). Understanding violence in contemporary and
    earlier gangs: An exploratory application of the theory of reasoned action.
    Journal of Black Psychology, 21(1), 71–81.

Eveleth, P. B., & Tanner, J. M. (1976). *Worldwide variation in human growth.*
    New York: Cambridge University Press.

Ewing, K. M., Richardson, T. Q., James-Myers, L. M., & Russell, R. K. (1996).
    The relationship between racial identity attitudes, worldview, and African
    American graduate students' experience of the imposter phenomenon.
    Journal of Black Psychology, 22(1), 53–65.

Fairchild, H. H. (1994). Whither liberation? A critique of a critique. *Journal of
    Black Psychology, 20*(3), 367–371.

Fanon, F. (1963). *The wretched of the earth* (C. Farrington, Trans.). New York:
    Grove Press.

Fanon, F. (1967). *Black skin, white masks.* New York: Grove Press.

Farrell, A. D., Meyers, A., & White, K. (2001). Evaluation of responding in peaceful
    and positive ways (RIPP): A school-based prevention program for reducing
    violence among urban adolescents. *Journal of Clinical Child Psychology, 30*(4),
    451–463.

Farrell, A. D., & White, K. S. (1998). Peer influences and drug use among urban
    adolescents: Family structure and parent-adolescent relationship as protec-
    tive factors. *Journal of Consulting and Clinical Psychology, 66*(2), 248–258.

Feigelman, S., Stanton, B., & Ricardo, I. (1993). Perceptions of drug selling and
    drug use among urban youth. *Journal of Early Adolescence, 13*(3), 267–284.

Feingold, A. (1990). Gender differences in effects of physical attractiveness on
    romantic attraction: A comparison across five research paradigms. *Journal
    of Personality and Social Psychology, 59,* 981–993.

Ferguson, G. O. (1916). *The psychology of the Negro: An experimental study.*
    New York: Science Press.

Fernander, A. F., Duran, R. E., Saab, P. G., & Schneiderman, N. (2004). John Henry
    active coping, education, and blood pressure among urban blacks. *Journal
    of the National Medical Association, 96*(2), 246–255.

Festinger, L., Schachter, S., & Back, L. (1950). *Social pressures in informal groups: A study of a housing community.* New York: Harper.

Fetzer Institute (2003). Multidimensional Measurement of Religiousness/ Spirituality for Use in Health Research. A report of the Fetzer Institute, National Institute on Aging Working Group. Kalamazoo, MT: Fetzer Institute.

Fiebert, M. S., Karamol, H., & Kasdan, M. (2000). Interracial dating: Attitudes and experience among American college students in California. *Psychological Reports, 87*(3, Pt. 2), 1059–1064.

Fields, J. (2003). *Children's living arrangements and characteristics: March 2002.* U.S. Bureau of the Census, Current Population Reports, P20-547. Washington, DC: U.S. Government Printing Office.

Fierros, E. G., & Conroy, J. W. (2002). Double jeopardy: An exploration of restrictiveness and race in special education. In D. J. Losen & G. Orfield (Eds.), *Racial inequity in special education.* Cambridge, MA: Harvard University Civil Rights Project.

Fischer, C. S. (2002). Ever-more rooted Americans. *City & Community, 1*(2), 177–198.

Fischera, S. D., & Frank, D. I. (1994). The health belief model as a predictor of mammography screening. *Health Values: The Journal of Health Behavior, Education, & Promotion, 18,* 3–9.

Fishbein, M., & Ajzen, I. (1975). *Belief, attitude, intention, and behavior: An introduction to theory and research.* Reading, MA: Addison-Wesley.

Fishel, L. H., & Quarles, B. (1970). *The black American: A documentary history.* Glenview, IL: Scott, Foresman.

Fisher, W. A., Fisher, J. D., & Rye, B. J. (1995). Understanding and promoting AIDS-preventive behavior: Insights from the theory of reasoned action. *Health Psychology, 14*(3), 255–264.

Fiske, S. T., & Taylor, S. E. (1991). *Social cognition.* New York: McGraw-Hill.

Flack, J. M., Amaro, H., Jenkins, W., Kunitz, S., Levy, J., Mixon, M., et al. (1995). Panel I: Epidemiology of minority health. *Health Psychology, 14*(7), 592–600.

Flaherty, M. J., Facteau, L., & Carver, P. (1999). The extended family. In R. Staples (Ed.), *The black family: Essays and studies.* Belmont, CA: Wadsworth.

Flaskerud, J. H. (1986). The effects of culture-compatible intervention on the utilization of mental health services by minority clients. *Community Mental Health Journal, 22*(2), 127–141.

Flemming, J. (1984). *Blacks in college.* San Francisco: Jossey-Bass.

Floyd, K. (1995). Gender and closeness among friends and siblings. *The Journal of Psychology, 129*(2), 193.

Foley, L. A., Evancic, C., Karnik, K., King, J., & Parks, A. (1995). Date rape: Effects of race of assailant and victim and gender of subjects on perceptions. *Journal of Black Psychology, 21*(1), 6–19.

Foner, E. (1988). *Reconstruction: America's unfinished revolution, 1863–1877.* New York: Harper & Row.

Ford, B. S., McDonald, T. E, Owens, A. S., & Robinson, T. N. (2002). Primary care interventions to reduce television viewing in African-American children. *American Journal of Preventive Medicine, 22*(2), 106–109.

Ford, D. Y. (1996). *Reversing underachievement among gifted black students: Promising practices and programs.* New York: Teachers College Press.

Ford, D. Y., Harris, J. J., III, Tyson, C. A., & Frazier Trotman, M. (2002). Beyond deficit thinking: Providing access for gifted African American students. *Roeper Review, 24*(2), 52–58.

Fordham, S., & Ogbu, J. U. (1986). Black students' school success: Coping with the "burden of acting white." *Urban Review, 18*(3), 176–206.

Forney, M. A., Forney, P. D., & Ripley, W. K. (1991). Alcohol use among black adolescents: Parental and peer influences. *Journal of Alcohol and Drug Education, 36*, 36–46.

Franklin, A. J. (1999). Invisibility syndrome and racial identity development in psychotherapy and counseling African American men. *Counseling Psychologist, 27*(6), 761–793.

Franklin, C. W., II. (1992). "Hey, home—yo, bro": Friendship among black men. In P. M. Nardi (Ed.), *Men's friendships: Research on men and masculinities* (Vol. 2, pp. 201–214). Newbury Park, CA: Sage.

Frazier, E. F. (1939). *The Negro family in the United States.* Chicago: University of Chicago Press.

Freid, V. M., Prager, K., MacKay, A. P., & Xia, H. (2003). *Health, United States, 2003.* Hyattsville, MD: National Center for Health Statistics.

Freire, P. (1989). *Pedagogy of the oppressed.* New York: Continuum. (Original work published 1970)

Frey, W. H., & Myers, D. (2002, July). Neighborhood segregation in single-race and multirace America: A census 2000 study of cities and metropolitan areas (Fannie Mae Foundation Working Paper). Washington, DC: Fannie Mae Foundation.

Frieman, M., Cunningham, P., & Cornelius, L. (1994). Use and expenditures for the treatment of mental health problems (Publication No. 94-0085). Rockville, MD: Agency for Health Care Policy and Research.

Gadsden, V. L. (1999). Black families in intergenerational and cultural perspectives. In M. E. Lamb (Eds.), *Parenting and child development in "nontraditional" families* (pp. 221–246). Mahwah, NJ: Erlbaum.

Gall, S., Beins, B., & Feldman, A. J. (1996). *The Gale encyclopedia of psychology.* Detroit, MI: Gale Research.

Garb, H. N. (1997). Race bias, social class bias, and gender bias in clinical judgment. *Clinical Psychology: Science & Practice, 4*(2), 99–120.

Gelles, R. J., & Straus, M. A. (1988). *Intimate violence.* New York: Simon & Schuster.

Geronimus, A. T. (1991). Teenage childbearing and social and reproductive disadvantage: The evolution of complex questions and the demise of simple answers. *Family Relations, 40*, 463–471.

Geronimus, A. T. (1996). Black/white differences in the relationship of maternal age to birth weight: A population-based test of the weathering hypothesis. *Social Science and Medicine, 42*, 589–597.

Gibbs, J. T. (Ed.). (1988). *Young, black and male in America: An endangered species.* Dover, MA: Auburn House.

Giles, M. W. (1978). White enrollment stability and school desegregation: A two level analysis. *American Sociological Review, 43*, 848–865.

Gingerich, K. J., Turnock, P., Litfin, J. K., & Rosen, L. A. (1998). Diversity and attention deficit hyperactivity disorder. *Journal of Clinical Psychology, 54*(4), 415–426.

Glanz, K., Resch, N., Lerman, C., & Rimer, B. K. (1996). Black-white differences in factors influencing mammography use among employed female health maintenance organization members. *Ethnicity and Health, 1*(3), 207–220.

Gluck, M. E., & Geliebter, A. (2002). Racial and ethnic differences in body image and eating behaviors. *Eating Behaviors, 3*(2), 143–151.

Good, T. L., & Brophy, J. E. (1987). *Looking in classrooms* (4th ed.). New York: Harper & Row.

Goode, W. J. (1982). *The family.* Englewood Cliffs, NJ: Prentice Hall.

Gooden, W. E. (1989). Development of black men in early adulthood. In R. L. Jones (Ed.), *Black adult development and aging.* Berkeley, CA: Cobb & Henry.

Goodstein, R., & Ponterotto, J. G. (1997). Racial and ethnic identity: Their relationship and their contribution to self-esteem. *Journal of Black Psychology, 23,* 75–292.

Gordon, R. (2003). Inside the Windhoek lager: Liquor and lust in Namibia. In W. Jankowiak & D. Bjradburd (Eds.), *Drugs, labor, and colonial expansion* (pp. 117–134). Tucson: The University of Arizona Press.

Gorman-Smith, D., & Tolan, P. (1998). The role of exposure to community violence and developmental problems among inner-city youth. *Development and Psychopathology, 10*(1), 101–116.

Gottlieb, N. H., & Green, L. W. (1987). Ethnicity and lifestyle risk. *American Journal of Health Promotion, 2*(1), 37–45.

Gottman, J. M., Levenson, R. W., Swanson, C., Swanson, K., Tyson, R., & Yoshimoto, D. (2003). Observing gay, lesbian and heterosexual couples' relationships: Mathematical modeling on conflict interaction. *Journal of Homosexuality, 45*(1), 65–89.

Goyette, C. H., Conners, C. K., & Ulrich, R. F. (1978). Normative data on revised Conners Parent and Teacher Rating Scales. *Journal of Abnormal Child Psychology, 6*(2), 221–236.

Grambs, J. D. (1965). The self-concept: Basis for reeducation of Negro youth. In W. C. Kvaraceus, J. S. Gibson, F. K. Patterson, B. Seasholes, & J. D. Brambs (Eds.), *Negro self-concept: Implications for school and citizenship* (pp. 11–51). New York: McGraw-Hill.

Gray-Ray, P., & Ray, M. C. (1990). Juvenile delinquency in the black community. *Youth & Society, 22,* 67–84.

Greene, B. (2000). Homophobia. In A. E. Kazdin (Ed.), *Encyclopedia of psychology* (Vol. 4, pp. 146–149). Washington, DC: American Psychological Assocation.

Greene, B., & Boyd-Franklin, N. (1996). African American lesbian couples: Ethnocultural considerations in psychotherapy. In M. Hill & E. D. Rothblum (Eds.), *Couples therapy: Feminist perspectives* (pp. 49–60). New York: Harrington Park Press/Haworth Press.

Greene, R. L. (1987). Ethnicity and MMPI performance: A review. *Journal of Consulting and Clinical Psychology, 55*(4), 497–513.

Greenfield, L. A. (1997). *Sex offenses and offenders: An analysis of data on rape and sexual assault* (Report No. NCJ 163392). Washington, DC: U.S. Department of Justice, Bureau of Justice Statistics.

Gregory, S. D., & Phillips, F. B. (1997). "Of mind, body, and spirit": therapeutic foster care—an innovative approach to healing from an NTU perspective. *Child Welfare, 76*(1), 127–142.

Greig, R. (2003). Ethnic identity development: Implications for mental health in African-American and Hispanic adolescents. *Issues in Mental Health Nursing, 24*(3), 317–332.

Grier, W. H., & Cobbs, P. M. (1968). *Black rage.* New York: Basic Books.

Grills, C. T. (2004). African psychology. In R. L. Jones (Ed.), *Black psychology* (4th ed.). Hampton, VA: Cobb & Henry.

Grills, C., & Longshore, D. (1996). Africentrism: Psychometric analyses of a self-report measure. *Journal of Black Psychology, 22,* 86–106.

Grover, P. L. (1998). *Preventing substance abuse among children and adolescents: Family-centered approaches* (DHHS Publication No. 3223). Washington, DC: Substance Abuse and Mental Health Services Administration, Center for Substance Abuse Prevention.

Gurin, P., Dey, E. L., Hurtado, S., & Gurin, G. (2002). Diversity and higher education: Theory and impact on educational outcomes. *Harvard Educational Review, 72*(3), 330–366.

Guthrie, R. V. (1998). *Even the rat was white: A historical view of psychology* (2nd ed.). Needham Heights, MA: Allyn & Bacon. (Original work published 1976)

Gutman, H. G. (1976). *The black family in slavery and freedom, 1750–1925.* New York: Pantheon.

Guttentag, M. (1972). Negro-white differences in children's movement. *Perceptual and Motor Skills, 35,* 435–436.

Gyekye, K. (1996). *African cultural values.* Accra, Ghana: Sankofa.

Hahn, E. J., & Rado, M. (1996). African American Head Start parent involvement in drug prevention. *American Journal of Health Behavior, 20,* 41–51.

Hale-Benson, J. (1986). *Black children: Their roots, culture, and learning styles* (2nd ed.). Baltimore: Johns Hopkins University Press.

Hale-Benson, J. (1990). Visions for children: Educating black children in the context of their culture. In K. Lomotey (Ed.), *Going to school: The African-American experience* (pp. 209–222). Albany: State University of New York Press.

Hall, G. C. N., Bansal, A., & Lopez, I. R. (1999). Ethnicity and psychopathology: A meta-analytic review of 31 years of comparative MMPI/MMPI-2 research. *Psychological Assessment, 11*(2), 186–197.

Hallinan, M. T., & Teixiera, R. A. (1987). Opportunities and constraints: Black-white differences in the formation of interracial friendships. *Child Development, 58*(5), 1358–1371.

Halpern-Felsher, B. L., Connell, J. P., Spencer, M. B., Aber, J. L., Duncan, G. P., Clifford, E., et al. (1997). Neighborhood and family factors predicting educational risk and attainment in African American and white children and adolescents. In J. Brooks-Gunn, G. Duncan, & J. L. Aber (Eds.), *Neighborhood Poverty: Context and consequences for children* (Vol. 1, pp. 146–173). New York: Russell Sage.

Hamilton, B. E., Martin, J. A., & Sutton, P. D. (2003). Births: Preliminary data for 2003. *National Vital Statistics Reports, 53*(9), 1–17.

Hamlet, J. D. (1998). *Afrocentric visions: Studies in culture and communication.* Thousand Oaks, CA: Sage.

Haney, W., Madaus, G., Abrams, L., Wheelock, A., Miao, J., & Gruia, I. (2004). *The education pipeline in the United States, 1970–2000.* Chestnut Hill, MA: Boston College, Center for the Study of Testing, Evaluation, and Educational Policy.

Hanson, M. J. (1997). The theory of planned behavior applied to cigarette smoking in African-American, Puerto Rican, and non-Hispanic White teenage females. *Nursing Research, 46*(3), 155–162.

Harrell, J. S., & Gore, S. V. (1998). Cardiovascular risk factors and socioeconomic status in African American and Caucasian women. *Research in Nursing & Health, 21*, 285–295.

Harris, M. I., Flegal, K. M., Cowie, C. C., Eberhardt, M. S., Goldstein, D. E., Little, R. R., et al. (1998). Prevalence of diabetes, impaired fasting glucose, and impaired glucose tolerance in U.S. adults: The Third National Health and Nutrition Examination Survey, 1988–1994. *Diabetes Care, 21*(4), 518–524.

Harrison, P. M., & Beck, A. J. (2003). *Prisoners in 2002* (BJS Report No. NCJ 200248). Washington, DC: U.S. Department of Justice, Bureau of Justice Statistics.

Harry, J. (1993). Being out: A general model. *Journal of Homosexuality, 26*(1), 25–39.

Harvey, A. R., & Hill, R. B. (2004). Africentric youth and family rites of passage program: Promoting resilience among at-risk African American youth. *Social Work, 49*(1), 65–74.

Harvey, J. C., & Katz, C. (1985). *If I'm so successful, why do I feel like a fake.* New York: Pocket Books.

Hasan, S. P., Hashmi, S., Alhassen, M., Lawson, W., & Castro, O. (2003). Depression in sickle cell disease. *Journal of the National Medical Association, 95*(7), 533–537.

Hatfield, E., & Walster, G. W. (1978). *A new look at love.* Reading, MA: Addison-Wesley.

Hathaway, S. R., & McKinley, J. C. (1940). A multiphasic personality schedule (Minnesota): I. Construction of the schedule. *Journal of Psychology, 10*, 249–254.

Hawkins, D. J., Catalano, R. F., & Miller, J. Y. (1992). Risk and protective factors for alcohol and other drug problems in adolescence and early adulthood: Implications for substance abuse prevention. *Psychological Bulletin, 112*, 64–105.

Haynes, N. (1995). How skewed is *The Bell Curve? Journal of Black Psychology, 21*(3), 275–292.

Hebl, M. R., & Heatherton, T. F. (1998). The stigma of obesity in women: The difference is black and white. *Personality and Social Psychology Bulletin, 24*(4), 417–426.

Helms, J. E. (1990). *Black and white racial identity: Theory, research and practice.* New York: Greenwood Press.

Henderson-King, D. H., & Veroff, J. (1994). Sexual satisfaction and marital well-being in the first years of marriage. *Journal of Social and Personal Relationships, 11*(4), 509–534.

Herrnstein, R. J., & Murray, C. (1994). *The bell curve: Intelligence and class structure in American life.* New York: Free Press.

Hill, H. M., & Madhere, S. (1996). Exposure to community violence and African American children: A multidimensional model of risks and resources. *Journal of Community Psychology, 24*(1), 26–43.

Hill, P. D., & Hood, R. W. (1999). *Measures of religiosity.* Birmingham, AL: Religious Education Press.

Hill, R. B. (1971). *The strengths of black families.* New York: Emerson Hall.

Hill, R. B. (1998). Understanding black family functioning: A holistic perspective. *Journal of Comparative Family Studies, 29*(1), 15–25.

Hilliard, A. G. (1983). IQ and the courts: Larry P. vs Wilson Riles and PASE vs Hannon. *Journal of Black Psychology, 10*(1), 1–18.

Hilliard, A. G. (1992). Behavioral style, culture, and teaching and learning. *Journal of Negro Education, 61*(3), 370–377.

Hofferth, S. L. (2003). Race ethnic differences in father involvement in two-parent families: Culture, context, or economy? *Journal of Family Issues, 24*(2), 185–216.

Hoffman, K., & Llagas, C. (2003). *Status and trends in the education of blacks* (NCES 2003-034). Washington, DC: U.S. Government Printing Office.

Hogan, D. P., & Lichter, D. T. (1995). Children and youth: Living arrangements and welfare. In R. Farley (Ed.), *State of the union: America in the 1990s: Vol. 2. Social trends* (pp. 93–139). New York: Russell Sage.

Hokanson, J. E., & Calden, G. (1960). Negro-white differences on the MMPI. *Journal of Clinical Psychology, 16*, 32–33.

Holbrook, C. T., & Phillips, G. (1994). Natural history of sickle cell disease and the effects on biopsychosocial development. *Journal of Health & Social Policy, 5*(3/4), 7–18.

Hollie, S. (2001). Acknowledging the language of African American students: Instructional strategies. *English Journal, 90*, 54–59.

hooks, b. (1993). *Sisters of the yam.* Boston: South End Press.

hooks, b. (1999). *Happy to be nappy.* New York: Hyperion.

Hopp, J. W., & Herring, P. (1999). Promoting health among black American populations. In R. M. Huff & M. V. Kline (Eds.), *Promoting health in multiracial populations: A handbook for practitioners* (pp. 201–221). Thousand Oaks, CA: Sage.

Horton, J. O., & Horton, L. E. (1997). *In hope of liberty: Culture, community and protest among northern free blacks, 1700–1860.* New York: Oxford University Press.

Huang, C. J., & Gunn, T. (2001). An examination of domestic violence in an African American community in North Carolina: Causes and consequences. *Journal of Black Studies, 31*(6), 790–811.

Hudson, C. G. (1988). The social class and mental illness correlation: Implications of the research for policy and practice. *Journal of Sociology & Social Welfare, 15*(1), 27–54.

Hughes, D., & Chen, L. (1997). When and what parents tell children about race: An examination of race-related socialization in African American families. *Applied Developmental Science, 1*(4), 200–214.

Hughes, M., & Hertel, B. R. (1990). The significance of color remains: A study of life chances, mate selection, and ethnic consciousness among black Americans. *Social Forces, 68*(4), 1105–1120.

Hummer, R. A., Rogers, R. G., Nam, C. B., & LeClere, F. B. (1999). Race/ethnicity, nativity, and U.S. adult mortality. *Social Science Quarterly, 80*(1), 136–153.

Huston, A. C., McLoyd, V. C., & Coll, C. G. (1994). Introduction: Children and poverty. Issues in contemporary research. *Child Development, 63*, 573–582.

Hyers, L. L. (2001). A secondary survey analysis study of African American ethnic identity orientations in two national samples. *The Journal of Black Psychology, 27*(2), 139–171.

Iceland, J., Weinberg, D. H., & Steinmetz, E. (2002). *Racial and ethnic residential segregation in the United States: 1980–2000* (U.S. Census Bureau, Series CENSR-3). Washington, DC: U.S. Government Printing Office.

Institute of Medicine. (1991). *Disability in America.* Washington, DC: National Academy Press.

Iscoe, I. (1974). Community psychology and the competent community. *American Psychologist, 29,* 607-613.

Jackson, A. P., & Sears, S. J. (1992). Implications of an Africentric worldview in reducing stress for African American women. *Journal of Counseling and Development, 71*(2), 184–191.

Jackson, J. S., Brown, T. N., Williams, D. R., Torres, M., Sellers, S. L., & Brown, K. (1996). Racism and the physical and mental health status of African Americans: A thirteen year national panel study. *Ethnicity and Disease, 6,* 132–147.

Jackson, M. S., Stephens, R. C., & Smith, R. L. (1997). Africentric treatment in residential substance abuse care. *Journal of Substance Abuse Treatment, 14,* 87–92.

Jacob (1990). Healing and prophecy in the black spiritual churches: A need for re-examination. *Medical Anthropology, 12,* 349–370.

Jagers, R. J., Smith, P., Mock, L. W., & Dill, E. (1997). An Afrocultural social ethos: Component orientations and some social implications. *Journal of Black Psychology, 23*(4), 328–343.

James, A. D. (1998). What's love got to do with it? Economic viability and the likelihood of marriage among African American men. *Journal of Comparative Family Studies, 29*(2), 373–386.

James, S. A. (1994). John Henryism and the health of African-Americans. *Culture, Medicine, and Psychiatry, 18*(2), 163–182.

James, W. H., & Johnson, S. L. (1996). *Doing drugs: Patterns of African American addiction.* Austin: University of Texas Press.

Jargowsky, P. (1997). *Poverty and place: Ghettos, barrios, and the American city.* New York: Russell Sage.

Jarrett, R. L. (1999). Successful parenting in high-risk neighrborhoods. *Future of Children, 9*(2), 45–50.

Jemmott, L. S., & Jemmott, J. B. (1991). Applying the theory of reasoned action to AIDS risk behavior: Condom use among black women. *Nursing Research, 40*(4), 224–228.

Jencks, C., & Mayer, S. (1990). The social consequences of growing up in a poor neighborhood. In L. E. Lynn & M. F. H. McGeary (Eds.), *Inner-city poverty in the United States* (pp. 111–186). Washington, DC: National Academy Press.

Jenkins, A. H. (1995). *Psychology and African Americans: A humanistic approach.* Boston: Allyn & Bacon.

Jenkins, E. J., & Bell, C. C. (1994). Violence among inner city high school students and post-traumatic stress disorder. In S. Friedman (Ed.), *Anxiety disorders in African Americans* (pp. 76–88). New York: Springer.

Jenkins, M. J., & Dambrot, F. H. (1987). The attribution of date rape: Observer's attitudes and sexual experiences and the dating situation. *Journal of Applied Social Psychology, 17*(10), 875–895.

Jenkins, R. A. (1995). Religion and HIV: Implications for research and intervention. *Journal of Social Issues, 51*(2), 131–144.

Jensen, A. R. (1969). How much can we boost I.Q. and scholastic achievement? *Harvard Educational Review, 39*(1), 1–123.

Jensen, A. R. (1985). The nature of the black-white differences on various psychometric tests: Spearman's hypothesis. *Behavioral and Brain Sciences, 8,* 193–219.

Jerald, C. D. (2001). *Dispelling the myth revisited.* Washington, DC: The Education Trust. Retrieved January 5, 2005, from http://www2.edtrust.org/NR/rdonlyres/ A56988EB-28DE-4876-934A-EE63E20BACEE/0/DTMreport.pdf

Jessor, R., & Jessor, S. L. (1977). *Problem behavior and psychosocial development: A longitudinal study of youth.* San Diego: Academic Press.

Jeste, D. V., Lindamer, L. A., Evans, J., & Lacro, J. P. (1996). Relationship of ethnicity and gender to schizophrenia and pharmacology of neuroleptics. *Psychopharmacology Bulletin, 32*(2), 243–251.

Johnson, E. H., & Gant, L. M. (1996). The association between anger-hostility and hypertension. In H. W. Neighbors & J. S. Jackson (Eds.), *Mental health in black America* (pp. 95–116). Thousand Oaks, CA: Sage.

Johnson, E. H., & Greene, A. F. (1991). The relationship between suppressed anger and psychosocial distress in African American male adolescents. *Journal of Black Psychology, 18*(1), 47–65.

Johnson, R. A., Hoffman, J. P., Su, S. S., & Gerstein, D. R. (1997). Growth curves of deviant behavior in early adolescence: A multilevel analysis. *Journal of Quantitative Criminology, 13,* 429–467.

Jones, A. C. (1991). Psychological functioning in African Americans: A conceptual guide for use in psychotherapy. In R. L. Jones (Ed.), *Black psychology* (3rd ed., pp. 577–589). Berkeley, CA: Cobb & Henry.

Jones, D. C., Costin, S. E., & Ricard, R. J. (1994). *Ethnic and sex differences in best friendship characteristics among African American, Mexican American, and Eurpoean American adolescents.* Poster session presented at the meeting of the Society for Research on Adolescence, San Diego, CA.

Jones, J. (1997). *Prejudice and racism.* New York: McGraw-Hill.

Jones, J. M. (1994). An exploration of temporality in human behavior. In R. C. Schank & E. Langer (Eds.), *Beliefs, reasoning and decision-making.* Hillsdale, NJ: Lawrence Erlbaum Associates.

Jones, R. (1989). *Black adolescents.* Hampton, VA: Cobb & Henry.

Jones, R. (1991). *Black psychology.* Hampton, VA: Cobb & Henry.

Jones, R. (1996). *Handbook of tests and measurements for black populations.* Hampton, VA: Cobb & Henry.

Jones, R. (1998a). *African American children, youth, and parenting.* Hampton, VA: Cobb & Henry.

Jones, R. (1998b). *African American identity development.* Hampton, VA: Cobb & Henry.

Jones, R. (1998c). *African American mental health.* Hampton, VA: Cobb & Henry.

Jones, R. (1999). *Advances in African American psychology.* Hampton, VA: Cobb & Henry.

Jones, R. (Ed.). (2004). *Black psychology* (4th ed.). Hampton, VA: Cobb & Henry.

Jordan, A. D. (1999). *The relative effects of socio-cultural factors on levels of obesity among African American women.* Unpublished dissertation, Virginia Commonwealth University, Richmond, VA.

Kaestner, R. (1998). *Does drug use cause poverty?* (Working Paper Series No. 6406). National Clearinghouse for Alcohol and Drug Information.

Kain, J. F., & Singleton, K. (1996, May-June). Equality of educational opportunity revisited. *New England Economic Review,* 87–112.

Kalmijn, M. (1991). Status homogamy in the United States. *American Journal of Sociology, 97*(2), 496–523.

Kambon, K. (1998). *African/black psychology in the American context: An African-centered approach.* Tallahassee, FL: Nubian Nation.

Kambon, K. (2003). *Cultural misorientation.* Tallahassee, FL: Nubian Nation.

Kandel, D. B., Kessler, R. C., & Margulies, R. Z. (1978). Antecedents of adolescent initiation into stages of drug use: A developmental analysis. *Journal of Youth and Adolescence, 7,* 13–40.

Kardiner, A., & Ovesey, L. (1951). *The mark of oppression: A psychosocial study of the American Negro.* New York: Norton.

Kardiner, A., & Ovesey, L. (1962). *The mark of oppression: Explorations in the personality of the American Negro.* Cleveland, OH: Meridian Books.

Karenga, M. (1988). *Introduction to black studies.* Los Angeles: University of Sankore Press.

Kaufman, J., & Rosenbaum, J. (1992). The education and employment of low-income black youth in white suburbs. *Educational Evaluation and Policy Analysis, 14*(3), 229–240.

Keith, V. M., & Herring, C. (1991). Skin tone and stratification in the black community. *American Journal of Sociology, 97,* 760–778.

Kessler, R. C., McGonagle, K. A., Zhao, S., Nelson, C. B., Hughes, M., Eshleman, S., et al. (1994). Lifetime and 12-month prevalence of DSM-III-R psychiatric disorders in the United States: Results from the National Comorbidity Study. *Archives of General Psychiatry, 51*(1), 8–19.

Kessler, R. C., & Neighbors, H. W. (1986). A new perspective on the relationships among race, social class, and psychological distress. *Journal of Health & Social Behavior, 27*(2), 107–115.

Kilpatrick, D. G., Acierno, R., Saunders, B., Resnick, H. S., Best, C. L., & Schnurr, P. P. (2000). Risk factors for adolescent substance abuse and dependence: Data from a national sample. *Journal of Consulting and Clinical Psychology, 68*(1), 19–30.

King, A. E. O. (1997). Understanding violence among young African American males: An Afrocentric perspective. *Journal of Black Studies, 28*(1), 79–96.

King, M. L., Jr. (1963). Letter from a Birmingham jail. In J. M. Washington (Ed.), *A testament of hope: The essential writings and speeches of Martin Luther King, Jr.* (pp. 289–302). San Francisco: Harper.

Klag, M. J., Whelton, P. K., Coresh, J., Grim, C. E., & Kuller, L. H. (1991). The association of skin color with blood pressure in U.S. blacks with low socioeconomic status. *Journal of the American Medical Association, 265*(5), 5990–6002.

Klepinger, D. H., Lundberg, S., & Plotnick, R. D. (1995). Adolescent fertility and the educational attainment of young women. *Family Planning Perspectives, 27,* 23–28.

Kliewer, W., Cunningham, J. N., Diehl, R., Parish, K. A., Walker, J. M., Atiyeh, C., et al. (2004). Violence exposure and adjustment in inner-city youth: Child and caregiver emotion regulation skill, caregiver-child relationship quality, and neighborhood cohesion as protective factors. *Journal of Clinical Child and Adolescent Psychology, 33*(3), 477–487.

Knox, D., Zusman, M. E., Buffington, C., & Hemphill, G. (2000). Interracial dating attitudes among college students. *College Student Journal, 34*(1), 69–73.

Koch, L. M., & Gross, A. (1997). Children's perceptions of Black English as a variable in intraracial perception. *Journal of Black Psychology, 23*(3), 215–226.

Kochanek, K. D., & Smith, B. L. (2004). Deaths: Preliminary data for 2002. *National Vital Statistics Report, 52*(13). Retrieved January 20, 2004, from http://www.cdc.gov/nchs/data/nvsr/nvsr52/nvsr52_13.pdf

Kochman, T. (1981). *Black and white styles in conflict.* Chicago: University of Chicago Press.

Kodjo, C. M., & Auinger, P. (2004). Predictors for emotionally distressed adolescents to receive mental health care. *Journal of Adolescent Health, 35*(5), 368–373.

Konner, M. (1991). Universals of behavioral development in relation to brain myelination. In K. R. Gibson & A. C. Petersen (Eds.), *Brain maturation and cognitive development: Comparative and cross-cultural perspectives* (pp. 181–223). Hawthorne, NY: Aldine de Gruyter.

Kozol, J. (1991). *Savage inequalities.* New York: Crown.

Krause, N. (2003). Race, religion, and abstinence from alcohol in late life. *Journal of Aging and Health, 15*(3), 508–533.

Kreider, R. M., & Simmons, T. (2003). *Marital status: 2000.* U.S. Bureau of the Census, Census 2000 Special Tabulation. Washington, DC: Government Printing Office.

Kretzmann, J. P., & McKnight, J. L. (1993). *Building communities from the inside out: A path toward finding and mobilizing a community's assets.* Chicago: Northwestern University, Institute for Policy Research.

Krieger, N. (1990). Racial and gender discrimination: Risk factors for high blood pressure. *Social Science and Medicine, 30*(12), 1273–1281.

Kumanyika, S. K. (1997a). Can hypertension be prevented? Applications of risk modifications in black populations: U.S. populations. *Ethnicity & Disease, 7,* 72–77.

Kumanyika, S. K. (1997b). The impact of obesity on hypertension management in African Americans. *Journal of Health Care for the Poor and Underserved, 8*(3), 352–365.

Kunjufu, J. (1984). *Developing positive self-images and discipline in black children.* Chicago: African American Images.

Kunjufu, J. (1985). *Countering the conspiracy to destroy black boys.* Chicago: African American Images.

Kupersmidt, J. B., Griesler, P. C., DeRosier, M. E., Patterson, C. J., & Davis, P. W. (1995). Childhood aggression and peer relations in the context of family and neighborhoods factors. *Child Development, 66*(2), 360–375.

Kurdek, L. A. (1998). Relationship outcomes and their predictors: Longitudinal evidence from heterosexual married, gay cohabiting, and lesbian cohabiting couples. *Journal of Marriage and the Family, 60*(3), 553–568.

LaFramboise, T., Coleman, H., & Hernandez, A. (1991). *Cross-Cultural Counseling Inventory–Revised (CCCI-R).*

Landrine, H., & Klonoff, E. A. (1992). Culture and health-related schemas: A review and proposal for interdisciplinary integration. *Health Psychology, 11*(4), 267–276.

Landrine, H., & Klonoff, E. A. (1994). The African American acculturation scale: Development, reliability, and validity. *Journal of Black Psychology, 20*(2), 104–127.

Landrine, H., & Klonoff, E. A. (1995). The African American acculturation scale II: Cross-validation and short form. *Journal of Black Psychology, 21*(2), 124–152.

Landrine, H., & Klonoff, E. A. (1996a). *African American acculturation: Deconstructing race and reviving culture.* Thousand Oaks, CA: Sage.

Landrine, H., & Klonoff, E. A. (1996b). The schedule of racist events: A measure of racial discrimination and a study of its negative physical and mental health consequences. *Journal of Black Psychology, 22*(2), 144–168.

Landrine, H., & Klonoff, E. A. (1999). Do blacks believe that HIV/AIDS is a government conspiracy against them? *Preventive Medicine, 28*(5), 451–457.

Langis, J., Sabourin, S., Lussier, Y., & Mathieu, M. (1994). Masculinity, femininity, and marital satisfaction: An examination of theoretical models. *Journal of Personality, 62*(3), 393–414.

Langreth, R. (1998, July 8). Black smokers' health may be affected as more nicotine is inhaled, studies say. *Wall Street Journal,* p. B6.

Lassiter, R. F. (1987). Child rearing in black families: Child-abusing discipline? In R. L. Hampton (Ed.), *Violence in the black family.* Washington, DC: Lexington Books.

LaVeist, T. A. (1993). Segregation, poverty, and empowerment: Health consequences for African-Americans. *Milbank Quarterly, 71*(1), 41–64.

LaVeist, T. A. (2003). Racial segregation and longevity among African Americans: An individual-level analysis. *Health Services Research, 38*(6), 1719–1734.

Lazarus, R. S., & Folkman, S. (1984). *Stress, appraisal, and coping.* New York: Springer.

Lee, B. A., & Campbell, K. E. (1990, August). *Common ground? Urban neighborhoods as survey respondents see them.* Paper presented at the annual meeting of the American Sociological Association, Washington, DC.

Lee, J. (2002). Racial and ethnic achievement gap trends: Reversing the progress toward equity? *Educational Researcher,* 31, 3–12.

Lee, J. W. (1999). Antecedents to the development of mainstream orientation, spirituality, and communalism in African American college students. *Dissertation Abstracts International, 60*(5-B), 2402.

Lefley, H. P., & Bestman, E. W. (1991). Public academic linkages for culturally sensitive community mental health. *Community Mental Health Journal, 27*(6), 473–488.

Lerner, R. M. (1991). Changing organism-context relations as the basic process of development: A developmental contextual perspective. *Developmental Psychology, 27,* 27–32.

Leventhal, T., & Brooks-Gunn, J. (2000). The neighborhoods they live in: Effects of neighborhood residence on child and adolescent outcomes. *Psychological Bulletin, 126*(2), 309–337.

Levin, J. S., & Taylor, R. J. (1997). Age differences in patterns and correlates of the frequency of prayer. *The Gerontologists, 37*(1), 75–88.

Levine, J. A., Pollack, H., & Comfort, M. E. (2001). Academic and behavioral outcomes among the children of young mothers. *Journal of Marriage and the Family, 63*(2), 355–369.

Levinson, D. J., with Darrow, C. N., Klein, E. B., Levinson, M. H., & McKee, B. (1978). *The seasons of a man's life.* New York: Knopf.

Lewandowski, D. A., & Jackson, L. A. (2001). Perceptions of interracial couples: Prejudice at the dyadic level. *Journal of Black Psychology, 27*(3), 288–303.

Lewis, D. K. (1975). The black family: Socialization and sex roles. *Phylon, 36,* 221–238.

Lewis Mumford Center. (2001). *Metropolitan racial and ethnic change—Census 2000.* Retrieved March 17, 2005, from http://mumford1.dyndns.org/cen2000/data.html

Lincoln, C. E., & Mamiya, L. H. (1990). *The black church in the African-American experience.* Durham, NC: Duke University Press.

Lindsey, K. P., & Paul, G. L. (1989). Involuntary commitments to public mental institutions: Issues involving the overrepresentation of blacks and assessment of relevant functioning. *Psychological Bulletin, 106*(2), 171–183.

Lipman, P. (2002). Making the global city, making inequality: The political economy and cultural politics of Chicago school policy. *American Educational Research Journal, 39*(2), 379–419.

Logan, D. D. (2000). *Africentricity among African Americans and its relationship to self-esteem, health, stress, and drug use.* Unpublished undergraduate thesis, Virginia Commonwealth University, Richmond, VA.

Logan, D. D., & Belgrave, F. Z. (1999). *Relationships between level of Africentricity in African Americans and European Americans and perceived health, self-esteem, stress, and drug use.* Paper presented at the 1999 Conference of the Association of Black Psychologists, Charleston, SC.

Losen, D. J., & Orfield, G. (2002a). Introduction. In D. J. Losen & G. Orfield (Eds.), *Racial inequity in special education* (pp. xv-xxxvii). Cambridge, MA: Harvard Education Press.

Losen, D., & Orfield, G. (2002b). *Racial inequity in special education.* Cambridge, MA: Harvard Education Press.

Lotkowski, V. A., Robbins, S. B., & Noeth, R. J. (2004). *The role of academic and non-academic factors in improving college retention* [Policy report]. Iowa City, IA: ACT Report. Retrieved March 16, 2005, from http://www.act.org/research/policy/pdf/college_retention.pdf

Loukissa, D., Farran, C. J., & Graham, K. L. (1999). Caring for a relative with Alzheimer's disease: The experience of African-American and Caucasian caregivers. *American Journal of Alzheimer's Disease, 14*(4), 207–216.

Lupus Foundation of America. (2001). Retrieved March 20, 2005, from http://www.lupus.org/

Lyna, P., McBride, C., Samsa, G., & Pollak, K. I. (2002). Exploring the association between perceived risks of smoking and benefits to quitting. *Addictive Behaviors, 27*(2), 293–307.

Maddux, J. E., & Lewis, J. (1995). Self-efficacy and adjustment: Basic principles and issues. In J. E. Maddux (Ed.), *Self-efficacy, adaptation, and adjustment.* New York: Plenum Press.

Madhubuti, H. R., & Madhubuti, S. L. (1994). *African-centered education: Its value, importance, and necessity in the development of black children.* Chicago: Third World Press.

Madu, S. N., Baguma, P. K., & Pritz, A. (Eds.) (2000). *Psychotherapy and African reality*. Sovinga, South Africa: University of the North Press.

Magnus, K. B., Cowen, E. L., Wyman, P. A., Fagen, D. B., & Work, W. C. (1999). Parent-child relationship qualities and child adjustment in highly stressed urban black and white families. *Journal of Community Psychology, 27*(1), 55–71.

Maiello, S. (1999). Encounter with an African healer: Thinking about the possibilities and limits of cross-cultural psychotherapy. *Journal of Child Psychotherapy, 25*(2), 217–238.

Marcia, J. E. (1966). Development and validation of ego identity status. *Journal of Personality and Social Psychology, 3*(5), 551–558.

Marcia, J. E. (1980). Identity in adolescence. In J. Adelson (Ed.), *Handbook of adolescent psychology* (pp. 159–187). New York: Wiley.

Marin, G., Burhansstipanox, L., Connell, C. M., Gielen, A. C., Helitzer, A. D., Lorig, K., et al. (1995). A research agenda for health education among under-served populations. *Health Education Quarterly, 22*, 346–363.

Mark, T. L., Palmer, L. A., Russo, P. A., & Vasey, J. (2003). Examination of treatment pattern differences by race. *Mental Health Services Research, 5*(4), 241–250.

Markus, H., & Kitayama, S. (1999). Culture and the self: Implications for cognition, emotion, and motivation. In R. F. Baumeister (Ed.), *The self in social psychology*. Cleveland, OH: Taylor & Francis.

Marsiglia, F. F., Kulis, S., & Hecht, M. L. (2001). Ethnic labels and ethnic identity as predictors of drug use among middle school students in the southwest. *Journal of Research on Adolescence, 11*(1), 21–48.

Martin, J. A., Hamilton, B. E., Sutton, P. D., Ventura, S. J., Menacker, F., & Munson, M. L. (2003). Births: Final data for 2002. *National Vital Statistics Reports, 52*(10), 1–113.

Masten, A. S., & Coatsworth, J. D. (1998). The development of competence in favorable and unfavorable environments: Lessons from research on successful children. *American Psychologist, 53*, 205–220.

Mathews, T. J., Curtin, S. C., & MacDorman, M. F. (2000). Infant mortality statistics from the 1998 period linked birth/infant death data set. *National Vital Statistics Reports, 48*(12). Hyattsville, MD: National Center for Health Statistics. Retrieved March 28, 2005, from http://www.cdc.gov/nchs/data/nvsr/nvsr48/nvs48_12.pdf

Mattis, J. S. (1996). Workings of the spirit: Spirituality, meaning construction and coping in the lives of black women. *Dissertation Abstracts International: Section B: The Sciences & Engineering, 56*(12-B), 7097. US: Univ. Microfilms International.

Mattis, J. S. (2000). African American women's definitions of spirituality and religiosity. *Journal of Black Psychology, 26*(1), 101–122.

Mattis, J. S., Hearn, K. D., & Jagers, R. J. (2002). Factors predicting communal attitudes among African American men. *Journal of Black Psychology, 28*(3), 197–214.

Mattis, J. S., Jagers, R. J., Hatcher, C. A., Lawhon, G. D., Murphy, E. J., & Murray, Y. F. (2000). Religiosity, volunteerism, and community involvement among

African American men: An exploratory analysis. *Journal of Community Psychology, 28*(4), 391–406.

Mayer, E., Kosmin, B. A., & Keysar, A. (2001). *American Religious Identification Survey.* Retrieved March 27, 2005, from http://www.gc.cuny.edu/studies/introduction.htm

Mbiti, J. S. (1970). *African religions and philosophy.* Garden City, NY: Anchor Books.

Mbiti, J. (1991). *African religions and philosophy* (2nd ed.). Portsmouth, NH: Heinemann.

McAdoo, H. P. (1993). The social cultural contexts of ecological developmental family models. In P. Boss, W. Doherty, & W. Schyumm (Eds.), *Sourcebook of family theories and methods: A contextual approach* (pp. 298–301). New York: Plenum.

McAdoo, H. P. (1998). African-American families: Strengths and realities. In H. I. McCubbin, E. A. Thompson, A. I. Thompson, & J. A. Futrell (Eds.), *Resiliency in African-American families* (pp. 17–30). Thousand Oaks, CA: Sage.

McAdoo, J. (1988). The roles of black fathers in the socialization of black children. In H. P. McAdoo (Ed.), *Black families* (pp. 257–269). Newbury Park, CA: Sage.

McBride, J. L., Arthur, G., Brooks, R., & Pilkington, L. (1998). The relationship between a patient's spirituality and health experiences. *Family Medicine, 30*(2), 122–126.

McCluskey, C. P., Krohn, M. D., Lizotte, A. J., & Rodriguez, M. L. (2002). Early substance use and school achievement: An examination of Latino, White, and African American youth. *Journal of Drug Issues, 2*(3), 921–944.

McCracken, L. M., Semenchuk, E. M., & Goetsch, V. L. (1995). Cross-sectional and longitudinal analyses of coping responses and health status in persons with systemic lupus erthematosus. *Behavioral Medicine, 20,* 179–187.

McCubbin, H. I., Fleming, W. M., Thompson, A. I., Neitman, P., Elver, K. M., & Savas, S. A. (1998). Resiliency and coping in "at risk" African-American youth and their families. In H. I. McCubbin, E. A. Thomson, A. I. Thompson, & J. A. Futrell (Eds.), *Resiliency in African American families* (pp. 187–323). Thousand Oaks, CA: Sage.

McDermott, P. A., & Spencer, M. B. (1997). Racial and social class prevalence of psychopathology among school-age youth in the United States. *Youth & Society, 28*(4), 387–415.

McKinnon, J. (2001). *The black population 2000* [2000 Census Brief]. Retrieved January 10, 2005, from http://www.census.gov/prod/2001pubs/c2kbr01-5.pdf

McKinnon, J. (2003). *The black population in the United States: March 2002.* U.S. Bureau of the Census, Current Population Reports, P20-541. Washington, DC: U.S. Government Printing Office.

McLanahan, S. S., & Casper, L. (1995). Growing diversity and inequity in the American family. In R. Farley (Ed.), *State of the union: America in the 1990s: Vol. 2. Social trends* (pp. 1–45). New York: Russell Sage.

McLoyd, V. C. (1990a). The impact of economic hardship on black families and children: Psychological distress, parenting, and socioemotional development. *Child Development, 61*(2), 311–346.

McLoyd, V. C. (1990b). Minority children: Introduction to the special issue. *Child Development, 61*(2), 263–266.

McLoyd, V. C. (1991). What is the study of African American children the study of? The conduct, publication, and changing nature of research on African American children. In R. L. Jones (Ed.), *Black psychology* (3rd ed., pp. 419–440). Berkeley, CA: Cobb & Henry.

McMillan, D. W., & Chavis, D. M. (1986). Sense of community: A definition and theory. *American Journal of Community Psychology, 14*(1), 6–23.

McMillan, T. (1992). *Waiting to exhale.* New York: Penguin Books.

McRae, M. B., Thompson, D. A., & Cooper, S. (1999). Black churches as therapeutic groups. *Journal of Multicultural Counseling and Development, 27,* 207–220.

Meraviglia (1999). Critical analysis of spirituality and its empirical indicators. *Journal of Holistic Nursing, 17*(1), 18–33.

Merriam-Webster. (1997). *Merriam-Webster medical dictionary* [online]. Retrieved from http://www.intelihealth.com/IH/ihtIH/WSIHW000/9276/9276.html

Merriam-Webster medical dictionary on Medline Plus. (2002). Medline Plus Health Information from the National Library of Medicine. Retrieved April 7, 2005, from http://medlineplus.gov/

Merriam-Webster online dictionary. (2004). Retrieved April 9, 2005, from http://www.m-w.com/

Mickelson, R. A. (1990). The attitude-achievement paradox among black adolescents. *Sociology of Education, 63*(1), 44–61.

Miller, J. L. (2001). Understanding achievement attribution and achievement motivation among African-American youth: Racism, racial socialization, and spirituality. *Dissertations Abstracts International, 61*(8-A), 3053.

Miller, T. Q., & Volk, R. J. (2002). Family relationships and adolescent cigarette smoking: Results from a national longitudinal survey. *Journal of Drug Issues, 2*(3), 945–972.

Millsap, M. A., Chase, A., Obdeidallah, D., Perez-Smith, A., Brigham, N., & Johnston, K. (2000). *Evaluation of Detroit's Comer Schools and Families Initiative: Final report.* Cambridge, MA: Abt Associates.

Molock, S. D., & Belgrave, F. Z. (1994). Depression and anxiety in patients with sickle cell disease: Conceptual and methodological considerations. *Journal of Health & Social Policy, 5*(3–4), 39–53.

Montgomery, D. E., Fine, M. A., & James-Myers, L. (1990). The development and validation of an instrument to assess an optimal Afrocentric worldview. *Journal of Black Psychology, 17*(1), 37–54.

Moore, K. A., Morrison, D. R., & Greene, A. D. (1997). Effects on the children born to adolescent mothers. In R. A. Maynard (Ed.), *Kids having kids: Economic costs and social consequences of teen pregnancy.* Washington, DC: The Urban Institute.

Moreland, C., & Leach, M. M. (2001). The relationship between black racial identity and moral development. *Journal of Black Psychology, 27*(3), 255–271.

Morgan, H. J., & Shaver, P. R. (1999). Attachment processes and commitment to romantic relationships. In J. M. Adams & W. H. Jones (Eds.), *Handbook of interpersonal commitment and relationship stability: Perspectives on individual differences* (pp. 109–124). Dordrecht, The Netherlands: Kluwer.

Mortenson Research Seminar on Public Policy Analysis of Opportunity for Postsecondary Education. (2002). Higher education equity indices by race/ethnicity and gender, 1940–2000. *Postsecondary Education Opportunity, 118.* Retrieved January 10, 2005, from http://www.postsecondary.org/rl/rl_02.asp

Moynihan, D. P. (1965). *The Negro family: Case for national action.* Washington, DC: U.S. Department of Labor, Office of Policy, Planning, and Research.

Moynihan, D. P. (1999). The study of black families. In R. Staples (Ed.), *The black family: Essays and studies* (6th ed.). Belmont, CA: Wadsworth.

Murdock, G. P. (1949). *Social structure.* New York: Free Press.

Musser, D. W., & Price, J. L. (1992). *A new handbook of Christian theology.* Nashville, TN: Abington Press.

Muus, R. (1988). *Theories of adolescence* (5th ed.). New York: Random House.

Myers, L. J. (1988). *Understanding an Afrocentric world-view: Introduction to an optimal psychology.* Dubuque, IA: Kendall/Hunt.

Myers, L. J. (1991). Expanding the psychology of knowledge optimally: The importance of worldview revisited. In R. L. Jones (Ed.), *Black psychology* (3rd ed., pp. 15–28). Berkeley, CA: Cobb & Henry.

Myers, L. J. (1992). Transpersonal psychology: The role of the Afrocentric paradigm. In A. K. H. Burlew & W. C. Banks (Eds.), *African American psychology: Theory, research, and practice* (pp. 5–17). Thousand Oaks, CA: Sage.

Myers, M. A., & Thompson, V. L. S. (2000). The impact of violence exposure on African American youth in context. *Youth and Society, 32*(2), 253–268.

National Center for Education Statistics. (2001a). *Digest of education statistics, 2000.* Retrieved January 7, 2005, from http://nces.ed.gov/

National Center for Education Statistics. (2001b). *Dropout rates in the United States: 2000* (NCES Report No. 2002-114). Washington, DC: U.S. Government Printing Office.

National Center for Education Statistics. (2001c). *Homeschooling in the United States: 1999* (NCES Report No. 2001-033). Washington, DC: U.S. Government Printing Office.

National Center for Education Statistics. (2002). *The condition of education 2002* (NCES 2002-025). Washington, DC: U.S. Government Printing Office. Retrieved January 5, 2005, from http://nces.ed.gov/pubs2002/2002025.pdf

National Center for Health Statistics. (1998). *Socioeconomic status and health chart book* (DHHS Publication No. 98-1232). Hyattsville, MD: National Center for Health Statistics.

National Diabetes Information Clearinghouse. (2002). *National diabetes statistics* (NIH Publication No. 02-3892). Retrieved April 4, 2002, from http://www.niddk.nih.gov/health/diabetes/pubs/dmstats/dr

National Urban League. (2004). National Urban League, Inc. Retrieved January 7, 2005, from http://www.nul.org/

Neal, A. M., & Wilson, M. L. (1989). The role of skin color and features in the black community: Implications for black women and therapy. *Clinical Psychology Review, 9,* 323–333.

Neighbors, H. W., & Jackson, J. S. (Eds.). (1996). *Mental health in black America.* Thousand Oaks, CA: Sage.

Neighbors, H. W., Jackson, J. S., Bowman, P. J., & Gurin, G. (1983). Stress, coping, and black mental health: Preliminary findings from a national study. *Prevention in Human Services, 2*(3), 5–29.

Neighbors, H. W., Jackson, J. S., Campbell, L., & Williams, D. (1989). The influence of racial factors on psychiatric diagnosis: A review and suggestions for research. *Community Mental Health Journal, 25*(4), 301–311.

Neighbors, H. W., Musick, M. A., & Williams, D. R. (1998). The African American minister as a source of help for serious personal crises: Bridge or barrier to mental health care? *Health Education & Behavior, 25*(6), 759–777.

Neufeldt, V., & Guralnik, D. B. (Eds.). (1996). *Webster's New World college dictionary.* New York: Macmillan.

Newburger, E. C., & Curry, A. E. (2000). Educational attainment in the United States (Update): March 2000. (Current Population Reports, P20-536). Washington, DC: U.S. Government Printing Office.

Newlin, K., Knafl, K., & Melkus, G. D. (2002). African-American spirituality: A concept analysis. *Advances in Nursing Science, 25*(2), 57–70.

Nickerson, K. J., Helms, J. E., & Terrell, F. (1994). Cultural mistrust, opinions about mental illness, and black students' attitudes toward seeking psychological help from white counselors. *Journal of Counseling Psychology, 41*(3), 378–385.

Nobles, W. (1976). Extended-self: Rethinking the so-called Negro self-concept. *Journal of Black Psychology, 11*(2), 15–24.

Nobles, W. (1980). African philosophy: Foundations for black psychology. In R. Jones (Ed.), *Black psychology.* New York: Harper & Row.

Nobles, W. W. (1986). *African psychology: Towards its reclamation, reascension, and revitalization.* Oakland, CA: Black Family Institute.

Nobles, W. W. (1991). African philosophy: Foundations of black psychology. In R. Jones (Ed.), *Black psychology* (pp. 47–63). Berkeley, CA: Cobbs & Henry.

Nobles, W. W. (2004). African philosophy: Foundations for black psychology. In R. Jones (Ed.), *Black psychology.* Berkeley, CA: Cobbs & Henry.

Nobles, W., & Goddard, L. (1993). An African-centered model of prevention for African-American youth at high risk. In L. L. Goddard (Ed.), *An African-centered model of prevention for African American youth at high risk* (DHHS Publication No. SMA 93-2015, pp. 115–129). Rockville, MD: U.S. Department of Health and Human Services.

Noguera, P. (2003). The trouble with black boys: The role and influence of environmental and cultural factors on the academic performance of African American males. *Urban Education, 38*(4), 431–459.

Nunn, K. B. (2002). Race, crime, and the pool of surplus criminality: Or why the "war on drugs" was a "war on blacks." *Journal of Gender, Race & Justice, 6*, 381–445.

Oakes, J. (1995). Two cities' tracking and within-school segregation. *Teachers College Record, 96*(4), 681–691.

O'Donnell, S. M. (1996). Urban African American community development practice. In I. Carlton-LaNey & N. Y. Burwell (Eds.), *African American community practice models* (pp. 7–26). New York: Haworth Press.

Oetting, E. R., & Beauvais, F. (1986). Peer cluster theory: Drugs and the adolescent. *Journal of Counseling and Development, 65*, 17–22.

Ogbu, J. U. (1999). Beyond language: Ebonics, proper English and identity in a Black-American speech community. *American Educational Research Journal, 36*(2), 147–184.

Okwumabua, J. O., Wong, S. P., Duryea, E. J., Okwumabua, T. M., & Howell, S. (1999). Building self-esteem through social skills training and cultural awareness: A community-based approach for preventing violence among African American youth. *Journal of Primary Prevention, 20*(1), 61–74.

Oldridge, N. B., & Streiner, D. L. (1990). The health belief model: Predicting compliance and dropout in cardiac rehabilitation. *Medicine and Science in Sports and Exercise, 22*(5), 678–683.

Oler, C. H. (1996). Spirituality, racial identity, and intentions to use alcohol and other drugs among African American youth. *Dissertation Abstracts International: Section B: The Sciences & Engineering, 56*(8-B), 4590. US: Univ. Microfilms International.

Oliver, W. (2001). Cultural racism and structural violence: Implications for African Americans. *Journal of Human Behavior in the Social Environment, 4*(2–3), 1–26.

Orfield, G., Losen, D., Wald, J., & Swanson, C. (2004). *Losing our future: How minority youth are being left behind by the graduation rate crisis.* Cambridge, MA: Harvard University Civil Rights Project.

O'Sullivan, M. J., Peterson, P. D., Cox, G. B., & Kirkeby, J. (1989). Ethnic populations: Community mental health services ten years later. *American Journal of Community Psychology, 17*(1), 17–31.

Oyserman, D., Harrison, K., & Bybee, D. (2001). Can racial identity be promotive of academic efficacy? *The International Society for the Study of Behavioral Development, 25*(4), 379–385.

Parham, T. A. (1992a). Cycles of psychological nigrescence. *The Counseling Psychologist, 17*(2), 187–226.

Parham, T. A. (1992b). *Issues in counseling African American clients.* North Amherst, MA: Microtraining Associates.

Parham, T. A., & Helms, J. E. (1981). The influence of black students' racial identity attitudes on preferences for counselor's race. *Journal of Counseling Psychology, 28*(3), 250–257.

Parham, T. A., White, J. L., & Ajamu, A. (1999). *The psychology of Blacks: An African centered perspective.* Upper Saddle River, NJ: Prentice Hall.

Parmer, T. (1998). Characteristics of preferred partners: Variation between African American men and women. *Journal of College Student Development, 39*(5), 461–471.

Parrish, T. (2002). Racial disparities in the identification, funding, and provision of special education. In D. J. Losen & G. Orfield (Eds.), *Racial inequity in special education* (pp. 15–37). Cambridge, MA: Harvard Education Press.

Pastore, N. (1946). A comment on "psychological differences as among races." *School & Society, 63,* 136–137.

Pavkov, T. W., George, R. M., & Czapkowicz, J. G. (1997). Predictors of length of stay among youths hospitalized in state hospitals in Illinois. *Journal of Child and Family Studies, 6*(2), 221–231.

Pearson, C. S. (1991). *Awakening the heroes within: Twelve archetypes to help us find ourselves and transform our world.* San Francisco: Harper.

Peplau, L. A., Cochran, S. D., & Mays, V. M. (1997). A national survey of the intimate relationships of African American lesbians and gay men: A look at commitment, satisfaction, sexual behavior, and HIV disease. In B. Greene (Ed.), *Ethnic and cultural diversity among lesbians and gay men: Psychological perspectives on lesbian and gay issues* (Vol. 3, pp. 11–38). Thousand Oaks, CA: Sage.

Perkins, K. R. (1996). The influence of television images on black females' self-perceptions of physical attractiveness. *Journal of Black Psychology, 22*(4), 453–469.

Peters, M. F., & Massey, G. (1983). Mundane extreme environmental stress in family stress theories: The case of black families in white America. *Marriage & Family Review, 6*(1–2), 193–218.

Peterson, G. W., Bodman, D. A., Rush, K. R., & Madden-Derdich, D. (2000). Gender and parent-child relationships. In D. H. Demo, K. R. Allen, & M. A. Fine (Eds.), *Handbook of family diversity* (pp. 82–103). New York: Oxford University Press.

Peterson, J. (1923). The comparative abilities of white and negro children. *Comparative Psychology Monographs, 1*(5), 141.

Peterson, J. L., & Marin, G. (1988). Issues in the prevention of AIDS among Black and Hispanic men. *American Psychologist, 43*(11), 871–877.

Peterson, R. D., Krivo, L. J., & Velez, M. B. (2001). Segregation and youth criminal violence: A review and agenda. In S. O. White (Ed.), *Handbook of youth and justice* (pp. 277–286). Dordrecht, The Netherlands: Kluwer.

Pettit, K. L. S., & Kingsley, T. (2003). *Concentrated poverty: A change in course.* Retrieved March 17, 2005, from http://www.urban.org/url.cfm?ID=310790

Phelps, J. (1993). *Black and catholic: The challenges and gifts of Black folk: Contributions of African American experiences and thought to catholic theology.* Milwaukee, WI: Marquette University Press.

Phinney, J. (1992). The Multigroup Ethnic Identity Measure: A new scale for use with diverse groups. *Journal of Adolescent Research, 7*(2), 156–176.

Phinney, J. (1995). Ethnic identity and self-esteem: A review and integration. In A. Padilla (Ed.), *Hispanic psychology: Critical issues in theory and research* (pp. 57–70). Thousand Oaks, CA: Sage.

Phinney, J. S., & Chavira, V. (1995). Parental ethnic socialization and adolescent coping with problems related to ethnicity. *Journal of Research on Adolescence, 5*(1), 31–53.

Pierce-Jones, J., Reid, J. B., & King, F. J. (1964). Adolescent racial and ethnic group differences in social attitudes and adjustment. *Psychological Reports, 5*(3), 549–552.

Plybon, L. E., Edwards, L., Butler, D., Belgrave, F. Z., & Allison, K. W. (2003). Examining the link between neighborhood cohesion and school outcomes: The role of support coping among African American adolescent girls. *Journal of Black Psychology, 29*(4), 393–407.

Plybon, L. R., & Kliewer, W. (2001). Neighborhood types and externalizing behavior in urban school-age children: Tests of direct, mediated, and moderated effects. *Journal of Child and Family Studies, 10*(4), 419–438.

Polakow-Suransky, S. (1999). *Access denied.* Ann Arbor, MI: Student Advocacy Center of Michigan.

Ponterotto, J. G., Sanchez, C. M., & Magids, D. (1991, August). *Initial development of the Multicultural Counseling Awareness Scale.* Paper presented at the annual meeting of the American Psychological Association, San Francisco.

Popkin, S., Rosenbaum, J., & Meaden, P. (1993). Labor market experiences of low-income black women in middle-class suburbs: Evidence from a survey of Gautreaux program participants. *Journal of Policy Analysis and Management, 12*(3), 556–573.

Porterfield, E. (1982). Black-American intermarriage in the United States. *Marriage and Family Review, 5*(1), 17–34.

Portney, K. E., & Berry, J. M. (1997). Mobilizing minority communities: Social capital and participation in urban neighborhoods. *American Behavioral Scientist, 40*(5), 632–645.

Potts, R. (1991). Spirits in the bottle: Spirituality and alcoholism treatment in African-American communities. *Journal of Training and Practice in Professional Psychology, 5*(1), 53–64.

Potts, R. G. (1996). Spirituality and the experience of cancer in an African-American community: Implications for psychosocial oncology. *Journal of Psychosocial Oncology, 14*(1), 1–19.

Potts, R. G. (2003). Emancipatory education versus school-based prevention in African American communities. *American Journal of Community Psychology, 31*(1–2), 173–183.

Powell, J. A. (1999). Achieving racial justice: What's sprawl got to do with it? *Poverty & Race, 8*(5). Retrieved March 17, 2005, from http://www1.umn.edu/irp/announce/PRRAC1999.htm

Prado, G., Feaster, D. J., Schwartz, S. J., Pratt, I. A., Smith, L., & Szapocznik, J. (2004). Religious involvement, coping, social support, and psychological distress in HIV-serepositive African American mothers. *AIDS and Behavior, 8*(3), 221–235.

Ptacek, J. T., & Dodge, K. L. (1995). Coping strategies and relationship satisfaction in couples. *Personality and Social Psychology Bulletin, 21*(1), 76–85.

Putnam, R. D. (1993, October). The prosperous community: Social capital and economic growth. *Current, 356*, 4–10.

Putnam, R. D. (1995). Bowling alone: America's declining social capital. *Journal of Democracy, 6*(1), 664–665.

Quarcoopome, T. N. O. (1987). *West African traditional religion.* Ibadan, Nigeria: African Universities Press.

Radziszewska, B., Richardson, J. L., Dent, C. W., & Flay, B. R. (1996). Parenting style and adolescent depressive symptoms, smoking, and academic achievement: Ethnic, gender, and SES differences. *Journal of Behavioral Medicine, 19*(3), 289–305.

Randolph, S. M., & Banks, H. D. (1993). Making a way out of no way: The promise of Africentric approaches to prevention. *Journal of Black Psychology, 19*(2), 204–214.

Rebach, H. (1992). Alcohol and drug use among American minorities. *Drugs and Society, 6*(1–2), 23–57.

Reiss, I. (1965). The universality of the family: A conceptual analysis. *Journal of Marriage and the Family, 27*(4), 443–453.

Reynolds, A. L., & Pope, R. L. (1991). The complexities of diversity: Exploring multiple oppressions. *Journal of Counseling and Development, 70*(1), 174–181.

Richardson, T. Q., & Helms, J. E. (1994). The relationship of the racial identity attitudes of black men to perceptions of "parallel" counseling dyads. *Journal of Counseling and Development, 73*(2), 172–178.

Ridley, C. R. (1984). Clinical treatment of the nondisclosing black client: A therapeutic paradox. *American Psychologist, 39*(11), 1234–1244.

Roberts, D. F., Henriksen, L., & Christenson, P. G. (1999). *Substance use in popular movies and music.* Washington, DC: Office of National Drug Control Policy.

Roberts, R. E., Phinney, J. S., Masse, L. C., Chen, Y. R., Roberts, C. R., & Romero, A. (1999). The structure of ethnic identity of young adolescents from diverse ethnocultural groups. *Journal of Early Adolescence, 19*, 301–322.

Robins, L. N., Helzer, J. E., Weissman, M. M., Orvaschel, H., Gruenberg, E., Burke, J. D., et al. (1984). Lifetime prevalence of specific psychiatric disorders in three sites. *Archives of General Psychiatry, 41*, 949–958.

Robins, L. N., & Reiger, D. A. (1991). *Psychiatric disorders in America: The Epidemiological Catchment Area Study.* New York: Free Press.

Rodgers-Farmer, A. Y. (1999). Parenting stress, depression, and parenting in grandmothers raising their grandchildren. *Children and Youth Services Review, 21*(5), 377–388.

Roebuck, J. B., & Murty, K. S. (1993). *Historically black colleges and universities: Their place in American higher education.* Westport, CT: Praeger.

Roen, S. R. (1961). Personality and negro-white intelligence. *Journal of Abnormal and Social Psychology, 61*, 148–150.

Rosenbaum, J. E., Kulieke, M. J., & Rubinowitz, L. S. (1988). White suburban schools' responses to low-income black children: Sources of successes and problems. *Urban Review, 20*(1), 28–41.

Rosenbaum, J. E., & Popkin, S. J. (1991). Employment and earnings of low-income Blacks who move to middle-class suburbs. In C. Jencks & P. Peterson (Eds.), *The urban underclass* (pp. 342–356). Washington, DC: Brookings Institution.

Rosenblatt, P. C., Karis, T. A., & Powell, R. D. (1995). *Multiracial couples: Black and white voices.* Thousand Oaks, CA: Sage.

Rosenthal, R., & Jacobson, L. (1968). *Pygmalion in the classroom.* New York: Holt, Rinehart & Winston.

Ross, L. E. (1997). Mate selection preferences among African American college students. *Journal of Black Studies, 27*(4), 554–570.

Rowe, D., & Gills, C. (1993). African-centered drug treatment: An alternative conceptual paradigm for drug counseling with African American clients. *Journal of Psychoactive Drugs, 25*(1), 21–33.

Rubin, D. F., & Belgrave, F. Z. (1999). Differences between African American and European American college students in relative and mathematical time orientations: A preliminary study. *Journal of Black Psychology, 25*, 105–113.

Rudner, L. M. (1999). *The scholastic achievement and demographic characteristics of home schooled students in 1998.* Report prepared under contract with HSLDA, Purcellville, VA.

Ruffin, J. E. (1989). Stages of adult development in black professional women. In R. L. Jones (Ed.), *Black adult development and aging.* Berkeley, CA: Cobb & Henry.

Rutter, M. (1990). Psychosocial resilience and protective mechanisms. In J. Rolf, A. Masten, D. Cicchetti, K. Nuechterlein, & S. Weintraub (Eds.), *Risk and protective factors in the development of psychopathology* (pp. 181–214). New York: Cambridge University Press.

Sagi, A., Lamb, M. E., Lewkowicz, K. S., Shoham, R., Dvir, R., & Estes, D. (1985). Security of infant-mother, -father, and -metapelet attachments among kibbutz-reared Israeli children. *Monographs of the Society for Research in Child Development, 50*(1–2), 257–275.

Salts, C. J., Lindholm, B. W., Goddard, H. W., & Duncan, S. (1995). Predictive variables of violent behavior in adolescent males. *Youth and Society, 26*(3), 377–399.

Sameroff, A. (1975). Transactional models in early social relations. *Human Development, 18,* 65–79.

Sampson, R. J., Morenoff, J., & Earls, F. (1999). Beyond social capital: Neighborhood mechanisms and structural sources of collective efficacy for children. *American Sociological Review,* 64, 633–660.

Sampson, R. J., & Raudenbusch, S. (1999). Systematic social observation of public spaces: A new look at disorder in urban neighborhoods. *American Journal of Sociology, 105*(3), 603–651.

Sampson, R. J., Raudenbusch, S. W., & Earls, F. (1997, August 15). Neighborhoods and violent crime: A multilevel study of collective efficacy. *Science, 277*(5328), 918–924.

Sanchez-Hughley, J. (2000). *The first session with African Americans: A step by step guide.* San Francisco: Jossey-Bass.

Sanders, M. G. (1997). Overcoming obstacles: Academic achievement as a response to racism and discrimination. *Journal of Negro Education, 66*(1), 83–93.

Saunders, J. M. (2000). Exposure to chronic community violence: Formal kinship, informal kinship, and spirituality as stress moderators for African American children. *Dissertation Abstracts International, A (Humanities and Social Sciences), 60*(12-A), 4333. US: Univ. Microfilms International.

Saylor, E. S., & Aries, E. (1999). Ethnic identity and change in social context. *The Journal of Social Psychology, 139*(5), 549–566.

Schafer, R. J. (1993). *Racial and ethnic groups.* New York: Harper Collins.

Schilling, R. R., & McAlister, A. (1990). Preventing drug use in adolescents through media interventions. *Journal of Consulting and Clinical Psychology, 58*(1), 416–424.

Schwartz, J. (1998, July 8). Blacks absorb more nicotine, suffer greater smoking toll. *Washington Post,* p. A3.

Schweinhart, L. J., Barnes, H. V., & Weikart, D. P. (1993). *Significant benefits: The High/Scope Perry Preschool Study through age 27.* Ypsilanti, MI: High/Scope Press.

Scott, J. W., & Black, A. W. (1989). Deep structures of African American family life: Female and male kin networks. *The Western Journal of Black Studies, 13*(1), 17–24.

Sellers, R. M., Rowley, S. A. J., Chavous, T. M., Shelton, J. N., & Smith, M. (1997). Multidimensional inventory of black identity: Preliminary investigation of reliability and construct validity. *Journal of Personality and Social Psychology, 73*(4), 805–815.

Semaj, L. T. (1996). Towards a cultural science. In D. A. Azibo (Ed.), *African Psychology in historical perspective and related commentary* (pp. 193–201). Trenton, NJ: Africa World Press.

Seppa, N. (1997). Children's TV remains steeped in violence. *APA Monitor, 28,* 36.

Shade, B. J. (1982). Afro-American cognitive style: A variable in school success? *Review of Educational Research, 52*(2), 219–244.

Shade, B. J. (1991). African American patterns of cognition. In R. Jones (Ed.), *Black psychology* (3rd ed., pp. 231–247). Berkeley, CA: Cobb & Henry.

Shade, B. J., & Edwards, P. A. (1987). Ecological correlates of the educative style of Afro-American children. *Journal of Negro Education, 56*(1), 88–99.

Shakoor, B. H., & Chalmers, D. (1991). Co-victimization of African-American children who witness violence: Effects on cognitive, emotional, and behavioral development. *Journal of the National Medical Association, 83*(3), 233–238.

Shaw, C., & McKay, H. (1969). *Juvenile delinquency and urban areas.* Chicago: University of Chicago Press.

Shockley, W. (1971). Models, mathematics, and the moral obligation to diagnose the origin of Negro IQ deficits. *Review of Educational Research, 41*(4), 369–377.

Shujaa, M. J. (1992). Afrocentric transformation and parental choice in African American independent schools. *Journal of Negro Education, 61*(2), 148–159.

Signorielli, N., Gerbner, G., & Morgan, M. (1995). Violence on television: The cultural indicators project. *Journal of Broadcasting & Electronic Media, 39*(2), 278–283.

Simon, K. J., & Das, A. (1984). An application of the health belief model toward educational diagnosis for VD education. *Health Education Quarterly, 11,* 403–418.

Simpkins, G. A., & Simpkins, C. (1981). Cross cultural approach to curriculum development. In G. Smitherman (Ed.), *Black English and the education of black children and youth: Proceedings of the national invitational symposium on the King decision* (pp. 221–240). Detroit, MI: Wayne State University, Center for Black Studies.

Slaughter, D. T., & Johnson, D. J. (Eds.). (1988). *Visible now: Blacks in private schools.* New York: Greenwood Press.

Slavin, L. A., Rainer, K. L., McCreary, M. L., & Gowda, K. K. (1991). Toward a multicultural model of the stress process. *Journal of Counseling and Development, 70*(1), 156–164.

Slavin, R. E. (1995). Enhancing intergroup relations in schools: Cooperative learning and other strategies. In W. D. Hawley & A. W. Jackson (Eds.), *Toward a common destiny: Improving race and ethnic relations in America* (pp. 291–314). San Francisco: Jossey-Bass.

Smith, E. P., & Brookins, C. C. (1997). Toward the development of an ethnic identity measure for African American youth. *Journal of Black Psychology, 23*(4), 358–377.

Smitherman, G. (2004). Talkin and testifyin: Black English and the black experience. In R. Jones (Ed.), *Black psychology* (4th ed., pp. 249–267). Berkeley, CA: Cobb & Henry.

Smith-Maddox, R. (1999). The social networks and resources of African American eighth graders: Evidence from the National Educational Longitudinal Study of 1988. *Adolescence, 34*(133), 169–183.

Snowden, L. R. (1998). Racial differences in informal help seeking for mental health problems. *Journal of Community Psychology, 26*(5), 429–438.

Snowden, L. R., & Hu, T. W. (1997). Ethnic differences in mental health services use among the severely mentally ill. *Journal of Community Psychology, 25*(3), 235–247.

Snowden, L. R., & Pingitore, D. (2002). Frequency and scope of mental health service delivery to African Americans in primary care. *Mental Health Services Research, 4*(3), 123–130.

Snyder, H. N., Sickmund, M., & Poe-Yamagata, E. (1996). *Juvenile offenders and victims: 1996 update on violence.* Pittsburgh, PA: National Center for Juvenile Justice.

Sodowsky, G. R., Taffe, R. C., Gutkin, T. B., & Wise, S. L. (1994). Development of the Multicultural Counseling Inventory: A self-report measure of multicultural competencies. *Journal of Counseling Psychology, 41*(2), 137–148.

Speight, S. L., Vera, E. M., & Derrickson, K. B. (1996). Racial self-designation, racial identity, and self-esteem revisited. *The Journal of Black Psychology, 22*(1), 37–52.

Spencer, M. B. (1982). Preschool children's social cognition and cultural cognition: A cognitive developmental interpretation of race dissonance findings. *Journal of Psychology, 112,* 275–286.

Spencer, M. B., Cole, S. P., Jones, S., & Swanson, D. P. (1997). Neighborhood and family influences on young urban adolescents' behavior problems: A multi-sample multisite analysis. In J. Brooks-Gunn, G. Duncan, & J. L. Aber (Eds.), *Neighborhood poverty: Context and consequences for children* (Vol. 1, pp. 200–218). New York: Russell Sage.

Spencer, M. B., Cross, W. E., Harpalani, V., & Goss, T. N. (2003). Historical and developmental perspectives on black academic achievement: Debunking the "acting white" myth and posing new directions for research. In C. C. Yeakey & R. D. Henderson (Eds.), *Surmounting all odds: Education, opportunity, and society in the new millennium* (pp. 273–304). Greenwich, CT: Information Age.

Spencer, M. B., Dupree, D., & Hartmann, T. (1997). A phenomenological variant of ecological systems theory (PVEST): A self-organization perspective in context. *Development and Psychopathology, 9*(4), 817–833.

Spencer, M. B., & Markstrom-Adams, C. (1990). Identity processes among racial and ethnic minority children in America. *Child Development, 61*(2), 290–310.

Spencer, M. B., McDermott, P. A., Burton, L. M., & Kochman, T. J. (1997). An alternative approach to assessing neighborhood effects on early adolescent achievement and problem behavior. In J. Brooks-Gunn, G. Duncan, & J. L. Aber (Eds.), *Neighborhood poverty: Context and consequences for children* (Vol. 2, pp. 145–163). New York: Russell Sage.

Spencer, M. B., Noll, E., Stoltzfus, J., & Harpalani, V. (2001). Identity and school adjustment: Revisiting the "acting white" assumption. *Educational Psychologist, 36*(1), 21–30.

Sramek, J., Roy, S., Ahrens, T., Pinanong, P., Cutler, N. R., & Pi, E. (1991). Prevalence of tardive dyskinesia among three ethnic groups of chronic psychiatric patients. *Hospital and Community Psychiatry, 42*(6), 590–592.

Stack, C. (1974). *All our kin: Survival strategies.* New York: Harper Torchback.

Stanton, B., Li, X., Cottrell, L., & Kaljee, L. (2001). Early initiation of sex, drug-related risk behaviors, and sensation-seeking among urban low-income African American adolescents. *Journal of the National Medical Association, 93*(4), 129–138.

Staples, R. (1982). *Black masculinity: The black male's role in American society.* San Francisco: Black Scholar Press.

Staples, R. (1999a). Interracial relationships: A convergence of desire and opportunity. In R. Staples (Ed.), *The black family: Essays and studies.* Belmont, CA: Wadsworth.

Staples, R. (1999b). Sociocultural factors in black family transformation: Toward a redefinition of family functions. In R. Staples (Ed.), *The black family: Essays and studies* (pp. 18–23). Belmont, CA: Wadsworth.

Steele, C. (1992, April). Race and the schooling of black Americans. *Atlantic Monthly, 269*(4), 68–78.

Steele, C. M., & Aronson, J. (1995). Stereotype threat and the intellectual test performance of African Americans. *Journal of Personality and Social Psychology, 69*(5), 797–811.

Steers, W. N., Elliot, E., Nemiro, J., Ditman, D., & Oskamp, S. (1996). Health beliefs as predictors of HIV-preventive behavior and ethnic differences in prediction. *Journal of Social Psychology, 136*(1), 99–110.

Steffen, P. R., McNeilly, M., Anderson, N., & Sherwood, A. (2003). Effects of perceived racism and anger inhibition on ambulatory blood pressure in African Americans. *Psychosomatic Medicine, 65*(5), 746–750.

Steinberg, L., Dornbusch, S. M., & Brown, B. B. (1992). Ethnic differences in adolescent achievement: An ecological perspective. *American Psychologist, 47*(6), 723–729.

Steinberg, L., Mounts, N. S., & Lamborn, S. (1991). Authoritative parenting and adolescent adjustment across varied ecological niches. *Journal of Research on Adolescence, 1*, 19–36.

Stevenson, H. C. (1995). Relationship of adolescent perceptions of racial socialization to racial identity. *Journal of Black Psychology, 21*(1), 49–70.

Stevenson, H. C. (1996). Scale of racial socialization adolescent version. In R. L. Jones (Ed.), *Handbook of tests and measurements for black populations* (Vol. 1, pp. 309–326). Hampton, VA: Cobb & Henry.

Stevenson, H. C., Cameron, R., Herrero-Taylor, T., & Davis, G. Y. (2002). Development of teenage experiences of raical socialization scale: Correlates of race-related socializations frequency form the perspectives of black youth. *Journal of Black Psychology, 28*(2), 84–106.

Substance Abuse and Mental Health Services Administration. (1999). *Summary of findings from the 1998 national household survey on drug abuse.* Rockville, MD: U.S. Department of Health and Human Services.

Substance Abuse and Mental Health Services Administration. (2002). *2002 National survey on drug use and health.* Rockville, MD: U.S. Department of Health and Human Services. http://www.oas.samhsa.gov/nhsda/2k2nsduh/Results/apph.htm#tabh.10

Sue, S. (1977). Community mental health services to minority groups: Some optimism, some pessimism. *American Psychologist, 32*, 616–624.

Sue, S. (1983). Ethnic minority issues in psychology. *American Psychologist, 38*, 583–592.

Suggs, D. N., & Lewis, S. A. (2003). Alcohol as a direct and indirect labor enhancer: In the mixed economy of the BaTswana, 1800–1900. In W. Jankowiak & D. Bjradburd (Eds.), *Drugs, labor, and colonial expansion* (pp. 135–148). Tucson: University of Arizona Press.

Sullaway, M., & Dunbar, E. (1996). Clinical manifestations of prejudice in psychotherapy: Toward a strategy of assessment and treatment. *Clinical Psychology: Science & Practice, 3*(4), 296–309.

Super, C. M. (1987). Cross-cultural research on infancy. In J. Oates & S. Sheldon (Eds.), *Cognitive development in infancy* (pp. 23–47). Hillsdale, NJ: Erlbaum.

Super, C. M., & Harkness, S. (1986). The developmental niche: A conceptualization at the interface of child and culture. *International Journal of Behavioral Development, 9*(4), 545–570.

Swartz, M. S., Wagner, H. R., Swanson, J. W., Burns, B. J., George, L. K., & Padgett, D. K. (1998). Comparing use of public and private mental health services: The enduring barriers of race and age. *Community Mental Health Journal, 34*(2), 133–144.

Swinney, J. E. (2002). African Americans with cancer: The relationships among self-esteem, locus of control, and health promotion. *Research in Nursing & Health, 25*(5), 371–382.

Tajfel, H. (1981). *Human groups and social categories.* Cambridge, UK: Cambridge University Press.

Takeuchi, D. T., Sue, S., & Yeh, M. (1998). Return rates and outcomes from ethnicity-specific mental health programs in Los Angeles. In P. Balls Organista, K. M. Chun, & G. Marin (Eds.), *Readings in ethnic psychology* (pp. 324–334). New York: Routledge.

Tanfer, K. (1987). Patterns of premarital cohabitation among never-married women in the United States. *Journal of Marriage and the Family, 49*(3), 483–497.

Taylor, H. U. (1989). *Standard English, Black English, and bidialectalism.* New York: Peter Lang.

Taylor, R. J., Chatters, L. M., Jayakody, R., & Levin, J. S. (1996). Black and white differences in religious participation: A multisample comparison. *Journal for the Scientific Study of Religion, 35*(4), 403–410.

Taylor, R. J., & Johnson, W. E. (1997). Family roles and family satisfaction among black men. In R. J. Taylor, J. S. Jackson, & L. M. Chatters (Eds.), *Family life in black America* (pp. 248–261). Thousand Oaks, CA: Sage.

Taylor, R. J., Leashore, B. R., & Toliver, S. (1988). An assessment of the provider role as perceived by black males. *Family Relations, 37*, 426–431.

Taylor, R. J., Tucker, M. B., Chatters, L. M., & Jayakody, R. (1997). Recent demographic trends in African American family structure. In R. J. Taylor, J. S. Jackson, & L. M. Chatters (Eds.), *Family life in black America* (pp. 14–62). Thousand Oaks, CA: Sage.

Taylor, S. E. (1991). *Health psychology.* New York: McGraw-Hill.

Tedin, K. L., & Weiher, G. R. (2004). Racial/ethnic diversity and academic quality as components of school choice. *The Journal of Politics, 66*(4), 1109–1133.

Terrell, F., & Terrell, S. (1984). Race of counselor, client sex, cultural mistrust level, and premature termination from counseling among black clients. *Journal of Counseling Psychology, 31*(3), 371–375.

Thomas, A. J., & Speight, S. L. (1999). Racial identity and racial socialization attitudes of African American parents. *Journal of Black Psychology, 25*(2), 152–170.

Thompson, S. H., Sargent, R. G., & Kemper, K. A. (1996). Black and white adolescent males' perceptions of ideal body size. *Sex Roles, 34*(5/6), 391–406.

Thompson, S. N., & Chambers, J. W. (2000). African self-consciousness and health-promoting behaviors among African American college students. *Journal of Black Psychology, 26*(3), 330–346.

Thompson, V. L. (1994). Socialization to race and its relationship to racial identification among African Americans. *Journal of Black Psychology, 20*(2), 175–189.

Thornton, M. C. (1997). Strategies of racial socialization among black parents: Mainstream, minority, and cultural messages. In R. J. Taylor, J. S. Jackson, & L. M. Chatters (Eds.), *Family life in black America* (pp. 201–215). Thousand Oaks, CA: Sage.

Thornton, M. C. (1998). Indigenous resources and strategies of resistance. In H. I. McCubbin, E. A. Thompson, A. I. Thompson, & J. A. Futrell (Eds.), *Resiliency in African American families* (pp. 49–66). Thousand Oaks, CA: Sage.

Thornton, M. C., Chatters, L., Taylor, R. J., & Allen, W. (1990). Sociodemographic and environmental correlates to racial socialization by black parents. *Child Development, 61,* 401–409.

Tonnies, F. (1925). The concept of Gemeinschaft. In W. J. Cahnman & R. Heberle (Eds.), *Ferdinand Tonnies on sociology: Pure, applied and empirical. Selected writings* (pp. 62–72). Chicago: University of Chicago Press.

Towns, D. P. (1996). "Rewind the world!" An ethnographic study of inner-city African American children's perceptions of violence. *Journal of Negro Education, 65*(3), 375–389.

Townsend, B. L. (2000). The disproportionate discipline of African American learners: Reducing school suspensions and expulsions. *Exceptional Children, 66*(3), 381–391.

Townsend, G. T., & Belgrave, F. Z. (2000). The impact of personal identity and racial identity on drug attitudes and use among African American children. *Journal of Black Psychology, 76*(4), 421–436.

Treisman, U. (1992). Studying students studying calculus: A look at the lives of minority mathematics students in college. *College Mathematics Journal, 23*(5), 362–372.

Triandis, H. C. (1995). *Individualism and collectivism.* Boulder, CO: Westview Press.

Troiano, R. P., Flegal, K. M., Kuczmarski, R. J., Campbell, S. M., & Johnson, C. L. (1995). Overweight prevalence and trends for children and adolescents. *Archives of Pediatrics and Adolescent Medicine, 149,* 1085–1091.

Tsao, B. P. (1998). Genetic susceptibility to lupus nephritis. *Lupus, 7*(9), 585–590.

Tsa-Tsala. (1997). Beliefs and disease in Cameroon. In S. N. Madu, P. K. Baguma, & A. Pritz (Eds.), *Psychotherapy in Africa: First investigation.* Vienna: World Council for Psychotherapy.

Tuch, S. A., Sigelman, L., & MacDonald, J. A. (1999). The polls-trends: Race relations and American youth. *Public Opinion Quarterly, 63*(1), 109–148.

Tuck, K., & Boykin, A. W. (1989). Verve effects: The relationship of task performance to stimulus preference and variability in low income black and white children. In A. Harrison (Ed.), *The eleventh conference on empirical research in black psychology* (pp. 84–95). Washington, DC: National Institute of Mental Health.

Tucker, C. M., & Herman, K. C. (2002). Using culturally sensitive theories and research to meet the academic needs of low-income African American children. *The American Psychologist, 57*(10), 762–774.

Tucker, M. B., & Mitchell-Kernan, C. (1999). Mate availability among African Americans: Conceptual and methodological issues. In R. L. Jones (Ed.), *Advances in African American Psychology* (pp. 129–163). Hampton, VA: Cobb & Henry.

Tyler, F. B., Brome, D. R., & Williams, J. E. (1991). *Ethnic validity, ecology, and psychotherapy: A psychological competence model.* New York: Plenum Press.

Ulbrich, P. M., Warheit, G. J., & Zimmerman, R. S. (1989). Race, socioeconomic status, and psychological distress: An examination of differential vulnerability. *Journal of Health & Social Behavior, 30*(1), 131–146.

United Church of Christ Commission for Racial Justice. (1987). *Toxic wastes and race in the United States: A national report on the racial and socio-economic characteristics of communities with hazardous waste sites.* New York: Author.

U.S. Census Bureau. (2000). *Census 2000 brief: Marital status: 2000.* Washington, DC: U.S. Government Printing Office.

U.S. Census Bureau. (2001a). *Current population survey, March demographic supplement.* Retrieved January 11, 2005, from http://www.census.gov/apsd/techdoc/cps/cpsmar01.pdf

U.S. Census Bureau. (2001b). *Income 2000.* Retrieved April 5, 2005, from http://www.census.gov/hhes/income/income00/inctab10.html

U.S. Census Bureau. (2002a). *Migration by race and Hispanic origin: 1995 to 2000.* Retrieved March 20, 2005, from www.census.gov/prod/2003pubs/censr-13.pdf

U.S. Census Bureau. (2002b). *Special tabulation.* Internet Release Date: March 16, 2004. Retrieved May 12, 2005, from http://www.census.gov/prod/2004pubs/censr–14.pdf

U.S. Census Bureau. (2003). *Current population survey, annual social and economic supplement.* Retrieved May 12, 2005, from http://www.agingstats.gov/chartbook2004/tables.economics.html

U.S. Department of Education, National Center for Education Statistics. (2002). *The condition of education 2002,* NCES 2002-025, Washington, DC: U.S. Government Printing Office. http://nces.ed.gov/pubs2002/2002025.pdf

U.S. Department of Health and Human Services. (2003). *National healthcare disparities report.* Washington, DC: Government Printing Office.

U.S. Department of Health and Human Services. (1985). Report of the secretary's task force on black and minority health. Washington, DC.

U.S. Department of Justice, Federal Bureau of Investigation. (2002). *Crime in the United States, 2001* (USGPO, pp. 252–254). Washington, DC: U.S. Government Printing Office.

U.S. Sentencing Commission. (2002). *Sourcebook of federal sentencing statistics.* Retrieved April 7, 2005, from http://www.ussc.gov/

Vega, W. A., Gil, A. G., & Zimmerman, R. S. (1993). Patterns of drug use among Cuban-American, African-American, and White non-Hispanic boys. *American Journal of Public Health, 83,* 257–259.

Ventura, S. J., Mosher, W. D., Curtin, S. C., Abma, J. C., & Henshaw, S. (2001). Trends in pregnancy rates for the United States, 1976–97: An update. *National Vital Statistics Reports, 49*(4), 5.

Veroff, J., Douvan, E., & Hatchett, S. J. (1995). *Marital instability: A social and behavioral study of the early years.* Westport, CT: Praeger.

Vygotsky, L. S. (1978). *Mind in society: The development of higher psychological processes.* Cambridge, MA: Harvard University Press. (Original work published 1934)

Wade, P., & Bernstein, B. L. (1991). Culture sensitivity training and counselor's race: Effects on black female clients' perceptions and attrition. *Journal of Counseling Psychology, 38,* 9–15.

Wade, T. J. (1996). The relationships between skin color and self-perceived global, physical, and sexual attractiveness, and self-esteem for African Americans. *Journal of Black Psychology, 22*(3), 358–373.

Walker, E. A. (2000). Spiritual support in relation to community violence exposure, aggressive outcomes, and psychological adjustment among inner-city young adolescents. *Dissertations Abstracts International: Section B: The Sciences & Engineering, 6161*(6-B). US: Univ. Microfilms International.

Walker, S., Belgrave, F. Z., Jarama, S. L., Ukawuililu, J., & Rackley, R. (1995). *The effectiveness of a support group intervention for increasing employment efficacy for ethnic minorities with disabilities.* Unpublished manuscript. Available from Faye Z. Belgrave, Department of Psychology, Virginia Commonwealth University, Richmond, VA.

Wallace, J. M., Brown, T. N., Bachman, J. G., & Laveist, T. A. (2003). The influence of race and religion on abstinence from alcohol, cigarettes and marijuana among adolescents. *Journal of Studies on Alcohol.*

Wallston, B. S., & Wallston, K. A. (1984). Locus of control and health: A review of the literature. *Health Education Monographs, 6,* 107–117.

Warren, N. (1972). African infant precocity. *Psychological Bulletin, 78*(5), 353–367.

Warren, N. C. (2002). *Should we have concerns about interracial marriages?* Retrieved September 29, 2002, from http://www.crosswalk.com/community/singles/1164789.html

Washington, B. T. (1896). The awakening of the Negro. *Atlantic Monthly, 78,* 322–328.

Washington, J. A. (1996). Issues in assembling the language abilities of African American children. In A. G. Kamhi, K. E. Pollack, & J. L. Harris (Eds.), *Communication development and disorders in African American children: Research, assessment, and intervention* (pp. 35–54). Baltimore: Brookes.

Washington, R. O., & McCarley, L. D. (1998). A postmodern perspective on black suicides in the United States. *Journal of Human Behavior in the Social Environment, 1,* 225–242.

Watkins, A. F. (2002). Learning styles of African American children: A developmental consideration. *Journal of Black Psychology, 28*(1), 3–17.

Way, N. (1996). Between experiences of betrayal and desire: Close friendships among urban adolescents. In B. J. R. Leadbeater & N. Way (Eds.), *Urban girls: Resisting stereotypes, creating identities* (pp. 173–192). New York: New York University Press.

Weinrich, S. P., Holdford, D., Boyd, M., Creanga, D., Cover, K., Johnson, A., et al. (1998). Prostate cancer education in African American churches. *Public Health Nursing, 15*(3), 188–195.

Wells, A. L. (2001). Ingredients for success: The factors that contribute to the internal motivation for achievement in African American women in non-traditional professions. *Dissertation Abstracts International: Section B: The Sciences & Engineering,* U*61*(12-B), 6726. US: Univ. Microfilms International.

Welsing, F. C. (1991). *Isis papers: The keys to the colors.* Chicago: Third World Press.

Whaley, A. (1993). Self-esteem, cultural identity, and psychosocial adaptation in African-American children. *Journal of Black Psychology, 19*(4), 406–422.

Whaley, A. L. (1998). Cross-cultural perspective on paranoia: A focus on the black American experience. *Psychiatric Quarterly, 69*(4), 325–343.

Whaley, A. L. (2001). Cultural mistrust of white mental health clinicians among African Americans with severe mental illness. *American Journal of Orthopsychiatry, 71*(2), 252–256.

White, J. (1970, September). Toward a black psychology. *Ebony Magazine.*

White, J. L. (1972). Toward a black psychology. In R. Jones (Ed.), *Black psychology.* New York: Harper & Row.

White, J. L. (1980). Toward a black psychology. In R. Jones (Ed.), *Black psychology.* New York: Harper & Row.

White, J. L. (1984). *The psychology of blacks.* Englewood Cliffs, NJ: Prentice Hall.

White, J. (2004). Toward a black psychology. In R. Jones (Ed.), *Black psychology* (pp. 5–35). Hampton, VA: Cobb & Henry.

White, J. L., & Parham, T. A. (1990). *The psychology of blacks* (2nd ed.). Englewood Cliffs, NJ: Prentice-Hall.

Whitehead, T. L., Peterson, J., & Kaljee, L. (1994). The "hustle": Socioeconomic deprivation, urban drug trafficking, and low-income, African-American male gender identity. *Pediatrics, 93,* 1050–1054.

Wierzbicki, M., & Pekarik, G. (1993). A meta-analysis of psychotherapy dropout. *Professional Psychology: Research & Practice, 24*(2), 190–195.

Wilson, B. (1999). Discussion, "The intersection of public policy and prevention/ promotion for children and families: Challenges for community psychology," symposium at the SCRA 7th Biennial conference on community research and action. Columbia, South Carolina.

Wilcox, S., Bopp, M., Oberrecht, L., Kammermann, S. K., & McElmurray, C. T. (2003). Psychosocial and perceived environmental correlates of physical activity in rural and older African American and White women. *The Journals of Gerontology Series: Psychological Sciences and Social Sciences, 58,* 329–337.

Williams A. L. (1996). Skin color in psychotherapy. In R. Perez Foster, M. Moskowitz, & R. A. Javier (Eds.), *Reaching across boundaries of culture and class: Widening the scope of psychotherapy* (pp. 211–224). Northvale, NJ: Jason Aronson.

Williams, D. R. (1992). Black-white differences in blood pressure: The role of social factors. *Ethnicity & Disease, 2,* 125–141.

Williams, R. (1974). A history of the association of black psychologists: Early formation and development. *Journal of Black Psychologists, 1,* 9–23.

Williams, R. A., Williams, R. L., & Mitchell, H. (2004). The testing game. In R. Jones (Ed.), *Black psychology* (pp. 465–485). Hampton, VA: Cobb & Henry.

Williams, R. L. (1997). The Ebonics controversy. *Journal of Black Psychology, 23*(3), 208–214.

Wilson, B. D. M., & Miller, R. L. (2002). Strategies for managing heterosexism used among African American gay and bisexual men. *Journal of Black Psychology, 28*(4), 371–391.

Wilson, J. Q., & Kelling, G. L. (1982, March). Broken windows: The police and neighborhood safety. *Atlantic Monthly, 249*(3), 29–38.

Wilson, M. N., Green-Bates, C., McCoy, L., Simmons, F., Askew, T., Curry-El, J., et al. (1995). African American family life: The dynamics of interactions, relationships, and roles. In M. Wilson (Ed.), *African American family life: Its structural and ecological aspects* (pp. 5–21). San Francisco: Jossey-Bass.

Wilson, S. M., & Miles, M. S. (2001). Spirituality in African-American mothers coping with a seriously ill infant. *Journal of the Society of Pediatric Nurses, 6*(3), 116–122.

Wilson, W. J. (1987). *The truly disadvantaged: The inner city, the underclass, and public policy.* Chicago: University of Chicago Press.

Wilson, W. J. (1997). *When work disappears.* New York: Knopf.

Wimberly, G. L. (2002). *School relationships foster success for African American students* [Policy report]. Iowa City, IA: ACT. Retrieved April 4, 2005, from www.act.org/research/policy/pdf/school_relation.pdf

Witherspoon, K. M., Speight, S., & Thomas, A. (1997). Racial identity attitudes, school achievement, and academic self-efficacy among African American high school students. *Journal of Black Psychology, 23*(4), 344–357.

Witty, P. (1945). New evidence on the learning ability of the Negro. *Journal of Abnormal and Social Psychology, 40*, 401–404.

Wong, C. A., Eccles, J. S., & Sameroff, A. (2003). The influence of ethnic discrimination and ethnic identification on African American adolescents' school and socioemotional adjustment. *Journal of Personality, 71*(6), 1197–1233.

Woods, L. N., & Jagers, R. J. (2003). Are cultural values predictors of moral reasoning in African American adolescents? *Journal of Black Psychology, 29*(1), 102–118.

Woodson, C. G. (1972) *The mis-education of the Negro* (Reprint). Washington, DC: Associated Publishers. (Original work published 1933)

Woolfolk, A. E. (1998). *Educational psychology* (7th ed.). Boston: Allyn & Bacon.

World Health Organization. (1999). *An overview of a strategy to improve the mental health of underserved populations.* Retrieved April 10, 2005, from http://www.who.int/mental_health/media/en/46.pdf

Worrell, F. C. (2003). Why are there so few African Americans in gifted education programs? In C. C. Yeakey & R. D. Henderson (Eds.), *Surmounting all odds: Education, opportunity, and society in the new millennium* (pp. 423–454). Greenwich, CT: Information Age.

Wright, B. J., & Isenstein, V. R. (1975). *Psychological tests and minorities.* Washington, DC: Government Printing Office.

Wright, R. C., & McCreary, M. L. (1997). The Talented Ten: Supporting African American male college students. *Journal of African-American Men, 3*, 45–68.

Wyatt, G. E. (1992). The sociocultural context of African American and White American women's rape. *Journal of Social Issues, 48*(1), 77–91.

Wyatt, G. E., Axelrod, J., Chin, D., Vargas Carmona, J., & Burns Loeb, T. (2000). Examining patterns of vulnerability to domestic violence among African American women. *Violence Against Women, 6*(5), 495–515.

Wyatt, T. (1995). Language development in African-American English child speech. *Linguistics and Education, 7*(1), 7–22.

Yancey, G. (2002). Who interracially dates: An examination of the characteristics of those who have interracially dated. *Journal of Comparative Family Studies, 33*(2), 179–190.

Yasui, M., Dorham, C. L., & Dishion, T. J. (2004). Ethnic identity and psychological adjustment: A validity analysis for European American and African American adolescents. *Journal of Adolescent Research, 19*(6), 807–825.

Young-Laing, B. (2003). *African American models of community organization: Toward a culturally competent theory.* Unpublished doctoral dissertation, Virginia Commonwealth University, Richmond, VA.

Yutrzanka, B. A. (1995). Making a case for training in ethnic and cultural diversity in increasing treatment efficacy. *Journal of Consulting & Clinical Psychology, 63*(2), 197–206.

Zack, N. (1995). *American mixed race: The culture of microdiversity.* Lanham, MD: Roman & Littlefield.

Zea, M. C., Quezada, T., & Belgrave, F. Z. (1996). Limitations of an acultural health psychology: Reconstructing the African influence on Latino culture and health related behaviors. In J. Garcia and M. Z. Zea (Eds.), *Psychological interventions and research with Latino populations.* Boston: Allyn & Bacon.

Zigler, E., Taussig, C., & Black, K. (1992). Early childhood intervention: A promising preventative for juvenile delinquency. *American Psychologist, 47*(8), 997–1006.

Author Index

Subject Index

Africentric Value Scale for
Children, 47, 52
Africentric worldview, 28-29, 53
contemporary African Americans
and, 40-42
continuum, 28
measurement of, 49-53
versus Eurocentric worldview,
28, 29
See also African American
psychologists, Africentric
psychology and; Africentric
psychology; Africentric
worldview dimensions
Africentric worldview dimensions,
34-42, 53
academic attitudes and, 44
balance and harmony with nature,
39, 53
collectivism, 35-36, 53
drug attitudes/use and, 45-46
health and stress and, 46
holism, 34
human authenticity, 40, 53
imposter phenomenon and, 44, 45
inclusive metaphysical
epistemology, 40
Maafa, 40, 53
Ma'at, 40, 53
orality, 38, 41, 53
racial identity and, 44
Sankofa, 40, 53
sensitivity to affect and emotional
cues, 38, 53
spiritness, 40, 53, 71, 83
spirituality, 34-35, 41, 53
time orientation, 36-37, 53
veneration of person assumes value
of all living things, 40, 53
verve and rhythm, 39, 53, 97
Africentric Worldview Scale, 44
Africentrism scale, 51-52
Afrocentric, 27
Aggression, 328
definition, 329
direct, 329
hostile, 329
indirect, 329

instrumental, 329
physical, 329
verbal, 329
See also Aggression and violence,
theories of; Violence
Aggression and violence, theories of,
331-337, 349
cultural theories, 335-337, 349
frustration reduction drive
theory, 332
innate, 332
See also Social learning theory;
Social organizational theory
Aid to Families with Dependent
Children, 240
Akbar, Na'im, 22, 30-31, 53
Alexander v. Sandoval, 88
American Civil Liberties Union, 108
American Psychological Association,
16, 25, 293, 294
African American presence in, 22
Division 45, 22, 293
Minority Fellowship Program,
21-22, 25, 294
mission, 22
Office of Ethnic Minority
Affairs, 22, 25
Office of Ethnic Minority
Affairs, 293
Research Office, 23
Society for the Psychological Study
of Ethnic Minority Issues,
22, 293
American Teachers Association, 16
Black psychologists committee, 16
Analytical learning style, 167,
168, 181
field independence, 168
reflectivity, 168-169
stimulus-centeredness, 168
Annie B. Casey Foundation, 124
Anokwalei Enyo, 279
Anomie and suicide,
Durkheim's, 115
Anti-Drug Abuse Act of
1986, 308
Archetypes, 115
Army Classification Battery, 12, 14

About the Authors

Kevin W. Allison is Associate Professor of Psychology and Director of Applied and Outreach Scholarship at Virginia Commonwealth University (VCU) in Richmond. He is also the Associate Director of the Center for Cultural Experiences in Prevention and the Center for the Promotion of Positive Youth Development at VCU. He completed his undergraduate degree in psychology at Notre Dame and his graduate work in clinical-community psychology at DePaul University in Chicago. Prior to joining the faculty at VCU, Allison worked at Penn State and served as Clinical Director of City Lights in Washington, D.C. His work focuses on understanding and addressing processes that support positive developmental outcomes for African American children and youth. This has included the examination of life skills and culturally informed interventions for youth and work with community-based human service providers.

Faye Z. Belgrave is Professor of Psychology at Virginia Commonwealth University in Richmond and Founder and Director of the Center for Cultural Experiences in Prevention. Her interests are in the areas of HIV/AIDS and substance abuse prevention, the role of culture and context in interventions, and gender and female-related issues. In collaboration with community partners, Belgrave has implemented several prevention programs for African American adolescents. These programs have been beneficial in increasing cultural attributes and in preventing or decreasing drug use and associated negative behaviors among adolescents.

Belgrave serves as an expert adviser on several national committees and agencies, including the National Institute of Drug Abuse, the Substance Abuse and Mental Health Services Agency, and the Center for Substance Abuse Prevention. She is the recipient of many national awards, including the Association of Black Psychologists Distinguished Psychologists Award and the Dalmas Taylor Award from the American Psychological Association, for a distinguished career in psychology. Belgrave received her Ph.D. degree from the University of Maryland, her M.A. degree from the University of Nebraska, Lincoln, and her B.S. degree from North Carolina A&T State University.